ANGLAIS SUP

New Starting up

Conforme au CECRL

BTS tertiaires, IUT, écoles de commerce, formation continue

Annie Goulvent
Professeur certifié en I.U.T.

Frédérique Le Graverend
Professeur agrégé en classes préparatoires scientifiques

Claude Mérour
Professeur certifié en classes de B.T.S.

Sophie Pedergnana
Professeur agrégé en collège et lycée

Laura Stewart
Professeur agrégé en classes préparatoires et en classes de B.T.S.

FOUCHER

Présentation du manuel

- *New Starting up* propose **18 unités de 10 pages** centrées sur des aspects du monde **socio-professionnel**.
- **Chaque unité** est structurée en **trois parties** : *Zooming on*, *Business Contacts* et *Keys to Success*.
- *New Starting up* favorise le travail **autonome**.
- *New Starting up* présente une grande **variété de supports** (texte, photos, graphiques, documents professionnels,...).
- *New Starting up* propose en fin d'ouvrage le corrigé des pages « Test yourself », **un précis grammatical et des repères culturels**.

Zooming on

▶ Une double page d'ouverture pour présenter le thème du chapitre

titre de l'unité

problématique

pictos du CECRL

des graphiques et des données chiffrées

support audio

support écrit

support visuel

question de synthèse

vocabulaire thématique

▶ Un texte et des activités pour travailler la compréhension de l'écrit et la production écrite

pictos du CECRL

première approche du texte

questions de compréhension

exercices de vocabulaire, de grammaire et de traduction grammaticale (version et thème)

une version

un exercice de production écrite

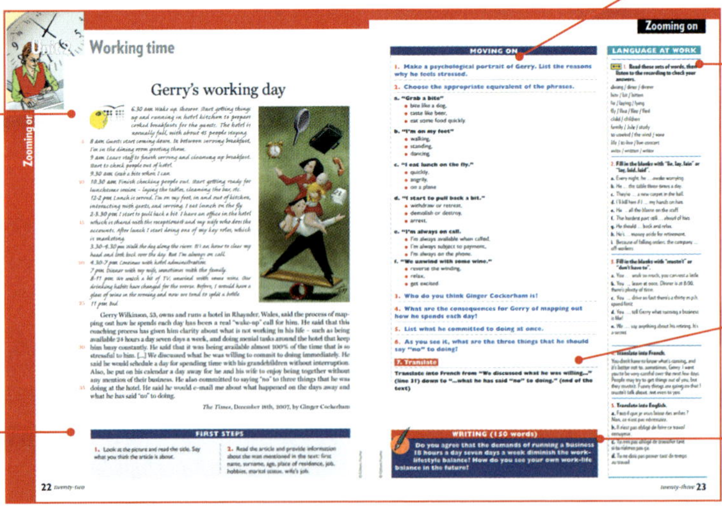

DANGER
LE PHOTOCOPILLAGE TUE LE LIVRE

« Le photocopillage, c'est l'usage abusif et collectif de la photocopie sans autorisation des auteurs et des éditeurs. Largement répandu dans les établissements d'enseignement, le photocopillage menace l'avenir du livre, car il met en danger son équilibre économique. Il prive les auteurs d'une juste rémunération.
En dehors de l'usage privé du copiste, toute reproduction totale ou partielle de cet ouvrage est interdite ».

ISBN 2-216-10801-5

Business Contacts

▶ Une ou plusieurs situations professionnelles pour développer les compétences professionnelles requises

votre poste

vos tâches

une production orale en continu ou en interaction

documents professionnels

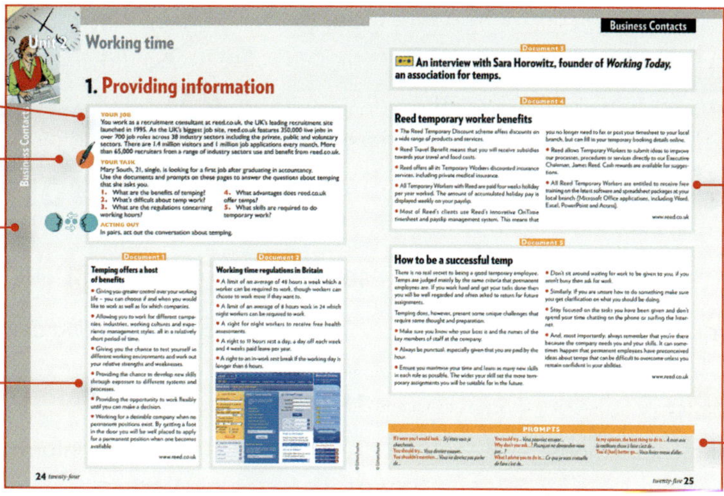

un ou plusieurs autres documents professionnels ou thématique

aide

▶ Un apprentissage écrit de la communication professionnelle

votre poste

vos tâches

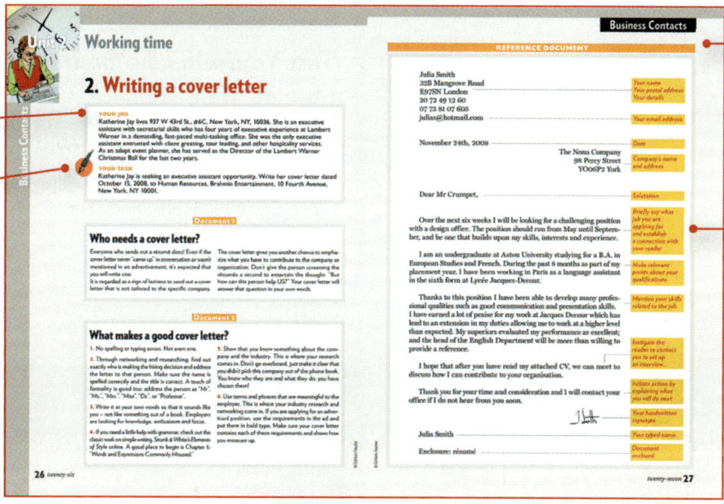

document servant de modèle

conseils pratiques

Keys to Success

▶ Un sujet d'examen et une évaluation pour s'entraîner en vue des épreuves

vérification des acquis de l'unité avec les corrigés en fin d'ouvrage

conseil méthodologique pour chaque type d'épreuves

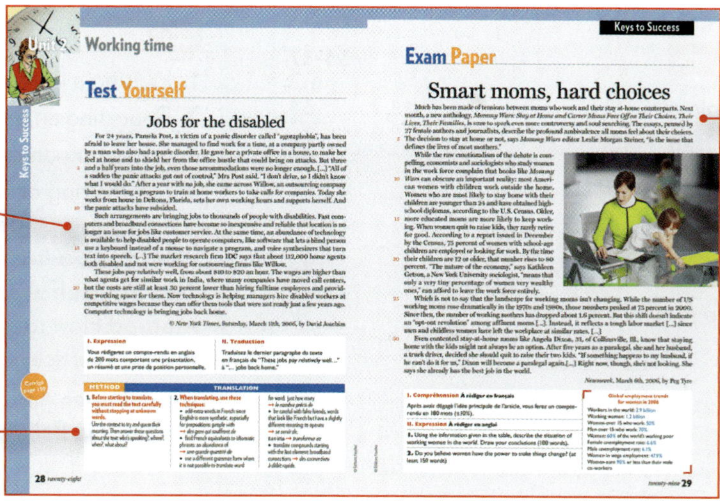

sujet type d'examen

Sommaire

Unit 1

Getting a job

Unit 2

Working time

Unit 3

Human resources

Unit 4

Industrial relations

Unit 5

Running a company

Unit 6

Corporate culture

Unit 7

Marketing

Unit 8

Advertising

Sommaire

Unit 9
Brand managing

Unit 10
Retailing

Unit 11
Sustainable development

Unit 12
Intercultural management

Sommaire

Unit 13

Consuming

Unit 14

Travelling

Unit 15

Business and ethics

Unit 16

Europe

Sommaire

Unit 17

Getting global

Unit 18

Money

Appendixes

New Starting up

Les CDs !

Les CDs proposent :

- **tous les documents de compréhension orale**
- **les exercices oraux**

Indispensable pour travailler en classe !

Le CECRL dans *New Starting up*

Le Cadre Commun de Référence pour les Langues (CECRL) est un document publié par le Conseil de l'Europe en 2001, qui définit des niveaux de maîtrise d'une langue vivante étrangère en fonction de savoir-faire dans différents domaines de compétence.
Ce document définit 6 niveaux communs de référence :

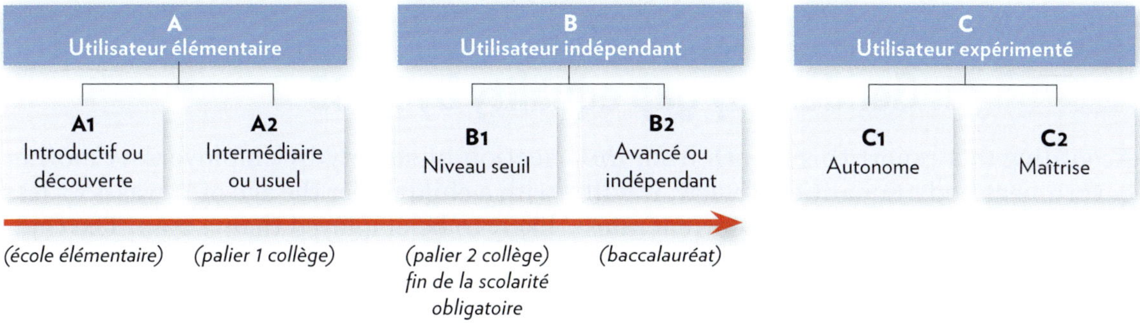

New Starting up permet à l'étudiant de consolider ses acquis du lycée (niveau B2) et de développer les compétences requises pour atteindre le niveau C1. Les activités de communication langagière relèvent de :

- la réception : écouter, lire ;
- la production : s'exprimer oralement en continu, écrire ;
- l'interaction : prendre part à une conversation ;
- la médiation : notamment activités de traduction et d'interprétation.

B2 – Niveau Avancé ou Indépendant : il implique la compréhension courante et la capacité à converser ; et prend en compte l'aptitude à émettre un avis et à soutenir systématiquement une argumentation.

- Je peux comprendre le contenu essentiel de sujets concrets ou abstraits dans un texte complexe, y compris une discussion technique dans sa spécialité.
- Je peux communiquer avec un degré de spontanéité et d'aisance tel qu'une conversation avec un locuteur natif ne comporte de tension ni pour l'un ni pour l'autre.
- Je peux m'exprimer de façon claire et détaillée sur une grande gamme de sujets, émettre un avis sur un sujet d'actualité et exposer les avantages et inconvénients de différentes possibilités.

C1 - Niveau Autonome : pour un usage régulier dans des contextes de difficulté raisonnable, il prend en considération la faculté à s'exprimer spontanément et couramment, et tient compte d'une bonne maîtrise de la langue.

- Je peux comprendre une grande gamme de textes longs et exigeants, ainsi que saisir des significations implicites.
- Je peux m'exprimer spontanément et couramment sans trop apparemment devoir chercher mes mots.
- Je peux utiliser la langue de façon efficace et souple dans sa vie sociale, professionnelle ou académique.
- Je peux m'exprimer sur des sujets complexes de façon claire et bien structurée et manifester mon contrôle des outils d'organisation, d'articulation et de cohésion du discours.

Pour chaque activité de *New Starting up*, vous trouverez un pictogramme indiquant la nature de la tâche.

Comprendre à l'oral	Lire	Écrire
Prendre part à une conversation	S'exprimer oralement en continu	

Unit 1 Getting a job

On today's tight job market, job seekers need to play the game and win. Having the right attitude, dress code, and techniques for landing that hallmark of a lifetime – a good job – is the key to success. What strategies work and why?

Zooming on

1. Gender pay gap equality by 2085

According to a report this month from the government body Equalities Review, it will take a further 78 years based on current rates to reach equality on pay between genders. The report found that presently there are clear regional differences in gender pay for full-time working across all industry sectors – the gap is as high as 17% in East Midlands and East Anglia, 14% in London but just 4% in Northern Ireland. Of specific interest to our readers, the report suggests that there is a 7% gender pay gap across all administrative and secretarial occupations.
This report also confirms that mothers with young children are the most discriminated section of society by employers. A mother with a child under the age of 11 was 45% less likely to be employed than a man. The findings will also make it clear that disabled people are one of the most disadvantaged groups in Britain and are 30% more likely to be out of work than non-disabled people with the same qualifications.

Executary News, March 31st, 2007

Read the text and have a look at the statistics.

1. Give the essential information.

2. Dress for success

According to Kim Zoller at Image Dynamics, 55% of another person's perception of you is based on how you look. Her *Dressing for Success* information gives some tips on how to look your best, without necessarily spending a lot of money. Here's a quick look at the basics:

Women's interview attire	Men's interview attire
• Solid colour, conservative suit • Coordinated blouse • Moderate shoes • Minimal jewelry • Neat, professional hairstyle • Tan or light hosiery[1] • Sparse make-up and perfume • Manicured nails • Portfolio or briefcase	• Solid colour, conservative suit • White long-sleeve shirt • Conservative tie • Dark socks, professional shoes • Minimal jewelry • Neat, professional hairstyle • Sparse after-shave • Neatly trimmed nails • Portfolio or briefcase

1. *bas, collants*

Read the document.

1. Comment on the table.

3. Find your competitive edge - and use it

Have you ever wondered what got you your job, or a premium client?

Good interview techniques, a top class curriculum vitae, a chance meeting, great contacts in your industry, being in the right place at the right time – or a combination?

Sometimes we think it is luck – but it is important to remember that luck is where opportunity meets preparedness.

In both business and sport it goes back to the basics of preparation, practice and play.

Before you know how to market yourself, or move yourself one rung up the ladder, you need to know where you want to go, and what you want to achieve along the way: start by finding your competitive edge.

Each of us has something special that elevates us above our peers, colleagues and competitors – a unique ingredient that creates distinction.

People are employed in positions for their positive attitude, rather than just aptitude.

Your personality is part of your package, and there is something special in you that sets you apart from others.

You have a name - if people are having trouble remembering it, it may be because you are not saying it with clarity.

Introducing yourself effectively is one step in the right direction.

Here are some brief pointers for making a good introduction:

Look someone in the eye when you introduce yourself, smile and say your name clearly.

Make sure your body language exudes positive energy – you will make more impact and get a better response.

A firm, friendly handshake is essential – no wet fish allowed! Women also enjoy a sturdy shake.

Have your opening line practised, without allowing it to sound rehearsed - just know it in your head.

If you cannot explain your position in eight words or less, you do not have a position!

Cape Times, September 27th, 2007

Read the text.

1. Say what is essential in selling yourself to a future employer, using modals to express your ideas.

4. A job interview

Listen to the recording and answer the questions.

1. Tell about the recruitment consultant's role.

2. Say how the interviewee should behave when answering questions.

3. Say what to do when the interview is over.

REPORTING

Is getting a job a question of being in the right place at the right time?

WORDS APART

Recruitment **L'embauche**

an applicant un(e) demandeur de poste
to give a piece of advice donner un conseil
to hire embaucher
hires des personnes embauchées
hiring success rates taux de réussite des embauches
a job board un tableau d'affichage de postes à pourvoir
a job offer l'offre d'embauche
online job posting affichage en ligne de postes à pourvoir
a referee la personne donnée en référence
a referral une lettre de référence
to resign donner sa démission
to screen filtrer
the selection/hiring process le processus de recrutement
the starting salary salaire de début de carrière
upbeat être positif, dynamique

Training **La formation**

business acumen le sens des affaires
to climb the career ladder grimper l'échelle hiérarchique du travail
a university graduate un diplômé de la faculté
a college université (US)
an intern stagiaire (US)
an internship un stage (US)
to major in se spécialiser en
on-the-job training la formation dans l'entreprise
a placement un stage (GB)
a professional journal une revue professionnelle
reliable fiable
a senior en dernière année (4 ans) d'études universitaires
a subject une matière
talented doué
top-notch top niveau
a trainee stagiaire (GB)

Applying for a job **La recherche d'emploi**

to alter modifier
to be effective être efficace
a business card carte de visite
businesslike de manière professionnelle
to downplay minimiser
fraudulent data des données truquées
job hunting la recherche d'emploi
a job hunter un chercheur d'emploi
a job interview un entretien d'embauche
a job seeker un chercheur d'emploi
strengths and weaknesses points forts et faibles
to land a job obtenir un poste
to play up mettre en valeur
the position le poste
to read the classifieds lire les petites annonces
a résumé un curriculum vitae (US)
a skill un atout
to target cibler

Portrait of an artist

Joyce Wan's whimsical art may not hang on the walls of the Smithsonian (yet), but it is ringing up sales in the museum's gift shop. At just 29, Wan finds that she needs to downplay[1] her full role at Wanart, her Hoboken, New Jersey-based company. "I've had a hard time getting people to take me seriously. To that point, I had 'president' printed on my business card, but I ended up taking it off because people would question me about my experience," she says. It is just one of the many challenges this young artist and businesswoman manages every day.

Wan, an architecture major, founded Wanart in 2003. The company produces greeting cards and soft goods like infant clothing, tote bags[2], and artists' notebooks, featuring art inspired by Wan's Chinese-American heritage. "I had been making greeting cards for my parents and they don't speak English all that well. The cards I did myself were bilingual and they really liked them. Then I realized that there was a big hole in the market for Asian themes that were contemporary," she says. She started the company while working full-time at a New York architecture firm; by summer 2004 she made the leap into full-time business owner. Wan's first line of greeting cards – and still her biggest seller – features modern takes on the Chinese zodiac figures. Later collections, such as her bamboo line, came from her childhood. "They are interpretations of images I grew up with in my home, (but) I never knew what they stood for. I did a lot of research and all the motifs I use have meaning behind them," she says.

Still, despite her marketable designs, starting a business from zero was tough, and it accounted for many sleepless nights. Even more difficult was learning how to divorce her artistic sensibilities from her newly acquired business acumen. "Your work is personal, it comes from inside you. And then you have to show your work at a trade show and open yourself to comment – it is like baring your soul," she says. "It was so hard. For a little while I thought, 'I can't sell my own product.' But you learn to do it," she concludes.

Wan's commitment is paying off. Her boxed cards and other products are sold at museum shops, including the Museum of Fine Arts in Wan's hometown of Boston, at stationery stores, and online at target.com in addition to Wanart.com. [...]

1. *minimiser* – 2. *des cabas*

Barnard Magazine, Fall 2007, by Allison Enright

FIRST STEPS

1. Read the title and say what the article might be about.

2. Describe the kind of artwork she produces.

3. Pick up the information you are given about Ms Wan's:

a. personal background,

b. professional background.

MOVING ON

1. Say how Joyce Wan got the idea for her company.

2. Pick out expressions used to describe:

a. people's reactions,
b. her own reactions.

3. Find the sources of inspiration for Joyce Wan's work.

4. Name three different places where customers can buy Wan's art.

5. Tick the right answer:

- Joyce Wan grew up in China.
- Joyce Wan grew up in New Jersey.
- Joyce Wan grew up in Boston.

- She started her business in an architecture company.
- She worked after studying architecture.
- She studied art and worked at home.

- Wan enjoys talking about her work.
- It has taken Wan time to be able to sell her own work.
- It is more difficult to create artwork than to sell it.

6. Say what it means:

a. "whimsical" (line 1):
humorous,
playful,
obscure.

b. "getting people to take me seriously" (line 4):
trying to look older than her real age,
making others think she was older,
convincing others that she was competent.

c. "baring your soul" (line 32):
telling your innermost secrets,
pretending not to exist,
exposing yourself to criticism.

7. Make a portrait of Joyce Wan, including her origins, her challenges, her success.

8. Translate

Translate the first paragraph into French, from "I've had a hard time getting people to..." down to "...this young artist and businesswoman manages every day."

WRITING (150 words)

Using Joyce Wan's success story as an example, explain the strategies that help young people overcome the difficulties getting started in their careers.

LANGUAGE AT WORK

1. Say if the following words are pronounced [tʃ], [ʃ], or [k]. Listen to the recording to check your answers.

challenge / architecture / Chinese / research / inertia / characteristic / Christmas / chain / chaos / chance / cheer / capricious / charming.

2. Use suffixes (*-tion* / *-ness* / *-ship* / *-ity*) to create nouns:

hard / serious / inspire / salesman / sleepless / imagine / creative / marketable.

3. Use 'like' or 'as' to complete the sentences.

a. Many of her designs look .... figures from the Chinese horoscope.

b. .... images often have a hidden meaning, they are useful.

c. Several museums, such .... the Smithsonian, are interested in Wan's work.

d. Wan feels .... a child when people judge her inexperience.

4. Translate into French.

a. Joyce started making her own cards when she was young.

b. She stopped working for the architectural firm in 2003.

c. Although she is successful, she doesn't enjoy working on her own every day.

5. Translate into English.

a. Joyce a dû faire croire aux gens qu'elle était compétente.

b. Elle a fait faire de la distribution par un sous-traitant.

c. Elle ne pouvait pas se faire comprendre par tout le monde.

d. A-t-elle réussi à faire vendre son œuvre par le musée de Boston ?

Unit 1 Getting a job

1. Analysing recruitment methods

YOUR JOB
You are a trainee currently looking for a job and are trying different methods in order to be effective in your job hunt.

YOUR TASK
You are asked to compile a list of different job search methods analysing their strong and weak points. Read the following documents to help you in your selection.

ACTING OUT
Report your findings to your fellow trainees.

Document 1

The hiring process

Survey data show that U.S. establishments use a variety of methods for publicizing the availability of job opportunities to potential workers. Newspaper advertisements and informal referrals from employees are used most frequently. Referrals are more often used together with other approaches than as a sole recruitment strategy; those establishments that rely exclusively on "network hiring" tend to be small, less formalized, and in the private sector. Professional referrals and advertisements are more typical approaches for high-prestige occupations than for low ones.

Increasingly, the most popular and effective recruiting strategy is the use of internships. Among employers that supplied internship data, nearly half increased their reliance on interns since 2004.

Document 2

Video resume becomes joke of Wall St.

College student Aleksey Vayner's video resume – with his weightlifting and dance moves – is getting him notice. But not the kind that may get him a job.

Another recruiting year, another job applicant humiliation. This season, Yale senior Aleksey Vayner went far beyond the usual misaddressed e-mail or keyboard-in-mouth embarrassment.

Vayner, an aspiring investment banker, sent a video entitled "Impossible is Nothing" along with an 11-page resume and glamour shot to financial services powerhouse UBS. Within hours scores of investment banks noticed his application, as bankers e-mailed the seven-minute video and turned Vayner into the biggest joke on Wall Street.

As long as there have been job applicants, there have been application gaffes. Today, with e mail as the preferred mode of corporate communication, that embarrassing camera phone picture quickly travels far beyond company walls. So too can a boastful resume or cover letter.

Younger employees, often devotees on MySpace and reality TV, are predisposed to online missteps in the workplace, says Castellini. "Voyeurism is an aspect of their lives," he says, "and they don't understand the ramifications of it." Employers often check out potential hires on social networking sites, so consider deleting that picture of you funneling beer or flashing the camera. "What we tend to tell our students about using new technologies," says University of Pennsylvania Career Services Director Patricia Rose, "is beware."

Document 3

Teleporting your CV to Dubai

We have a network of 1,000s of Recruiters, HR Managers & Company Directors in Dubai.

How does it work? The whole process is simple and takes just a few minutes.

1. You complete a brief and free registration.
2. Decide what contact details to give to recruiters.
3. Choose whether to send your details to agencies or direct employers.
4. Instantly send your details through our network.

Our Advance Match Technology (AMT) matches recruiters to you.

First, your details are instantly sent to all matched recruiters.

Then, recruiters will start calling you up with job opportunities.

Get your phone ringing in hours, start now!

Document 4

Top-notch in-house hotel training

The Mount Nelson Hotel's in-house training programme gives management trainees the chance to gain hands-on experience that leads to an approved certificate in hotel management. Four staff members are chosen every year. Candidates must have a Grade 12 certificate, a minimum of six months' work experience in any of the hotel's departments, and must be from a previously disadvantaged community [...]

Students are trained to deal effectively with real-life situations. Once they have completed the three-year theory course, trainees are appointed for a year in junior and supervisory positions to gain insight into the operational side of hotel management.

Hotel manager Andrew Cook says the Mount Nelson staff are talented and loyal and many have been with the establishment for several years. The hotel has found that providing high-quality training is a way of rewarding staff and ensuring ongoing high standards in the hotel. The programme converts talented, bright members of previously disadvantaged communities into competent future managers.

Cape Times, August 22nd, 2007

PROMPTS

one of the most effective methods... *une des méthodes les plus efficaces*

one of the least effective methods... *une des méthodes les moins efficaces*

nothing can replace practical experience such as in-house/on the job training... *rien ne peut remplacer l'expérience pratique de la formation en entreprise*

an entry-level position... *un poste de début de carrière*

new opportunities... *de nouvelles possibilités*

additional responsibilities *plus de responsabilité*

the pool of applicants *le tas de CV pour un poste*

career ladder *la hiérarchie des postes*

to think on your feet *la capacité de réfléchir et de réagir rapidement*

2. Writing your CV

YOUR JOB

You are in the job market again after a first job and have to rewrite your curriculum vitae (or résumé). You must be careful not to "stretch" the truth.

YOUR TASK

Use the documents provided to correctly target your résumé without exaggerating about your skills.

Document 1

CV fraud on rise in South Africa

People all over the world are lying on their CVs to secure jobs and South Africans are no different.

According to a recent survey released by Kroll, the world's leading screening and risk consultancy company, the trend is on the increase.

Kroll provides a wide range of investigative, intelligence and security services in more than 25 countries.

Ina van der Merwe, CEO of Kroll's South African associate, said credential verification has become an intrinsic part of most company's selection process.

"As applicants become aware that background screening will be done, we might see a drop in the number of fraudulent cases within the next 18 months," she said.

Kroll's national annual summary of fraudulent data, Hit Ratio Report and Industry Analysis, shows that most discrepancies were found in the employment and educational sectors.

It is reported that the number of potential employees who lie about their employment history had increased from 36.5 percent in 2005 to 49.4 percent in 2006.

Referring to people who do not tell the truth about where they have worked before, the transportation industry is the worst with 56.5 percent, the health care sector next with 50.1 percent, education 49.3 percent and the legal services 44.8 percent.

In addition, discrepancies in the educational sector have increased from 14.1 percent in 2005 to 21.5 percent in 2006.

Criminal record offences have increased from 8.5 percent in 2005 to 9.1 percent in 2006.

Most people in the construction industry lie about their criminal record, the report said.

Van der Merwe said: "Lies vary from a little lie where the candidate alters the symbols he or she has achieved on a matric certificate, to the gross lie where a candidate has never seen the inside of a university before."

She said certain universities open criminal cases where individuals were found guilty of bridging the truth.

Independent online, August 24th, 2007, by Jade Witten

Document 2

Being a 'geek' can help you land that job

Document 3

CV Tips

Most CVs are laced with spelling and grammatical errors. Have your CV read by as many people as you can. Give it to a professional proofreader and at least one person in the same industry. Don't annoy recruiters. CVs with job gaps, missing dates and lack of specifics will not make the short list. Poorly written and badly designed CVs are difficult to read and waste time.

REFERENCE DOCUMENT

Julia Smith
32B Mangrove Road
London E97 SN

Tel: 20 7249 1258
Mobile phone: 0773 8107 506
email: julias@hotmail.com
Date of birth: 31 May 19.... Age: 21
Female
Single, British

Personal details

Education

- 200.... to present: Aston University, Birmingham. B.A. European and French Studies to be completed in 2008
- 200.... to 200.... : Parker High School, Bristol, Avon – 3 A Levels
- 200.... to 200.... : Parker High School, Bristol, Avon – 8 O Levels

Dates, names of schools, addresses and diplomas

Experience

- September 2007-8: Language Assistant, sixth form, Lycée Jacques Decour, Paris, France. Assist and lead group discussion in English language classes. Prepare worksheets and organise individual remedial work.

Date of employment, name of organization

- August 200.. to February 200..: Administrative Assistant, Glastonbury Woodwork Designs, Birmingham. Handle telephone and written correspondence, provide customer service. Collect and classify data for upcoming promotional events.

Roles undertaken Responsibilities

Language

- English
- French: excellent mastery
- German: working knowledge

Language skills

Computer Literacy

- Daily use of Word, Excel, and PowerPoint

IT knowledge

Interests

- Community Service volunteer (Youth Reading Program)
- Photography
- Modern Jazz

References

Available upon request

Test Yourself

New world of networking

The success of Facebook has opened a new path to progress as our virtual lives begin to transform the landscape of career connections.

The popularity of social networking sites shows no sign of receding, and business networking sites such as LinkedIn.com have established the internet as a way to shake hands electronically with new contacts. Such is the hype around Web 2.0 that more and more specialist sites are springing up. So could tapping into an online community help you to find your next job?

The website i-resign.com started nine years ago as a hobby, a place to post jokes and famous resignation letters. It now serves about 15 million page impressions a year and has some seriously useful content for jobseekers. Registered members who intend to leave their job, post the details of the role, relevant contacts and the date that they are going to quit.

"Everybody knows about the regular job boards, but there is a whole market of hidden, unadvertised jobs and we think that posting these resignations is complementary to official job boards and classifieds," says Kauser Kanji, the website's general manager.

"People post their job up because they know that they are probably going to help someone else to find a job," he says. "It all sounds very altruistic, but I think that's the way it works. We don't entirely understand it because we don't incentivise or pay anybody to post their job up, but we get some 6,000 people a month telling us [that they are leaving their jobs]."

Laura, who works for one of the Big Four accountancy and professional services firms, has signed up as a "mole" with TheCareerMole.com. The website seeks to market personal referrals by putting jobseekers in touch with moles within a firm where they would like to work. The job hunter gains inside information about a particular company and the mole gets a financial bonus for a successful hire under their company's referral bonus scheme.

"It's quite good to have a big say in who you might be working with," says Laura, who wishes to remain anonymous. [...] "You can get a good idea of what someone is like by e-mail," she says.

It's a win-win for both parties, according to the website's co-founder, Kristian Hall. "Employers can reduce recruitment costs and improve employee retention by getting referrals from people they trust – the best possible filter. Employees, or moles, will be rewarded for referring quality candidates as well as gaining kudos from the boss for engaging in recruitment."

The Times, July 12th, 2007, by Clare Dight

Corrigé page 190

I. Expression

Après une lecture attentive du texte, vous rédigerez un compte-rendu en anglais de 150 à 200 mots maximum comportant une présentation, un résumé et une prise de position personnelle.

II. Traduction

Traduisez le texte en français de "Laura, who works..." to "their company's referral bonus scheme".

Exam Paper

Looking for a job in a speed-dating format, complete with charm

Love and money will hold hands in an upcoming event that will combine speed dating with job searching. And like a real date, students will have to impress companies with their devilish charm and wit.

Hosted by the Internship and career center and business fraternity Alpha Kappa Psi, the event, Networking for Success, is structured like speed dating so participants have guaranteed "alone time" with company recruiters. [...] Students are organized by their interests into groups of five, and each group has 15 minutes to talk and ask questions to one company before the bell sounds and the next round begins. After several rounds, approximately 60 minutes will be devoted to refreshments and time to mingle with all the companies. Wells Fargo, Target, Deloitte & Touche, Washington Mutual and the US Department of Commerce were among the 10 companies recruiting for various jobs or internship positions. Although students choose their top five choices for their "dates," their résumés are given to all visiting companies.

Ken Barnes, the program coordinator for the liberal arts and business at the Internship and career center, said that although the event is geared towards business students, it does not necessarily limit who can attend. "Business is broad, and these companies are looking for not just business majors, but business-minded people," he said. "Students have to present the big picture of themselves, not just GPA[1] or majors."

Barnes said he doesn't believe finding a job is any harder today than it was in previous years. However, job searching required just as much effort as studying for school, he said. "Most jobs are not advertised, so students have to actively look for them," he said. "This event will help students get more information since it is more relaxed than a career fair where you have 100 companies and the students waiting in line behind you." Cathy Wang, a member of the frat, has been organizing the event. She said the event is a practical follow-up to the recent career fair at UC Davis.

"I hope students will learn how to network with company recruiters, expose themselves to other recruiters and become more comfortable at selling themselves," she said.

californiaaggie.com, July 2007, by Katharine Lu

1. *Grade point average* : la moyenne annuelle

I. Compréhension À rédiger en français

Après avoir dégagé l'idée principale de l'article, vous ferez un compte rendu en 180 mots ±10%. Vous indiquerez le nombre de mots utilisés.

II. Expression À rédiger en anglais

1. Give your opinion about speed dating (pros and cons). (at least 100 words)

2. Say which method of recruitment works best in your opinion, and why. (at least 50 words)

Zooming on

Unit 2 Working time

In Japan they call it karoshi *and in China it is* guolaosi. *As yet there is no word in English for working yourself to death, but as more and more people put in longer hours and suffer more stress there may soon be.*

1. Average weekly working hours in Europe

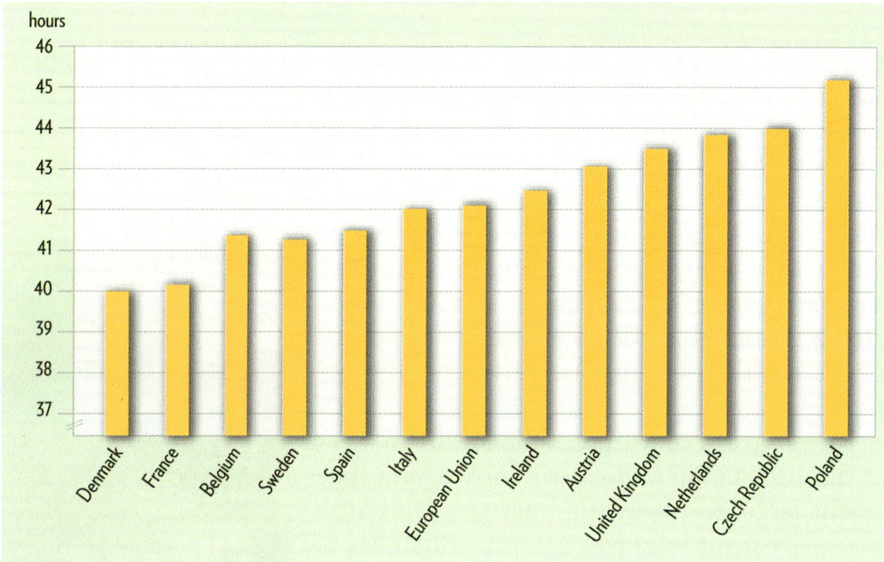

EU Labour Force Survey for 2004

Have a look at the statistics.

1. Say who works the longest and the shortest hours in Europe.

2. How can you account for it?

2. The long-hours culture in Britain

- Employees working more than 48 hours a week: **26%**.
- People working 60 hours a week: **15%**.
- Workers not using the full 60 minutes for lunch: **65%**.
- Average time for a break: **27 minutes**.
- Workers using up their full entitlement to annual leave: **44%**.
- The average British employee puts in a full working day in unpaid overtime every week – almost **£ 5,000** in unpaid salary every year.

Trade Union Congress, 2007

Have a look at the statistics.

1. Why can it be said that Britain has a long-hours culture?

3. Extreme jobs

Listen to the interview with Ann Hewlett who heads the Center for Work-Life Policy.

1. Give the definition of an "extreme job".

2. Why do people enjoy these jobs?

3. What are the negative consequences on **a.** children, **b.** companies, **c.** extreme workers themselves?

4. What is the solution?

5. "It's the American Dream on steroids." Explain and comment.

4. Shorter hours

The Chartered Institute of Personnel and Development (CIPD), claims that while there are indeed more people working over 48 hours a week in Britain than in other EU countries, the number working fewer than 30 hours is also greater than in other countries. "The average number of hours worked in the UK is actually slightly below the European average," said Mike Emmott, the CIPD's employee-relations adviser. "The UK labour market is characterised by far greater variation in working hours than other parts of Europe. This is partly because we have more part-time workers and because we are less governed by collective agreements." [...]

The CIPD also claims that most people who work long hours do so out of choice[1]. [...] "There's a social as well as an economic value to work and that is often overlooked in the long-hours debate." [...]

The assumption in the work-life-balance debate is usually that people want to spend less time at work and more time with their families, but research suggests that this may not always be the case.

The Times, June 10th, 2007, by Mary Braid

1. *par choix*

Read the text and answer the questions.

1. Why does the CIPD question the idea that Britain has a long-hours culture?

2. What makes people choose to work long hours?

REPORTING

"Do you believe that we live to work or that we work to live?" Ask the question to friends, relatives, school friends and teachers and report the results of your survey to the class.

WORDS APART

The work week — La semaine de travail

- **advancement** une promotion
- **the breadwinner** le soutien de famille
- **a clerk** un employé de bureau
- **to commute** aller de la banlieue au bureau
- **contracting** employer pour une durée déterminée
- **convenient** pratique
- **to earn money** gagner de l'argent
- **to earn one's living** gagner sa vie
- **full-time** à plein temps
- **the labour force** la main-d'œuvre
- **the minimum wage** le SMIC
- **an opportunity** une occasion
- **part-time** à temps partiel
- **the pay** la paye
- **qualified** qualifié
- **skills** des capacités
- **the staff** le personnel
- **temp(orary) work** l'intérim
- **a temp** un intérimaire
- **the 35-hour working week** la semaine de 35 heures
- **training** la formation
- **a venture** une entreprise

Employment — L'emploi

- **be on the payroll** être salarié de
- **competition** la concurrence
- **competitiveness** la compétitivité
- **to fire** renvoyer
- **flexibility** la flexibilité
- **to hire** embaucher
- **the income level** le niveau de revenus
- **job mobility** la mobilité de l'emploi
- **job security** la sécurité de l'emploi
- **labour costs** le coût de la main-d'œuvre
- **a layoff** un licenciement
- **on the black market** au noir
- **overtime** des heures supplémentaires
- **redundant** au chômage économique
- **to resign** démissionner
- **to sack** virer
- **a salary rise** une augmentation de salaire
- **shakeouts** licenciements
- **a trade union** un syndicat
- **unemployment** le chômage
- **unpaid** non payé
- **upward mobility** la mobilité sociale

Free time — Le temps libre

- **annual leave** les congés annuels
- **availibility** la disponibilité
- **a benefit** une allocation
- **a break** une pause
- **a couch potato** un téléphage
- **a day off** un jour de congé
- **entertainment** les distractions
- **a hobby/pastime** un passe-temps
- **holidays** les vacances
- **idle** oisif
- **leisure** les loisirs
- **a maternity leave** un congé de maternité
- **a pension** une retraite
- **a pensioner** un retraité
- **perks** les avantages
- **to reduce hours** réduire le temps de travail
- **to rest** se reposer
- **to retire** prendre sa retraite
- **a sickness leave** un congé maladie
- **stay-at-home** casanier, pantouflard
- **time off** du temps libre

Working time

Gerry's working day

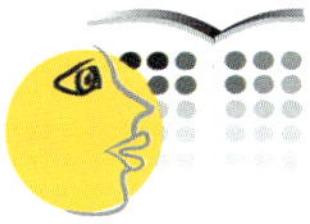

6.30 am Wake up. Shower. Start getting things up and running in hotel kitchen to prepare cooked breakfasts for the guests. The hotel is normally full, with about 45 people staying.

8 am Guests start coming down. In between serving breakfast, I'm in the dining room greeting them.

9 am Leave staff to finish serving and cleaning up breakfast. Start to check people out of hotel.

9.30 am Grab a bite when I can.

10.30 am Finish checking people out. Start getting ready for lunchtime session – laying the tables, cleaning the bar, etc.

12-2 pm Lunch is served. I'm on my feet, in and out of kitchen, interacting with guests, and serving. I eat lunch on the fly.

2-3.30 pm I start to pull back a bit. I have an office in the hotel which is shared with the receptionist and my wife who does the accounts. After lunch I start doing one of my key roles, which is marketing.

3.30-4.30 pm Walk the dog along the river. It's an hour to clear my head and look back over the day. But I'm always on call.

4.30-7 pm Continue with hotel administration.

7 pm Dinner with my wife, sometimes with the family.

8-11 pm We watch a bit of TV, unwind with some wine. Our drinking habits have changed for the worse. Before, I would have a glass of wine in the evening and now we tend to split a bottle.

11 pm Bed

Gerry Wilkinson, 53, owns and runs a hotel in Rhayader, Wales, said the process of mapping out how he spends each day has been a real "wake-up" call for him. He said that this coaching process has given him clarity about what is not working in his life – such as being available 24 hours a day seven days a week, and doing menial tasks around the hotel that keep him busy constantly. He said that it was being available almost 100% of the time that is so stressful to him. [...] We discussed what he was willing to commit to doing immediately. He said he would schedule a day for spending time with his grandchildren without interruption. Also, he put on his calendar a day away for he and his wife to enjoy being together without any mention of their business. He also committed to saying "no" to three things that he was doing at the hotel. He said he would e-mail me about what happened on the days away and what he has said "no" to doing.

The Times, December 18th, 2007, by Ginger Cockerham

FIRST STEPS

1. Look at the picture and read the title. Say what you think the article is about.

2. Read the article and provide information about the man mentioned in the text: first name, surname, age, place of residence, job, hobbies, marital status, wife's job.

MOVING ON

1. Make a psychological portrait of Gerry. List the reasons why he feels stressed.

2. Choose the appropriate equivalent of the phrases.

a. "Grab a bite"
- bite like a dog,
- taste like beer,
- eat some food quickly.

b. "I'm on my feet"
- walking,
- standing,
- dancing.

c. "I eat lunch on the fly."
- quickly,
- angrily,
- on a plane

d. "I start to pull back a bit."
- withdraw or retreat,
- demolish or destroy,
- arrest.

e. "I'm always on call.
- I'm always available when called,
- I'm always subject to payment,
- I'm always on the phone.

f. "We unwind with some wine."
- reverse the winding,
- relax,
- get excited.

3. Who do you think Ginger Cockerham is?

4. What are the consequences for Gerry of mapping out how he spends each day?

5. List what he committed to doing at once.

6. As you see it, what are the three things that he should say "no" to doing?

7. Translate

Translate into French from "We discussed what he was willing..." (line 31) down to "...what he has said "no" to doing." (end of the text)

WRITING (150 words)

Do you agree that the demands of running a business 18 hours a day seven days a week diminish the work-lifestyle balance? How do you see your own work-life balance in the future?

LANGUAGE AT WORK

1. Read these sets of words, then listen to the recording to check your answers.

dining / diner / dinner
bite / bit / bitten
lie / laying / lying
fly / flea / flee / fled
child / children
family / July / study
to unwind / the wind / wine
life / to live / live concert
write / written / writer

2. Fill in the blanks with "lie, lay, lain" or "lay, laid, laid".

a. Every night, he .... awake worrying.
b. He .... the table three times a day.
c. They're .... a new carpet in the hall.
d. I'll kill him if I .... my hands on him.
e. He .... all the blame on the staff.
f. The hardest part still .... ahead of him.
g. He should .... back and relax.
h. He's .... money aside for retirement.
i. Because of falling orders, the company .... off workers.

3. Fill in the blanks with "mustn't" or "don't have to".

a. You .... work so much, you can rest a little.
b. You .... leave at once. Dinner is at 8:00, there's plenty of time.
c. You .... drive so fast there's a thirty m.p.h. speed limit.
d. You .... tell Gerry what running a business is like!
e. We .... say anything about his retiring. It's a secret.

4. Translate into French.

You don't have to know what's coming, and it's better not to, sometimes, Gerry. I want you to be very careful over the next few days. People may try to get things out of you, but they mustn't. Funny things are going on that I mustn't talk about, not even to you."

5. Translate into English.

a. Faut-il que je vous laisse des arrhes ? Non, ce n'est pas nécessaire.
b. Il n'est pas obligé de faire ce travail ennuyeux.
c. Tu n'es pas obligé de travailler tant si tu n'aimes pas ça.
d. Tu ne dois pas passer tant de temps au travail.

Working time

1. Providing information

YOUR JOB

You work as a recruitment consultant at reed.co.uk, the UK's leading recruitment site launched in 1995. As the UK's biggest job site, reed.co.uk features 350,000 live jobs in over 700 job roles across 38 industry sectors including the private, public and voluntary sectors. There are 1.4 million visitors and 1 million job applications every month. More than 65,000 recruiters from a range of industry sectors use and benefit from reed.co.uk.

YOUR TASK

Mary South, 21, single, is looking for a first job after graduating in accountancy.
Use the documents and prompts on these pages to answer the questions about temping that she asks you.

1. What are the benefits of temping?
2. What's difficult about temp work?
3. What are the regulations concerning working hours?
4. What advantages does reed.co.uk offer temps?
5. What skills are required to do temporary work?

ACTING OUT

In pairs, act out the conversation about temping.

Document 1

Temping offers a host of benefits

- Giving you greater control over your working life – you can choose if and when you would like to work as well as for which companies.
- Allowing you to work for different companies, industries, working cultures and experience management styles, all in a relatively short period of time.
- Giving you the chance to test yourself in different working environments and work out your relative strengths and weaknesses.
- Providing the chance to develop new skills through exposure to different systems and processes.
- Providing the opportunity to work flexibly until you can make a decision.
- Working for a desirable company when no permanent positions exist. By getting a foot in the door you will be well placed to apply for a permanent position when one becomes available.

www.reed.co.uk

Document 2

Working time regulations in Britain

- A limit of an average of 48 hours a week which a worker can be required to work, though workers can choose to work more if they want to.
- A limit of an average of 8 hours work in 24 which night workers can be required to work.
- A right for night workers to receive free health assessments.
- A right to 11 hours rest a day; a day off each week and 4 weeks paid leave per year.
- A right to an in-work rest break if the working day is longer than 6 hours.

Document 3

An interview with Sara Horowitz, founder of *Working Today*, an association for temps.

Document 4

Reed temporary worker benefits

- The Reed Temporary Discount scheme offers discounts on a wide range of products and services.
- Reed Travel Benefit means that you will receive subsidies towards your travel and food costs.
- Reed offers all its Temporary Workers discounted insurance services, including private medical insurance.
- All Temporary Workers with Reed are paid four weeks holiday per year worked. The amount of accumulated holiday pay is displayed weekly on your payslip.
- Most of Reed's clients use Reed's innovative OnTime timesheet and payslip management system. This means that you no longer need to fax or post your timesheet to your local branch, but can fill in your temporary booking details online.
- Reed allows Temporary Workers to submit ideas to improve our processes, procedures or services directly to our Executive Chairman, James Reed. Cash rewards are available for suggestions.
- All Reed Temporary Workers are entitled to receive free training on the latest software and spreadsheet packages at your local branch (Microsoft Office applications, including Word, Excel, PowerPoint and Access).

www.reed.co.uk

Document 5

How to be a successful temp

There is no real secret to being a good temporary employee. Temps are judged mainly by the same criteria that permanent employees are. If you work hard and get your tasks done then you will be well regarded and often asked to return for future assignments.

Temping does, however, present some unique challenges that require some thought and preparation:

- Make sure you know who your boss is and the names of the key members of staff at the company.
- Always be punctual, especially given that you are paid by the hour.
- Ensure you maximise your time and learn as many new skills in each role as possible. The wider your skill set the more temporary assignments you will be suitable for in the future.
- Don't sit around waiting for work to be given to you, if you aren't busy then ask for work.
- Similarly, if you are unsure how to do something make sure you get clarification on what you should be doing.
- Stay focused on the tasks you have been given and don't spend your time chatting on the phone or surfing the Internet.
- And, most importantly: always remember that you're there because the company needs you and your skills. It can sometimes happen that permanent employees have preconceived ideas about temps that can be difficult to overcome unless you remain confident in your abilities.

www.reed.co.uk

PROMPTS

If I were you I would look... *Si j'étais vous je chercherais...*
You should try... *Vous devriez essayer...*
You shouldn't mention... *Vous ne devriez pas parler de...*
You could try... *Vous pourriez essayer...*
Why don't you ask...? *Pourquoi ne demandez-vous pas... ?*
What I advise you to do is... *Ce que je vous conseille de faire c'est de...*
In my opinion, the best thing to do is... *À mon avis la meilleure chose à faire c'est de...*
You'd (had) better go... *Vous feriez mieux d'aller..*

2. Writing a cover letter

YOUR JOB

Katherine Jay lives 937 W 43rd St., #6C, New York, NY, 10036. She is an executive assistant with secretarial skills who has four years of executive experience at Lambert Warner in a demanding, fast-paced multi-tasking office. She was the only executive assistant entrusted with client greeting, tour leading, and other hospitality services. As an adept event planner, she has served as the Director of the Lambert Warner Christmas Ball for the last two years.

YOUR TASK

Katherine Jay is seeking an executive assistant opportunity. Write her cover letter dated October 15, 2008, to Human Resources, Brahmin Entertainment, 10 Fourth Avenue, New York, NY 10001.

Document 1

Who needs a cover letter?

Everyone who sends out a résumé does! Even if the cover letter never "came up" in conversation or wasn't mentioned in an advertisement, it's expected that you will write one.

It is regarded as a sign of laziness to send out a cover letter that is not tailored to the specific company.

The cover letter gives you another chance to emphasize what you have to contribute to the company or organization. Don't give the person screening the résumés a second to entertain the thought: "But how can this person help US?" Your cover letter will answer that question in your own words.

Document 2

What makes a good cover letter?

1. No spelling or typing errors. Not even one.

2. Through networking and researching, find out exactly who is making the hiring decision and address the letter to that person. Make sure the name is spelled correctly and the title is correct. A touch of formality is good too: address the person as "Mr", "Ms.", "Mrs.", "Miss", "Dr.", or "Professor".

3. Write it in your own words so that it sounds like you – not like something out of a book. Employers are looking for knowledge, enthusiasm and focus.

4. If you need a little help with grammar, check out the classic work on simple writing, Strunk & White's *Elements of Style* online. A good place to begin is Chapter 5: "Words and Expressions Commonly Misused."

5. Show that you know something about the company and the industry. This is where your research comes in. Don't go overboard, just make it clear that you didn't pick this company out of the phone book. You know who they are and what they do: you have chosen them!

6. Use terms and phrases that are meaningful to the employer. This is where your industry research and networking come in. If you are applying for an advertised position, use the requirements in the ad and put them in bold type. Make sure your cover letter contains each of these requirements and shows how you measure up.

REFERENCE DOCUMENT

Julia Smith
32B Mangrove Road
E97SN London
20 72 49 12 60
07 73 81 07 605
julias@hotmail.com

Your name
Your postal address
Your details

Your email address

November 24th, 2008

Date

The Nona Company
98 Percy Street
YO06P2 York

Company's name and address

Dear Mr Crumpet,

Salutation

Over the next six weeks I will be looking for a challenging position with a design office. The position should run from May until September, and be one that builds upon my skills, interests and experience.

Briefly say what job you are applying for and establish a connection with your reader

I am an undergraduate at Aston University studying for a B.A. in European Studies and French. During the past 8 months as part of my placement year, I have been working in Paris as a language assistant in the sixth form at Lycée Jacques-Decour.

Make relevant points about your qualifications

Thanks to this position I have been able to develop many professional qualities such as good communication and presentation skills. I have earned a lot of praise for my work at Jacques Decour which has lead to an extension in my duties allowing me to work at a higher level than expected. My superiors evaluated my performance as excellent; and the head of the English Department will be more than willing to provide a reference.

Mention your skills related to the job

I hope that after you have read my attached CV, we can meet to discuss how I can contribute to your organisation.

Instigate the reader to contact you to set up an interview.

Thank you for your time and consideration and I will contact your office if I do not hear from you soon.

Initiate action by explaining what you will do next

J. Smith

Your handwritten signature

Julia Smith

Your typed name

Enclosure: résumé

Document enclosed

Test Yourself

Jobs for the disabled

For 24 years, Pamela Post, a victim of a panic disorder called "agoraphobia", has been afraid to leave her house. She managed to find work for a time, at a company partly owned by a man who also had a panic disorder. He gave her a private office in a house, to make her feel at home and to shield her from the office bustle that could bring on attacks. But three and a half years into the job, even those accommodations were no longer enough. [...] "All of a sudden the panic attacks got out of control," Mrs Post said. "I don't drive, so I didn't know what I would do." After a year with no job, she came across Willow, an outsourcing company that was starting a program to train at home workers to take calls for companies. Today she works from home in Deltona, Florida, sets her own working hours and supports herself. And the panic attacks have subsided.

Such arrangements are bringing jobs to thousands of people with disabilities. Fast computers and broadband connections have become so inexpensive and reliable that location is no longer an issue for jobs like customer service. At the same time, an abundance of technology is available to help disabled people to operate computers, like software that lets a blind person use a keyboard instead of a mouse to navigate a program, and voice synthesizers that turn text into speech. [...] The market research firm IDC says that about 112,000 home agents both disabled and not were working for outsourcing firms like Willow.

These jobs pay relatively well, from about $10 to $20 an hour. The wages are higher than what agents get for similar work in India, where many companies have moved call centers, but the costs are still at least 30 percent lower than hiring fulltime employees and providing working space for them. Now technology is helping managers hire disabled workers at competitive wages because they can offer them tools that were not ready just a few years ago. Computer technology is bringing jobs back home.

© *New York Times*, Saturday, March 11th, 2006, by David Joachim

I. Expression

Vous rédigerez un compte-rendu en anglais de 200 mots comportant une présentation, un résumé et une prise de position personnelle.

II. Traduction

Traduisez le dernier paragraphe du texte en français de "These jobs pay relatively well…" à "… jobs back home."

Corrigé page 190

METHOD — **TRANSLATION**

1. **Before starting to translate, you must read the text carefully without stopping at unknown words.**
Use the context to try and guess their meaning. Then answer these questions about the text: who's speaking?, where?, when?, what about?

2. **When translating, use these techniques:**
   - add extra words in French since English is more synthetic, especially for prepositions: people with → *des gens qui souffrent de*
   - find French equivalents to idiomatic phrases: an abundance of → *une grande quantité de*
   - use a different grammar form when it is not possible to translate word for word: just how many → *le nombre précis de*
   - be careful with false friends, words that look like French but have a slightly different meaning: to operate → *se servir de*, turn into → *transformer en*
   - translate compounds starting with the last element: broadband connections → *des connections à débit rapide*.

Exam Paper

Smart moms, hard choices

Much has been made of tensions between moms who work and their stay at-home counterparts. Next month, a new anthology, *Mommy Wars: Stay at Home and Career Moms Face Off on Their Choices, Their Lives, Their Families*, is sure to spark even more controversy and soul searching. The essays, penned by 27 female authors and journalists, describe the profound ambivalence all moms feel about their choices. The decision to stay at home or not, says *Mommy Wars* editor Leslie Morgan Steiner, "is the issue that defines the lives of most mothers."

While the raw emotionalism of the debate is compelling, economists and sociologists who study women in the work force complain that books like *Mommy Wars* can obscure an important reality: most American women with children work outside the home. Women who are most likely to stay home with their children are younger than 24 and have obtained high-school diplomas, according to the U.S. Census. Older, more educated moms are more likely to keep working. When women quit to raise kids, they rarely retire for good. According to a report issued in December by the Census, 75 percent of women with school-age children are employed or looking for work. By the time their children are 12 or older, that number rises to 80 percent. "The nature of the economy," says Kathleen Getson, a New York University sociologist, "means that only a very tiny percentage of women very wealthy ones," can afford to leave the work force entirely.

Which is not to say that the landscape for working moms isn't changing. While the number of US working moms rose dramatically in the 1970s and 1980s, those numbers peaked at 73 percent in 2000. Since then, the number of working mothers has dropped about 1.6 percent. But this shift doesn't indicate an "opt-out revolution" among affluent moms [...]. Instead, it reflects a tough labor market [...] since men and childless women have left the workplace at similar rates. [...]

Even contented stay-at-home moms like Angela Dixon, 31, of Collinsville, Ill., know that staying home with the kids might not always be an option. After five years as a paralegal, she and her husband, a truck driver, decided she should quit to raise their two kids. "If something happens to my husband, if he can't do it for us," Dixon will become a paralegal again.[...] Right now, though, she's not looking. She says she already has the best job in the world.

Newsweek, March 6th, 2006, by Peg Tyre

I. Compréhension **À rédiger en français**

Après avoir dégagé l'idée principale de l'article, vous ferez un compte-rendu en 180 mots (±10%).

II. Expression **À rédiger en anglai**

1. Using the information given in the table, describe the situation of working women in the world. Draw your conclusions (100 words).

2. Do you believe women have the power to make things change? (at least 150 words)

Global employment trends for women in 2006

Workers in the world: 2.9 billion
Working women: 1.2 billion
Women over 15 who work: 50%
Men over 15 who work: 70%
Women: 60% of the world's working poor
Female unemployment rate: 6.6%
Male unemployment rate: 6.1%
Women in wage employment: 47.9%
Women earn 90% or less than their male co-workers

Unit 3 Human resources

Employees make the company and should at the very least be heard. Profit is important for a company's survival and growth, but it is the people who make it happen. It is up to managers to listen to the staff and try to understand what it is that drives them to perform. The key is a solid foundation in win-win negotiations; how to empower, coach, and mentor; and how to lead and not just manage. Without the focus on human resources, the company is destined to doom.

1. You've got to laugh!

Forget salary, location, prospects – happiness is the new weapon in the drive to recruit the best and brightest new workers.

A new survey which set out to understand what makes for happy employees, found the most important factor is having friendly, supportive colleagues. Languishing in 10th place in the Happiness at Work index, conducted by a human resources consultancy, is a competitive salary. But happiness comes not just from having a laugh at work. Many employees want to know that they will be looked after, and that their employer has interests beyond the bottom line.

At an educational software company, an HR director said job seekers were increasingly interested in office atmosphere, extracurricular activities and company values.

Another Software developer Chris Munday said that when he was recruited seven years ago, the social aspects of working were emphasised. He added: "I remember watching a video of the last summer party and being impressed by the scale of the event being put on, to say thanks to the employees for their efforts." And it was persuasive!

BBC News, January 2007

Read the text.

1. What does the survey show?
2. What is important according to an HR director? And to Chris Munday?

2. On the job training

It is the responsibility of supervisors and managers to utilize available resources to train, qualify, and develop their employees. On-the-job training (OJT) is one of the best training methods because it is planned, organized, and conducted at the employee's worksite. OJT will generally be the primary method used for broadening employee skills and increasing productivity. It is particularly appropriate for developing proficiency skills unique to an employee's job. To have a successful OJT program, supervisors need to assign a coach to each employee involved in OJT.

US Department of the Interior

Read the article.

1. Say what the advantages of OJT are.
2. Find information about "lifelong learning" and the impact it has on the job market.

3. Why trade unions are powerful in Las Vegas!

Las Vegas is an unlikely stronghold of unionism, and not just because it is built on the promise of easy money. It lies in the "right-to-work" state, meaning that workers do not have to be members of a union to hold a particular job or be covered by a union contract. Its population is young and footloose – Nevada has been the fastest-growing state in the union for 19 out of the past 20 years – which does not encourage feelings of solidarity. And it hardly manufactures anything.

Las Vegas has become the symbol of "new" unionism, which is characterised by a missionary approach to recruitment. Membership of southern Nevada's carpenters' union has tripled in the past decade. Put that down to hotel owners' enthusiasm for blowing up perfectly good buildings and replacing them with fake tropical islands and European cities.

The most powerful outfit in the state is the 51,000-strong culinary workers' union, which represents hotel and casino employees.

Read the article.

1. Explain why it is unexpected to hear that Nevada is one of the most unionized states in the USA.

2. How can you account for this?

4. Selling equipment to monitor workplaces

Listen to the recording.

1. What are the pros and cons of monitoring workplaces?

2. Why do they mention Big Brother?

REPORTING

In the previous articles, pick out details that you think would contribute to making an ideal atmosphere in the workplace.

WORDS APART

The workforce **La main-d'œuvre**

- **an appraisal** une évaluation
- **an assessment** une appréciation, évaluation
- **a bias** un préjugé
- **career prospects** les perspectives d'emploi
- **a contribution** une cotisation
- **discrimination** une discrimination
- **a dress code** un code vestimentaire
- **a gender gap** un fossé entre les genres
- **glass ceiling** plafond (de verre) qui limite l'ascension professionnelle
- **manpower** la main-d'œuvre
- **membership** membres adhérents
- **the payroll** la masse salariale
- **a payslip** une feuille de paye
- **to reward** récompenser
- **to shortlist** sélectionner
- **training** la formation

Employee rights **Les droits des employés**

- **allowances** les allocations
- **to award damages** accorder des dommages et intérêts
- **benefits** des prestations
- **to be on social security** percevoir l'aide sociale
- **health care cover** une couverture médicale
- **an incentive** une stimulation
- **maternity/paternity leave** un congé de maternité, paternité
- **perks/fringe benefits** des avantages en nature
- **profit sharing** la participation
- **a retirement pension** une pension de retraite
- **a salary rise** une augmentation de salaire
- **severance pay** une indemnité de licenciement
- **sick leave** un congé de maladie
- **the welfare state** l'état providence
- **a works council** un comité d'entreprise
- **work/life balance** équilibre travail et vie

Industrial disputes **Conflits sociaux (direction/salariés)**

- **a claim/a demand** une revendication
- **collective bargaining** négociation collective
- **compensation** un dédommagement
- **a demonstration** une manifestation
- **dismissals/lay offs** licenciements
- **to downsize** dégraisser
- **to engender** engendrer
- **to exert pressure** exercer de la pression
- **grievances** plaintes
- **a notice** préavis
- **a riot** une émeute
- **a shop steward** un délégué syndical
- **social unrest** agitation sociale
- **to stage a strike** organiser une grève
- **to sue** poursuivre en justice
- **a union representative/delegate** un représentant syndical

Unit 3 Human resources

Zooming on

How to lose your job on your own time

Ms. Snyder's MySpace page featured a photograph of the student wearing a pirate hat and sipping from a plastic cup with the caption "Drunken Pirate". The university administrators deemed the image "unprofessional," and refused to award her an education degree and teaching certificate.

Were Henry Ford brought back to life today, he would most likely be delighted by the Internet: the uninhibited way many people express themselves on the Web makes it easy to supervise the private lives of employees.

In his day, the Ford Motor Company maintained a "Sociological Department" staffed with investigators who visited the homes of all but the highest-level managers. Their job was to dig for information about the employee's religion, spending and savings patterns, drinking habits and how the worker "amused himself." Home inspections are no longer needed; many companies are using the Internet to snoop[1] on their employees. If you fail to maintain amorphous "professional" standards of conduct in your free time, you could lose your job.

Employment law in most states provides little protection to workers who are punished for their online postings [...]. The main exceptions are workers who are covered by collective bargaining agreements or by special protections for public-sector employees; members of these groups can be dismissed only "for cause." The rest of us are "at will" employees, holding on to our jobs only at the whim[2] of our employers, and thus vulnerable.

A line needs to be drawn that demarcates the boundary between work and private life. When a worker is on the job, companies have every right to supervise activities closely. But what an employee does after hours, as long as no laws are broken, is none of the company's business.

In the absence of strong protections for employees, poorly chosen words or even a single photograph posted online can have career-altering consequences.

Stacy Snyder, 25, a senior at Millersville University, offers an instructive example. She filed a lawsuit in April this year in federal court contending[3] that her rights to free expression under the First Amendment had been violated. No trial date has been set.

© *New York Times*, December 30th, 2007,
by Randall Stross

1. *espionner* – 2. *caprice* – 3. *prétendre*

FIRST STEPS

Look at the picture and read the title of the article.

1. Say if the article deals with:
a. recruiting, **b.** dismissing, **c.** training.

2. Say if the threat concerns:
a. on the job activity, **b.** off the job activity.

MOVING ON

1. Why is Henry Ford mentioned here?

2. What did Henry Ford invent?

3. Explain what is meant by "home inspections are no longer needed".

4. Why do employees have to show "amorphous professional standards of conduct"?

5. Say if the following statements are right or wrong and justify your answer by quoting from the text.

a. In Ford's time all levels of management were under surveillance.
b. Employees are unlikely to be covered by the law for their online displays.
c. The public sector requires reasonable grounds to lay off people.
d. Companies are entitled to check employees' extra-professional activities.

6. Find words that mean the same as:

a. probably **b.** pleased **c.** extract **d.** entertained
e. lack **f.** laid off **g.** lawsuit

7. Say what the expression "career-altering (consequences)" means:

a. it may change your career,
b. it may endanger your career,
c. it may end your career.

8. Is Stacy Snyder's case:

a. a landmark,
b. an exception,
c. a model?

9. Translate

Translate from "In the absence of strong protections for employees..." (line 20) to "No trial date has been set." (end of the text)

WRITING (150 words)

What do you think of Ms Snyder's case?

Do you believe that one day nothing that is said online will be treated as embarrassing because we will have become so accustomed to everyone disclosing everything?
Where should the role of an HRM stop for you?

LANGUAGE AT WORK

1. In the following list of words, underline the syllable that is stressed, then listen to the recording and check your answers.

Administrators / uninhibited / supervise / sociological / department / investigators / information / professional / collective / vulnerable / bargaining / consequences.

2. What does the following sentence mean: "Were Henry Ford brought back to life?"

a. Why not imagine Henry Ford was still alive?

b. Suppose Henry Ford was brought back to life?

What word could you have used to start the sentence?

a. while, **b.** if, **c.** although.

3. What does the following sentence mean: "investigators visited the homes of all but the highest-level managers?"

a. even the highest-level managers were visited,

b. the highest-level managers were the only ones not to be visited.

What could you replace the word "BUT" by?

a. only, **b.** yet, **c.** except.

4. In the text, find nine verbs used in the passive form.

5. Fill in the blanks by using the correct form of the verbs in brackets.

Last year, she (give) a reward for her good services. This year, she could (lay off) for the bad image she (display) online. Next time she (be) more careful with the kind of documents that can (find) about her on the net. She (swear) she (not run) the risk again.

6. Translate the following sentences into French.

a. Had she guessed the consequences of her act, she wouldn't have even thought of doing it.

b. I wish we had warned her in advance not to use this kind of website. She would not have been spied on.

c. I'd rather you didn't post it before showing it to us. One never knows.

7. Translate the following sentences into English.

a. On dit qu'elle pourrait se faire licencier sans pouvoir expliquer son cas.

b. Votre vie privée peut être espionnée si vous ne faites pas preuve de suffisamment de prudence.

c. Il a été sanctionné alors qu'il n'avait rien fait du tout.

Unit 3 Human resources

1. Retaining employees

YOUR JOB

You work in the human resources department. Several resignations have been handed in. The Human Resources Manager asks you and your colleagues to devise a scheme which will better retain employees.

YOUR TASK

1. List the reasons why employees left, from the most obvious to the least probable reasons. **(See Doc. 1)**
2. Draw up a questionnaire to check employees' satisfaction. **(See Doc. 2)**
3. Prepare the schedule of meetings, assessment sessions, individual interviews.
4. Design a psychological approach to get to know the staff better (people's interests, ambitions, expectations, prospects...) **(See Docs. 2 & 3)**.

Document 1

Quitting jobs

Hiring good people is tough, but as every senior executive knows, keeping them can be even tougher. Indeed, most executives can tell a story or two about a talented professional who joined their company to great fanfare, added enormous value for a couple of years, and then departed unexpectedly. Usually such exits are written off. "She got an offer she couldn't refuse," you hear, or, "No one stays with one company for very long these days." Our research over the past 12 years strongly suggests that quite another dynamic is frequently at work. Many talented professionals leave their organizations because senior managers don't understand the psychology of work satisfaction; they assume that people who excel at their work are necessarily happy in their jobs. Sounds logical enough. But the fact is, strong skills don't always reflect or lead to job satisfaction. Many professionals, particularly the leagues of 20- and 30-somethings streaming out of today's MBA programs, are so well educated and achievement oriented that they could succeed in virtually any job. But will they stay?

Harvard Business Review,
by T. Butler and J. Waldroop

Document 2

Morale and not money

Document 3

Matching people to jobs

Job sculpting is the art of matching people to jobs that allow their deeply embedded life interests to be expressed. It is the art of forging a customized career path in order to increase the chance of retaining talented people. Make no mistake - job sculpting is challenging; it requires managers to play both detective and psychologist. The reason: many people have only a dim awareness of their own deeply embedded life interests. They may have spent their lives fulfilling other people's expectations of them, or they may have followed the most common career advice: "Do what you're good at." For example, we know of a woman who, on the basis of her skill at chemistry in college, was urged to become a doctor. She complied and achieved great success as a neurologist, but at age 42 she finally quit to open a nursery school. She loved children, demonstrating a deeply embedded life interest in counseling and mentoring. And more important, as it turned out, she was also driven by a life interest in enterprise control, the desire to be in charge of an organization's overall operations. It was a long time before she stopped remarking, "All those years wasted."

Harvard Business Review,
by T. Butler and J. Waldroop

Document 2

Employee retention: Why is it important?

As you know, it is getting more difficult to find and keep talented workers. U.S. businesses spend over $200 billion annually recruiting and replacing employees.

Estimates show 48 to 65 percent of the workforce is dissatisfied with their current employment situation and could leave for better positions as the economic situation continues to improve. Unemployment is the lowest it has been since 2000. By 2010 we could expect a shortage of nearly seven to ten million workers.

The Society of Human Resource Management (SHRM) and the Wall Street Journal website completed the Job Recovery Survey. The key findings revealed 64 percent of employees said they were extremely likely to begin or increase the intensity of their job search. An additional 19 percent said they were somewhat likely to increase their search.

Successful organizations realize employee retention and talent management is integral to sustaining their leadership and growth in the marketplace. Attracting, hiring, and retaining high-caliber employees in today's labor market challenges all organizations to manage talent at all levels.

Is your crew getting ready to abandon ship??
Don't let the good ones get away!
Retention programs are less expensive than recruitment programs.

2. Assessing yourself

YOUR JOB

You work in the Human Resources Department and are asked to carry out experimental approaches to help employees delineate their objectives and prospects with success.

YOUR TASK

You ask the group of employees you have decided to gather together to do the Kaleidoscope test.

1. After reading Documents 1 and 2, you give them a short account of what is expected from them in the following step: the Kaleidoscope test (**See Doc. 3**).

2. Then you write a short report to the Human Resources Manager to give him/her an account of the experiment.

Document 1

Career strategy

A fast-track 32-year-old software engineer with a second degree in sacred music feels that something is missing in her career strategy. She wants the life-style of a well-paid manager, but software doesn't feel as socially significant as playing the organ for a congregation. And she someday wants a house and a family. "Why can't I find the career path that will get me all of these things?" she wonders. "Are they really so unreasonable?"

Document 2

Managing oneself

To begin by asking yourself these questions:

"What are my strengths?"

To accurately identify your strengths, use feedback analysis. Every time you make a key decision, write down the outcome you expect. Several months later, compare the actual results with your expected results. What abilities do you need to enhance in order to get the results you want? What unproductive habits are preventing you from creating the outcomes you desire?

"How do I work?"

In what ways do you work best? Do you process information most effectively by reading it, or by hearing others discuss it? Do you accomplish the most by working with other people, or by working alone? Do you perform best while making decisions, or while advising others on key matters? Are you in top form when things get stressful, or do you function optimally in a highly predictable environment?

"What are my values?"

What are your ethics? What do you see as your most important responsibilities for living a worthy, ethical life? Do your organization's ethics resonate with your own values? If not, your career will likely be marked by frustration and poor performance.

"Where do I belong?"

Consider your strengths, preferred work style, and values. Based on these qualities, in what kind of work environment would you fit in best?

"What can I contribute?"

In earlier eras, companies told businesspeople what their contribution should be. Today, you have choices. To decide how you can best enhance your organization's performance, first ask what the situation requires. Based on your strengths, work style, and values, how might you make the greatest contribution to your organization's efforts?

The Harvard Business Review, by Peter F. Drucker

Document 3

The kaleidoscope strategy

Imagine the four components of success–happiness, achievement, significance, and legacy–to be four chambers of a kaleidoscope. Each goal you reach adds another brilliantly colored chip to a chamber, enriching your unique pattern over a lifetime. Only by setting and achieving goals in each area will you create a well-balanced mix.

Create your own kaleidoscope: Draw four intersecting circles and label them happiness, achievement, significance, and legacy. In each circle, jot down examples of your successes. Take your college degree, for instance. If your degree represents to you a mastery of skills, then write "college" in your achievement chamber. But if it holds special significance because you were the first person in your family to go to college, you might put it in your significance chamber. The point is to help you assess the various types of satisfactions you have already experienced and see what they add up to.

Analyze your success patterns:
- Are some of the chambers empty?
- Are others too full?
- Where am I devoting most of my time?
- Is that in line with the goals I want to achieve?

The Harvard Business Review,
by Laura Nash and Howard Stevenson

Unit 3 Human resources

Test Yourself

Wages rise in China

Working a 45-hour week, Mr. Zhang makes the equivalent of $263 a month; as recently as February, he was making just $197. Some of his higher pay comes from working more efficiently. "When I first started, I wasn't this fast," he said.

But a good portion reflects a raise Mr. Zhang got: to 1.45 cents for each bicycle seat from 1.32 cents. It is a small difference that signifies major change.

Chinese wages are on the rise. No reliable figures for average wages exist; the government's economic data are notably unreliable. But factory owners and experts who monitor the nation's labor market say that businesses are having a hard time finding able-bodied workers and are having to pay the workers they can find more money. And higher wages in China are likely to lead to higher prices in the United States - at the mall, at the grocery, even at the gas pump.

This summer, Mary Gallagher, a Chinese labor specialist at the University of Michigan, visited five sportswear factories near Shanghai and Guangzhou. She found them all struggling to hire and retain workers. One had shut one of its two main production lines because it had nobody to sew shirts and other garments.

"Basically half the factory was shut down and one dormitory was empty," Ms. Gallagher said.

In interviews, factory executives across the country complained of being forced to give double-digit raises in order to find and keep young workers at all skill levels. Chinese officials are quick to say that there is no overall shortage of labor - rather, there is a shortage of young workers willing to accept the low wages that prevailed in the 1990s.

Moreover, labor regulation is weak in China, as shown most vividly this year by the discovery that brick kilns in the north of the country had kidnapped and enslaved hundreds of children and mentally disadvantaged adults, working them under brutal conditions with little or no pay.

"It's easy to find a job with not a very high salary," said Chen Zheng, a 24-year-old auto worker and high school graduate in Ningbo. "It's not easy if you want a higher wage."

Corrigé page 190

I. Compréhension

Après une lecture attentive du texte, vous ferez un compte rendu en anglais en 150 mots maximum.

II. Traduction

Vous traduirez en français depuis: "Working a 45-hour week, Mr. Zhang...." jusqu'à : "at the mall, at the grocery, even at the gas pump."

Exam Paper

The feminine critique

Don't get angry. But do take charge. Be nice. But not too nice. Speak up. But don't seem like you talk too much. Never, ever dress sexy. Make sure to inspire your colleagues – unless you work in Norway, in which case, focus on delegating instead. Writing about life and work means receiving a steady stream of research on how women in the workplace are viewed differently from men. These are academic and professional studies, not whimsical online polls, and each time I read one I feel deflated.

What are women supposed to do with this information? Transform overnight? And if so, into what? How are we supposed to be assertive, but not, at the same time? "It's enough to make you dizzy," said Ilene H. Lang, the president of Catalyst, an organization that studies women in the workplace. "Women are dizzy, men are dizzy, and we still don't have a simple straightforward answer as to why there just aren't enough women in positions of leadership." Catalyst's research is often an exploration of why, 30 years after women entered the work force in large numbers, the default mental image of a leader is still male.

Most recent is the report titled "Damned if You Do, Doomed if You Don't," which surveyed 1,231 senior executives from the United States and Europe. It found that women who act in ways that are consistent with gender stereotypes – defined as focusing "on work relationships" and expressing "concern for other people's perspectives" – are considered less competent. But if they act in ways that are seen as more "male" – like "act assertively, focus on work task, display ambition" – they are seen as "too tough" and "unfeminine." Women can't win. [...] They are expected to be nurturing, but seen as ineffective if they are too feminine. They are expected to be strong, but tend to be labeled as strident or abrasive when acting as leaders. "Women have to choose between being liked but not respected, or respected but not liked." "Most of what we learn shows that the problem is with the perception, not with the woman."

In fact, Catalyst's next large project is to advise companies on ways they can combat stereotypical bias.

I. Compréhension

Après une lecture attentive du texte, rédigez une synthèse en français en 150 mots.

II. Expression **À rédiger en anglais**

Discuss what you think matters today in the recruitment process. Explain the importance of "dress code", for example, say if you think it is possible to combat stereotyped ideas… (150 words)

Unit 4 Industrial relations

When applying for a job, and once hired, the working place is far from being a bed of roses every day. Workers are regularly confronted with unfair regulations, injustice and abuse. Working together, however, remains the right way to socialize, understand each other, and improve one's position.

Zooming on

1. Skills and needs, an outdated recipe?

Die Zeit, 2004

Have a look at this photo.

1. Situate the scene.

2. Describe the main character.

This man is carrying a bill-board. Look at it.

1. Pick out the figures used in the message.

2. Associate each figure with the appropriate topic and explain what they mean.

3. This message contains a paradox; make it more explicit.

4. Imagine how the man on the street would react to such a CV.

2. Ethnic minorities on the brink

JOURNALIST: Now it's long been established that on average women are paid less than men, but the EOC has come up with some new statistics that show there's even a pay gap amongst women. Their research shows that black and Asian females are generally paid the least of all. Whilst the average discrepancy is 17%, some women from ethnic minorities are paid up to 28% less than their male counterparts.

BBC News, January 2007

Read the beginning of this report.

1. Say what specific issue is raised.

2. Pick out the statistics and comment on them. Give your conclusions.

Continue listening to the tape.

1. Give the reasons why Jenny investigated this topic.

2. List the categories of workers in unfair positions.

3. Women still waiting in the boardroom

In most developed economies, women make up slightly less than half of the work force. But the nature –and rewards– of their work vary widely between countries..

Newsweek, February 27th, 2006

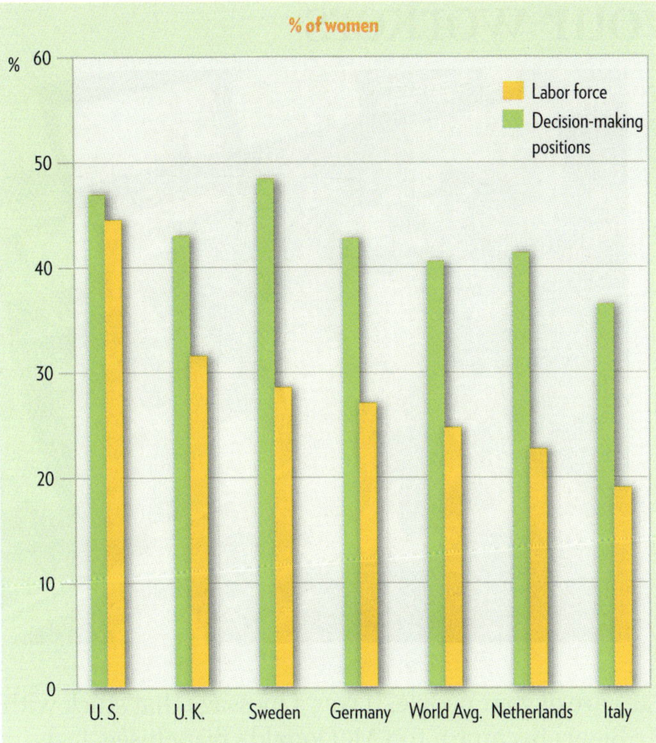

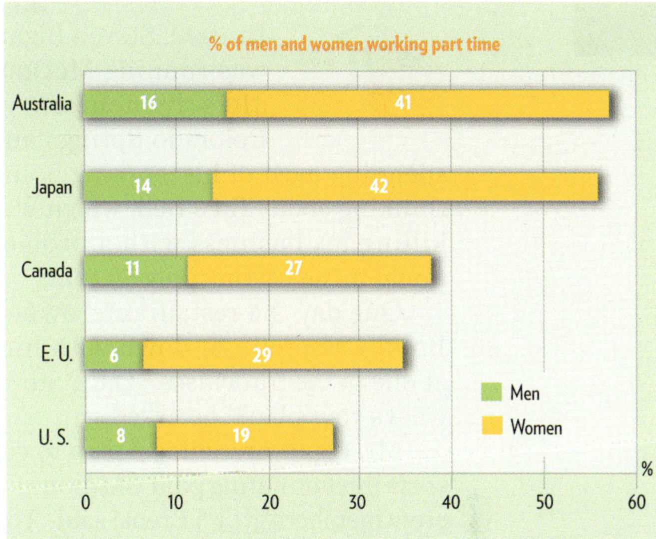

Look at the charts very carefully.

1. Comment on the bar-charts and compare the figures.

2. Account for the discrepancies: first from one country to another, then between genders.

REPORTING

The continent's boomers are retiring but the number of job opportunities still dwindles. The generation that comes next increasingly feels locked out of the European dream. Do you share this view?

WORDS APART

Drawbacks Les inconvénients

to be fired/laid off/sacked être licencié
to be in the red être à découvert
to be overworked être surmené
to be redundant être au chômage technique
to be underpaid être sous payé
to buy on credit acheter à crédit
a contribution une cotisation
the discrepancies les différences
the pay-gap le fossé des salaires
the gender gap le fossé entre les sexes
health expenditures des dépenses de santé
an industrial injury un accident du travail
to live on the fringe of society vivre en marge de la société
to raise ethnic issues soulever des problèmes racistes
sexual harassment harcèlement sexuel
the spendings les dépenses
unemployment/joblessness chômage

Advantages Les avantages

the earnings les gains
a golden handshake une prime de départ
a redundancy payment/severance package une prime de licenciement
to ask for a pay-rise demander une augmentation de salaire
to be awarded damages recevoir des dommages-intérêts
to be on the dole percevoir l'allocation chômage
to be on social security percevoir l'aide sociale
in cash or in kind en espèces ou en nature
to compensate s.o for indemniser qq'un
compensation un dédommagement
to lodge a complaint/to file a claim porter plainte
a maternity/paternity leave un congé de maternité/paternité
a pension fund une caisse de retraite
a retiree un retraité

In-betweens Les intermédiaires

an agreement un accord
an amicable settlement un corèglement à l'amiable
the Unions les syndicats
the spokesman le délégué
to demonstrate manifester
to be on strike être en grève
a striker un gréviste
the talks les pourparlers
a career break une interruption de carrière
to resign démissionner
to cancel résilier
a claimant/claimer un ayant-droit
social insurance une assurance maladie
the standard of living le niveau de vie
a time bomb une bombe à retardement
the academic records le cursus scolaire
a birth certificate un bulletin de naissance
a retirement home une maison de retraite
the elderly les personnes âgées

Industrial relations

Help your workers

In 1990, Steven Bigari was running McDonald's franchises in Colorado Springs and spending most of his working hours thinking about Taco Bell, which was killing his business with a promotional menu costing only 59 cents.

One day the restaurants' owner, Brent Cameron, sat down with him at one of the franchises. "O.K., Steve, what's your plan?" he asked.

Mr. Bigari presented a plan to cut costs by eliminating paid vacations for crew members. [...] "[Brent] said, 'You can afford to give up your vacation, but they can't, so I hope you have a better plan than that."

Mr Bigari said he got the message: take care of your people. It was a message that stuck with him even after Mr Cameron died and Mr Bigari became a top McDonald's franchisee. [...]

He created a system to help resolve the problems of the working poor who staffed his restaurants by pulling together an array of services, from day care to transportation to small emergency loans. The goal, he said, was to keep his employees on the job and focused on customers.

Now he is trying to persuade others to offer this kind of help to their workers, not as an act of kindness or charity but as a way to reduce employee turnover and increase profit. [...]

He had no such plans a decade ago, when he decided to continue Mr Cameron's practice of making small, short-term no-interest personal loans to his employees to help them pay their rent, buy tires or meet their immediate needs. [...]

By 2001, Mr Bigari was calling his programs McFamily Benefits, and it worked well, for his employees and for him. [...] All of the employees [...] said they felt motivated to work harder. [...]

Debra Powell, a divorced mother of five who managed one of Mr Bigari's restaurants, said the program helped many of her crew workers, which in turn made her job easier. She herself had money problems, and Mr Bigari found a budgeting course at a local non profit agency; it helped her so much that she required all the managers in her store take it, partly because many of them had never had checking accounts.

She used Mr Bigari's program in 2003 to get a loan for a personal computer and in 2004 to buy the first car she had ever purchased.

FIRST STEPS

1. Account for Mr Bigari's former and current positions at McDonald's.

2. Say what you learnt about Mr Cameron's position and the role he played in Mr Bigari's vision of the enterprise.

3. Define the industrial relations that link the manager to his staff in this article.

4. Comment on the example of Debra Powell.

MOVING ON

1. Read the title of the article and say why it sounds paradoxical.

2. Pick out the information showing Mr Bigari's business was a lame duck at the start.

3. What did he blame his employees for and how did he want to punish them to solve his problems?

4. Find the reason why his solution to boost his restaurant was a mistake.

5. Say whether these statements are true or false. Quote from the passage:

a. Mr Bigari didn't understand what Mr Cameron meant.
b. When Mr Cameron died, Mr Bigari laid off the staff.
c. His employees could borrow money from him.
d. He wanted to keep his employees loyal to the business.

6. What was the aim of this new industrial policy?

7. Pick out the elements showing Mr Bigari's policy benefits to both his employees and his outlet.

8. Define what McFamily Benefits consists of.

9. Would you agree and say that McFamily Benefits is a business within a business? Why or why not?

10. To what extent, does lending money generate a feel of good relation?

11. Mr Bigari's scheme seems to fit everybody's needs. Yet the workers' freedom is questionable. Give your opinion.

12. Translate

Translate from "He had no such plans..." (line 27) to "...or meet their immediates needs." (line 29)

WRITING (150 words)

Would you agree to work for a company that manages your bank account, your expenses and earnings? Can money make you loyal to your boss? Are you ready to lose your independence out of thankfulness?

LANGUAGE AT WORK

1. Read the following words containing the letter / u / and arrange them in 5 categories:

business / menu / cut / stuck / pull / customers / persuade / reduce / turnover / understand / continue / budget / computer / purchase.

2. Guess the French translation of the following word families:

a franchiser / a franchisee;
a trainer / a trainee;
an employer / an employee;
to retire / a retiree.

3. Use "to rise" or "to raise" to fill in the gaps. Use the appropriate form.

a. His boss has decided .... his salary by 10 per cent.

b. His staff turnover .... dangerously in this firm.

c. She got a promotion with an annual $1,000 pay-....

d. The loan rates have been .... dramatically by the bank.

4. Complete with a relative pronoun.

a. The worker .... asks for a loan eventually feels dependent.

b. They ran several franchises .... were set around the capital.

c. The owner .... restaurant closed down last month, is in trouble now.

d. The only thing .... he demanded was to be loyal to the firm.

5. Translate into French.

a. Mr Bigari is said to be a genuine leader, he works alongside minimum-wage workers.

b. In the same period, his profit margin rose more than three percentage points.

6. Translate into English.

a. Il espérait réduire les frais en supprimant les congés payés.

b. En ouvrant des crédits, les ouvriers amélioraient leur niveau de vie.

c. Grâce à leur patron, ils avaient la sécurité de l'emploi.

d. Pour éviter les absences de ses employés, il fallait les motiver.

e. Il l'aida à ouvrir un compte et à acheter un ordinateur à crédit.

Unit 4 Industrial relations

1. Writing a letter of complaint

YOUR JOB
You have been hired as a shop assistant at the deli counter in a Safeway branch near Canterbury.

YOUR TASK
You have been working there for three months and think that your working conditions are unacceptable.

1. Use the table below to list the arguments supporting your complaint.
2. Write a letter to Safeway's Personnel Manager.

ACTING OUT
Express your point of view to the Equal Opportunies Commission.

Pros	Cons
flexible hours / free time / bonus / profit-sharing / blocks of time / longer breaks / pay rise	overtime / unpaid extra hours / travelling expenses / limited promotion / danger / hygiene

2. Reporting an example of positive discrimination

YOUR JOB
You have been recruited as a member of an information team promoting the London Olympics in liaison with Manpower, the well-known job centre.

YOUR TASK
You are asked to design a leaflet showing the positive effects of the Olympics on employment. The leaflet should invite prospective female workers to apply. You have been given the recording of an interview and the framework below as a starter **(See Doc. 1)**.

Document 1

The London Olympics

3. Reporting on cases of discrimination

YOUR JOB
You are a journalist working for the Equal Opportunities Commission.

YOUR TASK
You have been asked to investigate new trends in discrimination at work and to write a one-hundred-word article reporting on cases of discrimination in the workplace.
1. Pick out the examples that you can cite in your report (**See Doc. 1 & 2**).
2. Combine these elements to write a press article with a title.

ACTING OUT
Present your point of view to the other students.

Document 1

Discrimination at work hits men too

Sexual discrimination is rife in certain professions but it affects men as well as women, according to research which challenges the traditional notion that women are the only victims of sexism in job applications.

Researchers found significant evidence of a bias against men in jobs for chartered accountants and computer analysts, which are already considered more gender neutral than some. While women are being passed over for engineering jobs because of their gender, men are even more likely to be turned away from secretarial posts. [...]

[Judy Rich, an economist at Portsmouth School, and Peter A. Riach] sent off two fake applications for more than 400 jobs in the four professions. Each applicant had equal experience, qualifications and age profiling but one bore a man's name, the other a woman's. They found women were half as likely to be invited for an interview for an engineering job compared with men, and men were nearly four times less likely than women to get an interview for the secretarial posts.

The pay gap between men and women currently stands at 17.1 [...].

© *Guardian*, News & Media Ltd 2006, 25 February 2006, by Polly Curtis

Document 2

Immigration hits young too

PROMPTS

I would like to lodge a complaint against X. *Je voudrais porter plainte contre X.*

I think it unfair to hire male staff only. *Je pense qu'il est injuste d'engager un personnel uniquement masculin.*

I really believe that the pay gap is unfair. *Je crois sincérement que la difference de salaire n'est pas justifiée.*

My colleagues' statements justify my claim. *Le témoignage de mes collègues justifie ma demande.*

I have listed unpaid overtime. *J'ai répertorié les heures supplémentaires non rémunérées.*

I hope an agreement will be reached to settle this problem. *J'espère que l'on trouvera un terrain d'entente pour régler cette affaire.*

I couldn't bear working there any longer that way. *Je ne pourrais pas travailler là plus longtemps de cette manière.*

Unit 4 Industrial relations

4. Downsizing or rightsizing?

"Want to improve your company's bottom line? Chances are you're thinking of cutting staff. Here are some tips you are offered to help 'rightsize' your staff..."

YOUR JOB

As a junior official at the Audit Office, you have been asked by Campbell's CEO to check the situation. Layoffs are foreseen in this packaging company.

YOUR TASK

The company is currently going through a financial downturn following a recent reshuffle, and you are asked to give the Board of Directors advice on the company management.

1. Read the tables (**See Doc. 1 and 2**) then match the "Guiding Values" to the corresponding headlines.
2. Do the Prompts exercises and select useful phrases.
3. Select at least three solutions from "Guiding Values" (**See Doc. 2**) to try and solve the problems.
4. Find the right words to convince your audience.

ACTING OUT

You are in the boardroom. Give your final advice and encourage the managers to adopt a new policy. Here are some guidelines.
Are the right staff doing the right things? Do they exhibit the right behaviour? Are they receiving the right rewards?

Document 1

Tracking headlines

Value experienced employees.	Look for signs of "wrongsizing."	Benchmark staffing levels.	Don't reward the wrong people.
Track productivity.	Educate your staff.	Offer incentives.	Consider part-timers.

PROMPTS

1. Fill in the blanks with the appropriate preposition.

a. It's no use cutting so many jobs .... reduce costs.
b. I was entrusted .... this mission two months ago.
c. I worked for Spencer's .... 10 years.
d. I was hired by Mr Jones .... ten years' experience.
e. I have been responsible .... the "Logon Project".

2. Use the verbs in brackets and turn them into the correct form.

a. I should (advise) you of the dangers of cutting jobs.
b. Why not (ask) your employees?
c. Some (be) on probation for several months.
d. They expect you (give) them a promotion.
e. They look forward to (earn) a higher salary.
f. They could be (motivate) by new incentives.
g. They might (agree) with our proposals.

Document 2

Guiding values

1. Count hours, not bodies. Add your staff's weekly hours, including their overtime, and divide by 40 to calculate the number of full-time staff members you employ per week. Compare your staffing ratios to those considered to be "best performers."

2. Keep a tab on staff for a few days to see how many tasks they perform. Use the data that can help you spot problems. If your productivity seems low, try to find out why. Perhaps a new staff member needs more training or your computer system is not working properly. Or you might find that staff members are being pulled away to do other tasks, like a billing team that sits right behind the front desk and ends up working the front end. The solution there might be to give them their own office and hire more receptionists.

3. If you have too few staff members, you are probably paying a lot of overtime, which hurts profits and burns out staff. Even firms that have enough staff can often do a better job with staff scheduling. Do you never have enough receptionists during peak times like Monday morning, but find staff standing around for most of Friday afternoon? So, adjust staff schedules to better match demand or hire part-timers to get the coverage you need.

4. If your most experienced employees spend their days filing or running a copier, you're not taking advantage of their expertise. For example, hiring a part-time billing person might free up a more experienced person to track down payment delays.

5. Try tapping into the part-time labor force of retirees, former employees looking for a second job and stay-at-home moms who want to work only a few hours a week. Full-time employees may balk at working on Saturday morning if you want to extend your hours, for instance. That position might be perfect for someone who wants to work part time.

6. While traditional conferences and seminars are one way to give employees new skills and knowledge, Ms. Larch urged groups to look for educational opportunities closer to home. Anyone who has worked at your firm for four years is an expert. Have him or her sit and talk about what he or she knows to other staff members over lunch or a snack.

7. Don't reward poor performance by continuing to shell out overtime to an employee who works too slowly. A skewed reward system can cost you good employees, especially if bigger workloads don't come with more benefits.

8. Employees are more motivated when they have a stake in financial results. Employees can get an incentive that can add up to an additional 10% of their base pay as a bonus for an individual performance but these 10% extra may be tied to the entire company's performance too. And don't make the mistake of trying to keep your incentive plan a secret. Keep any kind of incentive plan out in the open, particularly when it comes to salaries.

PROMPTS

I am persuaded/convinced. *Je suis convaincu.*
I strongly deter you from doing. *Je tiens à vous dissuader de faire.*
You'd better do... *Vous feriez mieux de faire...*
Why not do...? *Pourquoi ne pas faire... ?*
If I were you, I'd do... *Si j'étais vous, je ferais...*
What about doing...? *Que diriez-vous de faire... ?*
I'd rather you did... *Je préfèrerais que vous fassiez...*
You should/ought to. *Vous devriez.*

Test Yourself

A strike too many

Cheonju, South Korea, is thousands of miles away from Detroit. But the two cities have something in common: powerful labour unions. For nearly a year, the Korean automotive giant Hyundai has pushed to add a night shift at its plant in Cheonju to meet growing demands. But the union has repeatedly rejected the proposal. Annoyed by a 10-month backlog in orders, Hyundai management recently sent out a letter to union members warning them that if they didn't compromise, their work might go overseas. The union refused to budge.

[...] In fact with an annual salary of $60,000, Hyundai employees are among the highest-paid blue-collar workers in Korea, and make just a bit less than the average salary of their compatriots in Detroit. Hyundai, the world's sixth-largest automaker, is also plagued with many of the same problems that have driven American auto giants like GM and Ford to the brink of solvency in recent years. Hyundai's profits declined 35 percent last year [...].

[...] Hyundai's fall was unexpected. [...] Since the early part of this decade, the company has earned more than $1 billion in yearly profits. But rather than pouring that windfall back into new production-line technology and better engineering, the company gave disproportionate raises to workers. The end result was a huge productivity gap, not only with Japanese competitors, but also with the Americans. It takes 30 man-hours to make a car at Hyundai, compared with 22 hours at Toyota and 26 hours at Ford." Hyundai's labour costs are too high compared to its productivity," says [...] an auto analyst. "Its gap with Toyota is ever increasing." Meanwhile, things are improving at Ford and GM after massive layoffs and other cost-cutting.

Those companies are turning the corner in large part because workers confronted with the reality of pay cuts or no jobs at all have made major concessions on wages, health care and pensions.

Newsweek, February 26th, 2007.

I. Compréhension

Lisez attentivement l'article ci-dessus et faites-en un compte-rendu en anglais de 200 mots.

II. Expression

1. Explain why Hyundai is losing money today.

2. Give your personal opinion about the paradox: "their work might go overseas" (lines 9-10).

METHOD — HOW TO GIVE A WRITTEN ACCOUNT OF A PRESS ARTICLE

- First, look at the headline, the date, the author's name, and the origin are several elements that will help you present the document.
- Then, look at the title and pick out the keywords informing you about the topic.
- Read the article through to the end. Don't stop to check a word in your dictionary, you'll do it later.
- Check if the topic suggested in the title matches the contents.
- Write your introduction using the elements mentioned above.
- Second reading: highlight the word-groups belonging to the same family (places, figures, time, people, actions...).
- See if the different paragraphs are set in a logical order (cause, consequence, for example) or chronological order (first, second, with different dates).
- Pick out the guidelines to choose a plan and start writing regardless of the number of words. Avoid padding, enumerations, rewriting the text and repetitions; find synonyms, link sentences.
- Write a conclusion to underline your opinion and your knowledge of the subject.
- Comply with the requirements: number of words (some cutting may be necessary), balance between the different parts (the introduction must not be longer than the summary).
- Check your English: mind the verbs, the tenses; use phrases and vocabulary you learnt.
- Watch the time...

Corrigé page 190

Exam Paper

Accused over clothing factories standards in Bangladesh

Britain's second-largest supermarket chain last weekend launched an investigation into allegations that workers who make its clothes in Bangladesh are being forced to work up to 80 hours a week for as little as 4p an hour.

Asda, one of the three major discount clothing retailers accused of breaching international labour standards, said it would audit its suppliers in response to a report in the Guardian into the pay and conditions of Bangladeshi garment[1] workers who supply British companies. [...]

Employees of factories making clothes for George at Asda, Tesco and Primark said their wages were so low that, despite working up to 80-hour weeks, they struggled to provide for their families. There were also reports of physical and verbal abuse by supervisors and of workers being sacked for taking sick leave.

All but one of the eight workers interviewed, from seven different factories, claimed that they were forced to work 12-hour days and sometimes all night to finish an order. Workers from factories supplying all three retailers said they were refused access to trade unions and claimed that, in the past month, four colleagues had been dismissed for trying to organise a union.

Parvin, 25, a sewing machine operator making jeans for Primark said she felt "threatened and frightened" after witnessing a colleague being slapped by a supervisor for not meeting her target. Azizul, 28, who works in another factory producing items for Primark, said that he had been sacked and his wages withheld for taking two days off to take his baby daughter to hospital.

[...]

All three retailers have signed up to the Ethical Trade Initiative, a voluntary code of conduct that sets out basic rights for employees, including a working week of no more than 48 hours, voluntary overtime not exceeding 12 hours a week, and payment of a "living wage". They say they are doing their best to improve Workers' rights.

However, one factory owner in Bangladesh [...] told the Guardian that buyers gave him little choice but to keep wages low. [The Chairman of the Luman Group] said: "Buyers who come to Bangladesh tell us, 'we are businessmen; we want to make money. If we see cheaper prices in China we will go there.'"

© *Guardian* News & Media Ltd 2007,
July 20, 2007, by Karen McVeigh

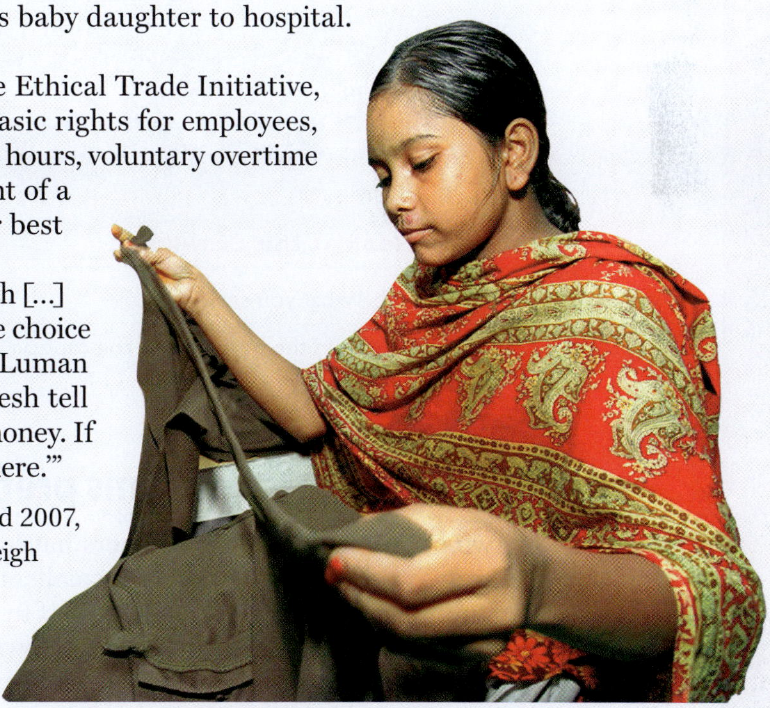

1. *vêtements*

I. Compréhension **À rédiger en français**

Lisez attentivement l'article ci dessus et faites-en un compte-rendu en anglais de 180 mots.

II. Traduction

Traduisez le troisième paragraphe depuis « Employees » jusqu'à « sick leave ».

III. Expression **À rédiger en anglais**

1. What profit do western countries draw from trading with the Third World? (100 words)

2. Imagine a contract in ten proposals that employers and employees could sign in these countries. (150 words)

Unit 5 Running a company

Today it isn't unusual to see companies coming from nowhere and disappearing in no time. Other facilities hold on while keeping their initial policies. Family firms find it hard to compete with mushrooming start-ups. Fortunately consumers have their say and businesses rely on the satisfaction of those for whom they produce.

1. Nose to the grindstone

Have a look at this drawing.

1. Describe what you see.

2. Comment on the beginning of the caption.

3. Say what you think about the boss's wishes.

2. Small firms prefer flextime

Two out of three business owners have adopted flexible working practices and the smaller the company, the more likely it is to allow staff to manage their working hours in their own way. Howard Venning, 51, commutes from Saffron Walden, Essex, every day to his job as Managing Director of specialist electronics distributor Aspen Electronics in Eastcote, North London; he prefers to start early and head home at 4pm to beat the traffic. He encourages his staff to adopt working times and practices that also suit their lives outside work.

The Mail on Sunday, January 28th, 2007

Read the following article.

1. Say why small firms prefer flextime.

Listen to the recording.

1. List the advantages this employer finds in flextime work.

2. Say why flextime is a way to make workers loyal to small firms.

3. Do you believe a small firm can be compared to a family firm? Say why or why not.

3. America's top 8 private companies in 2007

COMPANY NAMES	HEAD-QUARTERS	ACTIVITY	REVENUE	STAFF	CEO
Koch Industries http://www.kochind.com	Wichita KS	Chemicals, energy, technology	$90.bn	80,000	Charles Koch
Cargill http://www.cargill.com	Minneapolis MN	Agricultural commodities, food	$82.49bn	150,900	Gregory Page
Chrysler http://www.chryslerllc.com	Auburn Hills MI	Auto, truck manufacturing	$62.20bn	77,778	Robert Nardelli
GMAC http://www.gmacfs.com	Detroit MI	Financial services	$35.72bn	31,400	Eric Feldstein
Pricewaterhousecoopers http://www.pwc.com	New York NY	Accounting	$25.15bn	146,767	Samuel DiPiazza Jr
Publix Supermarkets http://www.publix.com	Lakeland FL	Supermarkets	$21.82bn	140,000	Charles Jenkins Jr
Ernst & Young http://www.ey.com	New York NY	Accounting	$21.16bn	121,000	James Turley
Mars http://www.mars.com	McLean VA	Confectioners (candy, pet food,)	$21.00bn	40,000	Paul Michaels

Look at the results of this survey.

1. Choose one of the companies above and make a presentation on it using complete sentences.

2. Say whether these eight companies supply goods or services.

3. Compare the locations of the head offices and the figures released by these businesses. Draw your conclusions.

REPORTING

Are you most attracted to working for a small medium-sized or large company? Give the reasons for your choice.

WORDS APART

The company La société
a branch une succursale
the cashflow la trésorerie
a factory / a plant une usine
a family firm une entreprise familiale
the headquarters le siège
a medium-sized firm une PME
the organization chart l'organigramme
overheads les frais généraux
a parent firm la maison mère
a Private Limited Company (LTD) une S.A.R.L.
a Public Limited Company (PLC) une S.A.
to run a company diriger une société
to set up s'installer
the turnover le chiffre d'affaires
a workshop un atelier

The staff Le personnel
an accountant un comptable
the Board of Directors le conseil d'administration
the Chairman and Manager le directeur
a civil servant un fonctionnaire
the clerical staff le personnel admisnistratif
a colleague un collègue
the Director (GB) / the C.E.O. (Chief Executive Officer) (US) le P.D.G.
the employees les employés
an entrepreneur un chef d'entreprise
the executives les cadres
a moonlighter un travailleur au noir
a partner un associé
the payroll l'effectif
seniority l'ancienneté
a trainee un stagiaire

The job L'emploi
to appoint nommer
business acumen le sens des affaires
to downsize / streamline dégraisser
the expertise la compétence
to generate profit produire des bénéfices
an internship un stage
knowhow le savoir faire
the labour force la main-d'œuvre
to make a decision prendre une décision
to meet the deadline respecter les délais
the minimum wage le SMIC
profitable rentable
to share in the profits participer aux bénéfices
training la formation
to work in shifts travailler en équipe

Unit 5 Running a company

Zooming on

Tony Ryan, founder of Ryanair

Tony Ryan founded Ryanair in 1986 with just a single 15-seat passenger aircraft and saw it grow within 20 years into Europe's largest low-cost airline. [...]

One of four children, he had ambitions to go to university. But his father died of a heart-attack when he was 18 and he suddenly became the family breadwinner. He liked to say that transport was in the family blood – even his grandfather had been a station master. [...] In any event, after leaving school, he joined the national flag carrier Aer Lingus in 1956, as a management trainee. He worked in management for the company for a number of years.

He always liked to say that the inspiration to go into business on his own account came to him on an evening in 1974 when he watched the painstaking care with which a South East Asian street food vendor went about the preparation and selling of his products. "I felt it a pity that such marketing, technical talent and energy was devoted to a process which produced a mere penny. Then and there I determined that when I went into business on my own account, I would apply my energies to developing and marketing a big-ticket product which could sell for vastly more."

The following year Ryan put up £5,000 of his own money, and borrowed a further £45,000 from Aer Lingus and the London merchant bank Guinness Peat Group. With this he set up his own aircraft leasing corporation at Shannon in the west of Ireland, which he called Guinness Peat Aviation, soon to be known simply as GPA. Over the next 15 years the business grew to be the largest aircraft leasing company in the world [...].

In 1986, Ryan had joined with two fellow businessmen to found the low-budget airline Ryanair, which in the following year began to operate flights between Dublin and London.

Under Ryan's protégé Michael O'Leary, who took over as chief operating officer in 1993, soon to become chief executive, Ryanair was to go from strength to strength, through [...] the new CEO's mastery of the principles of budget flights. It was O'Leary, for example, who first proposed getting rid of food on Ryanair. "The family were appalled," Ryan recalled. "We told him the passengers would go spare."

O'Leary was vindicated when, not only did no one complain, but crew were able to use the time saved to sell duty free. This year Ryanair is expected to carry some 52 million passengers.

The Times, October 5th, 2007

FIRST STEPS

1. Pick up the information you are given about Tony Ryan's :
a. family background,
b. professional background.

2. Find the reason why Tony Ryan decided to run a business of his own.

3. Describe the kind of company he founded.

MOVING ON

1. Present the document. Origin, title, date, & topic.

2. Say what events these four dates correspond to:

1956 – 1974 – 1986 – 1993.

3. Pick out the information given about Ryan's first plane.

4. Tick the right answer:

- Tony Ryan liked school.
- He wanted to work right away.
- His father helped him find a job.
- After his father's death, he left home.
- When his father died, he had to work.
- Fatherless Tony Ryan went to university.
- Tony Ryan was Irish.
- Tony Ryan was English.
- Tony Ryan was American.

5. Say what it means:

a. "he became the family breadwinner" (line 7)
- He found a job at the baker's.
- He had to support his family.
- He managed a pastry section in a store.

b. "transport was in the family blood" (line 8)
- Everybody in the family died of heart attack.
- Everybody was genetically fragile.
- Everybody worked in transportation companies.

c. "he joined the national flag carrier" (line 12)
- He landed a job in the army.
- He found a job in a state-owned airline company.
- His job consisted of carrying the Union Jack.

6. Where did Tony Ryan find the money to set up his own business?

7. Pick out the marketing device used to reduce the price of air-tickets.

8. Account for the company profits drawn from this strategy.

9. Translate

"He always liked to say that the inspiration to go into business on his own account came to him on an evening in 1974 when he watched the painstaking care with which a South East Asian street food vendor went about the preparation and selling of his products."

WRITING (150 words)

Tony Ryan was born on February 2, 1936. He died on October 3, 2007. His revolutionary concept of a low-budget airline gave Ryanair its image. Similar companies are jumping on the bandwagon.

Are you prejudiced against such companies? Why or why not?

LANGUAGE AT WORK

1. Read the first paragraph from "Tony Ryan" down to "master" and focus on the letter "o". Then, classify the corresponding sounds:

Tony / founded / grow / low / cost / one / four / go / to / transport / blood.

2. Guess the translation of the following compound words:

passenger aircraft / low-cost airline / heart attack / family breadwinner / station master / management trainee.

3. Use the verbs in brackets to fill in the gaps.

a. If he had been to university, he .... his company earlier. (found)

b. His father used .... in the Railway Company. (work)

c. He devoted his life to .... travel affordable. (make)

d. He was .... to be an ambitious man. (say)

4. Read the text once more and complete with the appropriate preposition.

a. He thought everybody would be interested ....cheap travel.

b. He explained .... the marketing manager that everybody could afford an air-ticket.

c. He had to borrow money .... several banks.

d. He often thought .... this street vendor.

5. Translate into French.

a. He dreamt of making plane trips affordable for decades.

b. Since 1986 thousands of people have chosen Ryanair.

c. The C.E.O. wanted to slash the ticket prices.

6. Translate into English.

a. Il travaille pour British Airways depuis 1990.

b. Il s'est installé à Londres voilà 10 ans.

c. C'est une entreprise familiale qui a été reprise par un groupe japonais.

d. Comme son chiffre d'affaires diminuait, il a décidé de vendre au plus offrant.

Unit 5 Running a company

1. Within a company

YOUR JOB
You have been hired as a temp to show groups of foreign managers around FastLink, a medium-sized company that specializes in transport and removal.

YOUR TASK
You have been informed that executives from a Japanese transportation company will visit FastLink next week. You have to prepare your presentation.

1. Read **Document 1** and list the different names and positions in the company.
2. Draw a plan on a board and locate each office in the premises.
3. Briefly define the main jobs. **(See Doc. 2)**

ACTING OUT
Guide your guests and comment on the different activities. Be ready to answer questions.

Document 1

An organizational chart

It is a chart that represents the structure of an organization in terms of rank. The chart usually shows the managers and sub-workers who make up an organization.

BOARD OF DIRECTORS

- Chairman of the board – Samuel Gordon
  - Managing Director – Don Cole
    - Personal Assistant – Jane Field
  - Marketing Manager – John Summer
    - Market Research – Lyn Klaser
    - Strategic Planning – Steven Palmer
    - Alliance & Partnerships – Eric Hill
    - Business Development – Louisa Calvez
  - Human Resources Director – Helen Stewart
    - Design & Resources – Laura Fletcher
    - Seminars, Trade shows & Events – Sarah Tool
    - Online commerce & Distribution – Richard Fair
      - Customer Development – Bill Fox
      - Public Relation – Michaele Donaway
  - Distribution Manager – John Meredith
    - Design & Resources – Douglas Bloomberg
    - Product Loading – Emily Preston
    - Product Pricing & Commercial Policies – Sean Evans
      - Product Managment – Charles Page
      - Product Management – Guy Loomis

PROMPTS

Welcoming *Accueillir*
I am delighted to welcome you to Fastlink. *Je suis ravi(e) de vous accueillir à Fastlink.*

I will be your guide for a couple of hours. *Je serai votre guide pendant une ou deux heures.*
I am at your disposal. *Je suis à votre disposition.*

Introducing *Présenter*
May I introduce you to Mr X? *Puis-je vous présenter à M. X?*
The C.E.O. would like to shake hands with you. *Le PDG aimerait vous saluer*

I will show you around the place. *Je vais vous faire visiter l'endroit.*
Would you please follow me? *Veuillez me suivre*

Document 2

Our skills

We provide professional shipping services for your furniture, belongings, cars and motorcycles throughout the country.

OUR EXPERTISE

- Free written estimates
- World-wide service
- Custom packing & crating
- Expertise in household & office relocation
- We transport automobiles, boats, motorcycles, etc.
- Electronics, tradeshow & exhibition service
- We transport unique and antique items with expert care
- Satisfaction guaranteed
- Agents in most major cities world-wide

OUR SERVICES

- All loose belongings need to be packed. You can do this yourself, pay the mover to do it all for you, or have the mover do partial packing (for example, pack only fragile items).
- Recycled boxes are available free from local stores, but they should all be clean, strong and able to close. (During your move, the boxes will be stacked on top of each other.)
- It is important to know how many boxes your move will require, both in terms of obtaining them and budgeting your time.

SHIPPING & DELIVERY

Processing time for an item is the time from when you submit your order to when the item leaves the warehouse.
Shipping time is from when the item leaves the warehouse to when it arrives at your door.
Only business days are taken into account.

www.AtoZtransport.com

PROMPTS

Explaining *Donner des explications*
Mr X is in charge of / is responsible for *M. X est responsable de*
Mrs X has been entrusted with this job. *On a confié ce travail à Mme X.*

She is the manager's right-hand woman. *Elle est le bras droit du directeur*
Drivers are expected to be prompt. *On demande aux chauffeurs de respecter l'horaire.*

Promoting *Faire la promotion de*
We are able to work around the clock. *Nous pouvons travailler 24 heures sur 24.*
Customers have never complained. *Nos clients ne se sont jamais plaints*

Flexible service is affordable. *On peut fournir une assistance modulable*
Should you need further information... *Si vous avez besoin de plus amples informations...*

2. Informing of a new business

YOUR JOB

You work as a trainee in the Customer Department of a discount clothing store called Causeway Mall.

YOUR TASK

You ask the group of employees you have decided to gather together to do the Kaleidoscope test.

The store will soon move to a commercial zone and you have been entrusted with the job of informing loyal customers of this change.

1. Read the information to find positive arguments on why people like discount clothing stores.

2. Read the reference document in the next page selecting useful words and expressions.

3. Write a letter to an imaginary regular customer to convince him/her to come and see the New Causeway Mall.

ACTING OUT

Stage an interview with your manager. You will outline the main information extracted from the documents and comment on it.

Document 1

A customer's testimony

Document 2

Loyalty cards

A loyalty card, rewards card, points card, or club card is a plastic or paper card, visually similar to a credit card or debit card. In the United Kingdom it is typically called a loyalty card, in Canada a rewards card or a points card, and in the United States either a discount card, a club card or a rewards card. Cards typically have a barcode that can be easily scanned. Small keyring cards are often used for convenience in carrying and ease of access. A retailer may issue a loyalty card to a customer who can then use it as a form of identification when dealing with that retailer. By presenting the card, the purchaser is typically entitled to either a discount on the current purchase, or an allotment of points that can be used for future purchases.

PROMPTS

- **I must stress that...** *Je dois mettre l'accent sur...*
- **I insist on...** *J'insiste sur...*
- **This aspect needs to be underlined.** *Cet aspect doit être souligné*
- **This detail is highlighted.** *Ce détail est mis en relief.*
- **I'd like to underline...** *Je voudrais souligner...*
- **It is worth noting.** *Cela mérite d'être souligné.*
- **I highlighted this idea.** *J'ai mis cette idée en valeur*
- **The emphasis is laid on this point.** *L'accent est mis sur ce point.*
- **I would like to explain in details...** *Je voudrais préciser...*
- **It is taken for granted that...** *Il va de soi que...*

REFERENCE DOCUMENT

JACKSON D.I.Y. Home Center 35 Main Street Hartford, CT 06103 U.S.A	Name and address of the sender
Jackson D.I.Y. Home Center	Logo of the company
September 22nd, 2008	Date
Dear Mr Butler,	Name of the addressee Opening salutation
We take pleasure in advising you that we shall be moving to new premises in the near future. We will be setting up our business in the new commercial area of Palm Square in the HUBzone.	Reason for writing: new location
Due to the fact that our business has expanded by some 20 per cent in the past year, we find that our current premises and car park have become too small. This move has become necessary as we would like to provide our loyal customers with the best possible service.	Reason for this change: better environment, better service
We are sure this change will cause no trouble in the weeks to come as the move will be happening from next month onwards. Our Sales Department will be at your disposal to help you and guide you throughout our new outlet. We do not anticipate a delay in supplying orders and our clients are welcome to keep on placing orders. Your current discount card still remains valid and will be changed at your first visit.	Business still going
Enclosed herewith are details of our new address and a map to show you the location of the new warehouse. We shall be commencing business there from November 12. In the meantime, kindly send any correspondence to our former address.	New references
We are looking forward to continuing doing business with you.	Future contacts
Yours sincerely,	Closing salutation
Carol Lewis	Signature
Carol Lewis Customer Department	Name and position in company
Enc: map & leaflet	Enclosures

Test Yourself

Working hand in hand

To judge by the entrepreneurial fire in Sheela's eyes, it seems that Percy Barnevik has been putting his multi-million-pound pension package to good use in the five years since his controversial departure from ABB, the Swiss-Swedish electrical engineering group.

"We want to expand to buy a packing machine and a fridge," said the 35-year-old business-woman, who is among eight shareholders in a bakery near Madras in southern India.

In a sweltering room containing two ovens and little fresh air, the women churn out 1,000 buns and 1,025 biscuits every day for the workers at a local textile company. Their toil is not in vain, as turnover rises 40 per cent a month to an estimated 120,000 rupees in July. By Christmas they will own the business outright, having repaid a 230,000 rupee (£2,785) start-up loan facilitated by Hand in Hand, a not-for-profit organisation backed up by Mr Barnevik. [...]

The bakery is one of 64,000 small to medium-sized enterprises in India founded – mainly by women from the lowest castes – under the auspices of Hand in Hand over the past three years. Every month, 4,000 new businesses are begun with the help of microfinance, a well-regarded lending mechanism, for the poor that cuts out loan sharks and fosters collective responsibility within small communities [...].

[...] Within five years, the 66-year-old Swede hopes to change the world in his retirement and aims to create 1.3 million jobs and 250,000 businesses in the state of Tamil Nadu alone, but by exporting a "five-pillar" model – mobilizing illiterate women, eliminating child labour, improving water and waste management, promoting health education and equipping citizens with the tools of democracy [...].

[...] "In South-East Asia, one billion people have made it out of poverty, but they didn't do it with aid. We have to replace the giving with lending and training," [Mr Barnevik said.]

While Mr Barnevik [...] has donated about £7million to Hand in Hand, he insists that the organisation should become self-supportive. "Everything we do must be sustainable, he said. We are just the facilitator and the trainer. As long as there are illiterate people behind the curve, we need to keep training. But it's like school – once you graduate, you are on your own."

The Times, July 21st, 2007

Corrigé page 191

I. Compréhension

Après une lecture attentive de l'article ci-dessus, vous en ferez un compte-rendu **en anglais** en 180 mots. Vous indiquerez le nombre de mots utilisés

II. Traduction

Vous traduirez **en français** le dernier paragraphe, depuis "While Mr Barnevik" ligne 24 jusqu'à "on your own" ligne 28.

III. Expression

1. Account for the role played by Mr Barnevik in the Indian economy. (at least 50 words)

2. Define the position and mission of Hand in Hand. What about the symbolism of its very name? (at least 50 words)

3. To what extent can "microfinance" represent an efficient means to support people in need? (at least 100 words)

Exam Paper

Autonomy helps create young C.E.O.'s

Michael S. Dell (of Dell Inc.) sold stamps to collectors when he was 12 and Bill Gates founded Microsoft when he was 19. Facebook, the social networking site, was the creation of Mark Zuckerberg, a Harvard University sophomore[1] at the time. A study by the Global Entrepreneurship Monitor shows that the United States is unusual among developed countries in having a higher business start-up rate among its 18-to 24-year olds than its 35-to 44-year olds.

But why has America produced so many successful young entrepreneurs like Bill Gates or Michael Dell?

Ben Casnocha, 19, author of the new book "My Start-up Life: What a very young entrepreneur learned on his journey through Silicon Valley," offers clues.

As he recounts in his book, Ben was 14 when he started Comcat Inc., a Web-based service for helping local governments manage customer service. [...] Some talented and busy people, presumably impressed by the young man, decided to support his enterprise. He also asked for outright grants to get his business off the ground and to help finance his version of the American dream.

American youths are so successful at entrepreneurship in part because so many older and wealthier people are willing to help them. The broader American success at philanthropy, then, lays the groundwork for American entrepreneurship.

[...] Ben surveyed his future customers and asked them what services they needed and how much they were willing to pay. He also had to persuade people to do business with a teenager. He had no formal education in marketing but, as a suburban American youth, he was exposed to intense commercial marketing every day. He decided to become an entrepreneur at the age of 12, he says, after being struck by the Apple "Think Different" ad. [...]

The fact that American schooling is less disciplined than that in other countries gives young creators the time and the energy to accomplish something outside their formal education. [...] Whenever he could, he used sick days to set up meetings for his business.

Relatively loose family structures have similar effects; American children are especially likely to be working on their own projects, rather than being directed by parents and elders.

It is a common American dream to want to start one's business, and this cultural influence spreads to the young. It sometimes replaces school and family as a driving force. [...]

In 2006, BusinessWeek ranked Ben as one of America's top young entrepreneurs, and he is only this fall enrolling at Claremont McKenna College in California. Whatever Ben does next, his story shows that economic advantages start early. On a national level, these successes are rooted in the commercial, competitive, philanthropic and open nature of American society.

1. *étudiant de 2e année*

I. Compréhension À rédiger en anglais

Après une lecture attentive de l'article ci-dessus, vous en ferez un compte-rendu en 200 mots +/- 10%. Vous indiquerez le nombre de mots utilisés.

II. Traduction

Vous traduirez depuis « As he recounts » ligne 15 jusqu'à « the American dream » ligne 18.

Unit 6 Corporate culture

The term "corporate culture" is used to define the character of a company: its core values, beliefs, ethics and rules of behaviour. It is expressed in the company's mission statement, in the architectural style or interior décor of its offices, by what people wear to work, by how people address each other and in the titles given to various employees.

Zooming on

1. "All I know is that it's part of our corporate culture."

"I don't know how it started, either. All I know is that it's part of our corporate culture."

Have a look at the cartoon.

1. Describe the setting and the characters.

2. Say where the humour stems from.

3. What is the implied criticism of corporate culture?

2. Companies need a strong culture

How does Black Diamond Equipment, in Salt Lake City, keep ahead of its rivals in the trendy rock-climbing-equipment industry? By filling its workforce with the sport's enthusiasts - the users of its products - and capitalizing on their passion. [...]

At Black Diamond, where competitive advantage depends on every employee doing product research and development, real responsibility for company success has been spread to every employee in the organization.

Companies with such strong corporate cultures have an almost unfair competitive head start. The work they do is invested with meaning. Their employees have reasons to care about how they perform. Even the challenges presented by mind-bending change – whether imposed by the marketplace or necessitated by internal growth – are easier to handle because a stable culture begets[1] a fast-moving, flexible company.

www.inc.com/magazine, John Case

1. *engendrer*

Read the text.

1. Pick out information about the company: name, place, economic sector.

2. What type of employees does it recruit?

3. What is the basis of the company's corporate culture? Write a message in one sentence that describes it. Present it to the class and state the reasons for your choice.

3. Uncovering a company's corporate culture is critical for job-seekers

Listen to the interview with Randall S. Jansen.

1. List the eight elements of a corporate culture you need to take into account when you are looking for a job.

2. How can you uncover a company's corporate culture?

4. Companies' statements about their corporate culture

AES Corporation operates electric-power-generating plants in 35 countries and plants millions of trees to make up for the carbon dioxide produced by its facilities. Materials-handling technicians negotiate contracts with coal suppliers, reducing the need for high-priced managers. Machine operators order replacement parts themselves, ensuring a minimum of downtime.

Southwest Airlines's corporate culture is based on hiring people with positive attitudes, who lend themselves to causes, have a good sense of humor and are interested in performing as a team. Communication is an important thing for people to feel fulfilled and happy. Management is proud of their people and interested in them as individuals. Everybody, from CEO Herb Kelleher to the newest gate attendant, makes sure that customers have a good time and that airplanes get unloaded and reloaded and back in the air fast.

W. L. Gore & Associates deals with fluoropolymer manufacturing, and delivers medical implants worldwide. We encourage hands-on innovation, involving those closest to a project in decision-making. Teams organize around opportunities and there are no chains of command. We communicate directly with each other and are accountable to fellow members of our multi-disciplined teams. Associates (not employees) commit to projects that match their skills with the guidance of their sponsors (not bosses) to offer personal fulfillment while maximizing their contribution to the enterprise. This environment combines freedom with cooperation and autonomy with synergy.

REPORTING

List the advantages for a company of having a strong corporate culture. Report to the class.

Read the text.

1. Say which company culture attracts you most.

WORDS APART

Corporate culture — **La culture d'entreprise**

- **to achieve something** réussir qqchose
- **ambition** l'ambition
- **behaviour** le comportement
- **to care** porter attention à
- **committed to** engagé à
- **competitive edge** l'avantage sur le concurrent
- **a core value** une valeur centrale
- **drive** le dynamisme, l'énergie
- **eagerness** le vif intérêt
- **entrepreneurial** entreprenant
- **expertise** les connaissances
- **to fit** aller bien, convenir
- **to focus on** se centrer sur
- **hands-on** mettre la main à la pâte
- **know-how** le savoir-faire
- **a prospect** une perspective
- **the rat race** la foire d'empoigne
- **skills** des capacités
- **success** la réussite
- **a task** une tâche
- **team spirit** l'esprit d'équipe
- **thriving on challenges** épanoui par les défis

The staff — **Le personnel**

- **a boss** un patron
- **the CEO** le PDG
- **a chief executive** un dirigeant
- **a consultant** un conseiller
- **an employee/a clerk** un employé
- **a firm/a company** une entreprise
- **a founder** un fondateur
- **hierarchy** la hiérarchie
- **junior** jeune
- **a leader** un meneur
- **a manager** un dirigeant
- **management** la direction
- **a partner** un associé
- **partnership** le partenariat
- **to perform** réussir
- **perquisites, perks** les avantages
- **the policy of** la politique de
- **the professions** les professions libérales
- **senior** principal
- **suppliers** les fournisseurs
- **a top executive** un cadre supérieur
- **work ethics** la conception du travail

Negative aspects — **Aspects négatifs**

- **biased** partial
- **to blackmail** faire du chantage
- **a breach of secrecy** une violation de secret
- **to bribe** soudoyer
- **to check on** vérifier
- **discriminatory** discriminatoire
- **to dismiss** rejeter, renvoyer
- **to fail** échouer
- **failure** l'échec
- **the gender gap** le fossé entre les sexes
- **to handle the pressure** faire face à la pression
- **the glass ceiling** impossibilité pour les femmes d'accéder aux postes de responsabilité
- **hostile** hostile
- **to investigate** enquêter
- **to intrude** on s'ingérer dans
- **prejudiced against** qui a des préjugés contre
- **to revamp** restructurer
- **quarrelsome** conflictuel
- **sexual harrassment** le harcèlement sexuel
- **womanizing** courir le jupon
- **the workload** la charge de travail

Unit 6 Corporate culture

Zooming on

How Bob Iger unchained Disney

Bob Iger (who became Disney's president in 2000) is a guy who says things like: "The story shouldn't be about me. It's about the team." Sounds like the false modesty of a media-trained CEO, no? But Iger really does prefer to hover in the background, letting the limelight stream over his lieutenants. He rules by consensus. [...] But by surrounding himself with smart people, including Jobs and the Pixar crew, and letting them get on with it, Iger has recreated a can-do culture at Disney. [...]

In 1974, Iger met the surrogate father who helped launch his career and instilled in him the management ethics he follows to this day. That man was Thomas S. Murphy, founder of ABC's then-parent, CapCities. Murphy, now 80 and retired from the Disney board, was a legendary figure who gave young talent the freedom to experiment. Iger calls it the Tom Murphy School of Management. "You put good people in jobs and give them room to run," he says. [...]

ABC chief Sweeney recalls Iger dropping by her office not long after he took over to talk about the network's future. She suggested coming up with an ABC site where viewers could get TV shows whenever they want. "We had a really interesting discussion of how you construct your own online network," says Sweeney. "Bob's parting words were: 'Go fast.'" A month later he announced the initiative at Disney's annual meeting.

If one thing separates Iger from other media moguls like Rupert Murdoch and Sumner M. Redstone, it's his belief that he doesn't need to go out and acquire a MySpace.com or YouTube Inc. While he hasn't ruled out buying an online property, Iger says he has the right content and world-class brands – Disney, ESPN, ABC – to lure eyeballs. The rollout in coming weeks of a reimagined Disney.com is central to Iger's plan to boost the company's online fortunes. The reconfigured site, which draws 21 million unique visitors each month, now features social networking and streamed TV shows aimed at young kids - another way to capitalize on that family vibe. The hope is that the site will get visitors to stay longer, allowing Disney to surpass the $700 million in digital revenues it projects for this year.

Business Week, February 5th, 2007

Johnny Depp, Keira Knightley in "Pirates of the Caribbean" (opus 3), 2007

FIRST STEPS

1. Look at the title and bottom of the document. Present the text.

2. Describe the picture. In which way is it linked to Disney?

3. Read the title and say what you think the article is about.

MOVING ON

1. Draw a portrait of Disney's new CEO:

a. first name, surname,

b. failings, qualities.

2. Explain what is meant by "a can-do culture at Disney".

3. Who did Iger take this style of management from?

Quote an example of Iger's management style.

4. Choose the equivalent of the following phrases.

a. "Iger prefers to hover in the background" means:
- to vacuum-clean the ground,
- to live underground,
- to remain unnoticed.

b. "Iger dropping by her office" means:
- he fell down in her office,
- he made things fall in her office,
- he came unexpectedly into the office.

c. "His parting words" means:
- what he said when he left,
- he said he was firing her,
- he spoke separating words.

d. "to lure eyeballs" means:
- to measure by sight,
- to seduce the audience,
- to shock people's eyes.

5. Name the companies Disney owns and those it has a deal with.

6. Which sector does Iger want to develop? How does he manage to do so? Who is the target audience?

7. Translate

Translate the third paragraph of the text into French from "ABC chief Sweeney..." (line 13) down to "... at Disney's annual meeting." (line 17)

WRITING (150 words)

How can Disney's new services contribute to the success of the company?

Think of the world of *Pirates* for instance, including two movies, three soundtracks available for downloading on iTunes, the film's sound track sampled for ring-tones, *Pirates* wallpaper with a skull-and-crossbones theme, games developed for Portable Multimedia Players...

LANGUAGE AT WORK

1. Say where the stress falls in each pair of words, then listen to the recording to check your answer.

a. corporate / corporation
b. electron / electronic
c. entertain / entertainment
d. legend / legendary
e. notoriety / notorious
f. person / personal
g. steady / steadily
h. strategy / strategic
i. technology / technological

2. Fill in the blanks with one of these adverbs: *actually, currently, hardly, mainly, obviously, paradoxically, theoretically, undoubtedly.*

a. .... loose-reign management gets better results than authority.
b. It is .... possible but is not likely to happen.
c. The staff is made up of .... young people.
d. He was .... the best candidate so he got the position.
e. I wasn't there. So I don't know what .... happened?
f. The Director cannot talk to you. He is .... having talks in LA.
g. .... a company cannot function without a strong corporate culture.
h. She can .... expect a pay rise.

3. Make compound adjectives.

a. a picture drawn by computer,
b. consequences that reach far,
c. a CEO who works hard,
d. a company that moves fast,
e. a business executive who is well equipped.

4. Translate into French.

a. a media-trained CEO,
b. world-class brands,
c. social networking and streamed TV shows.

5. Translate into English.

a. un film fait en Amérique ;
b. des employés bien payés ;
c. un autodidacte facile à vivre ;
d. des dirigeants étroits d'esprit ;
e. un film fait à la maison ;
f. un PDG de 29 ans aux yeux noirs ;
g. un exercice bien connu qui prend du temps.

1. Presenting a company's corporate culture

YOUR JOB
You work in the Marketing Department of Google.

YOUR TASK
You are asked to write a short memo that gives a clear and concise picture of Google's corporate culture. Follow the various steps.

1. Read Documents 1 and 3 taken from Google's website.
2. Listen to the recording and make notes on what seems essential to you.
3. For further information go to googleblog.blogspot.com, Google's official weblog, with news of new products, events and glimpses of life inside Google.
4. Prepare your memo.

ACTING OUT
Present your memo orally to the class and explain your choices.

Document 1

The Google culture

Though growing rapidly, Google still maintains a small company feel. Google's emphasis on innovation and cost containment means each employee is a hands-on contributor. There's little in the way of corporate hierarchy and everyone wears several hats: the international webmaster who creates Google's holiday logos spent a week translating the entire site into Korean; the chief operations engineer is also a licensed neurosurgeon.

Google's hiring policy is aggressively non-discriminatory and favors ability over experience. The result is a staff that reflects the global audience the search engine serves. Google has offices around the globe and Google engineering centers are recruiting local talent in locations from Zurich to Bangalore. Dozens of languages are spoken by Google staffers, from Turkish to Telugu.

As Google expands its development team, it continues to look for those who share an obsessive commitment to creating search perfection and having a great time doing it.

www.google.com

Document 2

Google Doodles

Listen to Dennis Hwang, the 28-year-old webmaster who designs the doodles that decorate google.com's website on special occasions.

Document 3

The Googleplex

Google's world headquarters building is located in Mountain View, California. While not all Google offices around the globe are equally well-stocked, these are some of the essential elements that define a Google workspace:

- **Lobby décor:** piano, lava lamps, and live projection of current search queries from around the world.
- **Hallway décor:** bicycles and large rubber exercise balls on the floors, press clippings from around the world posted on bulletin boards everywhere.
- **Recreation facilities:** workout room with weights and rowing machine, locker rooms, washers and dryers, massage room, assorted video games, Foosball, baby grand piano, pool table, ping pong, roller hockey twice a week in the parking lot.
- **Google café:** healthy lunches and dinners for all staff. Stations include "Charlie's Grill", "Back to Albuquerque", "East Meets West" and "Vegheads". Outdoor seating for sunshine daydreaming.
- **Googler offices:** Googlers work in high-density clusters remarkably reflective of our server setup, with three or four staffers sharing spaces with couches and dogs. This improves information flow and saves on heating bills.
- **Equipment:** most Googlers have high-powered Linux OS workstations on their desktops. In Google's earliest days, desks were wooden doors mounted on two sawhorses. Some of these are still in use within the engineering group.
- **Snack rooms:** bins packed with various cereals, gummi bears, M&Ms, toffee, licorice, cashew nuts, yogurt, carrots, fresh fruit and other snacks. Dozens of different drinks including fresh juice, soda and make-your-own cappuccino.
- **Coolest stop on the tour:** a three-dimensional rotating image of the world on permanent display on a large flat panel monitor in the office of the engineer who created it. A toggle switch allows you to view points of light representing real time searches rising from the surface of the globe toward space, color coded by language. Toggle and you can see traffic patterns for the entire Internet. Worth a trip to the second floor.

www.google.com

2. Writing a mailing

YOUR JOB

You work in the Marketing Department of Amy's Ice Creams, a ten-store chain of ice-cream parlours in Austin, Houston and San-Antonio, Texas. Founded in 1984, Amy's Ice Creams, now at $4.2 million, scoops out some 100,000 gallons of ice cream and grows about 20% a year. Amy's sells unique flavours such as Mexican vanilla, sweet cream, and for the truly Texan, Shiner Bock.

YOUR TASK

You are asked to write a mailing to announce that Amy's Ice Cream stores are celebrating the company's 25th anniversary.

1. Read the various documents and determine the elements that characterize the company's corporate culture.
2. Listen to the interview with owner Amy Miller **(See Doc. 2)**.
3. Write the mailing following the advice given in the reference document.

Document 1

Amy Miller's corporate culture

Amy Miller's strategy is to sell entertainment along with ice cream. Employees can be wearing pajamas (because it's Sleep-over Night) or masks (Star Wars Night); there might be candles (Romance Night) or strobe lights (Disco Night). They create fun, performing, juggling with their serving spades[1], tossing scoops[2] of ice cream to one another behind the counter, or break-dancing on the freezer top.

But the real secret to her company's success is its corporate culture. To create and nurture a culture that made that experience inevitable, she had to get the right people and get them to behave in the right way. And because their behavior needed to be inventive and self-initiated, she had to get them to know what the right way was, without being told.

www.amyicecream.com

1. *jouer avec des pelles à tarte* – 2. *lancer des boules*

Document 2

The White-paper-bag test

REFERENCE DOCUMENT

LUFTHANSA SAS AUSTRIAN AIRLINES

Reduce tour travel costs to Eastern Europe — *Object*

Groupe Partouche International
Rue du Marché Aux Herbes
1000 Bruxelles — *Name and address of the sender*

Dear Madam, dear Sir, — *Opening salutation*

In today's tough business climate every company, including the most profitable, is facing pressure to reduce operating costs. Every expense is under scrutiny and business travel is a major cost item. At the same time, business travel is essential for you. — *Background*

Start cutting your travel costs

We are convinced that we can help you to reduce your travel costs significantly. We have created a program especially designed to cut travel costs of companies that do business in Eastern and Central Europe. — *Efficiency*

Star Alliance brings together 15 of the world's finest airlines to offer an integrated network with one timetable. Austrian Airlines, Lufthansa and SAS – Star Alliance partner airlines – operate other 1,700 flights a week to 46 destinations in Eastern and Central Europe. — *Offer*

If you fly to this region with us in Economy or Business Class you are entitled to special tailor-made reductions. Our Reduced Fares Plan is customized to your company's needs, travel budget and travel patterns. It is unique and it is personalized. It is calculated to save you and your company the maximum amount possible. — *Reduction*

We would like to invite you to find out how much you can save, without obligation. Take a few minutes to complete the enclosed Reduced Fares Plan Fax and send it to us today – in return we will provide you, entirely free of charge, with a custom plan that we are sure will save your company money. — *Suggestion*

Frank Zoom
Manager for Belgium and Luxembourg — *Signature and position of the sender*

PS: Win your free flight. To reward you for your co-operation you are entitled to win a free round trip Business Class flight for two to St-Petersburg. You will find full details enclosed. — *Game*

Test Yourself

No-Sweat

Adam Neiman (left), Founder of No-Sweat Apparel.

Last September, Zander Sebenius decided he wanted to get involved with a business venture that could both help him develop his sales and marketing skills and make a difference. He turned to a family friend who shared his ideals: Adam Nieman, co-founder of No Sweat Apparel. No Sweat, a small Boston-based company, sells apparel manufactured in union-run factories. Last December, Nieman launched a line of T-shirts manufactured in Palestine, smack in the middle of the Israeli-Palestinian conflict. The factory, which Nieman said employs about 70 workers, is owned by a Christian and organized under a Muslim union. Nieman is Jewish. "All three religions have had a hand in creating this problem, and if the problem is to be solved, all three religions have to have a hand in solving it," Nieman said. The region in which the T-shirts are manufactured is home to an unemployment rate of more than 40 percent and a population of desperate citizens with access to weapons, but not jobs. No Sweat claims that the creation of jobs in the factory could be a deterrent to violence.

That's where Sebenius, who is Jewish, and his classmate and Muslim friend Tarek El Jahmi, come in. They have been building a network of clients, selling custom-printed T-shirts wholesale to schools and organizations. The two, who are trying to recruit other student resellers, receive a 4 percent commission on their sales. [...]

Zander Sebenius and El Jahmi have sold about 500 T-shirts so far, promoting the environmental benefits of organic cotton, the fair-labor benefits of a unionized shop and the diplomatic benefits of economic development in Palestine. They plan to keep working this summer, as El Jahmi attends wrestling camp in Iowa and Sebenius travels to Paris and Africa with his family. They're focused on fall orientations and school events, including, they hope, providing T-shirts for the Harvard-Yale football game.

Sebenius said he has joined the social entrepreneurship movement because he believes in doing good in the world and making money at the same time, something most people separate. He said he hopes that by showing it can be profitable to support the peace, fair labor and environmental movements, he will help them grow. "I used to think that there were some issues that were too big to tackle, no matter what you did," said Sebenius. "This has shown me that something as simple as buying a T-shirt can make an impact."

Cambridge Chronicle, July 25th, 2007, by Kristen Grieco

Corrigé page 191

I. Compréhension

Rédigez en anglais un compte-rendu de l'article en 160 mots à 10% près. Indiquez le nombre de mots utilisés.

II. Traduction

Translate the last paragraph of the text into French from "Sebenius said he has joined the social entrepreneurship ..." down to the end.

Exam Paper

Corporate blogs

SmugMug Inc is a Mountain View, Calif.-based company that operates an online photo-sharing site. It began its corporate blog about two years ago as a "blah, blah, blah blog that said: 'Our company is great and here's why,'" noted co-founder and President Chris MacAskill. But the first blog didn't generate much readership, he said. That all changed last year when Don MacAskill, Chris's son and the company's CEO posted a scathing[1] review of how Sun Microsystems's Sun Fire servers were performing in SmugMug's data center. The post made the front page of news aggregation website Digg.com. "The next thing we knew, our phone was ringing off the hook from senior vice-president of Sun," Chris MacAskill said. He added that Don MacAskill later met with Jonathan Schwartz, Sun CEO, – a prominent blogger himself – to discuss the Sun Fire servers, after which he helped Sun fix the performance problem he had cited and then ordered several new pieces of Sun hardware for SmugMug.

From that point on, both MacAskills have continued to blog about issues they think will engage readers, such as the differences in how the colors of photos appear on Windows PCs vs Macintosh systems. Readership of the blog has increased by a factor of 1,000, according to the elder MacAskill. Many outsiders are "just astonished" that the SmugMug executives are so open in the blog, Chris MacAskill said. But that approach "raises the profile of the company," he added.

Blogs like SmugMug's are still "marketing in disguise," Chris MacAskill acknowledged. "But you have to go into it with the notion that it is not marketing in order for the marketing to work. If we were to blog about the latest feature on SmugMug, everybody's eyes would glaze over[2]."

A blog can be a good way for a corporation to make itself more "humanlike." But companies shouldn't even attempt to blog if their public relations and legal teams don't agree to allow a genuine voice to be represented. "It has to be a realistic discussion about industry trends and issues that are important, potentially even issues that are antagonistic or troublesome," he said. Otherwise, "you look even more ridiculous than if you never attempted it."

www.computerworld.com

1. *acerbe* – 2. *devenir vitreux*

I. Compréhension **À rédiger en français**

Rédigez un compte-rendu de l'article en 180 mots à 10% près. Indiquez le nombre de mots utilisés.

II. Expression **À rédiger en anglais**

1. Read *Tips on corporate blogging*. What qualities should a good corporate blog have? (100 words minimum)

2. Do you agree that corporate blogs are "marketing in disguise" or do you believe they can actually bring something positive to consumers? (150 words minimum)

TIPS ON CORPORATE BLOGGING

- Develop internal policies about what can and cannot be discussed on corporate blogs.
- Have prospective bloggers read existing blogs to get a feel for a good "voice" to use in their posts.
- Make sure corporate bloggers are writing their own entries.
- Avoid editing blogs as much as possible to ensure that the voice of the author comes through.
- Try to maintain a two-way flow of information by deleting only obvious spam in the comments section.
- House blogs on your corporate Web site, not on third-party sites.
- Encourage authors to blog frequently and to link to other sources as often as possible.
- Use the spam filters that are available in most blogging software.

Unit 7 Marketing

Zooming on

For some time now, businesses have tried to get away from the idea of mass market and one-stop stores. Selling people things has become trickier than ever before, and so companies must endeavour to know their customers intimately and to market not only products, but also concepts such as "new experiences" or "green labels".

1. A new atmosphere in the English bio market

A TEXAN GROCER IS TRYING TO CHANGE THE FACE OF BRITISH RETAILING

The opening of yet another shop selling fancy food in one of Britain's richest neighbourhoods would normally merit little attention. But Whole Foods' entry is being closely watched by its competitors. The firm that started out as a hippy shop in Texas and still has fewer than 200 stores, has forced a transformation of American food retailing. [...]

As retailing polarises between stores that sell cheap goods and those that sell luxury stuff, Whole Foods has seized the top end. [...] It owes its success to exploiting two trends. The first is that people nowadays will pay a lot more for food they think is fresher and healthier.... The second is that shoppers are looking for entertainment, not just groceries.

Whole Foods aims to create the atmosphere of a festive street market with abundant displays of fresh food and tasting stations. More radically, its singles nights, massage centres and meditation classes make shopping seem less a chore than an adventure.

The Economist, May 24th, 2007

Have a good look at the photo.

1. Determine the name of the store and establish exactly what items they sell.
2. Analyse the way these items are presented to the customers.

Now read the text.

1. Two places are mentioned, explain how they are related in the article.
2. Why have they decided to open a shop "in one of Britain's richest neighbourhoods"?
3. Explain what the real originality of this store will be.

2. The blind leading the blind

The guests queue up single file, place one hand on the shoulder of the person in front and are then led to their table for a most unusual dining experience. Smoking is banned. So are flashlights, matches, lighters and even luminous watches. What makes the Blind Cow Restaurant in Zurich, Switzerland, unique is that it is completely staffed by blind people and operates in total darkness.

Listen to the recording.

1. What was at the origin of the project? How did it start?
2. Show how this project has now become a new marketing concept.
3. How are they trying to diversify the concept?

3. Shoppers at these stores urged to loiter, not buy

For its first store in the United States, Samsung, the Korean electronics company, took an unconventional route: it refused to sell anything.

NO SHOPPING, ONLY LOITERING.
Samsung called the new concept an "experience store" and, [...], the idea has proven a success.

[...] The era of Experience Shopping is upon us. The new stores are designed to put a piece of merchandise into customers' hands and teach them how to use it. The assumption is that after all the touching and feeling, customers will be willing to spend more.

[...] Those stores treated shopping as theater, transforming their vast sales floors into retail theme parks with demonstrations and educational seminars.

[...] There is evidence that this approach is working. In extensive surveys, Samsung says it has found that those who spend time in its experience store are far more likely to buy a Samsung product back at their local electronics retailer.

Read the short article.

1. Show what is unconventional in Samsung's New York store.
2. Explain why it is also totally different from other stores.
3. In your own words, show how this new concept works and why it is successful.
4. Would you go to such a place? If yes, what would your aim be?

REPORTING

Analyse why this concept of experience marketing is successful. Could it be used anywhere?

WORDS APART

Marketing techniques Les techniques du marketing

to build a brand name se faire un nom en tant que marque
competitive intelligence la veille concurrentielle
to deposit a cookie déposer un fichier espion
direct marketing le marketing direct
to express a brand's identity exprimer l'identité d'une marque
to fish for feedback vouloir obtenir un retour sur information
a focus group un groupe de consommateurs
to lure customers attirer des clients
to mass produce produire en masse
to master the art of influencing shoppers maîtriser l'art d'influencer les consommateurs
merchandising le marchandisage
to moderate a group animer un groupe
packaging emballage
a questionnaire un questionnaire
a survey une étude

One to one marketing and new experiences Le marketing personnalisé et de nouvelles expériences

a captive customer un client captif
to change the face of retailing changer la face du commerce en magasin
a chore une corvée
to cross-link croiser (des fichiers)
to customize an item fabriquer un article sur mesure
experience stores des magasins où l'on vit une expérience
to exploit a new trend exploiter une nouvelle tendance
to fit ajuster
a learning relationship with one's customers une relation qui permet d'accroître la connaissance que l'on a de son client
mass customization la personnalisation de masse
to meet a challenge relever un défi
a novelty une nouveauté
a tailormade product un produit sur mesure

Getting to know the consumer Apprendre à connaître le consommateur

to build customers' loyalty s'assurer de la fidélité des clients
to collect personal data rassembler des données privées
databases des bases de données
datamining le datamining
the end of privacy la fin de la vie privée
fickle desires des désirs changeants
to fill out profiles remplir des fiches de renseignements
to grant a privilege accorder un privilège
to know the shopping patterns connaître les modèles de consommation
to meet customers' expectations répondre aux attentes des consommateurs
to personalize the offer personnaliser l'offre
to spy on sb espionner quelqu'un
to switch brands changer de marques
to track suivre à la trace

Volume control

Julian Treasure isn't happy with what he hears. Standing in a coffee bar in London's Soho district, he's forced to raise his voice to list the noises bouncing around the café. [...] To Treasure, it sounds like money slipping away. "The soundscape is brutal," he says. "You're not likely to stick around here for a second cup." As head of the Sound Agency, a consultancy in London, Treasure wants companies to tune in to the realization that making the wrong noise can hurt business. [...]

It's long been known that sound can alter emotions and behavior. So why not use it to amplify profits? Treasure's agency acts like an audio interior designer, removing invasive noises or rescoring unappealing music. It seems simple, but while many businesses have mastered the art of influencing shoppers through sight (with alluring displays) and smell (say, by piping the odor of fresh coffee throughout a store), few have focused on the smart use of sound. [...]

But that's changing. [...]

Indeed, says Treasure, without some outside help, retailers often misjudge their customers. In 2005, for example, the Sound Agency swapped nursery rhymes and kiddie pop for relaxed classical music at a chain of British toy shops. The toy chain thought its stores were for kids, says Treasure, and forgot that the spending power belonged to parents who didn't want to be bombarded with Baa Baa Black Sheep. With the new music in place, he claims, sales jumped by up to 10%.

One rule seems clear for retail soundscapes: slow is good [...] a gently meandering[1] mix of classical music or soothing ambient noise encourages shoppers to slow down and relax. And, says Denison, an unhurried consumer is exactly what retailers want. "If customers are moving less quickly," he says, "they're more likely to engage with a product and make a purchase."

[...] Shopping psychologist Denison says growing competition for the attention of time-pressed consumers will force businesses to focus more on the total sensory experience they provide: "Retailers will have to make their stores more stimulating." The message, loud and clear: master the senses, and pump up the sales volume.

Time magazine, August 2nd, 2007, by Theunis Bates

1. sinueux, ici : diffusé doucement

FIRST STEPS

1. Introduce this text, using your own words.

2. Which country is involved here?

3. Have a good look at the photo and say where this man is sitting.

4. If you associate the picture with the title, try to define a possible subject for the article.

5. Who do you think this man is? Try to explain what his job consists of.

MOVING ON

1. Imagine the different noises Julian Treaure hears at the beginning of the text when he is sitting in the Soho coffee bar.

2. Why does he think that something must be done about them?

3. So far, which senses have been used in their marketing to boost sales?

4. Try and imagine examples of marketing techniques for each one, filling the grid.

Sense N° 1	Sense N° 2 ....

5. Using elements from the text, continue the grid for the 3rd sense analysed in the article.

Sense N° 3 ....

6. Imagine what could be done in a store with the two remaining senses.

7. Make a list of the different types of outlets using the volume control technique.

8. True or false. Justify your answer with a quote from the text.

a. More and more outlets are paying attention to their sound environment.
b. Consumers usually have plenty of time to make their purchases.
c. It has been proved that quick and energetic music urges people to buy more.
d. Stores for children mustn't forget parents in their sound approach.
e. Offering experiences involving the senses will help retailers selling more.

9. Translate

Translate into French from line 23 to 27: from "In 2005..." to "... up to 10%"

WRITING (150 words)

Put yourself in Julian Treasure's shoes in the Soho café and write the report he could have given the owner of the place in order to change the sound atmosphere of his restaurant for the better.

LANGUAGE AT WORK

1. In the first paragraph, spot the words containing the letter "u" in one of their syllables, and classify them by pronunciation into the grid.

[....]	[....]	[....]

2. Similar words do not always mean the same thing. Explain the differences between the following pairs.

Coffee (l.1) / café (l.2) - second (l.4) / second - head (l.4) / head - through (l.16) / thought (l.20) - smart (l.11) / smart.

3. Fill in the sentences with the appropriate term, chosen from the list: *sound (verb) - sound (noun) - noise - audio - music - volume.*

a. The .... of .... must be relaxing if you want customers to take their time and to buy more.
b. There was so much .... in the background that clients couldn't hear each other.
c. The .... control button must be kept low.
d. An .... tape is going to be played over and over in the store.
e. This idea of .... control .... very good to me.

4. Complete with the right form of the verb choosing between the present and the present perfect.

a. The idea of using sound in an appropriate way (be) .... quite new.
b. But in America, they (experience) .... it for a few years now, quite successfully.
c. People's biorhythms often (react) .... to the sounds around them.
d. Marketers (know) .... for a long time that sound (alter) .... emotions and behaviour.
e. With new music in the store, sales (jump) .... up by 10%.

5. Translate into French.

a. Julian Treasure, who used to be a musician in the 70s and 80s, has a lot of experience with the effect of sound on people.
b. Nowadays, people are used to doing their shopping in the midst of all sorts of noises.
c. Different sounds are used to increase profits.

6. Translate into English.

a. Le son fait changer l'humeur des gens.
b. Le travail de Julian Treasure consiste à faire changer le son ambiant.
c. Cela fera mieux vendre vos produits.
d. Cela fera rester les clients plus longtemps et donc ils consommeront plus.

1. Getting to know the consumer better and better

YOUR JOB

You are a marketing executive at Wal-Mart and you have selected 4 typical customers: a housewife with 3 children, a divorced working mother with 2 children, a single young working man, and a retired grandmother.

They have all agreed to take part in a test you are organizing with your team. For 3 weeks, they will use the handheld scanning system on their trolleys when shopping.

YOUR TASK

- Devise a short questionnaire to be given to the panel of selected clients after the 3-week test.
- Write up a report on their individual shopping patterns using their answers and the recorded data on the scanning handhelds.
- Finally, write a memo for the attention of your boss, proposing ways of using the collected information to fully personalize the offers, discounts and adverts proposed to each of them when they come back to the store. The aim, of course, is to use the system to the greater advantage of Wal-Mart.

ACTING OUT

Play an interview between one of the selected clients and a surveyor.

Document 1

Scanning handhelds

These machines have been installed by some supermarkets, such as Wal-Mart, on their trolleys so that customers can scan their own goods by themselves as they go along. At the check out, they only need to pay; there's no need to do anymore packing, therefore eliminating waiting queues.

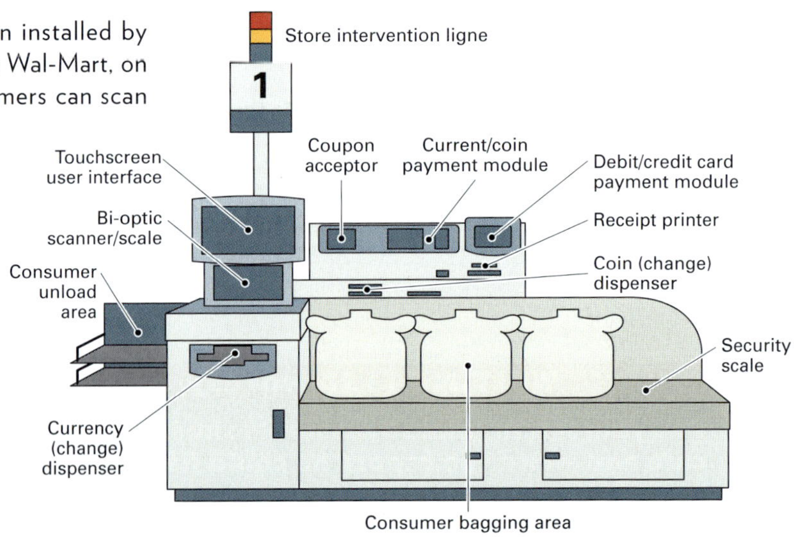

Document 2

Self-scanning checkout

Self-scanning checkout, also called «self-checkout» is an automated process that enables shoppers to scan, bag, and pay for their purchases without human assistance. Typically, a self-scanning checkout lane looks very much like a traditional checkout lane except that the shopper interacts with a computer's user interface (UI) instead of with a store employee.

The shopper begins the checkout process by touching the computer's welcome screen or, with some systems, by simply beginning to scan items. Once the checkout has been initiated by the shopper, the computer's animated voice provides the shopper with step-by-step instructions about how to scan their items and where to place them once they've been scanned.

When the shopper scans an item, the item's barcode provides the computer with the information it needs to determine what item is being scanned, as well as the item's weight and current price. If the store uses security tags, the system can also deactivate them during the scanning process. If the security tag is not deactivated, an alarm system sounds when the shopper leaves the store.

When the computer's animated voice directs the shopper to place the scanned item in a waiting shopping bag, the item is really being placed on a security scale. If you tried to fool the system by scanning a candy bar and putting a roast beef in your bag instead, the system would tell you to remove the item and scan it again. At the same time, the system would alert a cashier supervisor to pay attention to what was going on at that particular checkout stand. Typically, there is a cashier supervisor for every four self-scanning stations.

Depending on the system, payment at a self-scanning checkout can be made by debit card, credit card, or cash.

Document 3

Customers at the Edeka store near Munich which uses only Beetle iScan self-scanning equipment, like the technology.

Customers at the Edeka store near Munich which uses only Beetle iScan self-scanning equipment, like the technology.

[...] According to the study, 73% of the polled customers prefer the self-scanning solution over a traditional checkout. Around 70% of them said the self-scanning tasks, such as recording their own purchases, offered an enhanced experience factor. Another 64% of the polled customers said waiting time had been reduced. [...] 80% admitted that scanning their own goods offered more privacy.

Particularly noteworthy, the study showed older customers having a higher affinity to technology than younger ones, with 82% of over 50's preferring the new-style checkout as opposed to 69% of the under 50 group.

"The study shows that the new technologies are accepted by customers within a very short period of time when they are introduced to these technologies by service personnel", says Wincor Nixdorf marketing expert, Joachim Pinhammer.

Wincor Nixdorf website, report September 2006

2. Marketing surveillance

YOUR JOB

You work for the company Verizon Wireless as a marketing expert. This firm is seriously contemplating introducing a child-monitoring service to the market in the next few weeks.

YOUR TASK

You have been asked to lead a market survey amongst a sample of potential buyers i.e. busy parents of young children.
Read Document 2 to understand the product, its potential, and who it is aimed at.
Read the example of the questionnaire provided (**see Doc. 1**).

- Devise a pack of four to six identity cards defining a typical panel of parents who could be interested in this tracking system, define their jobs, working hours, number of children, the children's main activities, their parents' anxieties…
- Devise a questionnaire to be handed out to them. Remember that this questionnaire should be the decisive tool in order to launch this monitoring system or not.

ACTING OUT

- Pick out the panel of parents in the class. Each student chosen will have to study carefully the identity card he has been given in order to play his / her part.

Document 1

Leaner packaging

Email: ………… Today's date: …………

First name: ………… Last name: …………

Home Creations
2252 North Broadway Moore,
Ok 73160
info@homecreations.com

Age range:
☐ under 18 ☐ 18-25 ☐ 26-35
☐ 36-45 ☐ 46-55 ☐ 56 +

Gender: ☐ M ☐ F

Household income range:
☐ below $35,000 ☐ $35,000-$50,000
☐ $50,000-$75,000 ☐ 75,000-100, 000
☐ $100,000+

You: ☐ own your home ☐ rent a house
☐ rent an apartment ☐ other

If you rent, what is your monthly payment range?:
☐ less than $500 ☐ $500-650 ☐ $651-800
☐ $801-950 ☐ $951-1,100 ☐ $1,100+

How did you find out about Home Creations?:
☐ search engine ☐ radio ☐ newspaper
☐ family or friend ☐ billboard ☐ TV
☐ already own a HC home

Given the choice, would you take a tornado safety option even if it cost $1,000 more?

…………

If two homes had the same price and layout would you prefer the larger one with ordinary fixtures or the smaller one with higher quality fixtures?

…………

What features are important to you when considering a new home vs. an existing one?:
☐ Ability to customize floor plan
☐ Ability to customize design features
☐ Energy efficiency ☐ Monthly payment
☐ Lower insurance rates
☐ New home warranties
☐ Community features (picnic area, park, club house...).

Document 2

Selling surveillance to anxious parents

Kevin Reynolds, a real estate appraiser and father of two, is confronting a quandary: should he put his daughters under electronic surveillance?

It's a question more parents will face in the next months, thanks to new technology that lets them use cellphones to monitor their children's location.

Next month, Verizon Wireless plans to introduce a child-monitoring service[...]. The system tracks cellphones by satellite, allowing parents to look on the Internet to make sure their children arrived safely, say, at school or at a friend's house.[...]

These location-based services take advantage of technology built into dozens of the newest phones. It can instantaneously identify a phone's location by using satellites and the Global Positioning System.

For users, the technologies raise social, psychological, legal and interpersonal questions. A gadget that could save lives or bring peace of mind by identifying where a lost, rebellious or even kidnapped child is can also be viewed as a surveillance device, threatening one's privacy.

There is also the question of reliability. The network could fail, or the person with the phone could turn it off, making it futile as a monitor and perhaps causing more concern. [...]

Concerns about the services have not stopped Verizon from plunging ahead. The company aims to take the concept beyond spot-checks on a child's whereabouts. For $19.99, parents can program a child's phone with geographic boundaries (around a school, say). When a child leaves the area, the parent will get a text message indicating the perimeter has been breached.

[...]

The company calls the service "geo-fencing."

Test Yourself

They're making money from your kids

Do children need perfume or $30 haircuts? No, but smart entrepreneurs targeting affluent parents know how to make you think they do.

Moms and dads a generation ago might have laughed at these questions, but today there is a booming market for products and services targeting affluent parents willing to spend freely on their kids. [...]

"They're the most well-informed consumer group that you can look at", says Simon May, one of the four dads behind Bloom, a maker of high-end baby chairs. [...]

Bloom is just one example of how entrepreneurs [...] are profiting from the current wave of selling child-related products and services by appealing to parents. Other examples include clothing designers, writers, even nursery decorating consultants. Some of these businesses tap into parental concerns; [...] others target parents' political, physical, or social insecurities.

For example, concerns about childhood obesity, diabetes, and other nutritional problems prompted Shazi Visram to start HappyBaby four years ago. Visram identified a market of parents who want to feed their newborns and infants organic food but don't have time to prepare it. The company launched its line of organic, unprocessed frozen baby food on Mother's Day, 2006. A package of 12 frozen cubes retails for $4.99 at organic groceries such as Whole Foods and in more conventional markets such as Publix. "Parents just want to feel really secure that they're doing everything they possibly can to protect their babies", Visram says. [...]

The same market for child-centered grooming led Cozy Friedman to open Cozy's Cuts for Kids, a hair salon on Madison Avenue. [...] She has seen the market for her services grow steadily, with parents willing to pay $30 for a child's haircut if the child enjoys the experience.

BusinessWeek.com., by John Tozzi.

METHOD — **ANSWERING QUESTIONS IN ENGLISH**

1. Read all the questions and make sure you understand them well by underlining the key terms.

2. Verify if you have to use your own words only or if you also have to quote the text.

3. The questions can appeal to your imagination or to your personal knowledge or to both. Make sure you clearly define what you will use to answer them before actually writing.

4. Start writing ideas **in English** as quick notes for each question asked.

5. Then, tackle one question at a time, organize the contents of your answer and write it directly **in English**.

6. Take care of the presentation: neat paragraphs, skipping a line for any new important idea.

7. Read what you have just written again, making sure your account is complete.

8. Then concentrate on correcting any grammar, vocabulary or spelling mistakes.

Corrigé page 192

I. Compréhension **À rédiger en français**

Après avoir lu ce texte attentivement vous en ferez un résumé en 110 mots à 10% près. Vous indiquerez le nombre de mots utilisés.

II. Expression **À rédiger en anglais**

1. Explain why these kinds of products and services find their targets among the western population.

2. Enjoying these products and services could give children bad habits. Which ones? And what could be the negative effect on them?

3. What trap can parents fall into concerning their children's education if they indulge in material goods and services so much?

Exam Paper

Starwood hotels explore Second Life first

The hotel in Second Life is both a testing ground – a way to get public feedback on the designs developed in White Plains – and a marketing strategy aimed at tech-savvy, hip consumers.

Starwood, owner of the chic W brand as well as the Westin and Sheraton chains, is the first real-world hospitality company to open in Second Life, and joins a growing list of other companies who are using the online world to build their brand name, test products, or simply sell merchandise[...].

Created and run by San Francisco's Linden Lab, Second Life is a 3D digital universe with a growing population of some 400,000 people. [...]

Fishing for feedback. For Starwood, opening an aloft hotel in Second Life is a way to test-market the hotel's design and rapidly prototype the evolving concept. For instance, staffers will observe how people move through the space, what areas and types of furniture they gravitate towards, and what they ignore.

The project is also an effort to tap consumers for ideas. They're encouraged to post on a blog, which debuted on July 24 and features steady updates on the virtual hotel's design.[...]

The ultimate goal is, of course, to attract hip, youthful, tech-savvy customers. [...] For that reason, the virtual hotel will remain online, as an interactive marketing tool, even after the real-world buildings open.

Opening soon. "We're saving money. If we find that significant numbers of people don't like a certain feature, we don't have to actually build it", says McGuinness. "We don't have to have a painter here for 40 hours changing the color of a wall. We can reconfigure a detail. It is very parallel to rapid prototyping. "Starwood doesn't disclose the actual cost of producing the prototypes, both physical and virtual."

The first aloft hotels are scheduled to open in Lexington, Mass., Tucson, Ariz., Cherry Creek, Colo., and the San Francisco and Philadelphia airport. [...] there will be 500 aloft properties worldwide. [...]

While Starwood's approach to developing the aloft design is certainly innovative, the long-term test for the company will be to lure Second Lifers, and, more importantly, real life guests, toward the brand. Opening the doors of the aloft hotel in Second Life next month might be a big help in meeting the challenges ahead.

Innovation, August 23rd 2007, by Reena Jana.

I. Compréhension À rédiger en français

Après avoir lu l'article, vous en ferez un compte-rendu **en français** en 180 mots à 10% près. Vous indiquerez le nombre de mots utilisés.

II. Expression À rédiger en anglais

1. Answer the following questions in English. Allow 100 words for each answer.

a. In your own words, explain what Second Life is and give precise examples of what people can do in it.

b. What sort of alter ego would you create for yourself in Second Life?

c. As a Second Lifer, you are invited to spend a night at the new Starwood loft-style hotel. What remarks (positive and/or negative) would you post on the firm's blog to comment on their hotel.

2. You aimed at being hired by Starwood as a receptionist in their new Second Life hotel. Write your resume and a short motivation letter in order to be selected for an online interview.

Unit 8 Advertising

Zooming on

A common definition of advertising is an openly sponsored offering of goods, services, or ideas through any medium of public communication. The major criticisms of advertising are that it creates false values and impels people to buy things they neither need nor want.

Columbia Encyclopedia

1. Ads before all

"Well, gentlemen, we've got a stunning new logo and a marvellous publicity campaign ready. We just need to come on with a product."

Have a look at the cartoon and read the caption.

1. What, according to the cartoon, is more important: the product or the ad.

2. Say what the chairman's main concern is in the cartoon.

3. What is usually a firm's first concern?

2. The benefits and pitfalls of selling products by word of mouth

When it came to promoting its new video-game console, the Wii, in America, Nintendo recruited a handful of carefully chosen suburban mothers in the hope that they would spread the word among their friends that the Wii was a gaming console the whole family could enjoy together. Nintendo thus became the latest company to use "word of mouth" marketing. Nestlé, Sony and Philips have all launched similar campaigns in recent months to promote everything from bottled water to electric toothbrushes. As the power of traditional advertising declines, what was once an experimental marketing approach is becoming more popular.

After all, no form of advertising carries as much weight as an endorsement from a friend.

The difficulty for marketers is creating the right kind of buzz and learning to control it. Negative views spread as quickly as positive ones, so if a product has flaws, people will soon find out.

Read the article.

1. Say what selling "by word of mouth" means and what the pros and cons are.

3. Incentives to turn cars into billboards

Katz, 32, is one of the tens of thousands of motorists who have signed up to have their cars and trucks wrapped up in advertisements in exchange for a stipend of up to $800/month.

All you have to do is drive around town!

IHT August 28, 2007

Have a look at the picture.

1. What impact would you say car wrapping has?
2. How can you tell?
3. Would you accept to turn your car into a billboard?

4. Are you an ad-addict?

Listen to the following commercials.

1. Say which one deals with: mobiles, furniture, jobs, takeaway food, cars, solicitors, diet, tourism.

REPORTING

Do you feel brainwashed by ads in your everyday life? Give precise examples.

WORDS APART

Advertising **Faire de la publicité**

- **an adman** un publicitaire
- **to advertise** faire de la publicité
- **an advertisement/advert/ad** une annonce publicitaire
- **an advertiser** un annonceur
- **copy** un texte
- **a brandname/trademark** une marque
- **a catch-phrase** une phrase accroche
- **comparative advertising** publicité comparative
- **a criterion/criteria** un critère, des critères
- **a lay out** une mise en page
- **a line/a range** une gamme
- **a motto** une devise
- **to praise/to brag about** vanter
- **publicity** la publicité donnée à l'événement
- **to run an ad** faire passer une annonce
- **a sample** un échantillon
- **a slogan** un slogan
- **sponsorship** un parrainage

Targeting **Cibler**

- **an aim/a goal** un but
- **a consumer** un consommateur
- **creative** créatif
- **effective** qui fonctionne
- **to entice, coax, induce the consumer into buying** pousser le consommateur à acheter
- **glamorous** splendide
- **to inform** informer
- **innovative** innovateur
- **to market** commercialiser
- **misleading/deceptive** trompeur
- **performing** performant
- **promising** prometteur
- **reliable** fiable
- **seductive** séduisant
- **socio-professional categories** catégories socio-professionnelles
- **to target** cibler
- **undisputed, unchallenged** incontestable

Devices & Supports **Moyens et supports**

- **an advertising medium** un support publicitaire
- **an advertising space/time** un espace publicitaire
- **a billboard/a hoarding** un panneau
- **to broadcast a message** diffuser un message
- **a buying trend** une tendance
- **a commercial** un film publicitaire
- **a display/stand/rack** un présentoir
- **a fad** une mode
- **to highlight/to enhance** mettre en avant
- **a jingle** un indicatif sonore, chanson publicitaire
- **to launch a campaign** lancer une campagne
- **a leaflet/a flyer** un prospectus
- **a mailing** un envoi par poste
- **a market research** un étude de marché
- **prime time** heures de grande écoute
- **a poster** une affiche
- **to resort to devices** avoir recours à des techniques
- **a show/an exhibition** un salon

Company will monitor phone calls

Companies like Google scan their e-mail users' in-boxes to deliver ads related to those messages. Will people be as willing to let a company listen in on their phone conversations to do the same?

Pudding Media, a Web-based phone service is similar to Skype's online service – consumers plug a headset and a microphone into their computers, dial any phone number and chat away. But unlike Internet phone services that charge by the length of the calls, Pudding Media offers calling without any toll charges.

The trade-off[1] is that Pudding Media is eavesdropping[2] on phone calls in order to display ads on the screen that are related to the conversation. A conversation about movies, for example, will elicit movie reviews and ads for new films that the caller will see during the conversation. Pudding Media is working on a way to e-mail the ads and other content to the person on the other end of the call, or to show it on that person's cellphone screen. "We saw that when people are speaking on the phone, typically they were doing something else," said Ariel Maislos, chief executive of Pudding Media. So we said, 'Let's use that." The company's model, of course, raises questions about the line between target advertising and violation of privacy. Consumer-brand companies are increasingly trying to use data about people to deliver different ads to them based on their demographics and behavior online. Pudding Media executives said that scanning the words used in phone calls was not substantially different from what Google does with e-mail. Mr. Maislos said that Pudding Media had considered the privacy question carefully. The company is not keeping recordings or logs of the content of any phone calls, he said, so advertisements only relate to current calls, not past ones, and will only arrive during the call itself. [...]

As the company's software listens in on conversations, it filters out explicit words in determining which ads to select, so that content and ads will not be shown with those inappropriate words. While the calling service only works through computers for now, Mr. Maislos said he saw the potential to use it with cellphones. The company is offering the technology to cellphone carriers to allow their customers to enjoy free calls in exchange for simultaneously watching contextually relevant ads on their screens.

© *New York Times*, Sept 24, 2007, by Louise Story

1. *contre partie* – 2. *surprendre une conversation*

FIRST STEPS

1. Say if you think the article deals with:
a. how to use cell phones,
b. how to target phone users,
c. how to use a monitor.

2. Say what the main problem is:
a. urging people to consume,
b. infringing on consumers' privacy,
c. distracting people from their conversations.

MOVING ON

1. Reorder the following titles according to the article.

a. People fiddle while phoning.
b. Conversations are scanned.
c. People see ads related to their conversations on the screen.
d. Cell phones could soon do the same.
e. Key words only are recorded and not kept for long.
f. Some websites monitor mail.
g. Online conversations are paid for according to how long people talk for.

2. Say if these statements are Right or Wrong. Justify your answers by quoting the text.

a. Google monitors e-mail.
b. Skype keeps the users away from their correspondents.
c. Pudding Media is similar to any other website in most respects.
d. Phone users do all sorts of things while phoning.
e. Consumers' details are recorded and used by companies.
f. Pudding Media calls consumers during their calls.

3. Rewrite the following passage so that it corresponds to the article.

Pudding Media uses phone calls to log data just as Google does. Because Pudding Media felt concerned with consumers' privacy, they preferred to record old conversations rather than the latest ones to be more discreet. It would be inappropriate to send ads just by examining explicit words. Pudding Media is also paying for free calls in exchange for cell phone carriers' technology.

4. In the text find words that mean the same as:

scrutinize; eager to; connect; tax; show; enable; pertinent.

5. Translate

From "While the calling service only works through computers for now..." down to the end of the text.

LANGUAGE AT WORK

1. Classify the following words according to the pronunciation of the vowel "a", then listen to the tape to check your answers.

Ads, dial, related, media, trade, typical, are, software, any, message.

2. Pick out six adverbs in the text and say which ones are built on the adjective or the verb.

3. Find the English word for:

Autant ; contrairement ; pendant ; pendant que ; soit ; bien entendu ; alors que ; afin de ; en retour de.

4. Add « to » when necessary.

a. They refused .... let them .... monitor their phone calls but they allowed them .... read their emails.

b. Of course they were willing .... pay less but couldn't .... accept .... be spied on in their intimacy.

c. Nobody can make people .... do something they are reluctant .... do.

5. Translate the following sentences into English.

a. Est-ce que les consommateurs vont accepter d'avoir leurs conversations sur écoute ?

b. Les comportements des utilisateurs d'internet sont espionnés et répertoriés.

c. Malheureusement la publicité semble empièter sur la vie privée des consommateurs.

6. Translate into French.

a. As the company's software listens in on conversations, it filters out explicit words in determining which ads to select.

b. The company is offering the technology to cell phone carriers to allow their customers to enjoy free calls in exchange for simultaneously watching contextually relevant ads on their screens.

WRITING (150 words)

Explain and comment upon the following sentence extracted from the article:

"The company's model, of course, raises questions about the line between target advertising and violation of privacy."

Unit 8 Advertising

1. Launching an advertising campaign

YOUR JOB

As a product manager for an American-based company called Skincare you are responsible for the launch of an innovative advertising campaign meant to boost the sales of the company, which are currently plummeting.

YOUR TASK

1. Decide on a poster, catch-phrase, slogan, lay-out or body-copy.

2. Write a report to your company in which you explain your intentions and expectations.

- Determine the target (male/female/age).
- Define advertising approaches to break into the market (**See Doc. 1**).
- Figure out a slogan (e.g.: enticing, quickly comprehensible, playing on words, down-to-earth, innovative, eye-catching, glamorous...).
- Choose the best way to allocate the budget and select the appropriate media (**See Doc. 2, 3 & 4**) (e.g.: hiring a star, deciding on a high frequency of publication in newspapers, magazines, jingles on the radio, free samples, leaflets, trial offers, hoardings on bus shelters or taxis, direct mail, display stands, films, sandwich-men, internet...).

Document 1

Dos and don'ts

Target audience

Don't: if you don't want any customers, be sure to ignore your target audience.
Do: knowing your target audience is crucial to any successful ad campaign.

Planning

Don't: start advertising without thinking about your budget.
Do: prepare a well-conceived plan (identify your target audience, where to advertise, your ad budget).

Frequency

Don't: think your ad is so great that you can run it just once.
Do: frequency is the key if you want to gain customers.

Consistency

Don't: make each ad different.
Do: make an impression with customers. Use the same logo, tagline, colours so that your customers associate your company with the product.

Act now

Don't: think your clients will get back to you if you don't compel them to.
Do: tell your clients to act now. Hurry! This offer expires soon!

Budget

Don't: worry about the exact budget.
Do: plan out your ad budget to the penny. Think that if your budget is low, you may as well spend it in print rather than on one commercial. After all, frequency is the key.

Document 2

Google advertising programs

Reach people when they are actively looking for information about your products and services online, and send targeted visitors directly to what you are offering. With ADWords cost-per-click pricing, it's easy to control costs, and you only pay when people click on your ad.

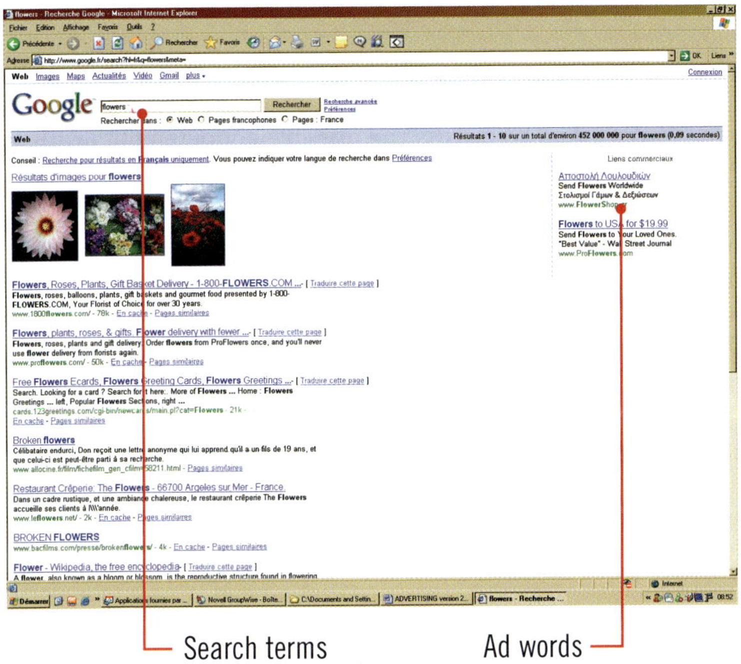

Document 3

Watching your every move

Adapted from *New York Times*, June 23, 2007

Document 4

Three golden rules

1

A mixed campaign is more effective than a single medium campaign with the same budget.

2

The choice of advertising medium depends on the user's profile.

3

The cost of the campaign is not the only criterion of efficiency.

2. Put your name on it!

YOUR JOB

You work for an IT company called Chip, which is willing to offer its best clients gifts with its logo.

YOUR TASK

1. You contact EMC and send them an E-mail.
Use: It would be nice if you could…, we need specifics…, make sure we get all the details…, please get back to us asap…, we'll be in touch.
2. You ask for the types of gifts, conditions, shipment.

PROMPTS

- **To be available for…** *être disponible pour…*
- **Contrary to…** *contrairement à…*
- **To make something in agreement with…** *faire quelque chose avec l'accord de…*
- **The launch of something…** *le lancement de…*
- **To be relevant to someone** *être pertinent pour quelqu'un*
- **To be proud of…** *être fier de…*
- **To be familiar with…** *être accoutumé à…*
- **Further to…** *suite à…*
- **For further information…** *pour plus d'informations*
- **To inquire** *s'enquérir/s'informer*
- **To supply** *fournir*
- **We would be happy to…** *nous serions ravis de…*
- **Please do not hesitate to contact us** *n'hésitez pas à nous contacter*
- **We look forward to doing business with you…** *dans l'attente de faire des affaires avec vous…*

3. Describing an ad

YOUR JOB

You work in the marketing department for a sportswear company, called Score. An advertising campaign for new sneakers is about to be launched, featuring either celebrities or children. You're asked to discuss the possible endorsements with your colleagues.

YOUR TASK

You organize a brainstorming session with your team.
Concentrate your attention on Nike's ad (next page), and analyse the ad.

1. List the pros and cons of alternative endorsements (**See Doc. 2**).
2. Envisage choices and their justifications.
3. Draft a memo.

ACTING OUT

Prepare an oral account to the Marketing Director.

Document 1

Companies ditch celebrity endorsements

From Michael Jordan to Shakira, Tiger Woods to Catherine Zeta-Jones, companies have always paid big bucks for a famous face to be associated with their products.

That's about to change. Many companies are shying away from big names and dumping celebrity endorsements altogether. Pepsi officials said the celebrities were too big (Beyoncé and Britney Spears), and the Pepsi brand didn't get the promotion out of the ad campaign that the stars were getting. Chrysler dumped Céline Dion from its new ad campaign. Insiders at Chrysler say the commercials featuring Dion driving a Pacifica produced great sales... for the singer, not the car.

Your guide to advertising,
by Apryl Duncan (About.com)

Document 2

Responsible advertising: ads and children

Article 16 is dedicated to advertising to minors.

Television advertising shall not cause moral or physical detriment to minors, and shall therefore comply with the following criteria for their protection:

a. it shall not directly exhort minors to buy a product or a service by exploiting their inexperience or credulity;
b. it shall not directly encourage minors to persuade their parents or others to purchase the goods or services being advertised;
c. it shall not exploit the special trust minors place in parents, teachers or other persons;
d. it shall not unreasonably show minors in dangerous situations.

www.iccwbo.org

The lay out, composition (how the image is positioned: camera angle, colours, background, body language, endorsement)
Are you sick of hearing "where do you find the time"?
The message (body copy, lines of appeal)
Is there a make-up kit in your gym bag?
Do you consider tri-athletes underachievers?
Does your kick-boxing trainer
make fun of your yoga instructor?
Have you ever done
crunches while waiting for pasta to cook?
Do you keep more than one pair of trainers
at work?
The target
Are you an All Rounder?
The logo (brand identity) website
Find yourself at
nikewomen.com
The catch phrase, slogan

Unit 8 Advertising

Test Yourself

Advertising and sexism

Before 1925 advertisements focused on the actual properties of the products being sold, but at about that time corporations realized that method did not generate enough capital so they tried a different approach: relating products to real human desires and emotions.

One of these basic human desires is sex. Advertising frequently uses the image of sex or sexual pleasure to sell a product that has nothing to do with sex. With this portrayal of sex in advertisements, women are almost always the ones to provide the sexual pleasure.

With women so frequently displayed as passive sexual objects, this has consequences for women in real life.

The fact is, while advertisements on the surface sell products, through their secondary discourse they sell normalcy, values, and ideas. The way we know that advertisements create culture rather than just reflect it, is by examining different cultures and time periods. Our concepts of gender are constructed and advertisements help construct it.

So why does advertising create gender stereotypes? To sell products of course, but that answer is too obvious. As I mentioned earlier, advertising sells normalcy, so not only does it tell society what a woman/man is, it creates an image of the perfect woman or man.

It does not end there. Women exposed to this system of advertising are not merely shown an ideal image that they cannot achieve, but they internalize it and there are real consequences. Eating disorders are a huge problem, with an estimated 5-10 million girls/women in the United States and 1 million boys/men affected. Not only does the unobtainable beauty stereotype create physical consequences, but perverse mental ones as well.

According to the National Eating Disorder Association, 80% of American women are dissatisfied with their appearance. Not only are they dissatisfied, women are obsessed with how they look and this prevents them from participating in other areas of life.

Trisha Grover' s article/*Duluth YSA*

I. Compréhension

Résumez l'article en français en 100 mots.

II. Expression (150 mots)

Trisha Grover also wrote: "*The average woman can never look like this, so how is she able to? By buying the products of course. Advertising needs women to feel insecure about themselves or they will not generate more capital, and that is what the system is about.*"

Explain and comment upon this.

Corrigé page 192

METHOD — **PREPARE FOR THE ORAL EXAM**

1. **Read the article**
   - **a.** Determine the topic.
   - **b.** Underline the key words.
2. **Make your own notes.**
   - **a.** State what the question debated is.
   - **b.** Pick out the link words.
   - **c.** Give the position of the journalist.
   - **d.** Identify the conclusion.
3. **Formulate a well-argumented composition.**
   Facts are facts, but there is also room for feelings, emotions, reactions, and ideas. We find ourselves faced with questions:
   - **a.** An ethical problem
     - Is business meant to be business regardless of who is involved or victimized?
   - **b.** The influence of fashion, trends, and clichés on business
     - Do fashion, trends, stereotypes generate business or is it the other way round?
     Fashion/trends generate business/ Business generates fashion/trends
   - **c.** The impact of advertising

Exam Paper

Selling television sets by turning up the glamour

An ad for Philips's Aurea television, shot by a fashion photographer, Vincent Peters. A five-minute film is actually an advertisement for a new television from Philips Electronics, a high-end flat-screen model called Aurea. The film, a spy story shot in Shanghai, will be shown in the Paris boutiques of the fashion label Lanvin and the jeweler Lorenz Bäumer – on Aurea televisions, of course. The decision to produce a short film with an art-house director shows how brands are trying to break away from their reliance on 30-second television spots, which some marketers fear have lost their effectiveness. Now, even televisions are being marketed without recourse to television. Meanwhile, the move by Philips to involve luxury goods purveyors like Lanvin and Bäumer reflects a desire by consumer electronics companies to differentiate their products in an intensely competitive marketplace by trying to give them some of the glamour of the fashion business. "The idea is to be more exclusive, to be very different from your traditional kind of advertising," said Sandrine Huijgen, Marketing Director for consumer electronics at Philips. "We don't see Dior advertising a lot on television." "There is a lot of female coding in this advertising," said Laura Jones, Global Client Managing Director at the advertising agency DDB, a unit of Omnicom Group. "Before, televisions have always been sold based on pixels or that sort of thing." Philips is not alone in moving away from a masculine approach to selling consumer devices, embracing the presumably more female world of fashion. LG, the South Korean electronics company, is selling a mobile phone under the Prada brand name. Philips trails Sony and Samsung in the market for flat-panel L.C.D. televisions. Samsung had 16.8 per cent of the market in the first quarter of 2007, compared with 12.6 per cent for Sony and 12.2 per cent for Philips, according to iSuppli, a market research firm. With its unusual ad campaign for the Aurea, can Philips close the gap? In the film by the art director, a female agent sent to kill a character named Light is instead seduced by him. Now, Philips must hope that not too many customers get similarly sidetracked – spending their money on Lanvin fashions or Bäumer jewellery instead.

© *New York Times*, August 14th, 2007, by Eric Pfanner

I. Compréhension À rédiger en français

Après avoir dégagé l'idée principale de l'article, vous ferez une synthèse en 100 mots. Vous indiquerez le nombre de mots utilisés.

II. Expression À rédiger en anglais (200 words)

The Gucci family slogan is: "Quality is remembered long after the price is forgotten."

a. Explain what that means.
b. Does this slogan apply to all sorts of products?
c. Illustrate your answers with precise examples.
d. Briefly say how you would choose a slogan.

Zooming on

Unit 9 Brand managing

One of the most important decisions a company must make is the image it wants to give of itself. Choosing a brand name and a logo for the company or finding a name for a new product has become all the more difficult as good trademarks are scarce.

1. Brand top 10s in 2007

PUBLIC'S TOP 10		EXPERTS' TOP 10	
1. Microsoft	6. British Airways	1. Google	6. BBC
2. Coca-Cola	7. Lego	2. Apple	7. Coca-Cola
3. Google	8. Guinness	3. iPod	8. Red Bull
4. BBC	9. Mercedes-Benz	4. Mini	9. Tesco
5. BP	10. Cadbury	5. eBay	10. Waitrose

Have a look at the results of the survey of 3,000 British consumers led by the brand monitoring group Superbrands in 2007.

1. Say who has been voted the UK's number one brand by the public. Compare with the list voted by experts.

2. Which three brands are in both the public's and experts' top 10 lists. Can you imagine the reasons why?

3. Say which brands are British and which are not?

4. Say in which sectors they operate: the Internet, the media, technology...

5. Prepare a similar survey in your class.

2. Gender and generation gaps

The public survey, conducted by YouGov, showed men and women ranked many of the same brands top. One of the notable differences in opinion saw champagne brand Moët & Chandon making the women's top 10, whilst Guinness made the men's list. "The greatest difference in voting positions between men and women confirms that women clearly rate high quality lifestyle brands while their male counterparts voted in considerably higher numbers for more everyday functional brands – Wall's ice cream tops this list with men placing the brand 265 places higher than the women; on the other hand more women than men voted Swarovski a Superbrand, placing it 355 places higher," the report says.

Young and older generations are set apart most markedly by alcohol. The 18-24 category included Smirnoff, Bacardi and Jack Daniel's in its top 10. The over-65s voted traditional brands including Wedgwood, Parker and Clarks into their top 10, but also picked Google and Nike.

Read the text

1. Say what the difference between men's and women's choices of brands is.

2. Say what sets generations apart.

3. Starbucks is leaving the Forbidden City

Starbucks had done its best to respond to criticism of its presence in a World Heritage Site, visited by nearly 9 million tourists a year. It removed its familiar green sign following earlier protests that began as soon as the outlet opened. [...] The coffee retailer was told it could remain only if it sold its coffee through a store operated by other brands, and without being identified as Starbucks. [...] Officially, Starbucks says it understands the reasons for the decision, and that its departure is "very congenial". The firm must be hoping that this does not portend further attacks on its operations in China, where it already operates nearly 200 outlets and plans to grow rapidly. [...]

The most positive interpretation of Starbucks' ousting from the Forbidden City is that it reflects the surprisingly rapid development of civil society in China. After all, resisting the pernicious spread of global brands is evidence of the existence of the most advanced phase of consumerism, based on refinement and superior tastes.

Have a look at the photo.

1. Say where you think it was taken.

2. What makes it particularly striking?

Read the article.

1. Say why Starbucks closed its outlet in Beijing's Forbidden City?

2. What does the popularity of the brand among Chinese consumers indicate about the state of the Chinese society?

4. Rui Chenggang

Listen to the anchorman for China's biggest TV network.

1. Say what the negative stereotypes associated with Starbucks are.

2. Give the name of the next brand he wants to target.

3. Do you agree with his arguments?

REPORTING

Draw a list of the advantages and dangers of the globalization of brands.

WORDS APART

A trademark Une marque déposée	**Marketing** La mercatique	**Launching a new product** Lancer un nouveau produit
available disponible	**advertising** la publicité	**challenging** stimulant
a brand une marque	**to advertise** faire de la publicité	**cost-sensitive** sensible au prix
a consumer un consommateur	**an after-sales service** un service après-vente	**a discount** une ristourne
competition la concurrence	**to appeal** to plaire à	**fashionable** à la mode
counterfeiting la contrefaçon	**brainstorming** le remue-méninges	**a guarantee** une garantie
craftsmanship la maîtrise d'un métier	**to cater to** s'occuper de	**high profile/upmarket** haut de gamme
a fake un faux	**to come up with** suggérer	**high-tech** la haute technologie
to file a complaint déposer une plainte	**a discount** une remise	**inexpensive** bon marché
the law la loi	**a gimmick** un gadget	**innovative** innovant
a lawyer un avocat	**globalization** la mondialisation	**latest** tout dernier
to name baptiser	**marketing people** les commerciaux	**low-price** à bas prix
a naming consultant un conseiller en nom de marque	**an open day** une opération porte ouverte	**packaging** l'emballage
an outlet un point de vente	**to pitch a service** établir un service	**promising** prometteur
a patent une licence	**to promote** faire la promotion de	**provocative** qui fait réagir
to register a name déposer un nom	**a rep** un représentant	**state-of-the-art** dernier cri
a sample un échantillon	**a travelling salesman** un VRP	**top-level** de haut niveau

Zooming on

Brand it like Beckham

David Beckham will soon be seen in U.S. commercials for Adidas, Walt Disney's, sports network ESPN and cell phone maker Motorola. He'll likely be on the cover of major U.S. magazines and papers, as well as leading sports reports and other television news coverage. David Beckham is already having an economic impact on U.S. professional soccer before his first game here, as he joins the Los Angeles Galaxy of Major League Soccer.

[...] For those soccer fans who have been patiently waiting for Americans to warm up to the world's favorite sport, this would seem to be their moment. While Americans have had only brief flirtations with soccer in the past, they've had a long-time meaningful love affair with celebrities and media superstars. And Beckham clearly qualifies as that, even among the 90 percent of fans here who can't tell you the name of a single U.S.-born male soccer player. The polling of Americans done by talent marketing agency Davie Brown Entertainment found that 51.9 percent of Americans know who Beckham is. Landon Donovan, who will be Beckham's teammate on the Galaxy, is known by only 9.1 percent of Americans, even though he's been in the league six years and has played for the American team in two World Cups.

Beckham is already one of the top athletes in terms of endorsements, with the *Times of London* estimating his deals are worth £20.5 million a year, or $41.3 million. [...] And he is cashing in with the Galaxy as well. His contract, which includes a share of ticket and merchandize sales, could net him $250 million in five years. To put that in perspective, that's about the same pay the Yankees, Alex Rodriguez is getting over ten years. Still, Beckham could wind up being a bargain for the Galaxy. His base salary of $5.5 million for this year has already been covered by increased revenue for the Galaxy. Beckham's first game, an exhibition match on July 21 against British team Chelsea, has already sold out the Home Depot Center, a soccer-only stadium that seats 27,000.

Chris Isidore, CNNMoney.com, July 6th, 2007

£ 10m a year from adidas

£ 4.5m from Motorola

£ 2m from Pepsi

£ 2-3m from Gilette

Source : Industry estimates

FIRST STEPS

1. Look at the bottom of the text and say where and when the article was published.

2. Look at the chart and name the companies David Beckham endorsed in 2006.

3. Read the article and match each sentence with a paragraph:

a. Beckham's future in the US is paved with gold.

b. The major league Soccer expects to make a lot of money out of Beckham.

c. Beckham is already a superstar in the US.

MOVING ON

1. Say what these figures refer to.

a. £20.5 **b.** $41.3 million **c.** $250 million **d.** $5.5 million

2. Say what these names refer to.

a. Adidas, Walt Disney's, ESPN and Motorola,
b. the Los Angeles Galaxy,
c. the Home Depot Center.

3. Say whether these statements are right or wrong. Justify your answers by quoting from the text.

a. Beckham has the potential to become famous in the U.S.
b. Beckham refuses to endorse brands.
c. Beckham will earn ten times as little as famous baseball players in the US.
d. Tickets to upcoming games with Beckham are sold out.

4. Choose the equivalent to the following phrases.

a. "Endorsements" means that Beckham:
- suffers from back pain,
- publicly declares his personal support of brands,
- gives money to brands.

b. "Merchandize sales" are sales of:
- products bearing a brand name or logo,
- manufactured products,
- bargains.

c. "His contract could net Beckham $250 million" means that
- he could earn $250 million on the sales,
- he could lose $250 million in revenue,
- he could sell 250 million T-shirts.

d. "Wind up being a bargain" means Beckham will:
- spend more money than he earns,
- bring in more money than he costs,
- cost more money than he brings in.

5. Translate

Translate the first paragraph of the text into French, from "David Beckham will soon be seen..." down to " ...the Los Angeles Galaxy of Major League Soccer." (line 10)

WRITING (150 words)

Can David Beckham transform himself from just another European sports star into a global brand?

Analyze what makes his image – his model good looks, a carefully managed star power, being married to Victoria Adams, the former Spice Girls singer – but also the difficulties –, most Americans have never seen Beckham play and have no interest in soccer, his metrosexual image does not go down well in Asia…

LANGUAGE AT WORK

1. Pick out all the nouns in the plural and classify them according to the way the -s is pronounced: [s], [z] or [iz]. Then, listen to the recording to check your answers and make out a rule of the way *-s* is pronounced.

2. Pick out the equivalents of the following from the text.

a. les publicités à la télé ;
b. couverture par la télévision ;
c. signatures ;
d. tirer des profits de ;
e. une part des ventes ;
f. une bonne affaire ;
g. des bénéfices accrus ;
h. tous les billets sont vendus.

3. Transform the sentences using *be likely to*.

a. Beckham will probably be on the cover of magazines.
b. He will probably be a popular player.
c. He will probably boost ticket sales.
d. He will probably sponsor brands.
e. He will probably be a bargain for the Galaxy.
f. MLS leaders are probably very happy with the deal.

4. Translate into English using *be likely to*.

a. Il sera vraisemblablement très heureux de l'affaire.
b. Les ventes de billets vont sûrement augmenter.
c. Il se pourrait bien que nous achetions un T-shirt des Galaxy.
d. Les joueurs vont probablement faire un stage d'entraînement.
e. Ils vont probablement bien s'entendre.
f. Ils ont sûrement acheté leurs billets.
g. Il va sûrement se plaindre s'il n'obtient pas une augmentation.

Unit 9 Brand managing

1. Designing a logo

YOUR JOB

You work for the Marketing Department of CleanWorld, a company that specializes in finding ways to recycle waste. Many documents (texts, graphs, letters, brochures, advertising material) are going to be circulated within the company and to its customers. CleanWorld wants to consolidate its image by adopting a new logo, which is the most visible element of the image the company gives of itself. The most successful logos are simple and easy to remember.

YOUR TASK

You are asked to define the new logo. Follow the different steps.

1. Look at Document 1. Say in which sector each company operates and if the logo is a drawing or a monogram. What image of the company does each logo give? Select the logo concept best adapted to the company.

2. Read Document 2 and choose the colours of your logo.

3. Read Document 3 about the evolution of the adidas logo and write a memo on the same model to describe your logo and justify your choices.

ACTING OUT

Use your notes to make an oral presentation of your choices for the logo to the class. Make sure your arguments are clearly presented.

Document 1

The logo concept

It can be :

- An image related to a business: a house for real estate, a car for a car dealer, a computer for a programming company. These logos are often very eye-catching, detailed and impressive and therefore expensive.
- An abstract image representing the company's philosophy: a pyramid for a stable, trustworthy company. Orbits, swooshes, sparks, or particles might be suitable for a very young, modern, high tech company. Think of Nike, AO...
- An iconic image: for example the Michelin Man, Kentucky Fried Chicken's Colonel Sanders since 1952...
- The company name: a unique font or unique layout style can make a great logo; for example: Sony, Kellogg's, Coca-Cola, IBM.

edf

bp

Gaz de France

Unilever

Document 2

Keep in mind, when selecting colours for your logo, that your colour scheme should be appropriate to your company. Everybody knows that colours have a symbolic and psychological meaning. Here are some of the values generally attached to colours.

WHITE	YELLOW	RED	ORANGE	BLUE	GREEN	BLACK
refers to purity, and makes other colours look brighter.	evokes energy, friendliness and gives an impression of warmth and well-being.	symbolizes life, danger, interdiction.	being a combination of red and yellow has all the qualities of the two colours.	is peaceful and refreshing, and often associated with water. Dark blue portrays comfort and relaxation.	obviously refers to nature, that is to say what is natural.	is the symbol of mourning and death, but also the distinctive colour for refinement and authority.

Document 3

adidas

Adi Dassler, the adidas company founder, created the 3-Stripes mark in 1949. Dassler created a symbol that could be immediately recognized when his footwear was used in athletic competition and associated with adidas. He emphasized the association with the slogan "The Brand with the 3 Stripes".

The above shape created in 1996 formed by the bars represents a mountain, indicating the challenge to be faced and the goals to be achieved.

In the late 1960s adidas expanded into the leisure and apparel sector, and this prompted Käthe and Adi Dassler to seek a new, additional identification mark for the brand. In August 1971, the Trefoil was born, out of more than 100 ideas. Inspired by the 3-Stripes, it is a geometric execution with a triple intersection, symbolizing the diversity of the adidas brand.

The adidas Sport Style logo was created in 2001. The inspiration for the symbol was the fast moving and ever-changing world we live in today. The world is represented with the globe whose speed is captured by the oval shape. adidas is indicated by the three stripes across the face of the globe, keeping pace with the speed and change of our world. The new logo is simple, clear, confident and shows leadership. It will support future business growth and is flexible enough to anticipate any unforeseen changes.

www.adidas-group.com

PROMPTS

CAUSE
- as *comme*
- for *car*
- since *puisque*
- due to *dû à*
- owing to *en raison de*
- because of *à cause de*
- the reason why *la raison pour laquelle*

CONSEQUENCE
- as a result *par conséquent*
- consequently *en conséquence*
- so *ainsi*
- then *alors*
- therefore *par conséquent*

INTERPRETING
- it appeals to *cela fait appel à*
- it evokes *cela évoque*
- it gives an impression of *cela donne l'impression que*
- it highlights *cela met en valeur*
- it means *cela veut dire*
- it refers to *cela se réfère à*
- it shows that *cela montre que*
- it suggests *cela suggère*
- it symbolizes *cela symbolise*
- it underlines *cela souligne*
- it reflects *cela reflète*
- it reinforces *cela renforce*
- it mirrors *cela reflète*

2. Launching a new product

YOUR JOB

You work for Leh Berry, a company which began operating in January 2006 in Gujarat state, India.

YOUR TASK

You are asked to announce that Leh Berry is entering the nectar market in a circular letter to be sent to customers. Follow the different steps.

1. Read the information about the new product. **(See Doc. 1 and 2)**
2. Read the circular letter sent by another company.
3. Prepare your letter.

- Address the person you are writing to by his or her name.
- Present the reason why you are writing from the start.
- Use positive adjectives to advertise the product.
- Make an attractive offer.
- Suggest making contact as soon as possible.

ACTING OUT

4. Prepare your notes for the phone conversation **(See Doc. 3)**.
5. Make the phone call in pairs.

Document 1

Range of Leh Berry nectars

Pineapple-apple	Blackcurrant
Apple-peach	Mango
Mixed fruit	Guava
Orange	Seabuckthorn

Document 2

Figures about the Indian juice market

Total juice market: $ 177.7
Nectar market: $ 66.63
Other players: Tropicana and Real
Target segment of the nectar market: 10%

Soft Drinks International

Document 3

M. S. Dhanota, President of Leh Berry

Listen to the recording and make notes of interesting phrases you could use when calling your customers:

- to make sure they have actually read your mail;
- to know whether they are interested in your offers;
- to encourage them to pass an order as soon as possible.

PROMPTS

POSITIVE ADJECTIVES

Low-priced/economical/inexpensive *à bas prix/économique/peu cher*
Providing value for money *fournir un bon rapport qualité-prix*
Innovative/challenging/provocative *novateur/stimulant/provocateur*
State-of-the-art/up-to-date *à la pointe de la technique/moderne*
Fashionable/latest *à la mode/tout dernier*

ATTRACTIVE OFFERS

To take an opportunity *saisir une opportunité*
An item *un objet*
A guarantee *une garantie*
To grant a discount *accorder une remise*
Special terms of payment *des conditions particulières de paiement*

REFERENCE DOCUMENT

DREADS INTERCONTINENTAL Ltd.
12 St John's Street
Manchester NX45 3SR England

Name and address of company

June 26th, 2008

Date

Dear Mrs Edwards,

Salutation

We are a leading manufacturer of hairdressers' equipment and we are pleased to send you a brochure about our new special line.

Reason for writing

Our latest shampoos, hairdyes and hair treatment are up-market, state-of-the art products that are certain to meet the needs of your most demanding customers. They are natural cosmetics that are produced with the utmost care and carry a two-year guarantee. In addition, our prices are unchanged from last year.

Positive presentation of product

Inside the brochure you will find a reply coupon to be completed and returned to us by September 30th for a 10% discount on the catalogue prices. We do hope that this offer will appeal to you.

Attractive offer

You can obtain more detailed information concerning these new products by contacting our agents at the above address. We are looking forward to doing business with you and can assure you that your order will be dealt with promptly.

Suggesting contact

Yours sincerely,

Complementary close

Janet Behan

Janet Behan
Marketing Department

Name and position in company

Enc: 1 brochure

Document enclosed

Brand managing

Test Yourself

Dianabilia takes over

A decade ago, Diana, Princess of Wales, became a powerful "Princess of Sales" as her death created a cottage industry of marketers cashing in with books, magazines, television shows and merchandise like figurines and coins. Diana is being recalled in an array of mementos, from TV shows and books to coins and porcelain plates.

Ten years later, the coming milestone anniversary is bringing a reprise as dozens of companies seek to capitalize on a renewed interest in Diana's life and legacy. And so far at least, the commemorative products have proved popular among consumers and advertisers alike. Among those taking part in the return of what the British call "Dianabilia" are blue-chip names that include Bertelsmann, Cablevision, Comcast, Discovery, Disney, General Electric, Hearst and Time Warner. Back, too, are the purveyors of trinkets like the Danbury Mint, with "an exquisite porcelain collector plate"; the Mystic Stamp Company, with a "Princess Diana colorized British penny"; and the Hamilton Collection unit of the Bradford Group, with a "limited edition" figurine devoted to "Diana, princess of our hearts."

It no longer raises eyebrows when celebrities are commercialized after their deaths. But just how quickly Diana became a potent global marketing phenomenon after she died on Aug. 31, 1997, took experts in building and licensing brands by surprise. The strength of her appeal then is a major reason, they say, that the merchandising of her memory has resumed now. "If you think of her as a product, she was able to accomplish a lot," said Burt Alper, principal at Catchword Branding, a consulting company. He added, "She was brilliant in reaching out and connecting to her audience in a way every brand would want to do." And Diana is "remembered as this young, captivating person, a beautiful princess who passed before her time," he said. "She did not go through a waning of her popularity and she did not go through the aging process." [...]

Another reason Diana may continue to intrigue is the unfolding lives of her sons. "You can't help but look at the boys and think about her," he added. William and Harry may even be living versions of line extensions, as brand offshoots are known in marketing circles. "They keep her alive in people's minds, which perpetuates her brand," said Mr. Alper. "It allows the legend to continue and provides a sequel."

Corrigé page 192

© *New York Times*, August 27th, 2007, by Stuart Elliot

I. Compréhension À rédiger en anglais

Rédigez un compte-rendu de l'article en 160 mots à 10% près. Indiquez le nombre de mots.

II. Traduction

Traduisez le dernier paragraphe du texte en français.

Exam Paper

The baby's called what?

Parents are increasingly, if subconsciously, "branding" rather than simply naming their children. Pamela Satran, who co-wrote the most successful series of baby-naming books in Britain and the US, says: "Companies stamp their names and initials on every single item of clothing. It's very much in the air. It is an influence. A parent wants to give their child individuality and competitive advantage. People have become conscious of the power of names and they want a name that is going to stand out in a world of Williams and Elizabeths. Parents are thinking far beyond how their friends will to react to their child's name."[...]

Prospective parents in search of a baby name should bear in mind the HobNob, says Graham Hales, the executive director of the corporate branding company Interbrand. Emotionally, it's a name that conveys so much more than chocolate-covered biscuit. Interbrand invented HobNob, Prozac and the Gillette razor Mach3. "When we think up a new name the primary function is for it to stand out, and I think the same can be said for how parents view children's names," he says. "Every parent wants their children to be successful, but how do we define success? Successful in our society is the ability to stand out from the crowd. That's not saying everybody wants their children to be a celebrity, but to call your son John would be very grey." [...]

In the US, the marketing men have gone one step further. I talked to Burt Alper, one of the founders of the corporate branding company Catchword, who hosts baby-name brainstorming sessions in his spare time for friends. "As a professional in the business, people expect great advice from us," he says. [...] Alper encourages parents to apply the three golden rules of brand-naming to children's names: "1. Don't tell people about what you are thinking about calling your baby or product. 2. Choose a name for your target audience as opposed to yourself. 3. Wait till you meet the baby before you choose the name. In the corporate world it would be like naming a company before you know what personality you want to give it."

That's all very well, but some brand names are successes, others are terrible failures. A parent is in no position to do the profiling it takes to create a brand. Corporations have enormous resources to do that. What do parents think they are going to do? Personally educate everyone in the world that Thor is a good name with positive associations?

Alongside the obsession with originality, the contempt for convention, the deliberate misspellings, the inventions and the abbreviations, are the sorely regretted mistakes.

The Times, July 31st, 2007, by Stefanie Marsh

I. Compréhension À rédiger en français

Après avoir dégagé l'idée principale de l'article, vous ferez un compte-rendu en 180 mots ±10%. Vous indiquerez le nombre de mots utilisés.

II. Expression À rédiger en anglais

1. Using the information given in the table, analyse the trend in baby names in Britain. Draw your conclusions. (100 words)

2. Do you believe a name has a personal meaning that can influence a child's character? (150 words)

Traditional names dominate the top ten: Olivia, Thomas, Jessica, William, Emily, Daniel
In 2006 in Britain were born:
864 Summers, 94 Myloses, 55 Autumns, 22 Spikes, 6 Blades, plus a handful of Kofis, Francos, Fds, Kikis, Brontes, Lunas, Uniques, Rorys, Florabellas, Harleys, Vices, Scorpios, Foxes and Cadences.
Rise in popularity:
Cruz (the Beckhams' youngest son) by 245%, Maddox (adopted son of Angelina Jolie) 88 places; Jayden (Britney Spears's youngest) 16 places to number 68; Lexie (Steven Gerrard's daughter) by 234%.
Figures from the Office for National Statistics

Unit 10 Retailing

The consumer seems to be the target of all sorts of merchants. Some decades ago they predicted the death of small shops in their struggle for survival against super stores.
Then e-commerce was accused of killing various kinds of outlets. Today we witness a retailing boom, whatever the area, closely connected to the spending spree of our western economy.

Zooming on

1. The call of the wild

Have a look at the two photos.

1. Describe them and comment on these contrasting situations.

2. List the advantages provided by these two kinds of retailers.

2. Cyber Monday

"Cyber Monday" is the Monday after Thanksgiving. The idea is that many people look in stores over the weekend. Then, to save time, they order online using the Internet at their jobs when they return to work.

Cyber Monday is a big day online. But market researchers at comScore Networks reported that the biggest day of the holiday season so far was December thirteenth. The company said people spent almost six hundred seventy million dollars at American sites that day. That did not include travel sites.

BBC Worldwide March 2007

Read the beginning of this report.

1. Say what Cyber Monday is.

Listen to the continuation of the tape.

1. Pick out the figures which account for the success of online selling.

2. Say what periods of the year show an online buyers' peak.

3. Spot the economic advantage of online shops over physical stores.

3. Has online shopping entered the dot calm era?

Online retail sales may reach $116 billion in the United States this year, or 5 per cent of all retail sales. But the rate of growth will keep slowing.

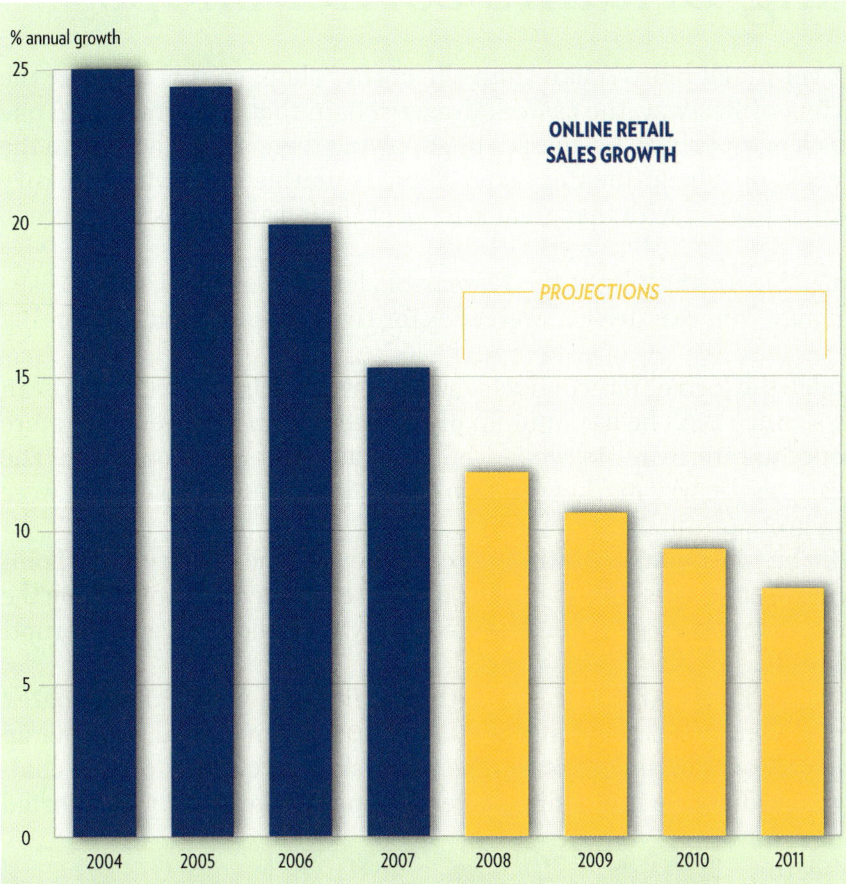

Jupiter Research.

Look at the bar-chart very carefully.

1. Explain in your own words what this graph is supposed to underline.

Account for the slowdown of e-commerce.

1. Compare online shopping with traditional shopping.

2. Give the retailer's viewpoint on both marketing devices.

3. Give the customer's viewpoint on these two means of buying.

REPORTING

Do you think online shopping is the best way to find what you are looking for without wasting your time? Weigh up the pros and cons before making your choice.

WORDS APART

Distribution **La distribution**

a branch/a subsidiary une filiale
a car dealer un concessionnaire automobile
a department store un grand magasin
a discount store un magasin à marge réduite
downmarket/upmarket bas de gamme/haut de gamme
a forklift truck un chariot élévateur
to meet the safety standards satisfaire aux normes de sécurité
one-stop shopping le commerce integré
online shopping la vente en ligne
an outlet un point de vente
retailing le petit commerce
a self-service store un libre service
to sell door-to-door faire du porte à porte
to set up s'implanter
a shopping arcade une galerie marchande
a shopping centre un centre commercial
to store entreposer
a supplier un fournisseur
a vending machine un distributeur automatique

Services **Les services**

an after-sales service un service après vente
to boost the sales dynamiser les ventes
the cashbox/check-out register, till la caisse enregistreuse
customer service le service clientèle
to deliver livrer
a drop in prices une baisse des prix
to expand a range/a line élargir une gamme
to freeze prices geler les prix
a good bargain une bonne affaire
handling la manutention
to load, unload charger, décharger
a loyalty card une carte de fidélité
maintenance l'entretien
to mark down démarquer
to pack, package emballer, empaqueter
to replenish réassortir
the scanning machine le lecteur électronique
to sell out brader
the servicing department le service réparation
to slash prices casser les prix

Consumer goods **Les biens de consommation**

available disponible
a barcode un code-barres
a brand leader un article pilote
best before date date limite de consommation
a can, a tin une boîte de conserve
cash on delivery payable à la livraison
to conduct a survey mener une enquête
a display rack un présentoir
frozen food les produits surgelés
a glass jar un bocal en verre
good value for money bon rapport qualité prix
an item un article
a label une étiquette
perishables les denrées périssables
the price tag l'étiquette de prix
a quality product un produit de qualité
the receipt le ticket de caisse
reliable fiable
a sample un échantillon
the shelf le rayon
a shopping cart/trolley un chariot
a spare part une pièce détachée
a wide choice un choix important

Supplying Britain's corner shops

You don't get much more Asian than the corner shop, so it is apt that the headquarters of Bestway, the cash-and-carry chain that has grown into one of Britain's biggest private businesses by supplying them should adhere to the central tenets of subcontinental taste. There is marble everywhere, luxury wallpaper and the car park is packed with that great symbol of Indian and Pakistani success, the Mercedes saloon.

"It's not an Asian thing," Sir Anwar Pervez, the 72-year-old founder and chairman insists. [...] "It's just value for money. You can drive a Mercedes for five years without it breaking down." [...]

[...] Few would begrudge the former bus conductor who arrived in Britain from Pakistan at the age of 21, a few toys. Since 1963 he has built up his business from a convenience store in Earls Court, West London, into Britain's second-biggest cash-and-carry operator. The decision to go into the cash-and-carry market came in 1976. At the time wholesalers were making about 10 per cent gross profit.

Sir Anwar thought that he could manage with 4 per cent and pass the saving on to whomever he supplied – allowing them to pass the saving on to their customers. It worked. By the mid-eighties Bestway had six warehouses. "When I started, everybody said, 'he'll go bankrupt'. But I am a millionaire now." [...]

According to The Sunday Times Rich List, he (with his family) is worth an estimated £543 million. Group profits were up 27 per cent in 2005 to 2006, on an annual turnover up 26 per cent over the same period. The numbers may be surprising, given the storm of challenges faced by Bestway, including the increasing power of supermarkets and the reported departure of many Asians from the convenience store sector. [...]

One of the ways in which Bestway has kept ahead is through acquisition. In January 2005, after a prolonged courtship, it bought Batleys, another cash-and-and-carry chain, for £100 million, which enlarged the group from 31 to 50 warehouses and increased its buying power. Unusually for a merger, Bestway has left the acquisition untouched, keeping the management, head office and brand.

The Times, Saturday July 21st, 2007

FIRST STEPS

1. Present the document (type, origin, date...).

2. Specify the kind of retailing that Bestway represents.

3. Give the main lines of Sir Anwar's marketing strategy.

4. Say what you think about the chain's name.

MOVING ON

1. Draw a portrait of Bestway's manager.

2. What do the following figures correspond to?

72 / 21 / £543m / 50.

3. Select the appropriate explanations of these quotes from the article.

a. "the central tenets of subcontinental taste" means
- the criteria the English like most,
- the criteria the Indian prefers,
- the atmosphere the Europeans appreciate.

b. "It's just value for money" means
- his car is worth the money it costs,
- his car should be more expensive,
- his car is very cheap for me.

c. "He'll go bankrupt" means
- he will open a bank,
- he will close his bank account,
- he will close down.

d. "the storm of challenges" means
- few managers could compete with him,
- he had to overcome lots of difficulties,
- he didn't have to vie with big chains.

4. Sir Anwar is the image of the successful immigrant. Pick out elements highlighting his path to success.

a. as a man,
b. as a manager,
c. as a businessman.

5. What changing picture of the current British retailing sector is presented?

6. What deal was struck in January 2005? Give details about this agreement.

7. Show how Sir Anwar proved to be a well informed entrepreneur in this merger.

8. Sir Anwar stands as the link between producers and retailers. What makes this position uncomfortable?

9. Translate

From 'Sir Anwar thought that he could manage with 4 per cent...' to '..."When I started, everybody said, I'll go bankrupt. But I am a millionaire now."'

WRITING (150 words)

Account for the assets suppliers have to accumulate in today's business world.

Do you think the retailling network can do without them?

LANGUAGE AT WORK

1. Read the following words included in the article. Underline the syllables which are stressed.

business / success / embarrass / supplying / allowing / expanding / Asian / Indian / Pakistani / conductor / operator / sector.

2. Find the translation of the following compound nouns.

headquarters / wallpaper / chairman / wholesaler / warehouse.

3. Complete with "used to" or "be used to".

a. He .... a bus conductor when he settled in Britain. (*to be*)

b. The small store retailers .... with him. (*to deal*)

c. The Board of directors .... every month. (*to meet*)

d. Before the merger he .... with Batleys. (*to compete*)

4. Complete with a compound adjective.

a. Sir Anwar is a .... manager. (*72 years old*)

b. Bestway used to be a .... chain. (*six warehouses*)

c. The company has reached a .... turnover. (*1.7 billion pounds*)

d. It proves to be a .... chain. (*which grows fast*)

5. Translate into French.

a. He provided his whole family with positions in the firm.

b. He will provide for them as long as he runs Bestway.

c. He has been supplying corner shops for over 20 years.

d. He usually supplies to stores within 24 hours after the orders.

e. The battery is not supplied with the torch.

6. Translate into English.

a. Il profite de ses vacances à Madrid pour rencontrer ses homologues espagnols.

b. Il profite de ses vacances, il les a bien méritées.

c. Son patron profite du dévouement de sa secrétaire.

d. L'entreprise profite du contexte économique favorable.

Unit 10 Retailing

1. Conducting a survey

YOUR JOB

You work as a market research consultant for Sainsbury's. Your company has decided to investigate the vending machines niche to diversify its points of sales.

YOUR TASK

You are asked to conduct an opinion poll about the role played by vending machines in the average consumer's life (**See Doc. 1**).

1. You will first design a questionnaire –use the prompts– to investigate the concept, the products, places, prices, quality and targets (**See Doc. 2**). Analyse the example in document 3.

2. You will then survey a sample of 20 people, collect their answers and classify them. Draw your conclusions.

3. You will write a letter to tell your boss about the prospective investments to be made or not.

ACTING OUT

You will present the results of this poll to a focus group and discuss them.

Document 1

What a survey is

- The survey is a non-experimental, descriptive research method.
- Surveys are used to assess attitudes and characteristics of a wide range of subjects.
- Surveys can be useful when a researcher wants to collect data on phenomena that cannot be directly observed.
- In a survey, researchers sample a population.

Document 2

Question design

It is important to design questions very carefully. A poorly designed questionnaire renders the results meaningless. Some pointers can guide you:

- Make items clear (don't assume the person you are questioning knows the terms you are using).
- Avoid double-barrelled questions (make sure the question asks only one specific thing). Respondents must be competent to answer (don't ask questions that respondents won't be able to answer accurately).
- Questions should be relevant (don't ask questions on topics that respondents don't care about or haven't thought about).
- Short items are best (so that they may be read, understood, and answered quickly).
- Avoid negative items (if you ask whether librarians should not be paid more, it will confuse respondents).
- Avoid biased items and terms (be sensitive to the effect of your wording on respondents).

As may be seen, designing good questions is much more difficult than it seems. One effective way of making sure that questions measure what they are supposed to measure is to test them out first, using small focus groups.

Document 3

What store promotions motivate Black Friday shoppers?

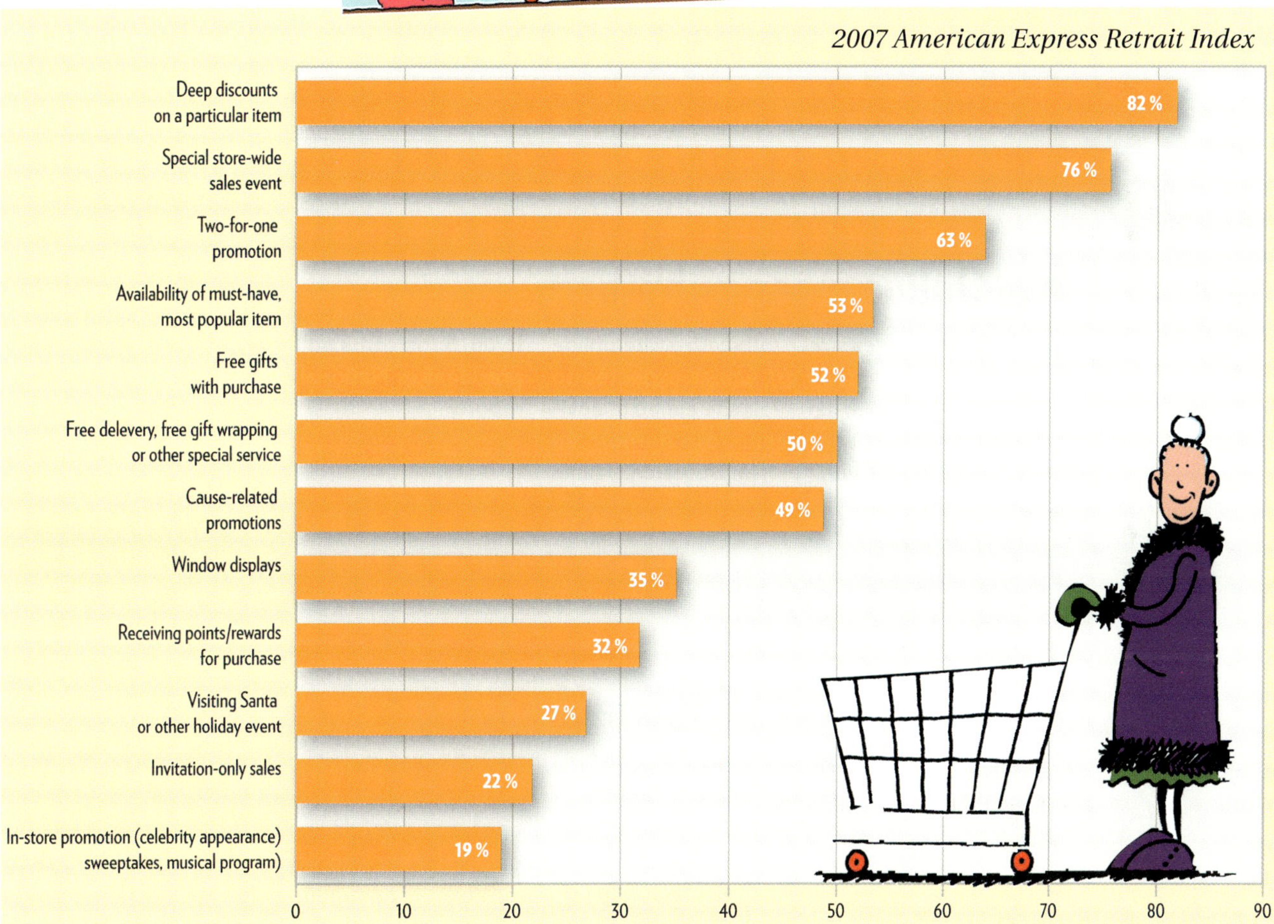

PROMPTS

Do you know what e-commerce means? *Savez-vous ce qu'est le commerce électronique ?*
Have you ever placed mail orders? *Avez-vous déjà passé des commandes par courier ?*
Would you buy over the net? *Accepteriez-vous d'acheter via internet ?*

Do you often buy goods from vending machines? *Consommez-vous souvent des produits issus de distributeurs ?*
Does the best before date frighten you? *Est-ce que la date de péremption vous fait peur ?*
Select the goods you would buy from vending machines. *Choisissez les produits que vous achèteriez dans un distributeur.*

Would you say such machines are convenient? Useful? Hype? *Diriez-vous que de tels appareils sont pratiques ? Utiles ? Des traquenards ?*
In your opinion were most countries right when they decided to ban these machines from schools? *Est-ce que à votre avis, la plupart des pays qui ont interdit ces machines dans les écoles ont eu raison ?*

2. Weighing up the pros and cons

YOUR JOB

You are an average consumer and you react to the inroads of new means of selling versus traditional retailing.

YOUR TASK

1. Do the prompts exercises.
2. Analyse the different types of retailing presented on both pages.
3. Design a blog relating a personal experience with one of these new devices.

ACTING OUT

You will defend your viewpoint in pair work.

Document 1

Online green publishers

Washington Post/Newsweek Interactive, the online arm of The *Washington Post Co.*, is expected to introduce Sprig.com, a new Web site aimed at environmentally conscious women. Josh Bernoff, an online media analyst with Forester Research, Jeanie Pyun, Sprig.com's editor in chief and Betsy Scolnik, president of National Geographic's online division report.

The International Herald Tribune,
April 23rd, 2007

Document 2

The convenience of online shopping

[...] One of the biggest factors in the growth of the online fashion retailer has been the proliferation of broadband. [...] The other key factor pushing increasing numbers online is convenience. "Girls don't have the time to go to the shops in their lunch hour. By shopping online they can get items delivered to their place of work, 96 per cent 15-year-olds have bought on line." [...]

In a cash-rich, time-poor society, shopping online would appear to be the ideal solution. The popularity of eBay, which announced that its annual profit soared by 52 percent to $377m this month, has shown the consumer's willingness to search for bargains online. [...]

According to new research on shoppers' habits, around half prefer to purchase consumer electronics online with just 30 per cent preferring to buy them in store. Similarly, more people want to buy gifts via e-commerce (42 per cent) compared with 28 per cent of consumers who want to buy gifts from a shop. However for clothing, footwear and jewellery the majority of people still prefer to visit the high street (63 per cent) as opposed to shop online (24 per cent). Yet, in a similar way to window shopping, consumers will research products on different websites before hitting the high street with their credit cards.

[...] A lot of people still want to look at things before they buy. They will do the research online then go and shop outside.

The Independent,
May 1st, 2007

Document 3

My blog about vending machine chips

Picture yourself. You're two thirds of the way through a journey in deepest, darkest north Norfolk. You're tired. The train leaving London was overcrowded due to the fact that it's the first train out of London that allows Saver tickets. So when you arrive at Norwich station and see a chip vending machine, you just have to give it a go!

There are very few things that I know about vending machines, but chief among them is that the contents tend to be pre-packaged. So that's cans and packets. You also have your drink dispensers which basically work by adding hot water to a variety of powders to lesser or greater success. But chips! That's a whole other proposition. The machine, supplied by McCain's, is supposedly filled with non-oil cooked chips. Instead hot air seems to be the method of heating the food up. Images of hairdryers pointed at oven-chips came to mind.

Document 4

Why people shop by mail order

There are various reasons why people shop by mail, and the trends point to an increase in mail order shopping over time.

1. Convenience: Everyone's busy these days with work, taking the kids to school, various sports and activities, etc. Being able to have the things you need come to you is very attractive.

2. Hard-to-find products: Some things are just not available in your local stores, or not available in the colours and options you need.

3. Better deal: Ordering by mail offers more competition than your local stores and may frequently offer a better deal by eliminating the retail overhead.

4. No pressure: There's no sales staff annoying you with bad advice or trying to steer you towards more expensive products.

5. Elderly: Mail order is more than a convenience. It's a life-saver, helping to keep up with everyone else. As more people live longer, this category of customer will continue to grow.

Lastly: Consumers can browse, compare and buy online 24 hours a day. They can also pay online and have their purchases delivered right to their door. No more parking problems or lining-ups at the till.

www.mailordering.com

PROMPTS

1. Fill in the blanks with relative pronouns.

a. I don't like these machines .... produce industrialized food.

b. The red light is flashing, ... means the chips are ready.

c. It's a device in .... frozen chips are stored.

d. .... is amazing is the price charged for a couple of chips.

2. How to get chips from a vending machine. Use the appropriate verb.

a. .... a coin into the slot.

b. .... large, medium or small.

c. .... the green button.

d. .... two minutes.

e. When the red light stop flashing, ... yourself.

Test Yourself

The great Wal-Mart of China

In the grocery section of a big store in north Beijing, shoppers struggle to catch a bargain. And a fish. "We'd still rather pick it out ourselves," says law student Guo Jiao, as she and a friend repeatedly plunge fishing nets into a tank full of slippery grass carp. [...] "I come here every day or two for the fresh stuff, they've got everything you need."

Such is life in the Great Wal-Mart of China. [...] For Wal-Mart, China represents the biggest frontier since it conquered America. China's voracious consumers are pushing retail sales to a 15 percent annual growth rate. [...] But the standard-bearer of American retailing has painstakingly discovered that success in China requires [...] going native. And now after a decade of ingratiating itself to Chinese consumers by adopting their customs and culture, Wal-Mart is making its move from a minor player to a dominant force. Word emerged last week that Wal-Mart is more than doubling its presence in China by spending $1 billion to acquire Trust-Mark, a Taiwanese-owned chain of more than 100 big-box stores in 20 Chinese provinces. The deal [...] will catapult Wal-Mart past its main foreign rival, Carrefour, which it outbid for Trust-Mart.

Company	Country	Market Share	Sales in millions (U.S. $)
Carrefour	France	8.8	2,167.0
Trust-Mart	**Taiwan**	**5.8**	**1,418.8**
A-Best	China	4.7	1,445.3
Lotus (Charoen) Pokphand Group	Thailand	4.1	1,006.5
Century Mart (Brilliance Group)	China	3.9	947.3
Hymail (Tesco)	Britain	3.7	897.4
Renrenie	China	3.6	891.3
Wal-Mart	**U.S.**	**3.1**	**764.0**

Measured as percent change in sales at only those stores open during the quarter listed and the same quarter the previous year.

Euromonitor international, retail forward, *Newsweek Research.*, 2006

Wal-Mart execs have long cited China as the best place on earth to export the U.S. merchandising miracle Sam Walton began 45 years ago. China represents the same wide-open retail landscape and burgeoning middle-class that mad Wal-Mart ubiquitous in the United States. [...]

China [however] remains an economy controlled by domestic retailers. Becoming the largest foreign retailer there will give Wall-Mart less than 9 per cent of the [...] market. [...] In fact, Wal-Mart will build more stores in America this year – 370 – than it will have managed to amass in China in 13 years.

At home, Wal-Mart is suffering a slowdown in sales as its relentless expansion finally reaches a saturation point and it increasingly confronts community backlash. "Wal-Mart is really hitting the wall in the U.S.". "So China is absolutely critical." [...]

Newsweek, October 30th, 2006

Corrigé page 193

I. Compréhension

Lisez l'article ci-dessus et faites-en un compte-rendu en français de 200 mots.

II. Traduction

Traduisez en français depuis "Wal-Mart execs..." jusqu'à "States" (lignes 24 à 26).

III. Expression

a. Read the title of the document, then Wal-Mart's current ranking. Identify Wal-Mart's eventual target. (80 words)

b. Give your opinion about Carrefour's position in this race for power. Imagine the near future of these giants. (100 words)

Exam Paper

Plug-and-pay toys are the latest fashion

FIRST BARBIE HAD KEN.
NOW BARBIE HAS A DOCKING STATION.

A new doll hitting retail shelves this week is familiar in many ways but she also has some unusual features. This Barbie, smaller and less shapely than her standard cousin, functions like an MP3 music player. When her feet are plugged into her docking station she unlocks pages of games, virtual shops and online chat functions on the BarbieGirls.com Web site.

The doll is a roundabout way of charging for online content. Instead of asking young Web surfers to punch in their parents' credit card numbers, BarbieGirls.com and other sites are sending customers to a real-world toy store first. Some of these sites, like the Barbie one, can be used in a limited way without purchasing merchandise – the better to whet young appetites – but others, like the popular Webkinz site, are of little use without a store-bought product or two. [...]

With children's leisure habits shifting online, toy companies are responding with new products that can be construed as fun both online and off. That Barbie in the docking station? Go to a physical store and buy her an extra outfit, and you get access to even more Web content. Products like these represent a new paradigm[1] not only in the design and function of toys, but also in how toy makers use their Web properties. Mattel, for instance, like many consumer goods companies, has until now treated Barbie.com and its 22 or so other Web sites as advertising forums, places to showcase toys with the hope that children will nag their parents for them.

Now, Mattel and others are trying to turn their sites into money-makers in their own right. About three million people have registered since April on the BarbieGirls Web site. [...] This concept behind Web-connected toys is not new. One noteworthy attempt came from The Learning Company, an educational software company that was owned for a short time by Mattel. But concepts like physical telescopes that could zoom to far-away islands when aimed at an Internet-connected computer failed to take off, in large part because Internet connections were too slow.

But times have changed tremendously. The starter set for the BarbieGirls site, sold $59.99, will be the main Barbie products this holiday season. Mattel will run some television ads for the product in the fall, but the site will be the primary driver of sales.

International Herald Tribune, July 23rd, 2007

1. *example*

I. Compréhension

Lisez attentivement l'article ci-dessus et faites-en un compte-rendu en anglais en 200 mots.

II. Traduction

Traduisez le premier paragraphe depuis "A new doll" (ligne 1) jusqu'à "Web site." (ligne 7)

III. Expression

a. Retailers take advantage of a brand image to devise and sell by-products. Why is it a lucrative market? (100 words)

b. Does the plug-and-pay policy make people dependent? Give your opinion. (100 words)

Unit 11 Sustainable development

In a sustainable world, society's demand on nature is in balance with nature's capacity to meet that demand. When resources are consumed faster than they are produced or renewed, they are depleted and eventually used up. Depletion is exacerbated by the growth in human population as well as by changing lifestyles.

Zooming on

1. Sustainable development quiz

1. The most widely used definition of sustainable development is: "Development that meets the needs of the present without compromising the ability of future generations to meet their own needs." In what text did this originate?

- ☐ Universal Declaration of Human Rights (1948)
- ☐ Brundtland Report (1987)
- ☐ UN Millennium Declaration (2000)
- ☐ Monterrey Consensus on Millennium Development Goals

2. Which of the following is an important factor or indicator of sustainable development?

- ☐ Equity between the present and the future
- ☐ Environmental impact of economic activity
- ☐ The costs of production and consumption on society
- ☐ All of the above

3. Gross domestic product, or GDP, is a poor indicator of sustainable development and is largely overvalued because it neglects which of the following fundamental factors?

- ☐ Increase in aggregate supply
- ☐ Depletion of natural resources
- ☐ Increase in prices
- ☐ Fluctuations in population

4. Which of the following countries contributes the highest rate of investment towards sustainable development as a percentage of GDP?

- ☐ United States ☐ United Kingdom
- ☐ China ☐ India

5. Roughly 100 birds and mammals have become extinct between 1900 and 2000, which is an extinction rate of one species per year. How much greater is this rate than the average extinction rate, or background rate, as measured in the geologic record?

- ☐ 3 times ☐ 33 times
- ☐ 333 times ☐ 3333 times

6. How many villages throughout Africa have been identified as hunger hotspots?

- ☐ 10,000 ☐ 40,000
- ☐ 100,000 ☐ 500,000

7. What percentage of the world's fish stocks are considered to be fully fished out or overexploited?

- ☐ 10% ☐ 25% ☐ 50% ☐ 75%

8. Since 1900, approximately how much has sea level risen?

- ☐ Sea level has not risen
- ☐ 6.7 to 7.1 inches
- ☐ 0.067 to 0.071 inches
- ☐ 1.5 to 2.1 inches

9. What is the approximate average life expectancy in sub-Saharan Africa?

- ☐ 34 years ☐ 46 years
- ☐ 65 years ☐ 71 years

10. Malaria, HIV/AIDS and tuberculosis account for how many deaths annually?

- ☐ 600,000 ☐ 1.6 million
- ☐ 5.6 million ☐ 10.6 million

www.earth.columbia.edu

Look at document 1.

1. Do the quiz individually.
2. Discuss your choices with the class.
3. Listen to the recording to check your answers.

2. 2005 World consumption cartogram

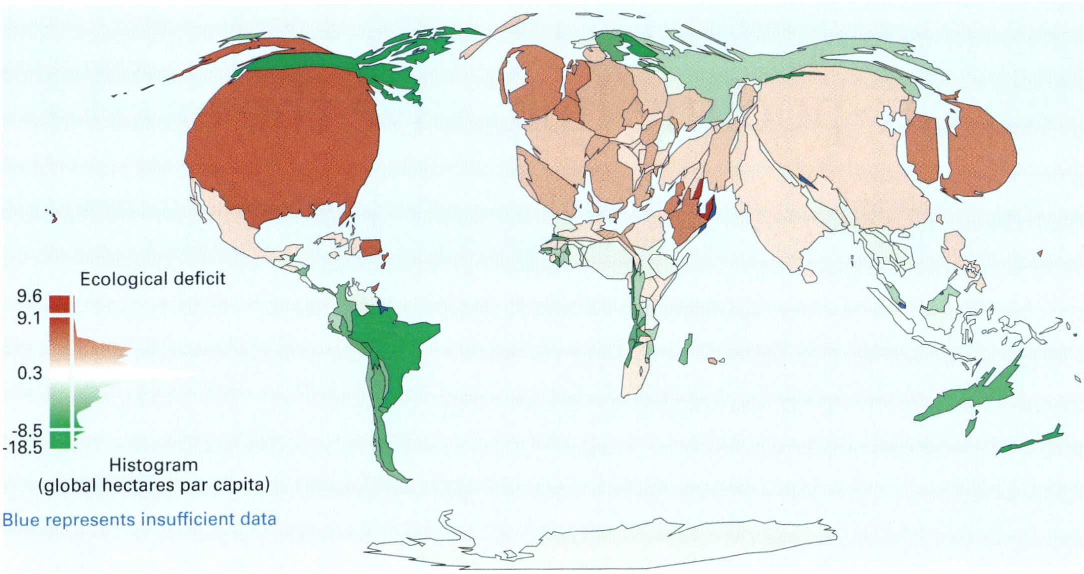

Have a look at the map.

1. Say in which countries the average ecological footprint is the highest and the lowest.

3. Carbon offsets

Listen to Mary Taylor, a campaigner at Friends of the Earth.

1. Pick out her two criticisms of the carbonoffset trading business.

2. What solution does she suggest?

REPORTING

Are you aware of climate change?
What are you personally ready to do to prevent it?
State your reasons.

WORDS APART

Pollution **La pollution**

acid rain les pluies acides
assault agresser
an assault une agression
chemicals produits chimiques
carcinogenic cancérigène
congested embouteillé
an earthquake un tremblement de terre
deforestation la déforestation
drought /au/ la sécheresse
to dump waste jeter des ordures
a flood /ʌ/ une inondation
fossil fuels énergies fossiles
fly-tipping dépôt illégal d'ordures
household waste les déchets ménagers
a landslide un glissement de terrain
the melting of the ice cap la fonte de la calotte glacière
natural disasters les désastres naturels
a pandemics une pandémie
pollutants des polluants
the rain forest la forêt primaire
rubbish/garbage les déchets
the soil le sol
wildlife la faune et la flore

The threat of climate change
La menace du changement climatique

carbon dioxide le dioxyde de carbone
the carbon footprint l'empreinte écologique
to damage the lungs endommager les poumons
deadly/lethal/mortal mortel
to deplete réduire
exhaust fumes les gaz d'échappement
foul air l'air souillé
global warming le réchauffement planètaire
greenhouse gases les gaz à effet de serre
harmful dangereux
noxious nocif
the ozone layer la couche d'ozone
a scheme un projet
smog (smoke + fog) le brouillard en ville
to spew cracher, rejeter
a stranded tanker un pétrolier échoué
toxic waste les déchets toxiques
to threaten menacer
a threat une menace
to unbalance/upset the balance déséquilibrer
to unload décharger
to use up resources épuiser les ressources
to wipe out anéantir, éradiquer

Sustainable development
Le développement durable

breathable respirable
car-pooling le co-voiturage
to clean up nettoyer
conservation la préservation
to curb juguler
an environmentalist/ecologist un écologiste
flex fuels les bio carburants
disposable jettable
to harness maîtriser
non-polluting non polluant
to offset compenser
plug-in hybrids (PHEVs) voitures hybrides
to recycle waste recycler les déchets
renewable energies les énergies renouvelables
to salvage récupérer
to save économiser
to tackle s'attaquer à
to spare épargner
survival is at stake la survie est en jeu
to unclog désembouteiller
a wind mill une éolienne
a wind farm un parc éolien

Unit 11 Sustainable development

Zooming on

Can car-pooling help save the earth?

Kate Sydney had never met me, but she unhesitatingly opened the door of her 1998 Nissan so I could ride to Target with her. The trip didn't take long, but it spared the world 10 pounds of carbon dioxide. Multiply that by millions, and you have one reason Robin Chase started GoLoco, an Internet-based service that uses social networking to create instant car pools. [...] Chase, 48, whose previous start-up was the Web-based car-rental service Zipcar, saw a big problem: 75 percent of all auto trips transporting only one human, driving Earth to ruin with toxic emissions. Her idea was to let drivers and riders use the Web to turn solitary rides into shared ones, saving fuel and cutting costs. She would also build a business by taking a cut of the fees that passengers on the site would pay drivers to share the costs.

When brainstorming the company, she saw three obstacles to her goal: A fear of strangers. The difficulty of finding rides. And a feeling that the effort really isn't worth it. That last concern, she asserts, is no longer valid: awakened by the threat of climate crisis, lots of people are now eager to win greenie points. The connection problem, she believes, will be solved by a virally[1] growing online network where members routinely post their intended commutes, trips and errands[2]. [...] The more people sign up to GoLoco, the better the chance that someone is going to the same place you are. Meanwhile, GoLoco will handle the payments that let riders pay their share, without cheesy[3] discussions of who owes what.

That leaves the safety issue. "It's all about framing," says Chase. When you sign up for GoLoco, you submit picture and share information about yourself from sites like Facebook and Flickr, as well as a list of groups you belong to. You speak into your computer mic[4] to describe your favorite breakfast so that potential ride-sharers can hear your voice. You also indicate what other Olos[5] you trust enough to ride with, so that others can see if you know people in common. Also, as you use GoLoco, drivers or passengers who accompany you will write reviews of your behavior, eBay style. After taking all that into consideration, Olo's can accept or pass on potential riders.

Newsweek, April 23rd, 2007, by Steven Levy

1. *qui se répand comme un virus* – 2. *les courses* - 3. *moche, médiocre* – 4. *(abbr.)* microphone – 5. *(abbr.)* On Line Opinion: *usagers de sites*

FIRST STEPS

1. Look at the title and bottom of the document. Present the text.

2. Read the title and say what the article is about.

3. Read the article and pick out the words connected with protection of the environment.

MOVING ON

1. Provide information about GoLoco

a. the service it provides,
b. what it is based on.

2. Choose the appropriate equivalent of the following phrases:

a. "Car-pooling" means travelling:
- several people in one car,
- each person in their own car,
- accumulate miles by car.

b. "Social networking" is:
- a system of lines that interconnect,
- a web of radio or TV stations,
- a group of people with similar interests who interact for mutual support.

c. In the text, "to ride" means:
- to travel by horse,
- to be carried in a car,
- to move as if on water.

3. Fill in the identity card of GoLoco's founder:

first name, name, age and former business.

Say what GoLoco lets drivers and riders do.

4. Say whether these statements are right or wrong. Justify your answers by quoting from the text.

a. A driver is alone in his car 75% of the time.
b. Car exhaust fumes are destroying the Earth.
c. Sharing a car-trip increases fuel consumption.
d. Car-pooling is more economical.

5. Name the three difficulties she anticipated.

6. How are the difficulties overcome?

7. Reorder the statements to describe the way "framing" works.

- You accept or pass on potential riders.
- You give a list of groups you belong to.
- You indicate what other Olos you trust enough to ride with.
- You share information about yourself.
- You sign up for GoLoco.
- You speak into your computer mic to describe your favourite breakfast.
- You submit a picture.
- You write reviews of riders' behaviour.

8. Translate

Translate the first paragraph of the text into French from "Kate Sydney had never met me..." down to "...to create instant car pools." (line 5)

WRITING (150 words)

Do you agree that people need to change their everyday habits to curb global warming?

LANGUAGE AT WORK

1. Say how *-ea* is pronounced: [e], [aː], [əː], [iː], [eə], [iːə], [ei], [iː ei] or [iːæ].
Then listen to the recording to check your answers.

Earth – reason – create – idea – fear – eager – really – threat – leaves – speak – breakfast – hear – reaction – bear – heart.

2. Fill in the blanks with these verbs:
accept, describe, give, indicate, pass on, share, sign up, speak, submit, write.

a. You .... for GoLoco.
b. You .... a picture.
c. You .... information about yourself from sites like Facebook and Flickr.
d. You .... a list of groups you belong to.
e. You .... into your computer mic to .... your favourite breakfast.
f. You .... what other Olos you trust enough to ride with.
g. You .... reviews of your behaviour.
h. You .... or .... potential riders.

3. *Let* or *make*?

a. I hope car-pooling will .... me richer.
b. The driver .... me wait for an hour!
c. The company .... drivers and riders choose.
d. I'll .... you regret being a polluter!
e. They refused to .... me get in the car.

4. Compare drivers' attitudes today and 30 years ago.

a. Thirty years ago, people didn't use to...
b. They used to make...

5. Translate into French.

The more commuters sign up to GoLoco, the better the chances of reducing global warming are. The less people use their cars, the more fuel they will save and the more they will cut costs.

6. Translate into English.

a. Avant, elle conduisait une grosse voiture mais elle l'a vendue pour économiser l'essence.
b. Autrefois, les gens ne prenaient pas leur voiture pour aller faire les courses.
c. Quand j'étais jeune, il y avait un bois ici. L'Amérique n'est plus ce qu'elle était !
d. Enfant, il passait toutes ses vacances à la campagne.

Unit 11 Sustainable development

1. Designing a leaflet

YOUR JOB

You work in the Marketing Department of the DeepBlue Aquarium in Atlanta. Your aim is to put an end to the debate about the fish living conditions so as to attract new visitors.

YOUR TASK

You are asked to design a leaflet that gives a clear and synthetic vision of the aquarium's 4R program for whale sharks: Rescue, Research, Relocation and Rehabilitation.
You need to underline all the actions and programmes led by the DeepBlue Aquarium:
– to reach the standards in term of sanitary care and public sensitization,
– to provide knowledge and resources to be used for the preservation of sea life outside the precincts of the aquarium.
Follow the various steps.

1. Read the documents on these pages. Pick out the pros and cons of aquariums.
2. Listen to the recording and make notes on what seems essential to you.
3. Prepare your leaflet.

ACTING OUT

Make an oral presentation of your leaflet to the class and explain your strategic choices.

Document 1

Welcome to the DeepBlue Aquarium

Now is the perfect time to experience the world's largest aquarium! With eight million gallons of fresh and marine water, and more aquatic life than found in any other aquarium, you are sure to see things you have never seen before!

At the DeepBlue Aquarium, we are committed to advancing the scientific community's understanding of whale sharks and growing public awareness of this species for sharks. By having whale sharks in the DeepBlue Aquarium, we raise awareness of the species, and encourage our guests to be stewards of the oceans.

Our interpreters have introduced nearly five million people face to face to whale sharks.

Our educators have taught nearly 100,000 students for the first time about whale sharks.

Our team has reached out through national and international media to teach hundreds of millions of people about whale sharks, many learning about the species for the first time.

Our Seafood Savvy program gives our guests the tools to make environmentally responsible decisions when eating seafood.

In cooperation with the College of Veterinary Medicine, the DeepBlue Aquarium's Center for Aquatic Animal Health is a veterinary teaching hospital advancing the understanding and care of aquatic animals.

Document 2

An interview with Jane Witherman

Executive director and president of the DeepBlue Aquarium.

Document 3

Humans are happy, but what about the fish?

Critics argue that aquariums have the opposite effect: more technologically sophisticated exhibits suggest that oceans are disposable. "What they say is the natural habitat doesn't matter," said Randy Malamud, an English professor at Georgia State University. "That the awe and mystery of animal life – which is so much dependent on the animal's living where it lives – that's all irrelevant and can be dispensed with for our convenient consumption."[...]

In January, Ralph the whale shark, an adolescent, died. The details of Ralph's death provided a glimpse of not so-luxurious life. Ralph, who stopped eating after the tanks were chemically treated for parasites, had been force-fed for months – apparently a common practice at aquariums, even for tiny creatures like sea horses.

"Sometimes in science we learn as much through death as through life," Mr Swanagan wrote. In Ralph's case we learned that he died of a perforated stomach, most likely caused by the feeding tube.

Document 4

Can man improve on nature's fishbowl?

John Fraser, the director of public research and evaluation for the Wildlife Conservation Society Institute, which oversees New York's zoos and aquariums, said that critique bears no relation to what he sees. "A lot of people would like zoos and aquariums to be a lot more aggressive in terms of our environmental advocacy," he said, but sociologists have learned that moral indignation is not the only motivator to action: there must also be emotional and cognitive connections. If institutions give those too little attention, he said, the result is something the educational theorist David Sobel called "ecophobia", a state in which the monumentality of the problem immobilizes the viewer.

An encounter with a living being, on the other hand, is a catalyst for action. "This," Mr. Fraser said, "is the place where the love starts."

Document 5

Guidelines for the layout

The leaflet must be 150 × 200 mm.

On the front side: logo, photo and sentence summing up the project.

At the back:
- address (25 Baker Street),
- telephone number (404-581-4000),
- e-mail address (visitorservices@deepblueaquarium.org),
- opening hours (Monday – Thursday: 10 a.m. – 5 p.m., Friday – Sunday: 9 a.m. – 6 p.m. 365 days a year),
- wheelchairs available at information desk,
- prices (adult: $29.50, senior – age 55 and up –: $25.50, Child – age 3-12 –: $22.00)
- and details about the various services.

2. Sending a press release

YOUR JOB

You work in the Marketing Department of Wal-Mart stores, the world's largest retailer. Every week, more than 175 million customers shop at Wal-Mart's 5,300 stores. Wal-Mart has promised to become "packaging neutral" by 2025. That means that, through recycling, reusing or perhaps even composting, it will try to recover as much material as was used in the packaging that flows through its stores. To reach that goal, it is enlisting the help of its 66,000 vendors to cut back on their packaging for the products themselves and by using less shrink-wrap or cardboard for shipping.

YOUR TASK

You are asked to write a press release about Wal-Mart's scheme to get rid of excess packaging. Follow the various steps.

1. Read the documents on these pages.
2. Listen to the recording and make notes of what seems essential to you.
3. Prepare the press release.

Document 1

The Wal-Mart effect

Wal-Mart has pledged publicly to reduce packaging 5 percent by 2013. Environmental Defense will assist the retailer in meeting this goal, and especially in creating and tracking metrics for understanding and communicating solid waste and greenhouse gas reductions and environmental health impacts of the packaging changes.

www.environmentaldefense.org

Document 2

Leaner packaging

Marketers usually boast about what they have added to their products. Increasingly, though, they are bragging about what they are taking out by cutting down on packaging and its impact on the environment. [...] Coca-Cola plans to cut the plastics in its Dasani water bottles by 7 percent over the next five years, just by tweaking the shape of the bottle and the cap "Waste of any kind is inefficiency, and inefficiency equals cost," said Scott Vitters, CocaCola's director of sustainable packaging.

The number of companies making such changes is growing sharply, as they try to reduce costs and address growing environmental concerns. [...] They do not expect consumers to buy their products purely for the package but they are hoping that "greener" packages will give them a competitive edge over similar products, even as they hold down costs.

© *New York Times*, June 30th, 2007, by Claudia H. Deutsch

Document 3

An interview with Cynthia Hampton

Listen to the Vice President for Marketing and Communications of Environmental Defense, an American non-profit organization which has been dedicated to protecting the environment since 1967 and represents more than 400,000 members.

REFERENCE DOCUMENT

UPS & ALLIANCE FOR ENVIRONMENTAL INNOVATION DELIVER GREENER PACKAGING

Headline announces news, under 80 characters

A unique corporate-environmental alliance has produced an action plan that will help UPS dramatically reduce the amount of natural resources needed to make its express packaging. The joint project, an eight-month review of UPS' packaging with the Alliance for Environmental Innovation, produced concrete, affordable changes for UPS' package production processes. Indeed, once fully implemented, the various changes are expected to actually save the company more than $1 million annually.

Give the most important information in the lead sentence. Answer the who, what, when, where, why and how questions.

The new packaging improvements announced today along with the reusable envelope introduced earlier this year will increase the use of post-consumer recycled materials by 22 percent, cut wastewater discharge by more than 15 percent and use 12 percent less energy compared to previous UPS packaging.

The rest of the press release elaborates on the information provided in the lead paragraph. It contains details about what makes it unique, controversial or provides information about a prominent person, place or thing.

The packaging results announced today cut across the spectrum of UPS express shipping packages. They include:
Nearly doubling the amount of post-consumer recycled material in the UPS box, and using at least 80 percent post-consumer recycled material in the Express Letter.
Eliminating the use of bleached paper in all express packaging, lessening pollution of water from chlorinated compounds.
Reducing overall waste and pollution from production of shipping materials by an average of 13 percent.
Introducing post-consumer recycled material into UPS' plastic PAK and reducing each PAK's weight by almost 10 percent.
Market testing reusable options for other packaging.

Keep sentences and paragraphs short.

The tone is neutral and objective, unlike an advertisement.

In addition, UPS has expanded its use of reusable packaging to include the A4 Next Day Air Letter. The A4 envelope is the standard envelope in most countries outside the United States - 3/4 of an inch longer than the standard, 9-by-12 inch US envelopes. It is now available for US and overseas shipments.

Avoid addressing the target audience directly. Do not use "I", "we" or "you".

The standard press release is 300 to 800 words.

http://www.environmentaldefense.org

Use a word processing program to check spelling and grammar before submitting it.

Test Yourself

How to protect rural England

You hardly need me to tell you how lucky you are to have what you have in this country. Being surrounded by such a sumptuous diversity of history and beauty is a delight and a privilege, of course, but it is also a great danger. When you have such an abundance of great things, it is easy to think of it as essentially inexhaustible and to persuade yourself that it can be nibbled away at without serious loss. I hate it when people think like that.

To me, the mathematics of the British landscape are wonderfully simple and compelling. Britain has about 60 million acres of land and about 60 million people. That's one acre for each of us. Every time you give up 10 acres of greenfield site to build a superstore, in effect 10 people lose their acres. To enjoy the countryside they must go and use other people's acres. By developing countryside you force more and more people to share less and less space. Trying to limit the growth of development in the countryside is common sense.

In the meantime there are three matters that I hope and intend to pursue. The first is litter and fly-tipping. [...] Second, pylons and overhead wires generally. To me, marching ranks of pylons are way too common in the countryside, and inexcusably alien and ugly. [...] In 1986, when electricity companies were being privatised, *the Economist* magazine calculated that if all the generating companies were required to devote one half of 1% of their turnover to burying overhead cables, we would be able to bury 1,000 miles of them every year. There are 8,000 miles of high voltage power lines in this country, so they would all be buried now. At a minimum there should be a presumption against pylons within sight of World Heritage sites, national parks or areas of outstanding natural beauty. But really they should just be taken away.

Corrigé page 193

Finally, number three, trees, forests, woodland. You can never have too many trees. The UK has less forest cover than almost any country in Europe. France has 28%, Germany 32%, Italy 34%, Sweden almost 70%. Britain has 12% – the fourth lowest amount in Europe. Even Cyprus has more. [...] I think we should be pushing forcefully for restoration and renewal of hedgerows. I am really worried about hedgerows. They define the English landscape and everywhere they are quietly fading away. Eventually you end up with no hedgerows at all and this is the fate that I fear is awaiting very large swaths of the countryside.

I. Compréhension

Rédigez en anglais un compte-rendu de l'article en 160 mots à 10% près. Indiquez le nombre de mots utilisés.

II. Expression

Translate the first paragraph of the text into French from "You hardly need me to tell..." down to "...people think like that."

Exam Paper

Cleaning up the air

London is still one of Britain's least pleasant places to go cycling. The capital's air is the dirtiest in the country and among the worst in Western Europe. Levels of nitrogen dioxide (a toxic chemical that damages the lungs) are above official limits throughout the city, and several areas exceed similar limits on particulate pollution (which may also carry carcinogenic chemicals). Foul air kills about 1,000 Londoners a year, for the most part by exacerbating lung diseases, and recent data suggest that the problem is getting worse. The main culprit is road transport, especially the diesel-powered variety. Traffic generates around two-thirds of London's fine-particle pollution and 40% of the noxious nitrogen.

Inspired by the success of his road-charging scheme in unclogging city-centre roads, Ken Livingstone, the city's mayor, has promised a similar approach to tackle air pollution. He plans to designate almost the entire city as a low-emissions zone (LEZ). Beginning in 2008, a network of automatic cameras would trigger charges of up to £200 on heavy diesel-powered vehicles (mainly buses and large lorries) that did not meet European emissions standards. In its public consultation on the scheme, Transport for London (TfL) put the public-health benefits as high as £460m.

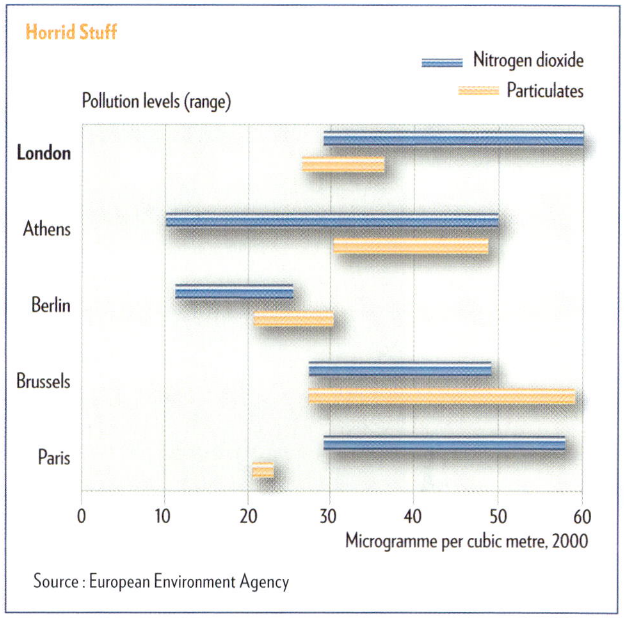

Everybody agrees that it would be nicer if the capital's air were more breathable but not everyone thinks that the Mayor has the right approach. London First, a business funded lobbying outfit, points out that the LEZ's cost-benefit ratio is the highest of any project that TfL is currently funding, appearing to fall outside central government guidelines. [...] Others worry that, although particulate emissions are thought to be the most harmful sort, other pollutants are not covered. The scheme takes no account of planet-heating carbon dioxide, of which diesel engines tend to emit less than petrol-powered ones. [...] Although the zone will bring cleaner air overall, many new engine designs obtain their low levels of particulate pollution at the expense of higher outputs of nitrogen dioxide.

The scheme's most striking flaw is that although it will be extended to light vans after 2012 there are no plans to charge private motorists. Officials cite technical difficulties and point out that, individually, cars produce fewer nasties than lorries. But there are far more cars on the roads than heavy goods vehicles, and in aggregate they produce roughly as much atmospheric muck as lorries do. Those in the know whisper that Mr. Livingstone is worried that London's motorists – already fed up with high parking charges and an unwanted westward extension of the congestion-charging zone – might rebel if they were to face pollution charges too.

I. Compréhension **À rédiger en français**

Après avoir dégagé l'idée principale de l'article, vous ferez un compte-rendu en 180 mots ±10%. Vous indiquerez le nombre de mots utilisés.

II. Expression **À rédiger en anglais**

1. Using the information given in the table, analyse the pollution in European cities. Draw your conclusions. (at least 100 words)

2. What are the solutions to reduce pollution in big cities? (at least 150 words)

Unit 12 Intercultural management

Marc Raynaud warns: "Until we come into contact with another culture, we are probably blissfully unaware of our own cultural identity-wherever we come from."

Zooming on

1. IKEA store

Beijing, April 2006. An opera performer waits for the opening of a new Ikea store in Beijing, the second largest Ikea store in the world.

Look at the picture and read the caption.

1. Describe what you see and say what you know about Ikea.

2. What does it show of Ikea's impact in China.

3. How much would you say Western countries are also influenced by Chinese design?

4. What conclusion could you draw?

2. Preventing culture clash

At the humorous level cultural differences provide very funny stories. However, when shock becomes clash, levels of efficiency are hit and companies and individuals can suffer.

Take the following example. The chief executive of a US multinational arrives in Paris to meet the managers of the French company it has just bought. His address to the audience of expectant French employees is couched in the language of transatlantic 'direct management'. He says: "There are two types of people in this room: those who will stay with us and those who will leave." In the US such a message would be interpreted as a ritual gauntlet throwing – a direct appeal for commitment to the new challenges ahead. In France it is decoded as a redundancy announcement. The result is trade union agitation and an immediate confidence crisis.

Corporate Relocation News, August 2001, by Marc Raynaud and Elizabeth Jardine

Read the article.

1. Contrast the American and French points of view.

2. What impact is this example of culture clash said to have on the French and the Americans?

3. What does it reveal of the two nations' mentalities?

3. What is left of India's cultural heritage?

Listen to Vijayendra Rao 24, from India who wanted to relocate from New York to India.

1. What makes Bangalore a magnet to foreign job seekers?

2. What are the drawbacks of having Western businesses and lifestyles invade Bangalore?

3. To what extent is India's cultural heritage harmed?

REPORTING

If you were asked to work in a foreign country how would you prepare yourself? Would that experience appeal to you? Say why or why not.

WORDS APART

Cultural awareness Conscience culturelle

- **to identify** repérer
- **to acknowledge** reconnaître
- **to be prejudiced** avoir des préjugés
- **to consider** considérer
- **to reject** rejeter
- **to appreciate** évaluer
- **to manœuvre** manoeuvrer
- **flexibility** flexibilité
- **preconceived ideas** idées pré-conçues
- **clichés** clichés
- **stereotypes** stéréotypes
- **preliminary** préliminaire
- **mutually** mutuellement
- **sensitive** sensible
- **confident** confiant
- **honest** honnête
- **constructive** constructeur
- **delicate** délicat

Handling conflicts Gérer les conflits

- **to compromise** faire un compromis
- **to make concessions** faire des concessions
- **to disapprove of** désapprouver qch
- **to clarify** clarifier
- **to further discuss** discuter plus amplement
- **to lose/save face** perdre/sauver la face
- **to overcome** surmonter
- **to deal with** traiter de
- **to take into account** prendre en compte
- **go ahead** allez-y
- **you're right/wrong** vous avez raison/tort
- **it depends on** cela dépend de
- **provided that** à condition que
- **although** bien que
- **a middleman** un intermédiaire
- **a misunderstanding** un quiproquo
- **culture clash** choc culturel
- **tough** dur

Negotiating Négocier

- **to challenge** défier
- **to bargain** négocier
- **to conduct negotiations** mener des négociations
- **to favour consensus** favoriser un consensus
- **to counter-propose** faire une contre proposition
- **to come to/to reach an agreement** tomber d'accord
- **to conclude** conclure
- **to suit** convenir
- **to value** valoriser
- **a short/long term relationship** une relation à court/long terme
- **a fallback position** une position de repli
- **deadlines** échéances
- **a win-win collaboration** gagnant des deux cotés
- **reliability** fiabilité
- **loyal** fidèle
- **it's a deal!** affaire conclue!

Unit 12 Intercultural management

Zooming on

To woo[1] Europeans, McDonald's goes upscale

A McDonald's in London.
The chain's European restaurants now have designer touches and more localized menus.

Sophisticated? McDonald's? The Golden Arches are going upscale. Aiming to create a more relaxed experience in a sophisticated atmosphere, McDonald's is replacing bolted-down[2] plastic yellow-and-white furniture with lime-green designer chairs and dark leather upholstery[3]. It is the restaurant chain's biggest overhaul[4] in more than 20 years and, with its franchisees, it plans to spend more than 600 million euros ($828 million), remodeling 1,280 European restaurants by the end of this year. The changes are more than cosmetic. McDonald's is introducing healthier foods and items that cater[5] to regional tastes, like caffè lattes. Hoping to attract more young adults and professionals, in addition to its core[6] customer base of children, the chain is also adding amenities like Internet access and rental iPods. The changes are paying off. The original impetus for the makeover was a European sales slump in the late 1990s, brought on by concerns about obesity and annoyance at unappealing décor and grumpy[7] employees. But the ideas for how to change came from Denis Hennequin, president of McDonald's Europe, the first non-American in that role. As head of McDonald's restaurants in his native France in the late 1990s, Mr. Hennequin had searched for ways to make fast food more appealing to a nation that prefers slow-simmered[8] cassoulets and likes to savor a meal. But now the success of makeovers comes with a challenge of its own: how much can you upgrade the image before McDonald's isn't McDonald's anymore? A separate food factory in Munich is trying to come up with new menus for the different tastes in the 41 European countries, including Russia, where McDonald's operates. In Britain, McDonald's restaurants started to serve porridge for breakfast. In Portugal, they offer soup and in France, cheese saga —burgers with French cheeses. McDonald's first adapted its menu to local tastes in the 1980s when it started to offer beer in some of its German restaurants. Paying attention to local European tastes has also helped McDonald's overcome some of the cultural hurdles[9] it faced as a large American fast-food chain. While head of McDonald's restaurants in France, Mr. Hennequin experienced opposition to American corporations firsthand in 1999 when José Bové, the firebrand leader of a French farmers union, organized a bulldozing of a McDonald's restaurant to protest the spread of American "hegemony".

© *New York Times*, Aug 25th, 2007, by Julia Werdigier

1. *rechercher les faveurs de* – 2. *vissés au sol* – 3. *cuir d'ameublement* – 4. *remaniement* – 5. *s'adresser à* – 6. *central* – 7. *grincheux* – 8. *mijoté* – 9. *obstacles.*

FIRST STEPS

I. Describe the atmosphere of this McDonald's restaurant.

II. Compare it with the ones you know in France.

MOVING ON

1. In this article McDonald's focuses its policy on:

a. better food,
b. new ad campaigns,
c. cross-cultural issues,
d. European design.

2. In the article find examples of modernization of McDonald's restaurants concerning:

a. decoration, **b.** food, **c.** target, **d.** equipment, **e.** eating habits in Europe.

3. Why did the President of McDonald's restaurants in Europe feel particularly concerned with embellishing restaurants?

4. In the text find words that mean the same as:

a. designing, **b.** appeal to, **c.** rewarding, **d.** recession, **e.** irritation,
f. bad-tempered, **g.** taste, **h.** modernize.

5. Find expressions that mean the opposite of:

a. the differences are superficial,
b. the restaurant tends to standardize flavours,
c. innovations fail,
d. the changes came after a sudden economic recovery abroad,
e. McDonald's good results are undisputed.

6. Explain what kind of cultural hurdles McDonald's had to overcome.

7. On the whole would you say that, in this article, McDonald's policy is:

a. harshly criticized/ **b.** seen as rather flexible/ **c.** described as radical.

What makes you say that?

8. Explain what the "spread of American hegemony" means.

9. What do you know about José Bové? What is your reaction to this kind of protest? State your reasons.

10. Can you think of other types of boycotts?

11. Translate

Translate the last paragraph into French from "paying attention to..." down to the end of the article.

WRITING (150 words)

Explain and comment upon the following sentence: "How much can you upgrade the image before McDonald's isn't McDonald's anymore".

Try to find more examples of challenges taken up by other companies in an attempt to be accepted in different countries.

LANGUAGE AT WORK

1. Classify the following words according to their pronunciation: [d]; [t]; [id]. Listen to the recording to check your answers and make out a rule out of the way (-ed) is pronounced.

simmered, relaxed, localized, sophisticated, searched, started, adapted, helped, experienced, organized.

2. Add the "-ed" or "-ing" form to the following adjectives and participles in the following passage.

To make it more appeal.... McDonald's is going to upgrade its soil.... image. A well-design.... decor is meant to create a more sophisticat.... image for unsatisfi.... customers will.... to experience a moderniz.... environment.

It's a challeng.... but most probably reward.... experience for McDonald's.

3. Translate the following sentences into English.

a. Pour plaire à tous les goûts, McDonald's envisage de rénover et moderniser ses restaurants.

b. McDonald's ne risque-t-il pas de perdre de sa notoriété et de modifier son image ?

c. McDonald's a souvent été accusé de vendre de la mauvaise nourriture et considéré responsable de problèmes d'obésité.

d. McDonald's a donc un défi à relever en Europe pour courtiser ses clients et élargir la cible de ses consommateurs.

4. Translate the following sentences into French.

a. The original impetus for the makeover was a European sales slump in the late 1990s, brought on by concerns about obesity and annoyance at unappealing décor and grumpy employees.

b. As head of McDonald's restaurants in his native France in the late 1990s, Mr. Hennequin had searched for ways to make fast food more appealing to a nation that prefers slow-simmered cassoulets and likes to savor a meal.

Unit 12 Intercultural management

1. Organising a visit

YOUR JOB

You work for Magic, a French toy company, and you are asked by the Marketing Director to organize the visit of two CEOs working in the same sector of activity, one from Germany and the other one from the USA. They envisage expanding abroad, particularly in France and would be interested in starting a partnership with your company.

YOUR TASK

Prepare the greetings, organize the visit of the two visiting managers.

1. Give a full schedule of the two days: planning of the mornings and afternoons, coffee breaks, meetings, presentations, lunches, dinners, evenings out **(See Doc. 1)**.

2. Practical details: arrange for a driver to pick them up (arrival, departure, appointments...), check restaurants and hotel bookings, send each participant a copy of the agenda in advance etc. Try to avoid culture clashes **(See Doc. 2)**.

3. Identify and overcome obstacles (language gap, choice of language, need of a translator?).

4. Set priorities, draw up a "time plan": time and length of each presentation, powerpoint, slides **(See Doc. 1)**.

Document 1

Sample schedule for a group interview

These schedules should give you a better idea of the types of things to expect in a company visit. Remember that your visitors are a focus of attention throughout the day.

February 14, 200...

5:00 p.m. Arrival at O'Hare Field, travel to Hyatt O'Hare.

7:30 p.m. Reception and Dinner, Fisheaters Restaurant, Hyatt O'Hare: Dinner speaker, Ms. Emily Jackson, Vice President for Administration Attire, business casual.

February 15, 200...

8:15 a.m. Check out of hotel and meet in lobby Ride to corporate headquarters.

8:30 a.m. Continental breakfast on site.

9:00 a.m. Opportunities with Wexford Widgets Karen Shocken, Director of College Relations.

10:00 a.m. Tour of facilities.

11:00 a.m. Interview: Bob Harlow, Manager of Customer Relations.

12:00 p.m. Group lunch with recent trainees.

1:30 p.m. Interview: Cathy Goodman, Customer Services Associate.

2:1 p.m. Wexford's Vision and Opportunities Howard Rice, Vice President of Marketing.

3:00 p.m. Group Open Forum and Discussion.

3:30 p.m. Wrap-up: Karen Shocken.

4:00 p.m. Departure for airport.

Document 2

Cases of multicultural conflicts

Situation	Title	Conflict	Comment
1. American-German	Alcohol at lunch in the US	At a business lunch in a club-house on the occasion of a high-level first exploration of common business opportunities, the only German asked for a glass of wine. The Americans where shocked.	The German thought, that for a fine meal, a white wine would be the most appropriate drink. The Americans do not have alcohol for lunch, only for dinner or later. Asking for alcohol during business hours is rude.
2. French-German	Alcohol at lunch in France	At a fine lunch on a very hot day, a German ordered a Coke. Shock for the French who had all ordered wine.	From the French side, ordering a drink that does not go with the quality of the meal showed very bad taste.
3. American-German	Open criticism out of own responsibility	A high-ranking US manager noticed that expensive individual hotel rooms had been reserved for a meeting, but not used. He made an open comment in this meeting to the German manager responsible for this meeting. The Germans accused the US manager of not being a team player and of being rude.	In a US company, open criticism is allowed. In a German company, it is seen as rude that a difference between two persons should be discussed in front of others who are not concerned. Secondly, a manager is responsible for his budget, but free to spend it the way he wants. As long as he is within the budget, he can allocate expenditure that seems useless to others.
4. All situations	Foreign food	A visitor is offered food that he thinks is absolutely disgusting.	Having a meal together is one of the oldest forms of socializing – it remains one of the most important ones!
5. French-German	French business lunches: length	A German manager tries to shorten or avoid a lunch with his French colleagues, because "he needs the time for business discussions". The meeting ends without the impact he had hoped for.	In France, lunch is not the end of a discussion, but part of the meeting. It allows for compromise and negotiation after having stated the facts. By avoiding the lunch, the negotiation phase never happened.

PROMPTS

Diplomacy! Transform the following sentences so as to make them more polite and diplomatic.

a. I refuse to accept this/I disagree with you.
b. Be realistic.
c. This is wrong. I won't take this anymore! This meeting is a waste of time.
d. Check your figures!
e. No way!
f. I don't understand, you're lying!

Here are a few examples of more polite expressions that you may use to be more moderate:

You could / may
Not quite / not exactly
I'd rather / I wish / why don't we
I would recommend / my suggestion is / if I were you
To a certain extent / up to a point
I am not in favour of / I am afraid
I wonder if / I see it differently

2. Writing a memo

YOUR JOB

The Marketing director of Magic asks you to write an account of the brainstorming session you had with your colleagues before the arrival of your visitors from Germany and the USA.

YOUR TASK

You give a brief account of the tone you and your colleagues have decided to adopt during the visit (a lot of listening, mutual understanding, building on others' ideas, asking open-ended questions, straightforward answers, transparency, clear explanations).
The recording **(See Doc. 1)** will help you focus on the most frequent bad French habits that may cause problems in intercultural management.

1. You list your objectives (mere discussion, or already a place for decision, B to B negotiation, limited bargaining zones or big concessions, specific offers, handling conflicts).
2. You decide of the strategy you want to use (you choose to present your products first or decide to try and identify their needs and requests first).
3. You establish your positions (deadlines).
4. You summarize the areas of agreement.
5. You suspend your judgement until a next visit is planned or you give an immediate feedback.

Document 1

About the French! The critical art of conversation

Listen to Terence Brake, president TMA-Americas

PROMPTS

Fill in the blanks with the right words from the list below:
Inhibit, training, wasting, unfamiliar, relationship, self-awareness, resources, skills.

If we are going to send some of our sales people into .... cultural territory, we should:

Select those who fully understand that selling is a .... .

Provide them with .... tools so that they can appreciate how their personality and background can foster or .... a cross-cultural relationship.

Provide them with .... and coaching to develop cross-cultural communication, presentation, and negotiation .... in general, and targeted to specific cultures.

Provide informational .... for just-in-time and ongoing learning.

If we don't do these things for our sales people, we are .... their time, our customer's time, and our resources.

REFERENCE DOCUMENT

Meeting on Monday, March 22ND 2008
from 9 am to 11 am

Writing a memo from a brainstorming session in Japan before a Franco-Japanese meeting (Renault-Nissan).

Members of the team

Mr Jones, Ms. Shan, M. Ung, Mr Xian, Mr Fu, Ms Cong and myself.

Topics

On the agenda

Preparation of the Franco-Japanese meeting in 2 weeks' time.

To avoid culture clashes

Recommendations

- As most Latin people, the French like contact, shaking hands, long lunch meetings, getting to know the person before making a deal.
- The French are much more sentimentally attached and **faithful** to their company: they like to put corporate relations on a personal basis... Within the company, the French keep the doors closed.
- In a French company, after a meeting, it's hard to say if a decision has been reached or not: for the French, "deciding" is giving the broad lines without getting into implementation "details"
- The French do not believe a **win-win** situation can exist ("if you win, it means I lose") and negotiations are always difficult when people do not try to reach a **consensus**...

Strategy

Objectives

- To have a clear vision of their requests, (open-ended questions, round tables, questionnaires).
- To make a presentation of our new products and a visit of the company (how to organise your data, how to structure the information, what support you need).
- To give them samples, glossy brochures, gifts.
- To start the negotiation at lunch time (the choice of a beautiful restaurant in a private dining room is a must).
- Afternoon meeting will fix the conditions of the deal with our bargaining zones, leaving room to an escape route (the French don't like to have too much pressure).
- To draft a written account of the brainstorming session (only written commitments are serious for the French).

To plan future visits before the signature of the contract.

Conclusions

A meeting will be held with the team Tuesday, March 23rd to poll the different reactions and ask for feedbacks.

Ideas and objections and suggestions will be listed before next month's meeting.

Test Yourself

Cultural edge

Taiwanese chain RT-Mart says it can prevail in retail battle with Western supermarkets. Hymall has been acquired by British retailer Tesco and Trust-Mart has been taken over by the United States giant Wal-Mart. What about the only remaining Tawanese chain, RT-Mart? The supermarket brand is committed to holding its flag high in the market, competing head-to-head with Western rivals, and one day seeking expansion to other countries. The retailing industry plays an important role in a country's economy. Developed nations use advanced and industrialized methods to operate supermarkets. While they are successful in their own countries, they often have a hard time in other places. Wall-Mart is strong in the US, but has lost the battle in Germany. Tesco is everywhere in Britain, but rarely seen in other European nations. French Giants Carrefour and Auchan never think of trying to take Wal-Mart's market share in the US market. Many Western retailers think coming to China is like entering several different countries, since the dialect, cuisine, and shopping behavior varies from place to place. The advantage of Taiwan retailers is their mastery of Chinese culture. RT- Mart's corporate culture has influenced almost every member of its staff –earning money is surely important, but building up a Chinese brand in the industry is the ultimate target. Wang Yao, vice secretary-general of China General Chamber of Commerce, says some Taiwan-based retailers were founded with the thought that they would merge or sell their operations for a large profit. The famous examples are Hymall and Trust-Mart, which were sold to large foreign chains. Two aspects differentiate Hymall and Trust-Mart from RT-Mart, which aims at long-term development in the market through management and personnel training. Wang says: "personnel resources are the key to maintaining sustainable growth in the sector".

China Daily, July 2nd, 2007

I. Compréhension

Rédiger en anglais un compte rendu de l'article en 150 mots.

II. Traduction

Traduire en français le passage suivant : "the retailing industry plays an important role..." down to "the ultimate target".

III. Compréhension orale

Listen to the recording and give an oral account of it as suggested below in Method.

Corrigé page 193

METHOD — GIVING AN ACCOUNT OF A RECORDED ARTICLE

1. Listening, understanding, eliciting, re-ordering.

a. First, listen carefully to the passage without writing anything.
b. Next, listen to it again and concentrate on the key words.(write them down).
c. Make your own notes. (Where? Who? When? What for?)
d. Define the topic and present the different aspects of it. (It is about, the different ideas are)

2. Clarifying, illustrating, challenging.

a. Explain more precisely what the document emphasizes (facts, solutions, impact...).
b. Illustrate with examples from the passage.
c. Discuss the arguments presented in the document (show the advantages or disadvantages, list the pros and cons).

3. Making your point.

a. Discuss the subject more generally (by expanding the debate, by suggesting risks, dangers, opportunities, solutions and by imagining possible consequences).
b. Agree or disagree with some of the arguments or simply give your opinion or your impressions (say if you approve of, disapprove of, share, side with, back...; say if you are optimistic, pessimistic, worried, concerned...).

Exam Paper

Developing global brand ambassadors

It was breakfast time in Tokyo; a sublime autumnal day. A perfect day, but one that would soon turn into a comedy of errors for one sale's executive.

Directly opposite my breakfast table were four businessmen engaged in what I will loosely describe as a sales meeting. One was a Western executive –I'll call him Mr. X– and the other three were Japanese. Mr. X is the seller. I overheard him making references to Ghana, Congo, South Africa and aluminium. Of the three Japanese, one is a senior gentleman –let me call him Y-San. He is accompanied by two young associates who do most of the talking while he listens –a typical scene in Japanese business. Let me jump ahead to the end of the sales meeting– the Japanese apologise profusely, but say they have to leave. Mr. X leaves the meeting empty-handed, frustrated, and confused. What went wrong? There were too many mistakes to detail here, but let me highlight four.

Superficial preparation: Mr. X appears to know little about Japanese culture except for the fact that gifts are sometimes exchanged. About three quarters of the way through the meeting, X is getting desperate because the Japanese are giving him no positive signals. As a last resort, he pulls three crushed and unwrapped gifts out of his bag and says, "I hear you people like to receive presents." The words chosen and his tone are insulting, and he has obviously given very little thought to the gifts. The whole exchange feels like a clumsy bribe.

Lack of empathy: X was speaking English so fast that I could barely understand what he was saying. One of the young Japanese was trying to translate, but his inability to keep up was obvious to everyone, except X. X had learned his sales pitch by heart.

No sense of humor: When X found he was misunderstanding the Japanese or being misunderstood he became defensive and hostile. "I know what I said. You're putting words into my mouth. That's absolutely not what I said." And so it went on. Rude, crude and utterly ineffective. In an age when reputation is so important, we must groom them to be brand ambassadors and not just frequent flyers.

Terence Brake,
President TMA-Americas

I. Compréhension À rédiger en français

Faire un compte rendu en français du texte en 100 mots.

II. Expression À rédiger en anglais

Use your knowledge of intercultural management to advise a brand ambassador and write the letter you would have sent to Mr X to help him prepare his visit to Japan to avoid these kinds of blunders. **(200 words)**

Unit 13 Consuming

The world's economy lies in people's purchasing power.
Patterns of consumption are constantly changing thanks to technological advances, new desires, and the emergence of a new wave of consumers from fast developing countries.
What will this new consumption pattern look like?

Zooming on

1. The future face of China's market economy

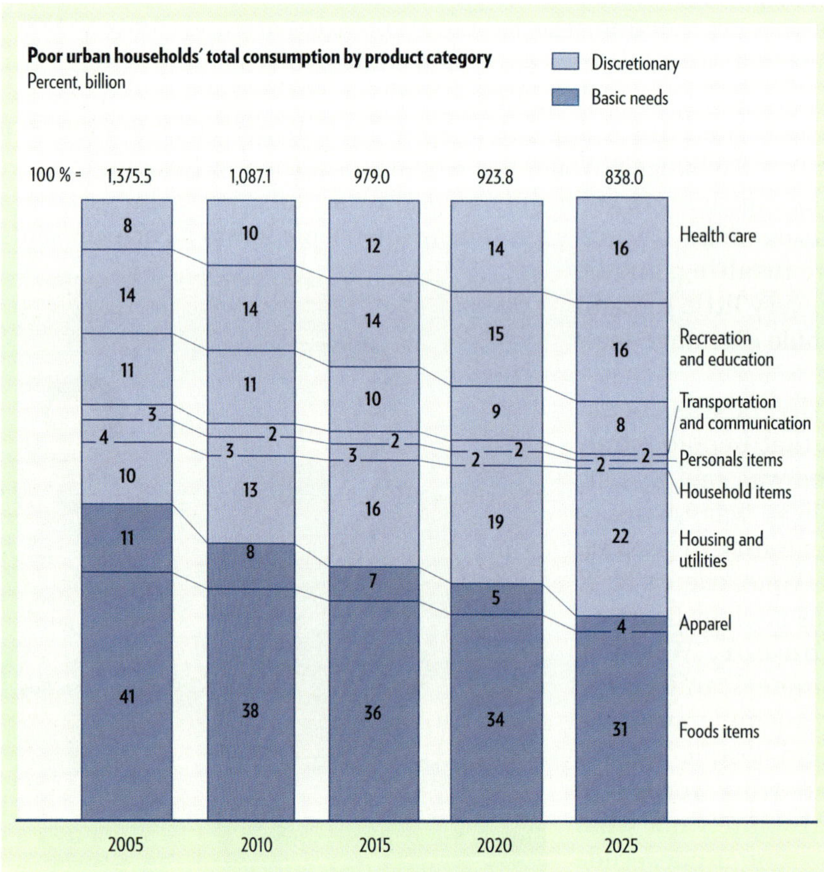

McKinsey Global Institute

Study this graph carefully.

1. Show what the very general trend in the consumption of Chinese people seems to be.

2. See which three sectors are going to increase the most and explain why.

3. Draw a portrait of the future average Chinese customer of 2025 compared to the one of 2005.

2. Buying from charity shops

Listen to the recording.

1. Having heard where this document comes from, say who Sarah Burnett could be.

2. Describe her latest shopping craze.

3. Show all the advantages of this new shopping experience.

4. Imagine what she will do with these books once she has read them all.

5. Show that this kind of attitude could change the status of the book. In what ways?

3. Spending more on cosmetic surgery

Botox is an increasingly popular option in the UK.

Image-conscious Britons are spending more than ever on being nipped, tucked and pumped with Botox, a report has found.

The number of cosmetic operations and treatments has risen by 92 per cent in just two years, and is set to break the £1 billion barrier next year, according to market analysts Mintel.

The non-invasive treatments of Botox and collagen wrinkle fillers have seen the biggest rise in popularity because they are viewed as less risky [...].

A total of 577,000 cosmetic operations and treatments were carried out in Britain this year, of which 472,000 were non-surgical. This compares with just 300,000 in 2005 of which 230,000 were non-surgical.

Mintel senior cosmetics analyst Alexandra Richmond said: "Today, the British perception of beauty is based on airbrushed images of models and photos of surgically enhanced celebrities, both young and old."

"For many the natural look simply can't compete and leaves them feeling inadequate."

© *Daily Mail*, December 19th, 2007

Read the text above.

1. Explain people's main motivation as given in the text.
2. How does this phenomenon drive people to cosmetic surgery?
3. Why are these interventions more possible today?
4. How can people afford them?

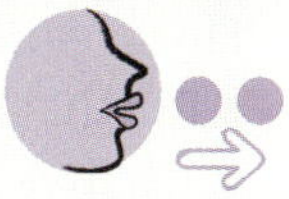

REPORTING

With the help of the three documents above, present a short analysis to the class assessing the main differences between old consumption patterns and new ones.

WORDS APART

People and general notions **Les personnes et notions générales**

Basic necessities produits de première nécessité
To be delivered être livré
A consumer un consommateur
Consumer goods des biens de consommation
Consumer society une société de consommation
Consuming/purchasing power le pouvoir d'achat
Consumption la consommation
Consumption patterns des modèles de consommation
A customer/a client/a patron un client
Discretionary items des articles non essentiels, laissés au libre choix du consommateur
A first-time consumer consommateur qui achète un produit pour la première fois
Household consumption la consommation des ménages
A label une étiquette
A loyal customer un consommateur fidèle
An order une commande
A price un prix
A repeat buyer un consommateur à répétition
A share buyer un consommateur qui partage un bien avec un autre
A shopper un acheteur
Wages/salary le salaire

What these people do **Ce que font ces personnes**

To afford pouvoir se permettre financièrement
To barter faire du troc
To buy online acheter en ligne, sur internet
To buy/to purchase acheter
To choose from choisir parmi
To consume consommer
To get one's money's worth en avoir pour son argent
To go on a shopping spree se laisser aller et consommer
To haggle marchander, discuter le prix
Hire-purchase une location-vente
To lease/to hire louer
To live on credit vivre à crédit
To make a bargain faire une bonne affaire
To make a bid/an offer faire une offre
To own posséder
To pay cash/credit card/instalments payer en liquide, par carte de crédit, à crédit
To pay for something payer quelque chose
To shop faire des achats
To spend money on something dépenser de l'argent pour quelque chose
To strike a good deal faire une bonne affaire, signer un contrat intéressant

When things go wrong **Quand les choses tournent mal**

To be in the red être dans le rouge, endetté
To be wronged by someone être spolié par quelqu'un
A class action une action commune de consommateurs
To complain se plaindre
Consumers' defence associations associations de défense des consommateurs
To get into debt s'endetter
To live beyond one's means vivre au-dessus de ses moyens
To lodge a complaint déposer une plainte
To overspend dépenser plus que ses moyens
To speculate spéculer
To sue / to take legal action intenter un procès, poursuivre en justice

Unit 13 Consuming

The tyranny of choice

Maybe your particular vulnerability is eggs (Barn? Free-range? Organic? Cotswold Legbar?). Maybe it's jam (Conserve? Preserve? Seedless? Low-sugar? High-fruit?).

Or milk (Whole? Skimmed? Semi-skimmed? Jersey? Goat? Sheep? Buffalo? Kangaroo?).

Whichever the aisle, we've all been there: a routine trip to the supermarket has ended up taking three times longer than it should because of the stupidly large range of varieties we have to wade through. If it's all for our benefit, how come it often ends up making us frustrated? [...]

Consider, for example, that in Tesco it is now possible to buy no fewer than 38 types of milk. Some of it is flavoured with strawberry, banana or Belgian chocolate; some has active bacterial flora; some has extra omega-3; [...]. And that's before you get to the aisle with 154 flavours of jam, or the one with 107 varieties of pasta. [...]

[...] We humans, in other words, are a bit like magpies. We're entranced by a myriad of bright, new, shiny things. But when the time actually comes to having to make sense of all this variety, our brains suffer option paralysis and cannot deal with it. [...]

What I do think we should strive to resist very vigorously, though, is the way that all this choice is exploited, both by government and big business, to tell us that we've never had it so good.

Note how supermarkets expect us to be supremely grateful that they're now selling more product lines – about 30,000 in a typical big one – than ever before.

But as we've all begun to realise, more doesn't always mean better. [...]. Having more varieties of ground coffee to choose from is no use if they all mostly taste of ground, burned acorns.

We need government to do its job and increase quality rather than quantity. We need supermarket buyers to use a bit of judgment and do the same.

In a busy, accelerating world, we haven't time for all this pointless decision-making. Give us three types of brilliant olive oil, not 300 mediocre ones.

FIRST STEPS

Have a good look at the picture.

1. Name the different items you can identify in it.

2. Associate the picture with the title and explain why this lady seems to be hesitant.

3. Guess the journalist's stance. What notion is he going to support?

MOVING ON

1. What sort of place is mainly examined in the text?

2. In your own words, sum up the main idea of the article.

3. Find the noun referred to by the following pronouns:

a. "taking three times longer than it should" (line 7),
b. "making us frustrated" (line 8-9),
c. "note how supermarkets expect us to be supremely grateful" (line 29),
d. "if they all mostly taste of ground, burned acorns" (line 32).

4. Find what the following figures refer to in the article.

38 / 30,000 / 300 / 154 / 3 / 107

5. In the list of products mentioned in the first lines of the text, try to find the kind of customer each type is aimed at.

6. Find the main reasons why supermarkets have adopted the technique of the widest possible choice?

7. Fill in a grid listing the advantages and drawbacks of so much choice.

8. Imagine a market test that will corroborate the idea that given too much choice, "our brains suffer option paralysis and cannot deal with it."

9. What could governments and consumers do to limit this sometimes copious offer.

10. When you are in a supermarket, for which product would you say you are a loyal customer? Conversely, for which ones would you welcome a wide range? Explain your reasons and motivations.

11. Translate

Translate into French from "Whichever the aisle" (line 6) to "making us frustrated" (line 9).

WRITING (150 words)

You don't usually go shopping for food but today you have been given the mission of going to the supermarket to refill the fridge.

Imagine the conversation you have with your mother (or father) on the phone when you realize that you don't really know what to buy faced with so many articles of the same product.

LANGUAGE AT WORK

1. Practice the pronunciation of these French-looking words with a good English accent:

conserve / fruit / routine / example / possible / types / active / option / resist / realise / decision / brilliant / mediocre.

2. Explain the differences between the following words:

Through / though / tough / thought.

3. Find the adjective at the root of the following adverbs:

Stupidly / actually / vigorously / supremely.

4. Form adverbs from the following adjectives:

particular / large / possible / active / bright / grateful / typical / busy / pointless / brilliant.

5. Match each verb to its preposition and then translate it.

Verb	Preposition	Translation
End	from	
Wade	to	
Get	with	
Make sense	of	
Deal	up	
Strive	to	
Choose	through	

6. Fill in the blanks with the verb "use" or an expression containing it.

a. It's no .... buying so many sorts of olive oil.

b. He .... seeing such a wide range of products in one shop. Where he comes from you are lucky when there is one type of each product!

c. If you .... logic, you'd find a solution.

d. They .... have only 2 or 3 types of honey on offer, now they have 12!

7. Translate into English.

a. L' Australie est treize fois plus grande que la France.

b. Il mange deux fois plus que moi !

c. Plus on a de choix, moins on sait quoi prendre.

d. Plus il y a de sortes de lait dans les rayons et plus on hésite au moment d'acheter.

8. Translate the different expressions with the verb "make".

a. It doesn't make any sense.

b. It makes me sad.

c. He made her buy this jam but she doesn't like it.

d. He was made a Lord by the Queen.

e. Go and make up to him.

1. Leasing versus owning

YOUR JOB

You are two customers, each ready to buy a new car but with different needs and means. You've both heard of the possibility of leasing a car instead of buying one with the help of a bank loan. You each personally want to assess the feasibility of such a project.

YOUR TASK

You go and see a car leasing agent at a car dealer's. With the help of the documents on the next page:

1. Invent the two portraits of the potential buyers with their different needs and means. One could need a new car for professional reasons, while the other could change his vehicle for personal reasons. One could get some financial or insurance help from his firm, while the other will only have his own income to buy or lease a car. These are only a few tips, but you can find other prerequisites for each customer.

2. List all the possible questions and objections you can put to the dealer.

ACTING OUT

1. In class, with the help of the document below, choose two students who will act as car leasing agents, and who will try to persuade you to lease your next vehicle.

2. Then act out the conversation between each client and the car leasing agents.

3. The "client" will state his/her final decision to the class i.e. if he/she will lease his/her next car, or rather buy it in the conventional way, justifying his/her stance.

Document 1

The Rifkin argument

Many of the objects surrounding us and that we use every day now get "old" in months and not decades, so why buy stuff that will need updating almost as soon as they are delivered? Rifkin argues that the desire to own things is disappearing from our lives.

Note on Rifkin:
Mr. Jeremy Rifkin is the founder and president of The Foundation on Economic Trends (www.foet.org) in Washington, DC. The Foundation examines the economic, environmental, social and cultural impacts of new technologies introduced into the global economy.

Document 2

Buying or leasing: a concrete case

A 1997 Honda Accord retails for about $19,500, but you could probably haggle the price down to $18,500. The average interest rate on a five-year loan for a new car is approximately 8.9%, and the monthly payments will be $345 if we pay 10% of the purchase price up front. As soon as we drive the car off the lot, it becomes a used car whose value is significantly lower than the amount we have just agreed to pay back over the next sixty months. The payments made in the early part of the loan mostly cover the interest, while those in the later stages cover more principal, so it takes some time for the value we could get for the car as a trade-in to be the same as the amount we have left to pay on the loan.

If we choose to lease this car instead, we would pay $259 per month for 36 months, and at the end of that time we would have three options. First, we could buy the car at a wholesale price determined when we signed the lease and guaranteed by the terms of the lease, in this case about $13,054. Second, we could trade it in to the dealer at a (higher) average trade-in price and buy or lease another car, trade-in value being about $14,200. Third, we could decide to buy the car at the wholesale price then sell it privately (without a dealer) at a presumably still higher price, about $15,900. We could also simply choose to conclude our payments and then walk away.

Document 3

The pros and cons

Apart from the obvious benefit of leasing (instant gratification of an affordable new car every three years), leasing also offers some unique benefits that purchasing does not. For example, leasing allows you to pay for the sales tax over the period of the lease, rather than all at once when you register the car, as is required in some states when you buy a car. Leasing also provides added insurance against unexpected losses.

But buying has its benefits, too. First, if you drive more than 15,000 miles per year, a lease can become quite costly. The lease agreement generally provides an allowance of 12,000 miles per year, and you must pay for every mile above the allotment, usually $0.15 per mile. [...] Also, if you tend to keep cars for more than five years, or are able to finance for shorter periods (if at all), then buying a car may be cheaper than leasing. [...] Here are a few points to keep in mind as you weigh your decision:

Leasing is best when you plan to put less than 15,000 miles per year on the car, and when you plan to replace the car every three to four years.

You may be able to negotiate a more favorable interest rate on a loan to purchase a car by going through a credit union, but they will require 10-20% of the purchase price as a downpayment.

Insurance payments for a financed new car should be about the same as those for leasing a new car.

A "zero money down" lease is a misnomer: it will usually cost at least $1,000 to drive away in your leased vehicle: first month's payment, $259; security deposit, $284 (monthly payment plus $25); "bank fee," $450–$500; "documentation/prep" fee, $75 (this is the same regardless of whether you buy or lease the car).

You still must pay to register a leased car, and the car must be registered in the name of the leasing company with you as the co-owner. You may therefore incur added costs to register the leased car than you would to register a car you own yourself because you cannot transfer the registration from your current vehicle.

Infoplease.com

2. Starting a class action

YOUR JOB

You are a consumer who has been wronged by a firm. This firm is an airline that didn't respect flight times nor treat its passengers correctly.
You have heard of the possibility of joining a class action against this company.

YOUR TASK

Read the documents below and don't hesitate to do some research on the Internet to further your knowledge (a very useful website is: www.consumeraffairs.com).
Using the indications given in the complaint form **(See Doc. 2)**, report on your bad experience when travelling with this particular airline **(See Doc. 3 & 4)**.
Working with your "lawyer", write up a thorough one-page report that will be added to the other complaints against the same firm.

ACTING OUT

Your complaint has been selected as being valid. In a role-play, act out the first meeting between the class action attorney and yourself. You will try to provide him/her with more details about your experience. He/she will tell you why you have a case and what outcome you could expect from the prosecution.

Document 1

What is a class action?

When many individuals have the same complaint to lodge and decide to sue the same company for it, it becomes a class action. The first step in filing this type of action is to find an attorney who is willing to study the case, and who will then take the risk of actually prosecuting.

Document 2

A complaint form

1. Give your full name and postal address, email, and home and work phone numbers.

2. Concerning the perpetrator, name the product, service, company, store, website or person that you are complaining about. Please be exact. Many businesses have similar names.

3. Say what happened in as much detail as you can.

4. Describe the consequences: the economic or physical damage that resulted.

5. Say if you do not wish to be contacted by an expert attorney about your complaint.

6. Submit your complaint

Thank you, that's all we need for now. Your report will be evaluated, and if more information is needed, we will contact you.

Document 3

American strands another planeload of passengers

Even after a wave of extended tarmac delays prompted Congress to consider a Passenger Bill of Rights, American Airlines flight 556 evolved from a two-and-a-half hour flight into an 11-hour nightmare.

Thunderstorms in Dallas-Fort Worth forced a diversion of the outbound Phoenix flight from Dallas to Midland, Texas. More than 200 passengers were left sitting in the plane for more than eight hours, an experience that mirrored other such incidents that occurred during the winter.

Fog, snow, and ice storms across the country caused problems in Denver Dec. 20, Dallas Dec. 29, New York and Philadelphia Feb. 14, and the Northeastern U.S. on March 16. Cancellations, delays, diversions, and long stretches of idling on tarmacs hit passengers of American, Delta, United, US Airways, and JetBlue, among others.

Passengers from some of those planes have testified before Congress about cabin conditions that included shortages of food and water plus non-working toilets and poor cabin ventilation. After nine of its planes were stranded at its JFK hub on Valentine's Day, JetBlue issued its own Passenger Bill of Rights.

Document 4

Potato chips not enough, passengers complain

In the latest event, American tried to ease the discomfort of passengers by sending pizza and potato chips to the stranded plane and attempting to roll a portable stairway to the aircraft. The former was insufficient for the number of people, however, while the latter was declared unsafe and therefore unusable.

Like JetBlue after the Feb. 14 fiasco, American has apologized to affected passengers and issued vouchers – good for $500 in this case.

Although several passengers from American 556 told USA TODAY their odyssey felt like a hijacking and kidnapping, the Air Transport Association gave the airline high marks for attempting to relieve their suffering.

According to the ATA's David Castelvetter, «By all accounts, American handled it well, given the severe weather conditions.»

As in previous incidents, passengers complained of poor communication from the airline during the time they were stranded. They said they were never told why they couldn't leave the plane, for example.

On the date of the incident, April 24, bad weather in its Dallas hub forced American to divert 129 flights, a record for any date other than Sept. 11, 2001, when all planes were grounded immediately after terrorists used planes to attack New York and Washington.

With the summer season approaching, airlines are warily watching the skies. Thunderstorms routinely cause more delays, cancellations, and diversions than winter weather conditions such as snow and ice storms.

Test Yourself

Gadgets for all of you

Alison Shepard, a marketing associate for a record label in Manhattan, straps an ultra-thin iPod Nano onto her arm before she goes for a run. When she returns to her apartment, she takes off the Nano and turns on the bulkier iPod that has replaced her home music system.

Ms. Shepard also owns two cameras – a point-and-shoot model she bought for $100 and a bulkier, far more expensive single-lens-reflex version that she says lets her be more creative. She has a laptop computer that can play DVDs, as well as a portable DVD player.

Electronic gadgets come in all shapes, sizes and descriptions to appeal to a range of tastes and requirements. For a growing number of consumers, that means buying two or more models to get every feature they want.

So much for one size fits all.

"I bought my 60-gig iPod, along with speakers, to replace my stereo, basically to minimize all the stuff in my apartment," Ms. Shepard said. "I didn't want to run with my 60-gig iPod on my arm because if I fell and broke it, it would be expensive to replace."

With the purchases of first-time gadget buyers leveling off, and even declining in some market segments, consumers like Ms. Shepard feed the industry's dream. The trend of buying more than one model of the same type of device – whether for personal use or as a gift – means revenue growth for manufacturers.

[...]

Repeat buyers bought about half of all digital cameras sold last year, for example, and are expected to overtake first-time digital camera buyers this year. In the personal electronics industry, companies expanded from marketing a single item to an entire household to marketing different products to different family members. [...]

Stephen Baker, vice president of industry analysis for the NPD Group, a market research firm, said that in the PC market, the trend started about four years ago with the rising popularity of notebook computers, which quickly turned one-computer households into multi-computer households.

I. Compréhension **À rédiger en français**

Après avoir dégagé l'idée principale de l'article, vous en ferez un compte rendu en 150 mots à 10 % près. Vous indiquerez le nombre de mots utilisés.

Corrigé page 194

II. Expression **À rédiger en anglais**

1. Analyse how this trend of repeat buyers evolved. Give several explanations. (60 words)

2. In the text, the reasons for and advantages of having more than one device for the same function are stressed. But what could the drawbacks be? (60 words)

3. Do you recognize yourself in this new trend? If yes, say how. If no, explain your attitude towards gadgets and electronic devices. (60 words)

Exam Paper

Not bound by anything

Now that books are being digitised, how will people read?

In secret locations and using secret methods, human beings are scanning lots and lots of books for Google, the world's largest web-search company. […].

As books go digital, new questions, both philosophical and commercial, arise. How, physically, will people read books in future? Will technology "unbind" books, as it has unbundled other media, such as music albums? […]

There is an obvious analogy between what Apple's iPods have done to CD players and what electronic books may do to the printed page, but the shift is unlikely to be quite so comprehensive. The simplest difference is that transferring one's old music CDs onto iPods is easy, whereas transferring one's old books onto an e-book is impossible. […]

[…] The Internet may indeed be to some book genres what Apple has been to music or what YouTube (now part of Google) has been to video. Among younger listeners albums are dead. They have been replaced by playlists of individual songs designed to be shared with friends.

In books this has already happened for encyclopedias. Wikipedia, which is free, collaborative and online, has eaten into sales of paper-bound alternatives. So books that people would not traditionally read in their entirety, or that require frequent updating, are likely to migrate online and perhaps to cease being books at all. […]

Certainly, some types of fiction […] are also likely to migrate online and to cease being books. Many fantasy fans, for example, have already put aside books and logged on to "virtual worlds" such as "World of Warcraft" […].

Most stories, however, will never find a better medium than the paper-bound novel. That is because readers immersed in a storyline want above all not to be interrupted, and all online media teem with distractions. […]

But even anthologies of short stories and poems, like longer novels, are unlikely to disappear. People want to be guided by others. They also want media suitable for unhurried reading in beds and bathtubs and on beaches. […] as Mr Godin puts it, they are "souvenirs of the way we felt" when we read something. That is something that people are likely to go on buying.

I. Compréhension **À rédiger en français**

Après avoir lu ce texte, vous en ferez un résumé en français en 120 mots à 10% près. Vous indiquerez le nombre de mots utilisés.

II. Expression **À rédiger en anglais**

Imagine how a twenty-year old consumer will "buy" his/her books in twenty years' time. (150 words)

Unit 14 Travelling

With the boom in the tourist industry, coupled with the growth of two superpowers, China and India, new forms of tourism are flourishing: from low-cost to high-end, from self-centered to global-centered mentalities, travelling has become increasingly complex.

1. Low-cost airlines in Asia

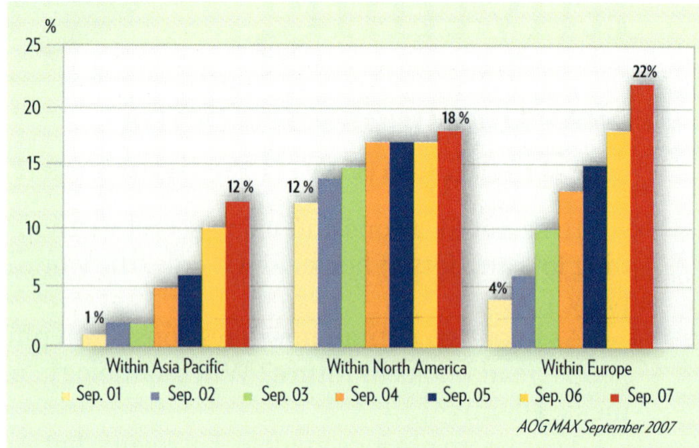

Since 2001, we have witnessed spectacular growth in air travel, thanks to the multiplication of the low-cost option. Travelling with no-frills airlines may be a far cry from the comfort of business class, but it makes travelling democratic – everyone can afford travelling these days. Now that low-cost airlines have been popping up in practically every country across Europe, it is time for the low-fare air travel option to become even more democratic and to stretch its wings across the Pacific to countries in Asia where emerging healthy economies mean more purchasing power for its populations, and thus more travel.

This year more new no-frills airlines will emerge in Asia than in any previous year since Air Asia launched in 2002. India, in particular, is expecting to see as many as twelve new low-cost airlines. In China, tentative low-cost airline projects include Yinglian and Spring and Autumn Airlines.

www.oag.com

Have a look at the graph. Read the text.

1. Compare the statistics concerning flights in 2002 and 2006.

2. Use 'whereas' to describe differences in growth in Europe and Asia.

3. Draw a conclusion about your findings.

2. Spreading the wealth

Across Eurasia, local middle-class travelers are increasingly choosing to vacation in their own countries. They've created a boom in domestic travel that has rapidly raised the level of accommodation and services. Many have traveled on package tours abroad, and are demanding the same amenities they found overseas, from spa treatments to high-thread-count sheets. And their demand for upscale travel is reaching even the most remote corners of the earth, from Tibet to Siberia, where posh hotels are opening in areas once hospitable only to backpackers. [...]

No country embodies the trend toward upscale domestic travel than China, where the purchasing power of the middle class has expanded at an astonishing pace over the last decade. Currently there are 320,000 millionaires in the country, worth a total of $1.6 trillion, whose free-spending ways have driven the country's luxury-goods market to grow by 28 percent a year.

Newsweek, May 7th, 2007.

Read the following text.

1. Pick out the facts about domestic travel in Asia.

3. Space: the newest frontier in extraordinary travel

Ride the Space Shuttle and board the International Space Station... without ever leaving the ground.

If you've dreamed of going on your own astronaut adventure, dream no more. Experience weightlessness, fly the Space Shuttle on re-entry and even walk on the moon (with help from NASA simulators) on two exhilarating space adventures. Join A&K Space at the U.S. Space & Rocket Center in Huntsville, Alabama, for an unforgettable adventure.

Family Space & Aviation Vacation

Imagine your family donning astronaut suits and repairing the International Space Station, or landing a Mach 1 jet on the deck of an aircraft carrier. With four days of science-based fun, education and action, this is a truly unique family getaway.

Abercrombie & Kent, e-News

Spaceship 1: a woman in her spacesuit came to witness the world's first private manned mission to space.

Read the text.

1. List the differences between ordinary and extraordinary travel.
2. Compare the importance of the means of transport to travellers.

4. Lost Luggage

Listen to the recorded conversation between the Troubleshooter and Mr Egeli.

1. Name the steps taken by Mr Egeli to retrieve his bags.
2. Pick out the details concerning the airline's agreement with passengers.
3. Say what travellers can do to protect themselves.

REPORTING

Are you interested in travelling?
Say what aspects are most important to you.

WORDS APART

Travel **Le voyage**

- **a bed and breakfast** chambre d'hôte
- **a cruise** une croisière
- **a family fun trip** des vacances en famille
- **a getaway** une escapade
- **a guided tour** une visite guidée
- **a package tour** un circuit tout compris
- **a packaged holiday** un séjour tout compris
- **a sea and sun holiday** un séjour balnéaire
- **a seaside resort hotel** un hotel-club en bord de mer
- **a short break** un long week-end
- **a sightseeing tour** un circuit
- **a stay** un séjour
- **a traveller** un voyageur
- **abroad** à l'extérieur du pays
- **accommodation** l'hébergement
- **business travel** le voyage des affaires
- **domestic** à l'intérieur, au pays
- **to go on holiday** partir en vacances

Transport **Le transport**

- **a caravan/a trailer** une caravane
- **a coach/a tour bus** un autocar
- **a houseboat/a barge** une péniche aménagée
- **a liner** un paquebot
- **aircraft carrier** porte-avion
- **airline company** une compagnie aérienne
- **car hire/rental** la location de voitures
- **carrier** transporteur
- **delivery times** délais de livraison
- **freight/cargo** le fret
- **hassles** les embêtements
- **jet lag** la fatigue due au décalage horaire
- **long-haul flight** un vol long courrier
- **low-cost/no-frills airline** compagnie aérienne à bas prix
- **package** colis
- **space shuttle** navette spatiale
- **the journey** le trajet
- **to file a complaint** déposer une plainte

Tourism **Le tourisme**

- **affordable/moderately priced** à prix raisonnable
- **amenities** les équipements
- **assets** les atouts
- **backpackers** randonneurs
- **budget** à petit prix
- **disposable income** revenu disponible
- **eco-tourism** l'écotourisme
- **extreme tourism** le tourisme extrême
- **facilities** les aménagements, les services
- **heritage** le patrimoine
- **lifestyle** le mode de vie
- **mass tourism** le tourisme de masse
- **niche tourism** le créneau du marché de tourisme
- **space tourism** le tourisme dans l'espace
- **standard of living** le niveau de vie
- **sustainable tourism** le tourisme durable
- **the tourist industry** l'industrie du tourisme
- **upscale/luxury/posh** haut de gamme

Unit 14 Travelling

Zooming on

Slow is beautiful

As work life becomes increasingly hectic[1], holidays are occupying a more important place in our lives; when we take a break, we want to truly step off the treadmill[2] – even as (or maybe because) we cling to our BlackBerrys. Just as the slow-food movement encouraged diners to savor meals and the way they are produced, the trend toward slow travel promotes a more thoughtful style of vacationing. It refers not only to leisurely and environmentally friendly modes of transport–train, boat, bike or foot–but also to the nature of the trips: smaller in scope and more off-the-beaten-path – a custom-crafted trek through niche sites rather than a top-10 group tour. [...]

More and more, people are living for vacation. They are using up every single allotted day off, and bargaining with their employers for more time to savor their travels. [...] "Today's tourists view travel as a form of self-expression. They don't want to come back with an object, or even a picture. They want to come back with a story."

The trend toward leisurely, in-depth holidays, like so many others, stems from the baby boomers. They've worked hard—their white-collar toil has largely driven the past few years of global productivity growth—and now they have the money and the time to enjoy themselves. [...] And why shouldn't the journey become the holiday? The private company that took over much of Canada's failing long-distance network in the '90s has seen traffic soar as sightseers return to the railways. "People want to get back to the way things were, before there were cell phones and computers," says Graham Gilley of Rocky Mountaineer Vacations. [...]

Still, it's important to note that slower holidays are a primarily Western phenomenon. While many Americans and Europeans can afford to take their time and plot their own paths, developing-world tourists are still trying to log enough hours and wages to afford the traditional one-week packaged tour. But there are signs that more leisurely travel is catching on even in emerging markets. Urban Chinese are taking weekend trips to country farms to de-stress[4]. Budget hotel chains catering to the growing number of domestic travellers in India and China are increasingly offering chill-out[3] amenities like spas.

Newsweek, May 7th, 2007

1. *mouvementé* – 2. *le tapis roulant* – 3. *pour décompresser*

FIRST STEPS

1. Present the document. Origin, title, date, topic.

2. Pick up the information you are given about the slow traveller's:
a. need for vacations, **b.** professional background.

3. Describe the niche this travel presents in tourism industry.

MOVING ON

1. Choose the appropriate equivalent for 'to step off the treadmill':

a. to take a break by practising sport,
b. to stop working altogether,
c. to change your lifestyle.

2. Compare the growth in low-cost air travel to this new trend. Are these two trends paradoxical?

3. Explain why "people want to get back to the way things were." (l. 18)

4. Give definitions for the following forms of tourism:

a. eco-tourism,
b. sustainable tourism,
c. heritage tourism,
d. mass tourism.

5. Tick the right answer.

a. 'environmentally friendly' means:
- that does not pollute,
- that studies nature,
- a group of ecologists.

b. 'off-the-beaten-path' characterises a:
- hiking trip,
- unique type of holiday,
- self-centred holiday.

c. a 'traditional holiday' would be a:
- personalised mountain trek,
- 10-city tour in 10 days,
- river cruise on the Indian backwaters.

6. Tick examples of transport when 'the journey' becomes the holiday. (l. 16)

a. a barge (péniche)
b. a luxury liner
c. a private jet
d. your family SUV (sports utility vehicle, a 4 × 4)
e. a low-cost flight

7. Translate

Translate from line 20: "Still, it's important..." down to the end of the text.

WRITING (150 words)

Describe your dream 'slow holiday'.

Give information about the destination, the time spent, the means of transport, and your motivations.

LANGUAGE AT WORK

1. Indicate the stressed syllables. Then listen to the recording to check your answers.

environmentally / primarily / increasingly / leisurely / traditionally / eventually / developing / thoughtfully / productivity / phenomenon / sightseers / amenities / traditional / domestic / personalized.

2. Fill in the blanks with the appropriate phrasal verb. Use the correct verb form:

to step off / to turn off / to take over / to take on / to get back to / to catch on / to use up / to take off / to come back

a. As soon as we .... the train, it was as if we were in another world.

b. When the plane ...., toxic gases are released from the engines into the air.

c. To save energy, you should .... all electrical appliances not in use.

d. Mr Sanders was unable to go on a short break because he .... all of his paid vacation time.

e. The Canadian rail company .... by a private company.

f. Businessmen have finally decided .... basics before it's too late.

3. Use the following compound nouns to complete the sentences.

backwaters/houseboat/treehouse/seafood/rice boat/bygone/shoreline.

a. When travelling to Kerala, you can spend the night in a .... if you aren't afraid of heights, that is.

b. Otherwise, the means of slow transport are either .... or .... .

c. Sailing along such beautiful ...., you will enjoy authentic .... dishes while gazing at the sunset along the glistening .... Your dream come true!

4. Translate into French.

a. Working hard enables travellers to play hard too.

b. Taking a weekend trip to the country is one of the best ways to relax.

c. We still do not know how Asian travellers will spend their time or their money.

5. Translate into English.

a. Si les Chinois préfèrent voyager à l'intérieur du pays, c'est qu'ils cherchent à mieux le découvrir.

b. Puisque les Américains et les Européens ont le temps et l'argent pour les voyages, ils deviennent de plus en plus exigeants.

c. De nos jours, la montée en puissance des pays en voie de développement a élargi le marché du transport à bas prix.

1. Presenting a brochure

YOUR JOB

You work for Tourindia, a small specialist tour operator, and you are in charge of promoting eco-tourism in Kerala. The development of nature resorts in Kerala– The Treehouses & Rain Forest eco-lodges in Green Magic Nature Resort – that were India's first eco-tourism product.

YOUR TASK

You must convince a group of experienced travellers to visit Kerala. Your presentation should include an introduction to the company **(See Doc. 1 & 2)**, an overview of the assets in Kerala, and show how unique this experience will be for the tourists **(See Doc. 3 & 4)**.

ACTING OUT

Introduce your tour operator and the product. Discuss the location, the accommodation, the overall interest of the product and give a few helpful tips.

Document 1

Tourindia

Tourindia, a specialist tour operator, started with a team of young people about 25 years ago. Tourindia pioneered the development of backwater tourism by introducing the first Kettuvallam (Rice Boat) for comfortable cruising in the canals. This boat enables tourists to enjoy the vestiges of a bygone era without endangering the fragile eco-system.

Document 2

The Tourindia project

We are now the exclusive promoters of this protection-oriented adventure trekking and camping programme, which was developed by the Kerala Forest Authority as a participatory ecotourism project.

The project has proved to be an excellent idea as people involved used to be poachers plundering forests. Over time they were converted to forest conservation work.

Document 3

Getting to know Kerala

With the Arabian Sea in the west, the Western Ghats towering 500-2700 meters in the east, Kerala enjoys unique geographical features that have made it one of the most sought after tourist destinations in Asia. With a pleasant climate, a long shoreline and serene beaches, Kerala exudes a sense of tranquility– you will see emerald backwaters, waterfalls and exotic wildlife. You can enjoy Ayurvedic* health holidays, enchanting art forms, magical festivals, as well as historic and cultural sights and events. An exotic cuisine will delight your palate. All of this offers you a unique experience.

*"knowledge of life" in Sanskrit

Document 4

Unique Kerala

- Backwaters are one of the unique attractions of Kerala, a chain of canals extending about 1500 kms, with a network of 44 rivers, lagoons and lakes. Most of it is naturally formed. Canals are remade for continuous traffic of men and materials.
- Super Deluxe Houseboat: SURYA.
- Backwaters form an inherent part of life in Kerala.
- These houseboats are known for their unique design use of local material like bamboo poles, coconut fiber ropes, bamboo mats and carpets. They invite you to enjoy the fascinating beauties of backwaters in a fabulous way.
- Their languid grace and quaint design adds another dimension to your cruise on the shimmering blue waters.
- Each boat has a fully equipped kitchen and an experienced cook to prepare authentic Kerala cuisine with seafood and fresh vegetables.
- Here man and nature find a balance of harmonious co-existence beyond the temptations of modernity.

- The guest can go for a short expedition by cycle or on the modified bullock carts which are available to take you higher and higher to enjoy the beauty of the village scenarios.

Kerala Tourism.

PROMPTS

- **best time to visit** *meilleure époque pour visiter*
- **high season** *la haute saison*
- **monsoon** *la saison des pluies, la mousson*
- **travel wear** *garde-robe pour le voyage*
- **credit cards** *cartes de paiement*
- **currency** *devise*
- **temple dress** *code vestimentaire à l'intérieur des temples*
- **visitor's tips** *conseils aux touristes*
- **wildlife sanctuaries** *réserves d'animaux sauvages*

2. Confirming a reservation

YOUR JOB
You organize group bookings for the large hotel chain Xu Hui in Shanghai. You are in charge of communicating with the British sportswear company, Golfer, who is seeking a reservation for its sales representatives attending a sales convention in September. You have received the following letter **(See Reference doucment)**.

YOUR TASK
You write a letter in response to the company's enquiry, confirm the reservation, but cannot ensure the discount requested. You can, however, offer a complimentary coffee service during their lunch seminar.

ACTING OUT
You are one of the sales representatives attending the convention, but in order to meet a deadline, your arrival will be delayed. Since you must quickly change your reservation, you decide to make a telephone call **(See Doc. 1)**.

Document 1

Making arrangements for a reservation

PROMPTS

I'm interested in booking a room... *J'aimerais réserver une chambre...*
I'm looking for accommodation in the downtown area... *Je cherche un hébergement en centre-ville*
If there are any cancellations... *Si jamais il y a une annulation...*
I'm afraid we are fully booked... *Je regrette. Nous sommes complets.*
Could you recommend another hotel? *Pourriez-vous me conseiller un autre hôtel ?*
I'll call back later... *Je rappellerai plus tard.*
I'll confirm my booking by e-mail within 48 hours... *Je vous confirmerai ma réservation par courriel d'ici 48 heures.*
Further to your enquiry... *Suite à votre lettre...*
We are pleased to confirm your reservation for... *Nous avons le plaisir de vous confirmer votre réservation pour...*
In order to best suit your needs... *Afin de mieux adapter à vos besoins...*
Our prices are extremely competitive. *Nos prix sont très compétitifs.*
Not only does this include... but it also includes... *Cela comprend non seulement... mais aussi*
Should you require any further information, please do not hesitate to contact me. *Pour plus d'informations, n'hésitez pas à nous contacter.*

REFERENCE DOCUMENT

GOLFER Ltd	*Logo of the company*
26 Chelmsford Road Essex CM2 L3U ENGLAND	*Name and address of the sender*
17 March 2008	*Date*
Reservation Manager Xu Hui Hotel 3 Square Xu Hui Shanghai CHINA	*Title of the addressee*
Dear Sir or Madam	*Opening salutation*
I am writing to enquire on the availability of 15 single rooms for our company's sales team, who will be attending the Sportswear Convention in Shanghai this September. We will arrive in Shanghai on Monday, 10 September 2008, and plan to return on the following Sunday (16 September).	*Reason for writing*
As we will be attending the Convention, we shall also require conference room facilities at least twice during the week. Would this be possible? We should also like to know whether a catered lunch could be provided by the hotel.	*Additional requests for service*
Seeing that we plan to purchase some local sportswear, could you provide information on how to send the merchandise back to England duty-free if possible?	*Transport questions*
Finally, I would like to know if your hotel would grant a group discount, as we normally are granted a 20% rebate on room rates for conventions.	*Sales argument to obtain a better price*
If your hotel is fully booked, could you please recommend another hotel in the vicinity? Thank you in advance.	*Assistance required*
Yours faithfully	*Closing salutation*
R. Nelson Travel Manager	*Signature Name and position*

Test Yourself

Road to Everest: China says environment first priority

Allaying India's fears that the metalled highway to the heart of the Himalayas will result in ecological damage, China on Wednesday said it will "strictly monitor" the number of tourists treading that road.

"We want to develop both tourism and the environment. But when we have to choose between the two, environment will be our first priority," Chairman of National Tourism Administration, Shao Qiwei, told a group of visiting Indian journalists.

Brushing aside allegations that China cared little about environment when it comes to implementing state interests, Shao argued the environment itself was important to attract tourism to China.

"If we do not protect our environment, we cannot expect to attract tourists here." Shao argued the state actually does not have to make big efforts to prevent an anticipated tourist overflow.

"The very climate of the Himalayas is such that not many tourists will be fit enough to reach that distance," he said.

"This we have discovered when we built the Quinghai-Lhasa high altitude train. Many people got breathless when they reached that altitude in the train. Mount Qomolangma (Everest) is much higher than that," he said.

"Moreover, we have very strict environmental laws; we will strictly monitor the number of people wanting to travel on that road," Shao said, adding that violators will be penalised.

Environmentalists in India and elsewhere have protested China's move to convert a 110 kilometre long sand-and-gravel path into a "black-topped, metalled road, lined with guardrails" for athletes to take the Olympic torch to the summit.

The Times of India, July 12th, 2007

I. Compréhension

Résumez le texte **en anglais** en 120 mots (± 10%). Vous indiquerez le nombre de mots utilisés.

II. Expression

1. Explain how countries attract tourists.

2. What is the future of China as a tourist destination?

METHOD — **SUMMARY**

1. A summary is a short version of the text, reduced to its main components. It is also called a 'contraction'. You must use your own words, but follow the text closely.

a. Highlight the key information (Who? What? When? Where? How?)

b. Pick out linking words to show contradictions and transitions.

c. Do not write an introduction or a conclusion.

d. Follow the chronological order of the text, keeping to essential facts.

e. Avoid quoting.

f. Express the author's point of view and not your own.

g. Respect the number of words required, and indicate this number clearly.

Corrigé page 194

Exam Paper

Window seats

The sun is shining and the waves are lapping at the sand. Just beyond the lounge chairs and palm trees, a gaggle[1] of beautiful people with perfect tans and lush hair gyrate[2] to music wafting from a pair of seaside speakers. It is, in short, a dream holiday. What's more, it's free, 100 percent eco-friendly and available any time. All you need is... a broadband connection.

Old-fashioned travelers might bristle[3] at the notion of a cyberspace beach resort, where the beauties in bikinis are the animated avatars of people sitting behind computer screens (and probably wearing sweat pants). But to the more than 5 million players in the absorbing world of the online game Second Life (SL), where shimmering oases do exist, this is nothing less than a real vacation. Cyber resorts, they argue, come with all the escapist benefits of any real-world holiday: a new perspective, stunning scenery and plenty of ready romance. But these vacations also promise things that real travel can't: no jet lag, hassles or crowds, perfect companions and the chance to visit Hollywood, Cairo and Rome all in the same day.

A growing number of cutting-edge cyber-entrepreneurs are betting that virtual reality could soon be the hottest holiday destination of all. Last fall, Italian travel journalist Mario Gerosa launched Synthravels (synthravels.com), the world's first virtual-reality travel agency, offering hip[4] personalized guides for almost 30 online worlds, including World of Warcraft and Matrix Online. Since then, the phenomenon of online travel guides has generated a buzz in cyberspace, with companies like SL Travel and Tours, SL Tourguides and Tour/Fun Guide—which, unlike Synthravels, each specializes in one world—attracting all kinds of new business. Although hard numbers are difficult to come by because the industry is so new, the fact that some top guides are now charging as much as $50 an hour for their services suggests a serious market already exists. "I try to give my clients a feel for the culture of the world we're in," says Gerosa. "I consider Second Life a continent, not a game."

It may not be a traditional holiday, but the classic traveler's adage still applies: "When in Rome..."

Newsweek, May 5th, 2007

1. *un groupe* – 2. *danser en se tortillant* – 3. *se hérisser* – 4. *branché*

I. Compréhension À rédiger en anglais

Après une lecture attentive de l'article ci-dessus, vous en ferez un compte-rendu en 200 mots +/- 10%. Vous indiquerez le nombre de mots utilisés.

II. Traduction

Vous traduirez depuis "A growing number" ligne 18 jusqu'à "new business." ligne 26.

Unit 15 Business and ethics

Ethics in business has increasingly been taken into account by many firms worried about their reputation and image. They have adopted a code of conduct towards consumers, workers, or the planet under the name of CSR (corporate social responsibility).
However, one can wonder if this is not just a smokescreen enabling companies to do more business with a clearer conscience.

1. The growing of GMOs

GMO growing worldwide
(Millions Hectares)

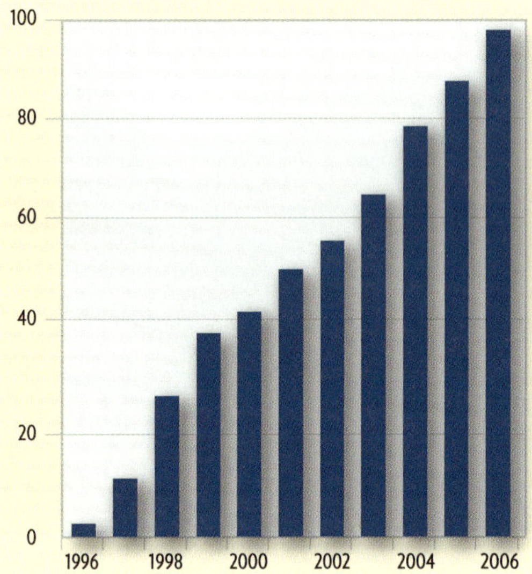

http://www.gmo-compass.org

Global Area of Genetically Engineered Crops, 1996 to 2006: By Country (Millions Hectares)

Country	USA	Argentina	Brazil	Canada	China	Paraguay
1996	1.5	0.1	...	0.1	...	...
1997	8.1	1.4	...	1.3	0.0	...
1998	20.5	4.3	...	2.8	<0.1	...
1999	28.7	65.7	1.4*	4.0	0.3	...
2000	30.3	10.0	3.6*	3.0	0.5	...
2001	35.7	11.8	5.7*	3.2	1.5	...
2002	39.0	13.5	6.3*	3.5	2.1	...
2003	42.8	13.9	3.0	4.4	2.8	...
2004	47.6	16.2	5.0	5.4	3.7	1.2
2005	49.8	17.1	9.0	5.6	3.3	1.8
2006	54.6	18.0	11.5	6.1	3.5	2.0

*Legal cultivation of gmos: calculated area

Look at the graph and the table.

1. Describe the main trend in the cultivation of GM crops.

2. Comment on the distribution per country and try to analyse why it is so.

3. Find out about France.

4. Do you think we are right in our attitude?

5. What is France's latest decision on GM crops?

2. Soya king changes face of pampas

Read the vocabulary notes and then listen to the recording.
Reap/harvest: *récolter* – Drive: *énergie* – Dashing: *jeunes et dynamiques* – Slums: *bidonvilles* – Fleet: *la flotte*.

1. In which country is it? Who is the main character and above all, what did you understand about his job?

2. What are all the advantages of GM soya mentioned in the text?

3. What are the two main drawbacks? Can you think of others?

4. What sort of society is emerging in that country?

3. We should farm cloned animal

The creator of Dolly the sheep has called for farmers to take up cloning as a way of producing cheap food...

The US expects to be eating cloned-farmed burgers, pork and bacon within two years and supporters of the method say Europe must follow suit.

Campaigners insist that meat and milk from cloned offspring is identical to the food in supermarkets and should not be labelled.

However, any attempt to deny families the right to decide whether they want to eat food produced in this way would be highly controversial.

One of the biggest concerns is the high number of clone animal pregnancies that lead to abnormalities, miscarriages and stillbirths. Even in the most successful cloning systems, twice as many piglets are born dead – around 20%.

Clone offspring cows, would be bigger and able to produce more milk than those from current breeding techniques. Pigs might also be much bigger, leaner or faster growing, so making them easier and cheaper to produce.

Perter Melchett said: "the fact that supporters of cloning are not prepared to support labelling and want to keep the whole thing secret, says it all. It stinks."

© *Daily Mail*, July 2007, by Sean Poulter

Read the text.

1. In your own words, explain the main topic of this article.
2. Explain what a cloned animal is.
3. List the pros and cons of the project as described in the text.
4. Think of other drawbacks for the consumers and the animals involved.
5. What would be totally unethical about this idea?
6. What unethical deviation could be coming next?

REPORTING

Should we worry about the food we buy and eat in Europe?

WORDS APART

Ethics and nature Éthique et nature

Breeding techniques des techniques d'élevage
clone farming élevage d'animaux clonés
to cut down on pesticides réduire les pesticides
an environmentalist un écologiste
to feed the world nourrir le monde
genetically engineered (GE) food nourriture génétiquement modifiée
genetically engineered (GE) seeds semences génétiquement modifiées
genetically modified (GM) crops récoltes génétiquement modifiées
genetically modified organisms (GMOs) organismes génétiquement modifiés (OGM)
to release polluting agents rejeter des polluants
sustainable development développement durable
traceability traçabilité
to trigger allergies provoquer des allergies

Ethics and workers Éthique et travailleurs

abuse maltraitance
allegations accusations
to be bullied être maltraîté
to be forced to work overtime être forcé de faire des heures supplémentaires
exploitative working conditions conditions de travail abusives
to fund a project financer un projet
to harass sb harceler quelqu'un
to improve the welfare of workers améliorer les conditions de vie des travailleurs
low wages bas salaires
to provide school facilities fournir des équipements scolaires
to support a project soutenir un projet
a sweatshop un atelier où les ouvriers sont exploités
to treat fairly/unfairly traiter équitablement ou injustement
unattainable production targets visées de production irréalisables

Ethics and business Éthique et affaires

to buy ethically acheter de manière éthique
a checking system un système de contrôle
to donate money faire des dons d'argent
to enforce quality and safety assurer la qualité et la sécurité
to go carbon neutral ne plus rejeter de gaz carbonique
a green product un produit écologique
a green initiative une initiative écologique
to outsource/to delocalise production délocaliser la production
a paperless bank account un relevé bancaire en ligne
to recall a product rappeler un produit
to reduce carbon emissions réduire les émissions de gaz carbonique
to refund carbon emissions rembourser ses rejets de gaz carbonique
to remove counterfeited goods retirer du marché des produits de contre-façon
to take a product off one's list enlever un produit de son catalogue

Unit 15 Business and ethics

Zooming on

The sweatshop high-street[1]

Two of Britain's major high-street retailers launched inquiries last night into allegations that factory workers who make their clothes in India are being paid as little as 13p per hour for a 48-hour week, [...].

India's largest ready-made clothing exporter, Gokaldas Export, which supplies brands including Marks & Spencer, Mothercare and H&M, confirmed that wages paid to garment workers were as low as £1.13 for a 9-hour day.

Garment workers for factories owned by exporters who supply to Gap, Matalan and Primark, told the Guardian they were paid similar wages and regularly forced to work overtime of between six and eighteen hours per week. The ETI[2] code states that workers shall not be regularly be required to work more than 48 hours per week, that overtime should be voluntary and that it should not exceed 12 hours per week.

Texport Overseas, which supplies Gap and Matalan, denied that workers were forced to do overtime.

Employees of factories owned by exporters who supply Gap and Matalan, claimed they were often made to work extra hours without pay to meet unattainable production targets.

They claimed the mostly female workforce was harassed and bullied by male production managers and supervisors for not achieving targets.

Another tailor who makes clothes for H&M, said that when she could not achieve her production targets, the clothes were thrown in her face. She said up to 15 workers a day collapsed and had to be given medical attention.

In February, a young woman hanged herself in the toilets of one factory owned by Gokalkas Exports. [...]

KP Gopinah, the director of Civiped, an Indian workers' rights group said: "When we speak to the workers, they tell us all they want is to be treated like human beings. They need a living wage to live in dignity, to get running water, to get a better education for their children."

He said a report by the Garment and Textile Workers union estimated a living wage in Bangalore to be at least £2.50 a day.

© *Guardian*, New & Media Ltd 2006, September 3rd, 2007, by Karen McVeigh

1. *rue principale, grande enseigne* – 2. *Ethical Trading Initiative*

FIRST STEPS

1. Have a look at the illustration. Name brands that have been targeted as such.

2. Present this article in a few sentences and say which countries are involved.

3. What is the main problem discussed?

4. Explain the words "sweatshops" and "high-street retailers".

5. List the brands involved and match them with the names of their suppliers.

MOVING ON

1. Match the following numbers with what they represent in the text:

13 – 9 – 1.13 – 48 – 15 – 12 – 2.50

2. Are the main allegations contained in the article true or false. Justify your choice.

a. Workers in India are paid 0.20 euros per hour or 2 euros a day.
b. They work twice as much as the average French worker.
c. Some are compelled by their employers to do many extra hours without being paid.
d. Women are more protected than men.
e. Many employees can't take the stress and hard work.

3. Fill in the table concerning the violation of the ETI code.

ETI Code	How it is violated in these factories

4. Is there any control of the working conditions in those delocalised factories. If yes, who does it?

5. How can these different brands react to the allegations and improve the conditions of work in the factories producing their goods.

6. Consumers' reactions.

a. What is your personal reaction to the problem analysed in this article?
b. As a consumer, find five ways or actions consumers could try to make the situation better.
c. Do you think consumers can really influence big brands into making them act more ethically towards their workers?

7. Could the British government do something?

8. Examine the great dilemma in this issue.

9. Translate

Translate into French from line 14 to 17: "Employees of factories..." for not achieving targets.

WRITING (150 words)

Imagine the continuation of the story of the young woman who committed suicide in the toilets: how her family coped and how they reacted, her employer's reaction...

LANGUAGE AT WORK

1. In the first paragraph, write the phonetic sign for all the "o" vowels.

2. Listen to the recorded words and write them down.

3. In the text, find the English equivalents to:

a. distributeurs de marques connues ;
b. accusations ;
c. salaire ;
d. heures supplémentaires ;
e. exportateur ;
f. fournisseur.

4. Find six irregular verb forms in the article and write all the other forms for each verb.

5. Find six passive forms in the article and turn them into active forms.

6. Write the following sentences, using the given prompts but keeping the same meaning.

a. The textile workers' union stated that a living minimum wage in Bangalore should be £2.50 a day, but it is always less than that.
Although ....
b. They can do extra hours on the condition that it is not more than twelve a week.
As long as ....
c. Some retailers make some effort to check the working conditions in their Indian factories but there are still many problems.
In spite of ....

7. Translate into French.

a. One worker claimed that security guards patrolled the toilets, harassing the women inside to get back to work.
b. Exploitation of workers in developing countries such as India is a very common phenomenon.
c. Many highstreet brands declared that such methods were unacceptable and and that they would take measures to ensure better working conditions.

8. Translate into English.

a. Le Guardian a mené une enquête sur les salaires et les conditions de travail à Bangalore, en Inde.
b. Cette enquête a révélé des conditions terribles, comme celles décrites dans les romans de Dickens.
c. La mondialisation n'a pas que des bons côtés. Beaucoup de travailleurs pauvres ont besoin d'être protégés officiellement.

Unit 15 Business and ethics

1. Presenting a project

YOUR JOB

You work for the Waitrose Fairtrade Foundation and you are in charge of the project currently developed in South Africa.

YOUR TASK

This partnership is already well established but you are now asked to complete it by setting up a meeting between the South-African producers benefiting from the program and some of Waitrose's already selected customers.

1. Read the different documents and visit Waitrose's website if you can to complete your information.

2. Devise a set of overhead transparencies to show the full-scale project to the selected Waitrose customers and enhance its positive aspects.

ACTING OUT

In the class choose some "Waitrose customers" and some "South African visitors" and act out the presentation of the project and the meeting of the two parties.

Document 1

Supermarket chain's scheme to help African growers bear fruit

Fruit growers in South Africa have seen more than £330,000 ploughed back into their communities over the past year by the supermarket group Waitrose, which is hoping to raise a further £500,000 to fund educational projects over the next six months.

The cash has been raised as part of the food retailer's initiative to return a sizeable proportion of profits it earns on sales of citrus fruits to the farmers who grow them. The scheme has proved more successful than had been hoped and now, the Waitrose Foundation, which operates as a partnership between the supermarket and members of the supply chain, is adding avocados to the grapefruit, lemons and clementines on offer.

Some 25 educational schemes have already been launched on ten citrus farms across South Africa, including training in literacy and IT, as well as classes in craft work to enable farm workers to earn an income out of season. The citrus season is only six months long so it is vital to teach new skills to the growers.

Waitrose's managing director, Steve Esom, who was in South Africa last month visiting some of the projects, said: "...I was 100% convinced this is the right thing to do before I went; now I am 110% convinced. It is absolutely clear that it's trade not aid that will work."

[...] Mr Esom is delighted with the response of the company's customers who, he says, "feel a strong link" with those who produce the food they buy. He is keen to bring some of the farmers to Britain to meet customers. The initiative is supported by the South African government.

[...] The Waitrose Foundation was set up as a long-term response to South Africa's social and economic problems and its work has been welcomed by the South African authorities.

[...]

Mr Esom is keen to see the scheme extended. "There's an opportunity in grapes and maybe in processed products. And it could be extended to wine, although that is a long way down the road. It's a big idea and we are only at the foothills."

© *Guardian*, News & Media Ltd, 2006,
May 29th, 2006, by Fiona Walsh

Document 2

About the foundation

In just two years since its creation the Waitrose Foundation is transforming thousands of lives.

The initiative, a partnership between all parties in the supply chain (Waitrose, exporters Green Marketing and a number of importers) was formed out of a desire to take role in spearheading[1] the management of the land reform process in South Africa.

Under the unique funding model, a proportion of the profits from South African citrus fruit, grapes, stone fruit and avocado are ploughed into[2] a fund to improve the lives of farm workers and their communities and develop their skills in line with the South African Government's aspirations for black empowerment.

While the Foundation is administered by a board of directors, the farm workers themselves decide what projects are needed most by their own communities: this could range from somewhere for children to do their homework, sports pitches, organised crèches or community centres.

This "bottom up" process of distributing Foundation funding dovetails[3] closely with the South African Government's evolving AgriBEE (Black Economic Policy), which has proposed that 30% of land should be owned by black South Africans by 2014. Consequently there are two distinct elements to the Foundation programme. The first stage looks at social issues and aims to ensure essential knowledge, through methods such as education programmes – both basic literacy and agricultural production.

The second stage will ultimately entail the ownership of some land by farm workers, whereby Foundation grants will be used to buy land to be held in trust on behalf of farm workers.

1. *être le fer de lance de* – 2. *réinvestis* – 3. *concorder*

Document 3

A foundation for the future

A spectacle of music and colour explodes from the midday heat at a remote citrus farm in South Africa's Eastern Cape.

The workers – dressed in vibrant outfits of lime and tangerine – are singing loudly with what seems like uninhibited joy.

One of the English speaking farm staff translates the workers' song from the local Xhosan language.

She explains: "They are singing 'Waitrose we welcome you. You have given us everything.'"

Continue listening to the tape.

2. Recalling defective items

YOUR JOB

You work as a communications manager for MATTEL UK, the toy company. You deal especially with consumers.

YOUR TASK

You have been asked to tackle the delicate matter of recalling potentially dangerous Chinese-made toys. Thus, you have been specifically asked to write a letter of recall that will be put on the website and also published in the press. As this is quite an embarrassing situation for Mattel, you will have to be both very precise in your wording as well as very cautious.

1. Read **Document 1** to understand which toys are concerned by this recall.
2. Read the tips and the standard recall letter on the next page.
3. Write the letter which must be informative and apologetic, insisting on Mattel's sense of responsibility and concern for safety.

ACTING OUT

Write a short radio communication that will be broadcast on all the main UK radio stations.

Document 1

Mattel recalls millions of hazardous toys

In what is believed to be one of the biggest product recalls the UK has seen, the company recalled hundreds of thousands of Polly Pocket and Batman toys because of fears that magnets could come lose and be swallowed by young children.

It is also recalling 49,000 Chinese-made toy cars, which may contain excessive levels of lead paint.

Many of these toys were made up to five years ago, but parents are being urged to take back any of the affected toys to a shop to get a full refund. The latest scare also involves toys with unsafe paint. Nearly 50,000 die-cast Sarge cars – from the hit animated film Cars – made in China between May and July this year were found to have "impermissible levels of lead", the company said.

The other toys – 1.9 million in the UK – have small magnets that could come loose [...].

Polly Pocket, a favourite among young girls, is the most badly affected by the recall with 53 different lines having problems. Batman, Barbie and Doggie Day Care are the other magnetic toys affected, all of which were made between 2001 and earlier this year.

It comes after Mattel introduced a new checking system in the wake of problems with paint used by a Chinese sub-contractor.

Mattel's chief executive Robert Eckert said: "The safety of children is our primary concern, and we are deeply apologetic to everyone affected.

"Mattel has rigorous procedures, and we will continue to be vigilant and unforgiving in enforcing quality and safety."

REFERENCE DOCUMENT

A Special Message to Our Education Customers

On August 24, 2006, Peach announced the jBook G4 and FlowerBook G4 Battery Exchange Program.

Peach has determined that certain lithium-ion batteries containing cells manufactured by Sony Corporation of Japan pose a safety risk that may result in overheating under rare circumstances.

the problem with the product, including whether it has breached product safety standards, and the effects resulting from this problem

The affected batteries were sold worldwide from October 2003 through August 2006 and were used with 12-inch jBook G4 and 12-inch FlowerBook and 15-inch FlowerBook G4 computers. Peach is voluntarily recalling the affected batteries and has initiated a worldwide exchange program to provide customers with a replacement battery, free of charge.

the dates the product was on sale

Recognizing that your school or institution may own or lease the above noted computers that use these batteries, we want to make sure you know about this battery exchange program. To view complete program details and begin the exchange process, please visit http://support.peach.com/batteryprogram/.

the immediate action to take, such as cease use, safe storage instructions

It's important to note that only certain jBook G4 and FlowerBook G4 batteries are affected. The chart below will help you identify the battery models and serial numbers that apply to your jBook or FlowerBook. To view the model and serial numbers labeled on the bottom of the battery, you must remove the battery from the computer. The battery serial number is printed in black or dark grey lettering beneath a barcode.

Computer model Battery model Battery serial number range
12-inch jBook G4 A1061 ZZ338 – ZZ427
6N601 ending with THTC

The product including its name, make, model, colour, batch or serial number

When you receive the replacement battery, please use the same shipping packaging and the included prepaid shipping label to return the recalled battery to Peach.

How to get a refund, replacement or have the product repaired
Where to return the product

If you do not have access to the website listed above, or if you have more than three batteries to exchange, please contact your Peach Account Manager or call Peach at 1 800 263-3394 between 9:00 a.m. and 9:00 p.m. Eastern Standard Time, seven days a week, for further assistance.

A contact phone number for further information, preferably toll free.

In closing, we want you to know that Peach takes product quality and customer satisfaction very seriously.

We appreciate your cooperation, ongoing business, and continued support.

Sincerely,

Peach

Unit 15 Business and ethics

Test Yourself

Counterfeit goods, a borderless problem

With the global economy, the companies being counterfeited are spending a lot of money to try to stop the problem. But have they been successful?

The Daily Times of Pakistan is reporting:

A long campaign to remove pirated goods from shop fronts in Asia is finally having an impact but the crackdown has also changed the nature of the problem and new outlets are flourishing. The results of police raids, a slate of new laws and increased prosecutions can be seen across the region on the back streets of Beijing, Hong Kong, Taipei, Singapore [...].

To counter the authorities, black market buccaneers are shifting their goods from roadside stalls and shopping malls to the Internet. In other words, the people behind counterfeiting are very adept at mutating their method of operation and carrying on.

Of course, we in the West can blame Asia and the third world for this activity, but if weren't for people in the West buying these goods, I doubt it would have grown into an international problem.

And the companies being counterfeited probably have something to worry about. With the popularity of Internet auctions, the business of counterfeiting goods is likely to grow. Internet auctions are big business and sites, such as eBay refuse to accept blame for the actions of their members. The sale of counterfeit goods is rampant on these sites and Tiffanys and Microsoft are spending a lot of money bringing legal action to try to curb it.

Some of these companies might be contributing to the problem in another way. After all, do you think all the $100.00 tennis shoes we buy are made in North America, or Europe? Not very likely in the global economy. In the quest for cheap labor, long regarded as one of the major expenses of doing business, many of our goods are produced in the same countries that produce the counterfeits. The end result is counterfeits of about the same quality as the item being counterfeited.

We can blame and prosecute counterfeiters in far-away lands, but as long as there is a demand and a ready means to distribute these goods, the problem isn't going away.

Sunday, April 30th, 2006

In China, a man offers rides on a poney disguised as a zebra.

Corrigé page 194

I. Expression

Après lecture de cet article, vous en ferez un compte rendu en français en 180 mots.

II. Compréhension

Puis vous répondrez en anglais aux questions suivantes:

a. What ethical reasons can urge companies to fight this multi-billion-dollar trade?

b. How unethically could the profits of this business be used?

c. Do you believe consumers have a great responsibility in the counterfeited goods boom?

Exam Paper

How the big five banks are learning to reap rewards

UK banks are making a concerted effort to prove they have as many ethical and environmentally friendly credentials as the companies in the next sector. In fact they are doing better than several other sectors, according to research by Covalence, a Geneva based company that tracks the ethical reputation of multinationals....

Antoine Mach, a Covalence director, attributes the good results partly to the fierce competition within the sector. Ethical standing, he says, "is becoming more and more important for banks as a way for them to differentiate themselves from each other. [...]

Among the 25 banks analysed by Covalence, HSBC came top and Barclays and Royal Bank of Scotland came fourth and ninth respectively [...]

Banks' efforts to improve their eco reputation is not a new phenomenon... In fact, many high-street banks have had environmental policies in place for a number of years. The difference is they are "stepping" their efforts".

This change is reflected by the fact that the big five make it a point to announce their efforts publicly.

Barclays recently issued a Barclays Breathe Card and stated 50% of the profits would go towards projects aimed at reducing carbon emissions...

But ask the average customer on the high street which bank is the greenest and you are likely to hear HSBC.

"HSBC was an early mover. Their CEO quickly grasped that this went beyond a publicity exercise and would be a strategic issue.

HSBC was the first big bank to go carbon neutral in early 2005 and recently announced a $100m donation to four environmental charities and groups. Its most recent environmental policy is to offer customers migration to a paperless green current account which offers discounts on environmentally friendly purchases.

But Mr Propper is skeptical about how effective the banks' green initiatives will prove: "they are comfortably talking about energy use and recycling, but they don't know what to do about the bigger issues." [...]

Anthea Lawson, campaigner at Global Witness, says that it's all very well banks undergoing green makeovers, but they need to look at all aspects of their business.

She says HSBC is a joint arranger in helping the Malaysian timber company Samling sell a 23.3% stake in its business on the Hong Kong stock exchange....

"So [...] while the bank is planting trees to reward its customers for requesting online statements, Samling is cutting them down."

[...]

For consumers looking for a green and ethical bank, Ms Clifton suggests doing some research to "root out" those banks whose practices may contribute to climate change or environmentally destructive causes.

I. Compréhension À rédiger en français

Après avoir lu ce texte attentivement, vous en ferez un résumé en français en 125 mots à 10% près.

II. Traduction

Traduire en français depuis : "Banks' efforts to improve their eco reputation" (ligne 10) jusqu'à "aimed at reducing carbon emissions." (ligne 15)

Unit 16 Europe

"What we share are common values and ambitions, such as sustainable development, solidarity and cohesion, equal opportunities and the fight against all forms of discrimination, universal access to health and education, quality of life and quality in work. And to achieve that, we need a competitive and open Europe..."

President Barroso

Zooming on

1. The economic consequences of the rise of English

In recent years Brussels has been a fine place to observe the irresistible rise of English as Europe's lingua franca. For native speakers of English who are lazy about learning languages (yes, they exist), Brussels has become an embarrassingly easy place to work or visit. English is increasingly audible and visible in this scruffily charming Belgian city, and frankly rampant in the concrete-and-glass European quarter. The union now boasts 27 members and 23 official languages, but the result has been the opposite of a new tower of Babel. Only grand meetings boast interpreters. At lower levels, it turns out, when you put officials from Berlin, Bratislava, Bucharest and Budapest in the same room, English is by far the easiest option. Is this good for Europe? It feels efficient, but being a native English-speaker also seems to many to confer an unfair advantage. It is far easier to argue a point in your mother tongue.

Read the article.

1. Say what the advantages of the rise of English are for the European Union.

2. Now list the drawbacks and the drastic consequences it has had on the job market.

2. Europe's baby shortage starts to move Eastwards

Listen to the recording.

1. What is Jelena's complaint?

2. What is the current issue in Czechoslovakia?

3. Why is it linked to the European Union?

3. The EU Treaty. What Lisbon contains

Eurocrats like to talk about building Europe "step by step". Critics accuse Brussels of slicing away[1] national sovereignty, treaty by treaty. Both versions are correct. [...]

Fans of the Lisbon treaty say it is designed to make EU institutions more efficient and to "streamline[2]" decision-making after the union's enlargement to 27 nations. What does that mean in practice?

The EU's voting system will become simpler and more reflective of a nation's population size. [...]

The treaty creates a full-time standing president of the European Council (which represents national leaders). This figure, probably an ex-prime minister, will be elected by serving heads of government for a two-and-a-half-year stint[3], renewable once, and will prepare and host four or more summits a year.

A new foreign minister will be created by merging two existing posts. Working for both governments and the European Commission, he will have political clout[4], money and his own diplomatic service. He will speak for the EU in places like the United Nations, whenever governments have agreed on a foreign policy position. [...]

The treaty gives legal force to the Charter of Fundamental Rights, a sweeping catalogue of social and civil rights. It is hard to predict how much it will matter. It talks of things such as a right to strike, or a "right of access to preventive health care", that are not in the EU's gift: the Union has few direct powers to regulate industrial disputes or national health services. [...]

National parliaments will be allowed to protest if they consider a proposed EU law unnecessary.

1. *démanteler* 2. *rationaliser* 3. *part de travail* 4. *poids*

Read the text.

1. What is the relevance of the Treaty of Lisbon in terms of foreign policy?

2. What is the use of the Charter of Fundamental Rights?

REPORTING

Do you feel that you are losing part of your national identity because you are a European citizen?

WORDS APART

Institutions **Institutions**

- **border** frontière
- **the Charter of Human Rights** Charte des Droits fondamentaux
- **European Economic Community** Communauté économique européenne
- **European Central Bank** Banque centrale européenne
- **Economic and Monetary Union** Union économique et monétaire
- **European Union** Union européenne
- **eurosceptics** eurosceptiques
- **European Parliament** Parlement européen
- **to hold a referendum** tenir un référendum
- **foreign policy** politique étrangère
- **a summit** un sommet, une réunion
- **single currency** la monnaie unique
- **single market** le marché unique
- **a treaty** un traité

Agreements **Accords**

- **to advocate** être partisan
- **approval** approbation
- **applicant countries** les pays candidats
- **to devise** élaborer
- **to draft** ébaucher
- **enlargement** élargissement
- **a framework** un cadre
- **free flow** la liberté de circulation
- **to join** rejoindre
- **labour market** le marché du travail
- **membership** appartenance
- **rebate** le rabais (britannique)
- **subsidies** les subventions
- **taxation** la fiscalité

Policies **Politiques**

- **To abide by** respecter
- **brain drain** la fuite des cerveaux
- **to break the law** enfreindre la loi
- **commitment** l'engagement
- **decision making process** processus de prise de décision
- **environmentally friendly** la protection de l'environnement
- **to implement** mettre en application la loi
- **to infringe** violer la loi
- **to liberalize** libéraliser
- **migration policy** politique migratoire
- **a patent** un brevet
- **a policy** une politique
- **a proposal** une proposition
- **think tank** une cellule de réflexion

Unit 16 Europe

Why Europe loses in the global competition for talent

Desperate Africans and Asians risk their lives in the Atlantic or the Mediterranean each year in the hope of finding a low-skilled job somewhere in Europe. But why are so few high-skilled engineers, technicians or doctors banging on the door? The best educated seem keener to go almost anywhere but the European Union. In Australia nearly a tenth of the employed population are highly qualified foreigners, in Canada more than 7% and in America just over 3%. The EU manages a paltry[1] 1.7%, or roughly 70,000 highly skilled non-Europeans in the workforce, says Franco Frattini, the commissioner for justice, freedom and security.

That is a problem. Europe's economies, along with everyone else's, increasingly rely on talented workers. But not only are too few ageing natives equipped with the necessary scientific, engineering and other skills; many who are qualified choose to go elsewhere. [...] With skilled labour ever more footloose[2], getting migrants to fill the gaps is essential.

This week the European Commission launched a plan to provide a "blue card" (yes, for the colour of the flag) to help would-be migrants with suitable job offers, and their families, to get into Europe faster. Once inside, the holders could swap[3] jobs, come and go from the EU and, after a while, move freely between countries. Although valid, at first, for just two years, the card would also make it simpler to get long-term residency. [...]

All good in theory, but do not expect much of a threat to America's green (in fact, pink) card. For a start, many European governments are jealous of their control of migration policies and will resist any harmonising effort by Brussels. Look out for possible German or British vetoes. And even if the card would make it easier to get in, it would do nothing to make Europe's economies more attractive in themselves. As long as those economies remain relatively undynamic, the most talented (especially English-speakers) will use their wits to look for work elsewhere.

1. dérisoire – 2. facilité – 3. changer

FIRST STEPS

1. Read the article once and say if it is about:
a. European trade;
b. the European labour market;
c. European trade-unions.

2. Say what the main problem is for Europe:
a. finding jobs; **b.** attracting workers;
c. refusing jobs.

3. Read the article a second time and say who considers Europe a magnet and who doesn't.

MOVING ON

1. Cross out one sentence that does not correspond to what is said in the article.

1st § – lack of skilled workers in Europe
- talented workers avoid Europe
- high-skilled workers head for Europe
- high-skilled workers flee Europe

2nd § – modern economies require brains
- brain drain is a topical issue
- migrant workers are wanted
- Australia experiences a shortage of skilled workers

3rd § – measures are taken at a European level
- a "blue card" is meant to help migrant workers with a job
- only valid migrants could obtain the card
- the blue card would enable the migrants to stay longer.

4th § – the blue card is a myth
- the blue card will be like the green card
- the blue card is not the most important problem
- European countries will have to find other measures

2. In the text find words that mean the same as:

a. knocking, **b.** eager, **c.** trust, **d.** empty space, **e.** procure, **f.** adequate, **g.** change, **h.** menace

3. Compare the attitude of the low-skilled migrants going to Europe with that of the highly skilled.

4. Does the sentence "they go almost anywhere but the European Union" mean:

a. they would go to European countries
b. they wouldn't go there if they could
c. they would choose any other destination?

5. What countries are said to be the most reluctant to welcome migrant workers?

6. What are English speaking workers said to prefer? Why?

7. Translate

From "For a start, many European governments..." (line 21) to "...more attractive in themselves." (line 24)

WRITING (150 words)

Comment on the following passage extracted from *The Economist* (11/2/07)

"Immigration already accounts for most of the limited population growth in Europe. Ageing populations, combined with the natives' lack of ability, or inclination, to do many jobs, mean that more foreign workers are likely to be needed. By one estimate Europe's native-born workforce will shrink by 44m by the middle of the century. Skilled workers will be in especially short supply. Those calling most fiercely for foreigners to go home may come to regret what they wished for."

LANGUAGE AT WORK

1. Pick out verbs in the article with "ed" endings and classify them according to their pronunciation [d]; [t]; [id]. Now listen to the recording and check your answers.

2. Put the verbs in brackets into the correct form.

a. If they (know) in advance, they (choose) not to travel that far.
b. If only they (be) skilled enough, they (have) a great job in Europe! What a pity!
c. If Europe (make) efforts in the future, it (be) the end of the brain drain.

3. Fill in the blanks using either somewhere, anywhere or nowhere.

a. Low-skilled workers would go ...., provided they were given .... to stay.
b. There was .... he could go without qualifications.
c. He would choose .... in Europe if he had .... else to live.

4. Fill in the blanks with a word from the list below: *criteria, member, ageing, welfare, budgetary, enlargement, global.*

The Commission emphasises that all 25 EU .... countries face similar issues of .... populations and related .... problems, ... competition and the need to modernise .... systems. The key factor in the smooth absorption of economic changes brought by .... is careful preparation to help the eight former communist countries to meet the .... for membership.

5. Translate the following sentences into English

a. Bien qu'il n'ait pas de diplôme, il veut travailler aux USA.
b. On lui a conseillé de travailler ailleurs comme il était peu qualifié.
c. Elle était hautement qualifiée alors que lui ne l'était que très peu.

6. Translate the following sentences into French.

a. As long as you don't infringe the law, you can stay.
b. You can stay, provided you have a green card.
c. Given that you own a green card you're welcome to work here.
d. Even though you have a passport you can cross the border.
e. Unlike its neighbours, this European country has become more and more intolerant.

Unit 16 Europe

1. Internship in Europe

YOUR JOB

You study international marketing at a university in France and decide to apply for a work placement in a company in another European country.

YOUR TASK

You write a letter of application responding to the job offer **(see Doc. 1)** you found advertised in "European Student Placement"

Before answering the ad you need to know more about European Student Placement (what you are entitled to get, what documents you need, the answers to different questions about the country, what to expect) **(see Doc. 2 & 3)**.

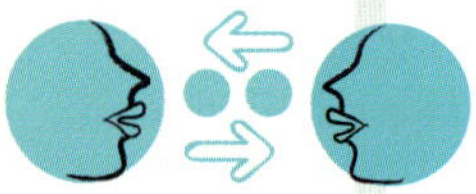

ACTING OUT

You call European Student Placement to ask a few questions first.

Document 1

Job offer

Home | Search

Job title: Marketing Assistant

Company description: Bio-security & Water Treatment solutions Kelso, Scottish Borders

Start date: November/December 2007

Duration: 6 months

Remuneration: £200 per month plus accommodation and travel costs provided (to help with accommodation and living costs)

Job description

- This exciting placement opportunity will give good practical experience to a marketing undergraduate or Masters student. You will be working for an internationally renowned business that has taken students on placement on a regular basis and provides accommodation and travel expenses as well as a small training allowance.
- Carry out general marketing functions, including preparation and editing of sales literature and advertising materials
- Produce customer & prospect mailings
- Produce and distribute press releases and other PR materials
- Assist with promotions & exhibitions
- Carry out market research and prepare targeted prospect databases

Essential requirements

Excellent written & spoken English
French language skills
Knowledge & experience with desktop publishing software
Coursework in marketing theory and practice
Communicative, organised, confident and self-motivated team player, able to work independently

Document 2

A guide for students applying for a placement

Applications

Never use a standard letter to apply which bears no relationship to the position.

Always state why you want to work for this particular company and what you believe you can offer them.

Always check for spelling mistakes and poor grammar in your letter – including spelling the name of the company incorrectly. Get someone else to proof read your letter before sending it.

Preparing for the initial interview

Before you call, think about why you would like to be considered for the position or what you can bring to the role.

Make sure you have read the remuneration details and you are happy with them. Understand that this is a placement/internship – not a holiday job.

When you telephone, try to call from a quiet location, where you are not going to be disturbed and can therefore concentrate on the phone conversation.

Remember to introduce yourself.

Remember the reference code of the placement/s you have applied for.

Understand the Essential Requirements of the role and that you can fulfil them.

Relax, the preliminary interviews are about how you come across and sound over the phone and to check you meet the basic requirements of the role.

Interview with company

Never say anything like: "So what do you do here?" It will show that you haven't been bothered to research them.

Make sure that you have read your own application again just before the interview. This is especially important if there has been a long time between you writing it and the interview – or if you have submitted applications for other jobs at the same time.

Remember, "Attitude is key", to really stand out from the rest. Genuine interest in the company, as well as the job on offer, is vital to getting the placement.

Document 3

Frequently asked questions

2. Your first job abroad

YOUR JOB

You participate in a mobility initiative to experience your first job abroad. You've just read the following ad campaign:

"An initiative to celebrate 50 years of working together"

On the occasion of 50 Years of the Treaty of Rome, which created the European Community, the European Commission will help 50 Europeans to find a first job in another European country. The initiative is launched through Eures, the European jobs network." **(see Doc. 1 & 2)**

YOUR TASK

Visit the Eures website and fill in a Europass CV.

The EU has adopted a European Standard Curriculum Vitae. Suitable for both vocational and academic graduates, this Europass CV gives a clear picture of a candidate's aptitude and skills across EU borders. This CV format is currently available in 20 EU languages in EURES CV-Online.

Send a short description of the reasons why you would like to work abroad, and what experience you expect to gain. **(See Doc. 3 & 4)**

ACTING OUT

Work with a friend in the classroom and simulate a job interview. **(See Doc. 5)**

Visit the Eures website and choose a job offer in the country of your choice. Ask your friend to be the interviewer and to prepare a few questions. Then swap roles.

Document 1

What is Eures?

Eures helps workers to cross borders. EURES – European Employment Services – is a cooperative network designed to facilitate the free movement of workers within the European Economic Area. Switzerland is also involved. Partners in the network include public employment services, trade unions and employers' organisations. The network is coordinated by the European Commission.

The main objectives of Eures are:

- to inform, guide and provide advice to potentially mobile workers on job opportunities as well as living and working conditions in the European Economic Area,
- to assist employers wishing to recruit workers from other countries,
- to give advice and guidance to workers and employers in cross-border regions.

Document 2

Required conditions to participate to the Mobility Initiative

In order to apply, you must be a citizen of one of the Member States of the European Union, or of a country of the European Free Trade Association (Norway, Iceland, Switzerland, and Liechtenstein). The competition is only open to people who have not had a job, studies or internship outside their home country before. In order to register, you must take up a job in another European country for at least four months, and be at least 18 years old.

The European Commission, together with Eures will then select fifty workers proposed for a First Job Abroad. There should be at least one national from each of the thirty-one participating countries.

The main prize is the job you will find and the regular wage that goes with it.

In addition, you will be invited to record your mobility impressions through a blog or an electronic diary. All winners and all hosting organisations will also be invited to a joint celebration event in 2008 in Brussels or in another central EU location. This event will be hosted by the European Commission who will provide plane or train tickets plus hotel accommodation to the winners.

Document 3

Hints and tips

Document 4

Testimony of a student on his return

Document 5

Job interview

You prepare for a job interview

As in your home country, you should prepare yourself thoroughly for a job interview. Make sure you have background information on the firm and be ready to ask questions both about it and particular aspects of the job. You will also be expected to prove your command of the host country's language and illustrate how your key skills and attributes fit in with the employers' requirements for that particular job. Many large firms throughout the EU use assessment centres to judge how potential employees would perform in real-life situations.

Documents you should bring to the interview.

- several copies of your CV in the appropriate language,
- a certified translation of your diploma (usually available from
- your educational institute or the relevant ministry), photocopies of your school leaver's certificate, university degree or other qualification,
- your passport or a valid identity card,
- a copy of your birth certificate,
- the appropriate E-form entitling you to health care coverage (eg. E111); and some passport photos.

Test Yourself

Work moves to jobseekers

The 'brain drain' – the loss of skilled labour through emigration – has in recent years affected many of the new EU Member States – also Poland. Many of the country's workers have moved to Western Europe to look for higher salaries and better working conditions. A recent World Bank report shows that around 35% of all Polish companies indicate shortage of skilled work staff as an obstacle to their performance.

One of them is ROMAG, a producer of design and manufacturing machinery and equipment for the car industry, situated in Pozna in west-central Poland. The country's accession to the European Union in 2004 and the progressive opening of the EU labour market for Polish workers left the company with a lack of qualified technical staff and no short-term solution.

A window of opportunity opened in person of Rainer Dambach, mayor of Pasewalk, a small town in northern Germany, close to the Polish border. Dambach was on a tour to promote his city to Polish employer associations, where he pointed out that many of the former East-German *Länder* are characterised by low salary levels, good infrastructure and a very well trained work force.

While Poland fights with the 'brain drain', Germany's recent and positive economic growth simply caused higher demand of skilled labour than the domestic market could supply.

But the German employment agency was able to offer a tailored solution. Employment advisor Djane Jennricke proposed to organise in cooperation with EURES targeted schooling programmes for local jobseekers and thus provide them with the sought-after skills. It was even possible to identify training facilities that used the same machinery as ROMAG in Poland. A successful cooperation was established.

With public financial support, ROMAG finally opened this autumn its new Pasewalk factory. Educated with the support of EURES, a first group of 10 local jobseekers found a new job and more are to be hired. This positive development has motivated many other producers, not only from Poland, to consider establishing branches in Germany's East – a different success story in Europe's labour market, where mobile employers move to their staff.

http://ec.europa.eu/eures/newsOnPortal, 2007.

Corrigé page 195

I. Compréhension

Write a summary of the article in French. (100 words)

II. Expression

How can you explain the last sentence of the article? What does it show about the European labour market? Is it the vision you have of it? How do you see the European labour market in the near future? (150 words)

Exam Paper

Microsoft is yielding[1] in European antitrust fight

Microsoft has given up its nine-year fight against antitrust regulators in Europe, saying yesterday that it would not challenge a court judgment from last month and would share technical information with rivals on terms the software giant had long resisted. The European competition commissioner, Neelie Kroes, negotiated the terms for Microsoft to share information with rivals. European regulators and some software groups in Europe hailed[2] the deal as a breakthrough that should open the door to freer competition. The agreement was struck in Europe, but it will have consequences worldwide because the terms for licensing Microsoft's intellectual property will be extended to competitors in the United States and in other markets. If the new terms enhance competition, as the regulators say, consumers could benefit from lower prices and faster innovation in software. What is clear is how much Microsoft's room for legal manoeuvering was limited by the ruling last month by the Court of First Instance in Luxembourg. The court reaffirmed that Microsoft, the world's largest software maker, had abused its market power and said the company must obey a 2004 European Commission order to share confidential computer code with competitors.

Microsoft has paid nearly 1 billion euros ($1.43 billion at current exchange rates) in fines[3] since the commission's initial ruling and could face fines of up to 1.6 billion euros more that began accumulating in December 2005 after Microsoft did not start sharing technical information as freely as the European Commission had demanded. Ms. Kroes said she would decide before the end of the year whether Microsoft must pay the additional fines. But as of yesterday, she said, "The major issues concerning compliance have been resolved."

© *New York Times*, October 23rd, 2007, by Steve Lohr and Kevin J. O'Brien

1. *céder* – 2. *saluer* – 3. *amendes*

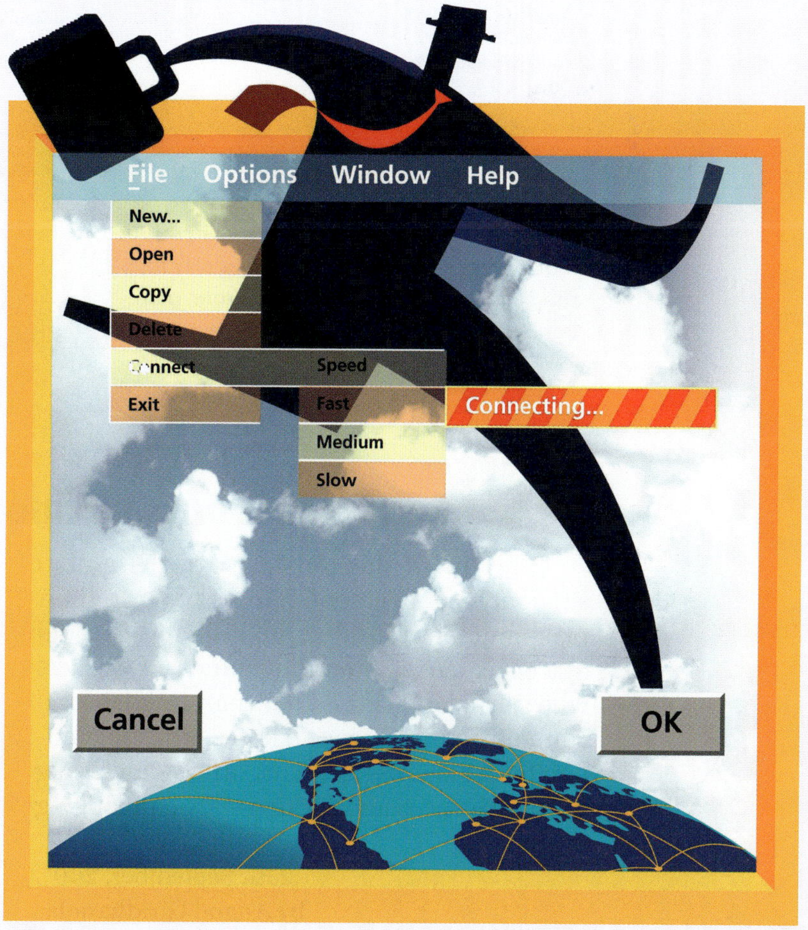

I. Compréhension

À rédiger en français

Write a summary of this article in French. (100 words)

II. Expression

À rédiger en anglais

1. What do you think of Microsoft's sentence handed down by the European Commission?

2. State your reasons. What are the foreseeable consequences?

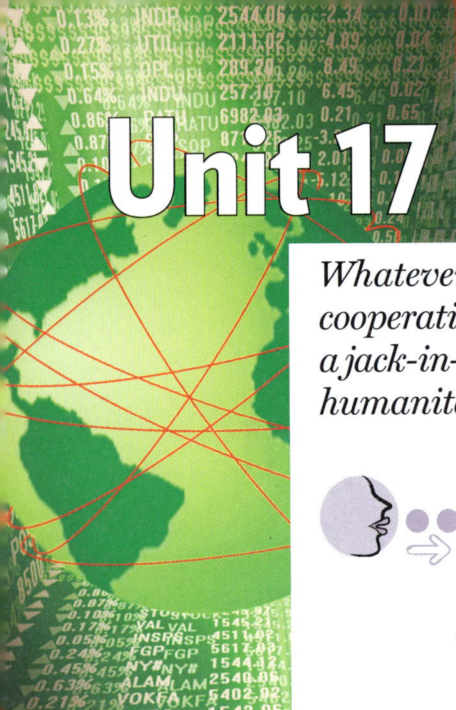

Unit 17 Getting global

Whatever the topic – merger, relocation, population flows, international cooperation or economic exchange – the word globalization springs out like a jack-in-the-box. Not only has it become a password to provide economic and humanitarian help, but also the touchstone for more underground designs.

1. A genuine global patchwork

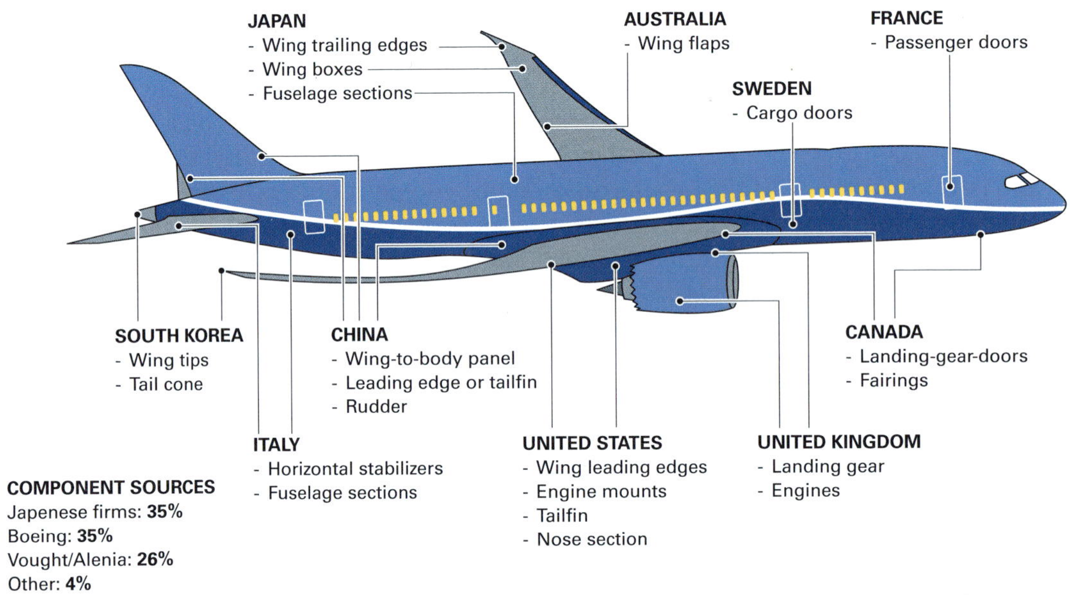

Have a look at the picture.

1. I. List the countries mentioned in this mock-up plan. What role did they play in the building of this plane? Draw your own conclusions.

2. Did you expect Boeing to be made by so many countries? Why or why not?

3. List the reasons why big planes are increasingly "made in the world"?

2. India is outsourcing outsourcing

[...] One of the constants of the global economy has been companies moving their tasks and jobs to India. But rising wages and a stronger currency here, demands for workers who speak languages other than English, and competition from countries seeking to emulate India's success as a back office – including China, Morocco and Mexico – are challenging that model.

25th September, 2007,
by Anand Giridharadas

Read this presentation very carefully.

Give a definition of "outsourcing" and say why outsourcing is changing.

Continue listening to the recording.

1. Give as much information as you can about Infosys: location, payroll, role, etc.

2. Why are language abilities paramount at Infosys?

3. India's consumer boom

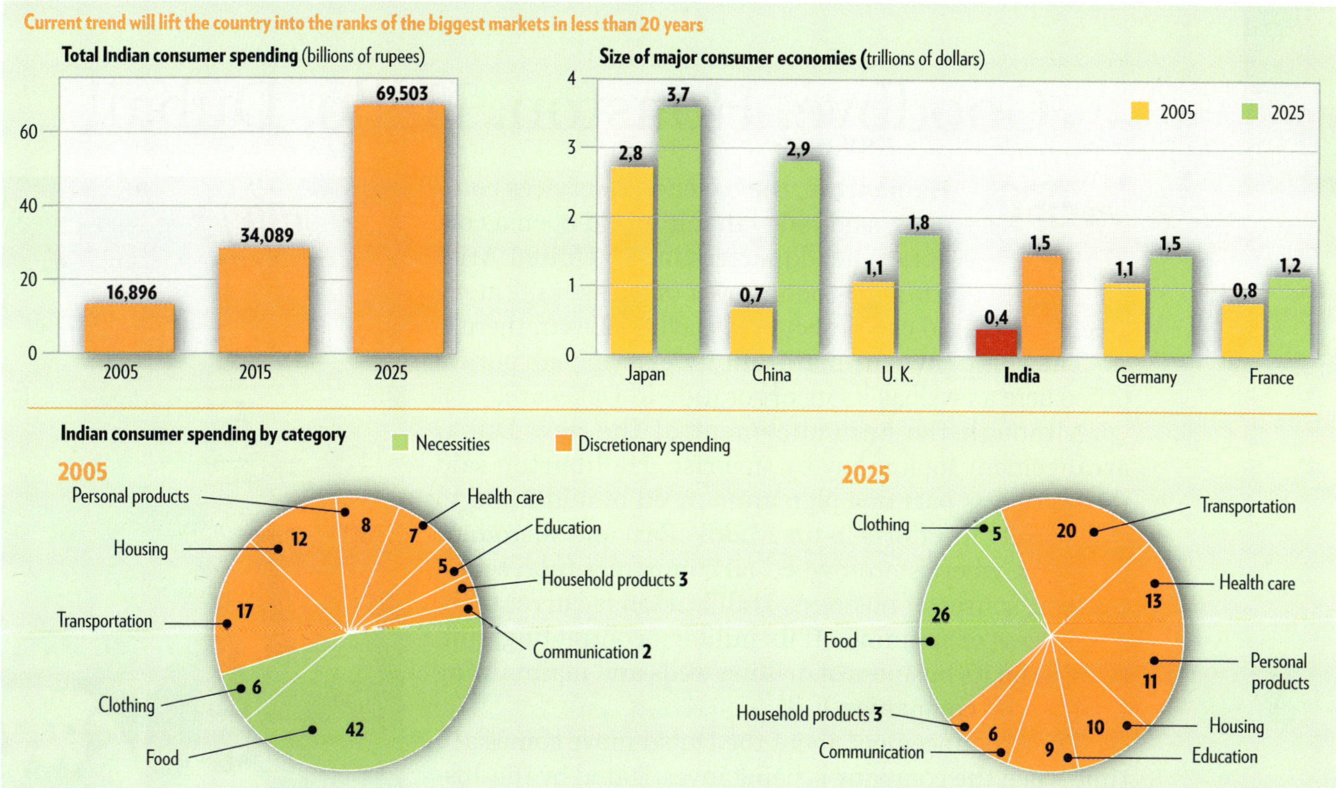

Newsweek, 28th May, 2007

REPORTING

Rich countries represent good opportunities for poor countries, and poor countries represent good opportunities for rich countries. Does that actually result in a win-win outcome?

Read this prospective study.

1. Say what it is all about.
2. Comment on the first bar chart.
3. Define the position of India in the second bar chart.
4. Look at the pie charts and say why India's goals are specific to a booming economy.

WORDS APART

The causes Les causes

- **budget deficit** déficit budgétaire
- **to compete with** concurrencer
- **a downturn** une régression
- **a drop/decline** une baisse
- **the economic situation** la conjoncture
- **forecasts** les prévisions
- **a global corporation** une multinationale
- **insider trading** opération d'initié
- **a lobby** un groupe de pression
- **rates** impôts locaux
- **a slowdown** un ralentissement
- **a subsidiary** une filiale
- **tax evasion** une fraude fiscale
- **unfair competition** concurrence déloyale
- **Value-Added Tax (VAT)** Taxe à la valeur ajoutée (TVA)

The means Les moyens

- **bribes** des pots-de-vin
- **a buyout** un rachat d'entreprise
- **developing countries** pays en voie de développement
- **to freeze prices** bloquer les prix
- **to fund** financer
- **a grant** une subvention
- **to invest abroad** investir à l'étranger
- **a merger** une fusion
- **supply and demand** l'offre et la demande
- **relocation** la délocalisation
- **a takeover** une prise de contrôle
- **tax-free** exempt d'impôt
- **a tax heaven** un paradis fiscal
- **the Third World** le tiers monde
- **the welfare state** l'État-providence

The goals Les cibles

- **abroad/overseas** à l'étranger
- **to capture, tap, corner a market** s'emparer d'un marché
- **economic** qui a trait à l'économie
- **economical** qui réduit les frais
- **foreign trade** le commerce extérieur
- **globalization** la mondialisation
- **growth** la croissance
- **home trade** le commerce intérieur
- **to increase/boost/spur/bolster** dynamiser/augmenter
- **the monopoly** le monopole
- **outsourcing** la délocalisation
- **profitability** la rentabilité
- **the recovery** la reprise économique
- **to settle** s'implanter
- **the standard of living** le niveau de vie

Unit 17 Getting global

Zooming on

Goodbye, Houston. Hello, Dubai!

Halliburton, the big energy services company, said today that it would open a corporate headquarters in the United Arab Emirates boomtown of Dubai and move its chairman and chief executive, David J. Lesar, there.

The company will maintain its existing corporate office here as well as its incorporation in Delaware.

Although the announcement of the new Dubai arrangement took many by surprise, Halliburton said the move was part of a plan announced in mid-2006 to concentrate its efforts in the Middle East and surrounding areas, where state-owned oil companies represent a growing source of business. Halliburton is currently in the process of spinning off its military-contracting unit, to focus on its business of drilling wells and maintaining fields for oil companies. [...]

The announcement about the Dubai move comes at a time when the company is being investigated by the Justice Department for allegations of improper dealings in Iraq, Kuwait and Nigeria. Halliburton has also paid out billions in settlements in asbestos litigation.

Halliburton officials did not elaborate today on what the shift of its top executive might mean. The move seemed to raise questions about whether Halliburton might gain tax advantages or other benefits from shifting into a foreign country with pro-business regulations.

On the face of it, the decision to move Mr. Lesar abroad appeared to have less to do with unwelcome headlines than with shifting epicentres for big energy construction projects and exploration from mature fields in North America toward the Middle East and Africa. The move especially underscores the arrival of Dubai as a center for energy deal-making and commerce, a role once solidly filled by Houston.

"My office will be in Dubai, and I will run our entire worldwide operations from that office," Mr. Lesar said at a conference in Bahrain. "The eastern hemisphere is a market that is more heavily weighted toward oil exploration and production opportunities. Growing our business here will bring more balance to Halliburton's overall portfolio." [...]

Mayor Bill White of Houston learned of Halliburton's move only shortly before the company's announcement this morning, "It is such an international business; the most senior guys are always on the airplanes. Having a corporate group located in the city is different than it used to be. We do not expect Halliburton move to have a big impact on employment here."

FIRST STEPS

1. Present the document. (Origin, date, title, etc.)

2. Have a look at a map and locate Dubai and Houston. Give extra information about these two places.

3. Re-read the title and make "Hello" and "Good-bye" more explicit.

MOVING ON

1. Read the first lines of the article and say what you learn about Halliburton company.

2. List the elements showing Halliburton keeps rooted in the U.S.A.? What does "incorporated" mean to US legislation?

3. Find the words synonymous with the following:

Today / drop /bore / hole/ change / overseas / highlight / manage / bias / equilibrium.

4. Underline the right statement:

a. "The United Arab Emirates boomtown of Dubai" means
- Dubai is a dangerous town.
- Dubai is a fast-developing town.
- Dubai is a very noisy town.

b. When the move to Dubai hit the news, ...
- a lot of people were surprised,
- everybody expected that,
- everybody knew it.

c. The company chiefly focuses on
- developing its military branch,
- competing with European companies there,
- tapping new oil markets.

d. The company is currently accused of...
- illegal transactions in the Middle East,
- still using asbestos,
- producing too much oil.

e. Some even think the company set up there in order to...
- help the United Arab Emirates,
- escape Uncle Sam,
- promote its executives.

f. Houston Mayor thinks the move...
- is dramatic for the town,
- will increase the number of jobless,
- will have no impact on the town economy.

5. Dubai is 17,000 miles from Houston. What problem does that distance raise?

6. Why do state-owned oil companies represent a growing source of business? What about their future? Compare them with the "Seven Sisters".

7. Does this investment abroad make sense? Why or why not? To what extent could it be detrimental to Houston?

8. Translate

Translate from "Halliburton officials..." (line 22) to "... Foreign country with pro-business regulations." (line 25)

WRITING (150 words)

Do you think relocation is one of the means to give a company a new start?

LANGUAGE AT WORK

1. Spot the stress in the following series of words.

a. litigation / regulation / construction / decision / exploration / operation / production.

b. Africa / America / Nigeria.

c. energy / company / military.

2. Guess the translation of the following verb-noun families:

a. to announce, the announcement,

b. to maintain, the maintenance,

c. to regulate, the regulation,

d. to settle, the settlement,

e. to arrive, the arrival.

3. Fill in the gaps with 'said' or 'told'.

a. Halliburton was ... to be hiding the truth.

b. The Chief executives .... it was necessary to move.

c. We are .... many national companies try to challenge the leader.

d. They .... the debunkers that the distance wasn't an obstacle.

4. Complete with the appropriate tenses.

a. U.S. Petroleum Companies .... in the Middle East several years ago. *(set up)*

b Experts predict that national companies .... international giants in the near future. *(challenge)*

c. They .... in Dubai since last year. *(be)*

d. The C.E.O. announced that he .... a decision next week. *(make)*

5. Translate into French.

a. Jack wasn't listening, that's why he couldn't answer.

b. While they were deciding about the new location of the plant, a higher bidder struck the deal.

c. They have been arguing for hours.

d. The C.E.O. had been keeping in touch with Arab countries to prepare the ground.

6. Translate into English.

a. Cette nouvelle n'aurait pas dû étonner les Américains.

b. La société devrait s'implanter dans le centre de la ville.

c. Je pense que des intermédiaires ont dû intervenir avant ce changement.

Unit 17 Getting global

1. Striking a deal

YOUR JOB
You work in the P.R. Department of the company eBay.

YOUR TASK
The company manager bought the free Internet telephone service Skype for $2.6 billion. After several meetings, D-day has come and both Boards of Directors are to meet in the next few weeks to strike a deal.

1. Choose the place, date, and time of the meeting and the officials invited.
2. Devise the card to be sent to the guests. Use the prompts.
3. Write a hundred-word article to be sent to the press. Use the prompts and **Documents 1, 2 and 3**.

ACTING OUT
You will write down the speech to be read by the C.E.O. on that day and deliver it in front of the class. Use the prompts and **Document 2**.

Document 1

The power of three

At its annual "eBay Live" convention, the company will announce plans to integrate Skype into its U.S marketplace for the first time. Sellers can choose to include Skype buttons in their auctions for a few carefully chosen product categories such as cars, real estate and diamond solitaire rings. CEO Meg Whitman hopes that this time-honored sales technique – good old-fashioned conversation – will generate more trust between buyers and sellers, and increase the number of sales – and eBay's commissions. [...]

Whitman, 49, has responded to eBay's new challenges by aggressively diversifying the company. She bought not just Skype but payment firm PayPal in 2002 and online retailer Shopping.com last year, and last month introduced eBay Express, which lets customers purchase new books, clothes and consumer electronics for fixed prices.

Newsweek, 19th June, 2006

Document 2

Celebrating a merger

Document 3

Spotlight

eBay Headquarters:
2145 Hamilton Avenue
San Jose, California 95125

eBay is a popular online auction site where users can sell almost anything around the world.

Founded in 1995, eBay Inc. connects hundreds of millions of people around the world every day, empowering them to explore new opportunities and innovate together. eBay Inc. does this by providing the Internet platforms of choice for global commerce, payments and communications. Since its inception, eBay Inc. has expanded to include some of the strongest brands in the world.

http://www.ebay.com

PayPal Headquarters
Park North 2211 North First Street
San Jose, CA 95131

Founded in 1998, PayPal, an eBay company, enables any individual or business with an email address to send and receive payments online securely and easily using a bank account, credit card or stored balance.

Because PayPal allows customers to shop online without sharing their financial information with merchants, privacy is built into the service. PayPal has nearly 143 million accounts and is available to users in 190 markets around the world.

https://www.paypal.com.

Skype Headquarters
Skype Technologies S.A.
22/24 Boulevard Royal, L-2449 Luxemburg

Skype was founded in 2003 by Niklas Zennström and Janus Friis. Skype created a little piece of software that makes communicating with people around the world easy and fun. With Skype you can say hello or share a laugh with anyone, anywhere. And if both of you are on Skype, it's free. Skype is available in 28 languages and is used in almost every country around the world. It is based in Luxemburg.It's considered easy to download and use, and works with most computers. Once you download, register and install the software, you'll need to plug in a headset, speakers or USB phone to start using Skype.

Skype was acquired by eBay on September 12, 2005.

http//www.skype.com

Shopping.com Headquarters
2145 Hamilton Avenue
San Jose, California 95125

Shopping.com wants you to compare before you shop. The company operates a leading comparison shopping Web site where users can check prices on millions of retail items and read product reviews. The site aggregates product and pricing information from thousands of online merchants and redirects interested buyers to the merchant's Web site to make their purchase. Revenue comes from lead referral fees based on the number of times a user clicks through to a merchant's Web site from Shopping.com.

The company was acquired by online auction operator eBay in 2005.

http//www.shopping.com

PROMPTS

- You are welcome *Vous êtes bienvenus*
- I'm delighted to meet you *Je suis enchanté de vous rencontrer*
- Can I introduce you to Mr X? *Puis-je vous présenter M. X ?*
- Here's Mr X. *Voici M. X*
- Glad to meet you *Ravi de vous rencontrer*
- I was looking forward to seeing you *J'étais impatient de vous rencontrer*
- I've heard of you *J'ai entendu parler de vous*
- Here's our new partner *Voici notre nouvel associé*
- To applaud/to clap one's hands *Applaudir*
- To shake hands with someone *Serrer la main à quelqu'un*
- To sign a contract *Signer un contrat*
- To drink a welcoming toast *Porter un toast de bienvenue*
- To wish good luck *Souhaiter bonne chance*

Unit 17 Getting global

2. Comparing documents

YOUR JOB
You are a tour operator working in Britain. You have been asked to investigate a new loophole: more and more people are looking for new working opportunities – dream businesses – abroad.

YOUR TASK
You have to promote some destinations. Read and listen to the five documents.
1. Design a short incentive document.
2. List the advantages and drawbacks expatriates might meet.
3. Analyse each document connected to a location and draw conclusions.
4. Make your choice.

ACTING OUT
Justify your viewpoint orally.

Document 1

The Spanish dream

The most popular choice amongst those leaving Britain is to find a business for sale in Spain. There are many reasons as to why this is such a relocation hotspot including the beautiful beaches, towns and cities, as well as many well established ex pat communities that make running a business in Spain appealing. With Spain being a major tourist destination many of the businesses for sale in Spain include bars, nightclubs and restaurants. However there are other businesses in Spain advertised for sale including beauty salons and hairdressers. As is to be expected most of these businesses are located in the popular tourist areas, so you can make the most of the tourist trade.

http://www.vault.com
Published on 26 September 2007

Document 2

Getting a job in Ireland

http://www.vault.com
Published on 30 October 2007

Document 3

Working in France

By Finn Skovgaard,
14 December 2007

Document 4

Buy a business in the sunshine state

One of the easiest ways of living year round in Florida is by means of an *E-2 Treaty Investor Visa* which requires the purchase of a qualifying business. You can choose from a wide range of businesses that can provide you with a good income and a new life in the sun. Investment in the business can be from as little as $100,000 and with the help of a good business broker in Florida you should be able to find that perfect business and the opportunity to do something that you really want to do.

John Wise is a business specialist with Real Estate Professionals of America, which is part of the *Century 21 Group* - the largest Real Estate Company in the world. For many years John has specialised in assisting British clients to relocate and here are the businesses most in demand.

Pool Service – hard but enjoyable work in which the business takes care of private or commercial pools. There are more than 1 million private pools in Florida and thousands more being built every year. Easy to run and expand and can produce good profits.

Lawn or Tree Service – most homeowners prefer to get someone else to look after their lawns and gardens. Hard work in the summer but easy in the winter months.

Property Management – always one of the most popular businesses but difficult to get E-2 visas in recent years. However, we currently have a limited number of property management franchise opportunities in Orlando, offered by a large organization and all to date have received E-2 visas. Retail - the most popular are gift shops and flower shops but we can usually find anything that you prefer.

Food Related – Coffee Shops and Tea Rooms are always in demand and restaurants of every kind are always available.

Contractor – If you have a trade we have a business for you. We sell lots of painting, plumbing, mechanic, air conditioning, electrical, building, and carpentry businesses.

Manufacturing – small and medium size manufacturing companies can often be easy to run and produce good profits.

Taxi and Limousine services – these are usually available throughout Florida.

Hair Salons and Day Spas – one of our most popular types of business.

For More Information – Contact John Wise
Real Estate Professionals of America

Email: info@realestateprofessionals.co.uk

Document 5

Doing business the Chinese way

Now that China, the most enormous market in the world has opened up to business outsiders, entrepreneurs have new opportunities to grow almost without limits. But you should know, a clock is ticking. What are the opportunities in China? China is the cheapest manufacturing hub of the world, it makes:

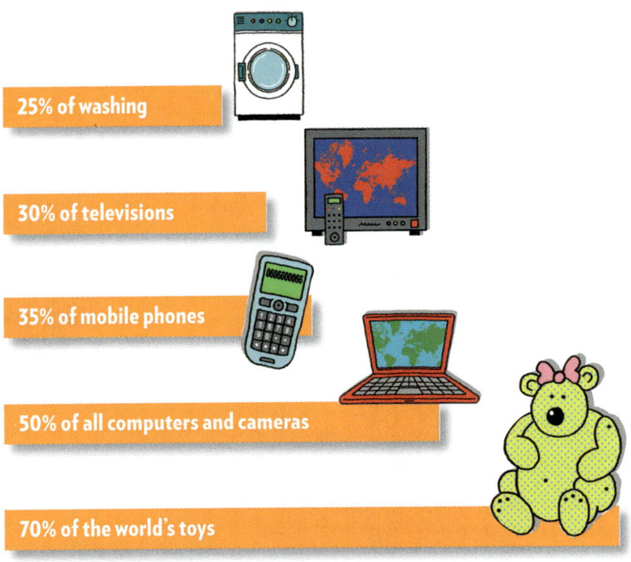

There is opportunity in China for entrepreneurs, specifically in these industries:

- Telecommunication equipment
- Information technology
- Medical equipment
- Oil and gas
- Biotechnology and pharmaceuticals
- Environmental protection

http://www.startupnation.com

Unit 17 Getting global

Test Yourself

Lost in translation

[...] Five years ago there were 10 call centers in the Philippines; today there are 108 employing 200,000 Filipinos, mostly in their mid-20s. Last year the industry generated $2.3 billion in revenues. Call centers account for about 80 per cent of the players in the business-process-outsourcing (BPO) industry. [...]

What is not mentioned is that down in the trenches, the burgeoning BPO industry is already encountering growing pains. The problem: many call centers can't keep up with demand because they can't find enough employees who speak "proper" English. "For every 100 people that apply in the call centers, only three to five are accepted. Most are rejected because of poor English communication skills. Almost all Filipinos understand English, but when we test the applicants with simulated phone calls, they take a while to reply because they translate the words into Tagalog (the local language) in their minds first. Weak English is an issue for even the largest call centers, which traditionally attract the most promising talent from the country's best schools. [...]

Now, to become more globally competitive, the government is scrambling to promote English to young people as the ticket to a good career. Three years ago the Department of Education reinstated English as the primary language of instruction in schools. Various business groups, including both the U.S. and European chambers of commerce, are sponsoring public-relations programs lauding the career benefits of English; one of the campaigns is called "English is cool" and is designed to break people of their habit of speaking "Taglish" – a mix of English and Tagalog. In addition, in a recent speech in Manila, president Gloria Macapagal Aroyo has promised to set aside $9.6 million to help put so-called near hires through a 100-hour English refresher course. [...] Just imagine the problem we get when an American says to one of our call-center employees, 'Get outta here,'" jokes Mitch Locsin, executive director of the Business Processing Association of the Philippines. "And the call-center employee responds, 'Sir, you want me to put down the phone already?"

Newsweek, May 29th, 2006

I. Compréhension

Après une lecture attentive du document ci-dessus vous en ferez un compte rendu **en français** de 180 à 200 mots. Vous indiquerez le nombre de mots utilisés.

Corrigé page 195

II. Expression

1. Why does Indian BPO industry worry about its operators? (50 words)

2. Do you support the idea that English should be the necessary passport to get a job? (120 words)

Exam Paper

Made in China: tainted food, fake drugs and dodgy paint

China is facing a global crisis of consumer confidence as the country's food safety watchdog acknowledged this week that almost a fifth of the domestic products it inspects fail to reach minimum standards. Following a number of contamination scandals in the US, the world's biggest exporter is struggling to prove that it can match quality with quantity. [...]

Officials said hundreds of bottles of fake human blood protein were found in hospitals and excessive amounts of additives and preservatives were detected in children's snacks. Shi Ying, 50, a businesswoman, said she was so concerned about food safety that she found it difficult to shop. "I dare not eat farmed fish or meat because most are fed with growth pills or pumped with bad additives. I worry about vegetables in case they are tainted with pesticide. I even think twice about the water I drink because it might contain heavy metals." [...]

While the worst violations are in the domestic market, the repercussions are felt beyond the country's borders. China fills the shelves of Wal-Mart, Tesco and Sainsbury's with low-price products. But as its world presence has grown, so have concerns about safety.

First, there was a mysterious spate of cat and dog deaths in the US this year that more than 1m Thomas & Friends toy trains coated with poisonous lead paint from China. Then, Independence Day fireworks were withdrawn in the US because of their dangerously unpredictable sense of direction. [...]

Other countries have also expressed concern. Last year, European customs officers seized fake birth control pills and HIV drugs from China. According to Mr Mandelson, the EU trade commissioner, half the counterfeit goods found in the EU originate in China. [...] In an attempt to quell concerns, the Chinese government closed 180 food factories in the first half of this year and seized tonnes of sweets, pickles, crackers and seafood tainted with formaldehyde, illegal dyes and industrial wax.

But the government also stands accused of reacting slowly to scandal rather than dealing with the root causes: a lack of trust in the safety standards of a country with a profit-first economic policy and a secretive political system. [...] Last month, the former head of China's food and drug agency was sentenced to death for accepting 6.5m yuan (£425,000) in bribes from pharmaceutical companies to expedite the approval of new drugs.

I. Compréhension **À rédiger en anglais**

Après une lecture attentive du document ci-dessus vous en ferez un compte rendu de 180 à 200 mots. Vous indiquerez le nombre de mots utilisés.

II. Traduction

Vous traduirez le deuxième paragraphe, depuis "Officials said..." (ligne 5) jusqu'à "heavy metals" (ligne 10)

Unit 18 Money matters

Money talks and money matters!
Even if new means of payment, the launch of new currencies, investing facilities, and new accounting codes have changed our relationship to money, we are still faced with financial scandals, personal and economic crises, crashes, bankruptcies and corruption in today's world.

Zooming on

1. Banks bid for green credentials

From credit cards to current accounts, new financial products are being launched – all hawking their environmental credentials.

But critics suggest banks are simply dusting off run-of-the-mill financial products and giving them a "greenwash".

The biggest green product to be launched of late has been Barclaycard's Breathe credit card. It pledges to plough 50% of the profits it makes from Breathe into carbon reduction initiatives. Yet, the only way to boost those profits is for customers to build up credit card debt at an interest rate of 14.9%. The rate, although competitive, is a long way from being a best buy."It is quite a strange way to contribute to the environment, building up expensive debt," says the spokeswoman for a financial information firm.

"Surely if people want to help with carbon reduction they should go for a marketplace best buy and give a little to charities in the sector."

HSBC has pledged to pay £5 to environmental causes for each current account customer who moves to a paperless account. Paperless not only means joining the "no statement" trend - but also dispensing with a chequebook.

Meanwhile, Britannia building society has launched a children's investment product, called the Planet Saver. For every new account opened between July and September, Britannia says, a tree will be planted.

The child gets a paper certificate telling him or her that they have adopted a new tree. As a result, several thousand trees are likely to be planted.

BBC News, July 9th, 2007,
by Julian Knight

2. New means of payment

Read the article.

1. Say what the three banks are and what policy they are adopting.

2. Explain why some kind of hypocrisy is suspected in this ethical behaviour.

Listen to the recording.

Say what the new means of payment are. Their purpose?The risks?

3. Enron's second coming?

In May 2005 NYSE Magazine portrayed Angelo Mozilo, the chairman and C.E.O. of Countrywide Financial, the nation's largest mortgage lender as a heckuva guy — a man from a humble background determined to help other people, especially members of minority groups, achieve the American dream of homeownership.

The article didn't mention one of Mr. Mozilo's other distinguishing characteristics: the extraordinary size of his paychecks. Last year Mr. Mozilo was paid $142 million.

These days, of course, Mr. Mozilo doesn't look like such a wonderful guy, after all. Instead, he's starting to bring back memories of other people who used to be praised not just as great businessmen but as great human beings — people like Enron's K. Lay and WorldCom's B. Ebbers.

In late 2006, even as Countrywide began using shareholders' money to buy back its own stock at more than $40 a share — it's now worth only $19 — Mr. Mozilo was selling.

Again, unless the stock sales lead to insider-trading charges, there's nothing in this story that involves illegality. Still, how can it be that so soon after Enron, WorldCom and other scandals rocked the business world, we're once again hearing about executives cashing in just before their companies are revealed as less successful than advertised? The answer, of course, is that we never dealt properly with those scandals.

© *New York Times*, October 1st, 2007, by Paul Krugman

Read the article.

1. Explain what Angelo Mozilo did. What is suspected?
2. What do they compare Countrywide with? Why?
3. Have you heard of other financial scandals?

REPORTING

Banks and financial institutions are offering more and more "services" to the public nowadays. What are the advantages and/or dangers to consumers?

WORDS APART

Accounting Comptabilité

- **assets** actifs
- **balance** sheet bilan
- **chartered accountant** un expert comptable
- **deadline** échéance
- **expenses** dépenses
- **intangibles** immobilisations incorporelles
- **ledger** livre comptable
- **liabilities** passifs
- **overheads** frais généraux
- **offshore** hors contrainte d'une zone monétaire
- **to pay by instalments** fractionner les paiements
- **profit and loss account** compte de résultat
- **to purchase on credit** acheter à crédit
- **a tax haven** un paradis fiscal

Banking operations Opérations bancaires

- **balance** le solde
- **cash dispenser** distributeur automatique
- **current account** compte courant
- **debit** débit
- **deposit** dépôt
- **fees** frais, agios
- **interest rate** taux d'intérêt
- **to lend** prêter
- **a loan** prêt
- **a mortgage** une hypothèque
- **an overdraft** un découvert
- **to pay off** rembourser
- **a savings account** compte épargne
- **a withdrawal** un retrait

Investing Investir

- **bear market** marché à la baisse
- **a bond** une obligation
- **blue chip** valeur vedette
- **a broker** courtier
- **a bull market** marché à la hausse
- **a crash** crack boursier
- **a currency** une devise
- **insider trading** délit d'initié
- **an investor** un investisseur
- **a magnate/tycoon** un magnat de la finance
- **a shareholder/stockholder** un actionnaire
- **to speculate** spéculer
- **the stock exchange** la bourse
- **to quote** coter en bourse

Unit 18 Money matters

Zooming on

When balance sheets collide with the new economy

At issue is a growing collection of crucial resources known as intangibles[1]: assets or liabilities[2] that have no obvious physical presence, but that represent real value or vulnerabilities.

Patents[3], trademarks, copyrights and brand recognition are most commonly recognized as intangibles. But as the nature of doing business has changed, the list has grown. For example, the most valuable assets of an innovation-based company today – its intellectual property, software investments, staff and managerial expertise, research and development, advertising and market research, and business processes – have no natural home on the balance sheet[4]. They can be recorded as expenses or sometimes, in the case of intellectual property, as liabilities, says Nir Kossovsky, the chief executive of Steel City Re, which assesses and insures companies' intangible assets. But often, they do not make their way onto the accounting ledger[5] at all.

Reputation is one such intangible asset; ask Mattel about its value, after its third recall of toys this summer. What's more, the market is demanding that companies prove that their business conduct is environmentally and socially conscious – not on the basis of ideology, but because to do otherwise exposes them to financial risk. The vulnerability of a global economy to cataclysmic risk, from terrorism to pandemics and extreme weather, is also pushing companies to disclose processes and strategies they have to ensure continuity after a disaster.

But because accountants have found it impossible to determine the value or the risk of such assets with certainty or objectivity, official financial accounting rules give intangibles a wide berth[6].

Yet today's markets are being transformed by intangibles, and a growing number of companies are scrambling to find the methods that will help them better use, develop and communicate about them. "In the last three years, investors have been looking at how social and environmental issues translate directly to market value," said Jed Emerson, a senior fellow at the Generation Foundation. [...]

"Today, it's about AIDS and education systems in South Africa, and things that you wouldn't have historically heard major C.E.O.'s voicing concern about." Stakeholders in emerging markets "want to know how investment translates to jobs, environmental concerns, etc."

© *New York Times*, September 9th, 2007, by Denise Caruso

1. *immobilisations incorporelles* – 2. *actifs, passifs* – 3. *brevets* – 4. *bilan* – 5. *livre comptable* – 6. *zone de manœuvre*

FIRST STEPS

1. Read the text once and say if the main topic of the article is:
a. accounting, **b.** investment, **c.** marketing.

2. Say if the account is:
a. informative, **b.** subjective, **c.** debatable

MOVING ON

1. In the following list circle what is said to matter more today in the "new economy":

Skills / reputation / tradition / customer loyalty / quarterly reports / innovation / marketing / deadlines / equipment / accountability / management.

2. Explain the effect it has on the balance sheet.

3. Say if the following statements are right or wrong, and justify by quoting from the text.

a. Intellectual property can be accounted for, contrary to other intangibles.
b. Mattel's reputation was tarnished when they renamed their products.
c. A socially and environmentally-friendly attitude could endanger companies, financially speaking.
d. Companies need to resort to all kinds of techniques in case of natural catastrophes.
e. It's difficult to account for today's intangibles.

4. Find words that mean the same as:

a. acknowledged **c.** besides **e.** epidemics
b. increased **d.** aware **f.** struggling

5. Explain what is meant by:

"In the last three years, investors have been looking at how social and environmental issues translate directly to market value."

6. What is at stake now in South Africa is?

a. to make sure ethical issues are respected,
b. to contribute to more investments,
c. to satisfy stakeholders.

7. What is the stakeholder's major concern today in these countries?

8. How can you explain it?

9. How can you account for the title of the article after a closer analysis of the text?

10. Translate

Translate from "What's more, the market is demanding that companies prove that their business conduct is environmentally and socially conscious..." (line 14) to "...they have to ensure continuity after a disaster." (line 18)

WRITING (150 words)

Explain the following passage and give your opinion.
Do you think that it is important that intellectual property and patents should be protected?
Can you give examples of countries which do not respect this right?
To what extent would you say that not respecting property rights is comparable to stealing? Give precise examples to state your reasons.

LANGUAGE AT WORK

1. Read the following words and underline the stressed syllable(s), then listen to the tape and correct your answers.

Environmentally / historically / vulnerability / intellectual property / insurance / valuables / terrorism / intangibles / reputation / tremendous.

2. Use words from the list below to fill in the blanks: *broker, return, bearish, bullish, shareholder, profit, blue chips.*

a. If the market is .... don't expect a big .... on your investment.

b. As a ...., ask your .... to help you buy .... when the market is .... and then try to sell them at a .... .

3. Use "make" or "do".

a. I need to .... out a cheque to my banker to .... sure I am not in the red.

b. If you want to .... business and .... profit, you must .... the difference between you and your competitors.

c. .... me a favour, don't .... a fuss about all this, just .... it and I'll .... with it.

4. Fill in the blanks with a word from the following list: *ledger, invoice, balance sheet, expenses, bookkeeper.*

a. A .... keeps track of financial transactions in the .... .

b. A reminder of the .... needs to be sent when a customer has not settled his account.

c. When a company is audited all the .... are checked and the .... is thoroughly examined.

5. Translate the following sentences into English.

a. J'aimerais faire un prêt bancaire. Pouvez-vous m'indiquer le meilleur taux d'intérêt que je puisse obtenir ?

b. Attention de ne pas être à découvert si vous ne voulez pas payer des agios bancaires.

c. Si vous aviez eu connaissance de la situation plus tôt vous n'auriez pas emprunté autant d'argent !

6. Translate the following passage into French.

Remember the days when loans were discussed over lunch at the Rotary Club and sealed with a handshake? Pretty soon, the idea of a banker knowing the name of the person he is lending to – let alone inside details of his credit history – could be as quaint a feature of banking's past as bowler hats and Bonnie and Clyde.

© *The Economist*, Newspaper Limited, London, May 19th, 2007

1. Asking for offshore services

YOUR JOB

You, John Meryll, Assistant Financial Director, work for a US company that deals with service and wants to conclude a new service contract for a business in Italy. It is contract work, and your company wants to use Mr Jonhson's services, an independent IT consultant, by sub-contracting him out to one of your clients in Italy.
You're asked by the financial manager to investigate the possibilities of reducing the company's income tax exposure in Italy (rates up to 45%) by using an offshore company. After having collected information about offshore companies, and having weighed up the pros and cons of going offshore, you send an email to Ocra, an offshore company **(see Doc. 1)**, to explain your request. **(see Doc. 2)**
Ocra's answer to your email **(see Doc. 3)** gives you full details of the possible solutions they can suggest.

YOUR TASK

Having discussed it with your financial director, you now write Ocra a short letter to confirm your decision, insisting on the reasons for your choice and your exact request.

ACTING OUT

You call Ocra's Consulting Department and ask them to send you their complete offshore file (including full details, guarantees, legal framework, financial documents and correspondents).

Document 1

Ocra Worldwide: a personal service company

Our core skills are the establishment and administration of secure and efficient corporate trust structures to reduce tax, protect wealth and facilitate international business. Specifically, we deliver private and cost-effective offshore and onshore company management and trustee services.

"The reasons and benefits for going offshore are many."

The motivations for individuals and corporations to utilise offshore planning and offshore companies include the desire to:

- Reduce tax
- Protect assets
- Manage risk
- Reduce costs
- Maintain privacy
- Avoid bureaucracy
- Enhance assets

www.google.com

Going Offshore: the reasons	Offshore companies applications
Security of property rights	Trading
Accessing low cost areas	Investment
Banking privacy	Holding
Availability of offshore experts	Financing
Enhanced privacy	Professional services or consultancy
Customs and duty exemptions	Patent, royalty and copyright holding
Higher yields and returns	Ship management and yacht owning
Reduced taxation	Personal and corporate tax planning
The availability of sophisticated banking facilities	

Document 2

Email written to Ocra

From: John Merryl
Date: March 15th 2008
Object: Offshore Services
To: Octa

We are an American corporate service company located in Oregon, and are about to sign a contract with one of our clients in Italy. We have a deal with Mr Jonhson, an independent IT consultant who works for us.

We are thinking of using an offshore company to try and reduce our tax exposure. Could you please send us information and suggest possible solutions?

John Merryl
Assistant Financial Director
Easytime corporate service company
Oregon

Document 3

Ocra's answer

From: Ocra
Date: March 25th 2008
Object: Re: Offshore Services
To: John Merryl

Dear Mr Merryl,

We suggest that you set up a new personal service company in a country which has a good tax treaty with Italy, thus ensuring – with some proper structuring – that any fees paid for Mr Johnson's work in Italy are taxed in the country of residence of the service company. The company makes him available for work in Italy.

The personal service company is fully owned by a personal service company set up by Mr Johnson under offshore jurisdiction. Thus, it is necessary that the service company is established in a country which does not levy a withholding tax on dividends paid abroad.

A country meeting these conditions is Malta. Although the Italian-source fees received by the Maltese company are subject to tax at a rate of 35%, two-thirds of the Maltese tax will be refunded upon the distribution of the dividends offshore, thus reducing the tax burden in Malta to 11.67%. Malta does not levy a withholding tax on dividends.

We remain at your disposal for any further information.

Please send us confirmation of your acceptance by email stating your precise request.

Ocra's Consulting Department

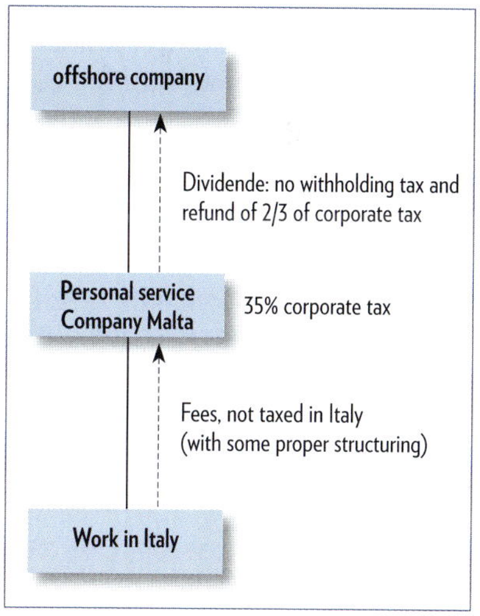

2. Describing graphs and charts

YOUR JOB

You work for an internet company that is carrying out surveys about online research driving offline sales. You have gathered information about online channels and are asked to give a clear account of the figures you found.

YOUR TASK

First study carefully the reference documents on page 187 and the information they contain. Then do the following tasks.

- Comment on Document 1 below. Sum up in a few sentences the most important information it contains.
- Draw your conclusions.

ACTING OUT

Now read **(See Doc. 2)** and comment on the evolution from 2007 to 2012.
Read it to the class as you would do when delivering your results to your supervisor.
What conclusion should marketing executives and business strategists draw from these surveys, according to you?

Document 1

Here comes the "Precision Shopper."

Any retailer who isn't using the online channel to promote offline sales—as well as online sales—is missing a sizable opportunity.

Looked at another way, for every $1 in online sales, the Internet influenced $3.45 of store sales. "Online consumers are becoming precision shoppers," says Jeffrey Grau, eMarketer Senior Analyst and author of the new report, Multi-Channel Retailing, "They are availing themselves of the wealth of information resources online to discover and evaluate products, compare them and find where they can be purchased."

US WEB-INFLUENCED RETAIL STORE SALES VS. RETAIL E-COMMERCE SALES, 2007 & 2012 (BILLIONS AND CAGR*)

	2003	2004	2005
Web influenced store sales	$470.7	$1,124.0	19.0%
Retail e-commerce sales	$136.4	$240.2	12.0%

Note: eMarketer benchmarks its retail e-commerce sales figures against US Department of Commerce data, for wich the last full year measured was 2007; excludes travel sales.

* CAGR = compound annual growth rate

eMarketer, February 2008

Document 2

Web-influenced stores combined with e-commerce sales

According to eMarketer estimates, combined Web-influenced store sales and retail e-commerce sales accounted for 15% of retail sales in 2007.

US WEB-INFLUENCED RETAIL STORE SALES AND RETAIL E-COMMERCE SALES AS A PERCENT OF TOTAL RETAIL INDUSTRY SALES, 2007-2012

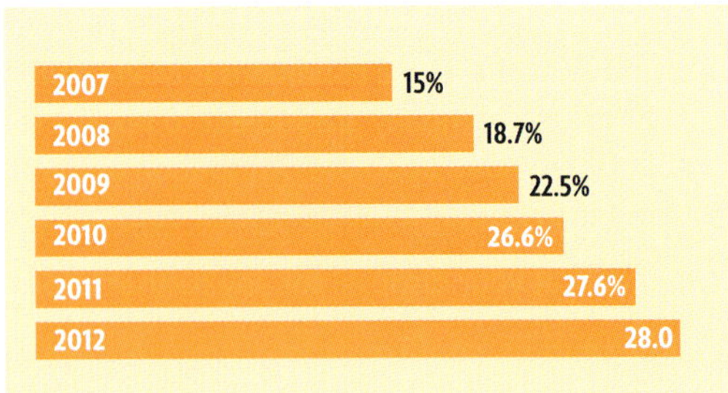

Note: eMarketer benchmarks its retail e-commerce sales figures against US Department of Commerce data, for wich the last full year measured was 2007; excludes travel sales.

eMarketer, February 2008

REFERENCE DOCUMENT

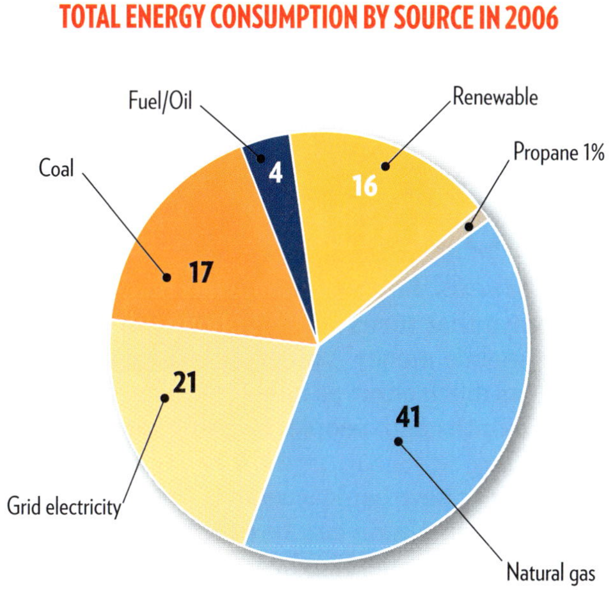

A pie chart is the best way of visualizing figures, essentially proportions or shares.

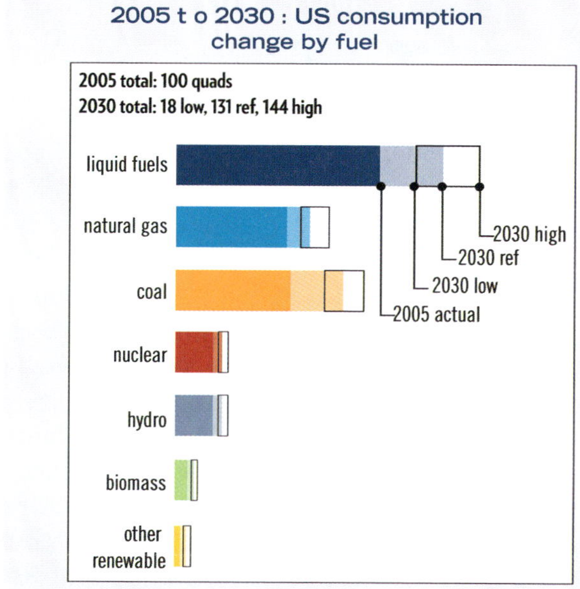

A bar chart is useful to present a trend, to compare few elements

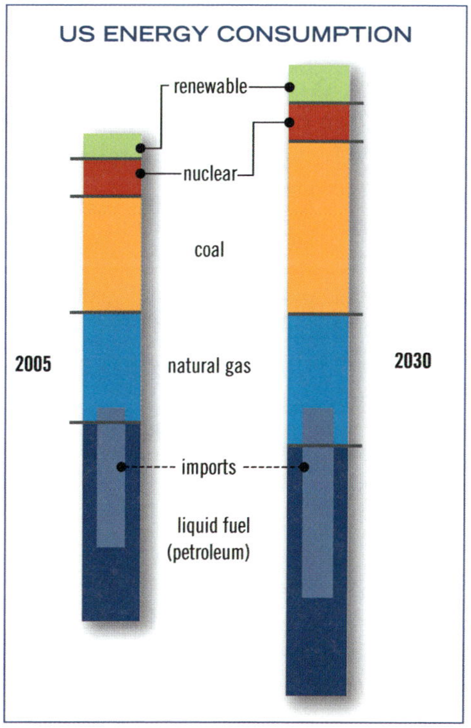

A customized bar chart provides the right visual representation of data.

A line chart is often used to show a trend or changes on a longer term that on a bar chart. It may show two (or more) evolutions on the same graph.

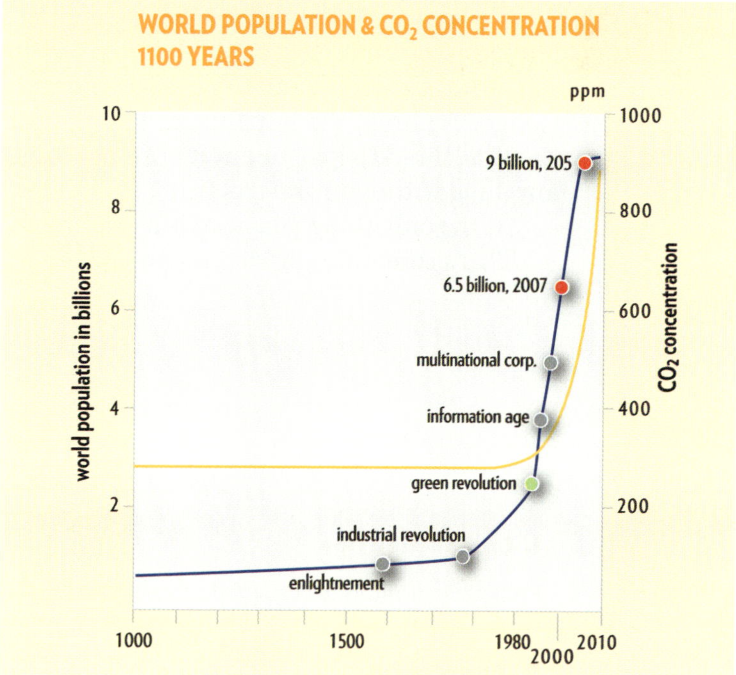

Source : Global Metrics

Test Yourself

Mobile money

Cell phones have been booming in Africa for years, but Susie Lonie has bigger ambitions. Lonie ran a pilot program for Vodafone in Kenya that turns the cell phone into a device for transferring funds. With M-Pesa (Swahili for "mobile money"), anybody with a phone and an account can send and receive funds with about as much effort as it took to write this sentence. In Kenya, where M-Pesa was launched three months ago, people are using phone money to buy goods and services from each other.

Many Kenyans – and most Africans – still do not have bank accounts. The costs of moving money through traditional institutions like Western Union can be prohibitively expensive. M-Pesa's virtual money, by contrast, is tied to real money held in the user's account and transferred for a small commission. Kenyan ministries are moving to allow users to pay electricity and water bills via cell phone.

Vodafone plans to expand its network of 450 agents in Kenya to 5,000 by March. It's also targeting Tanzania and Afghanistan, where a similar mobile-money pilot program is underway. Vodacom, meanwhile, is also hoping its mobile-money service can be used to tap into the $90 billion African remittance market. In July the firm will launch a program to test remittance payments from Britain to Kenya. If it works, it plans to expand the program to India, Greece and Albania.

The mobile-money trend is catching on elsewhere in Africa as well. In Zambia, a company called Celpay is conducting more than $10 million per month in business-to-business transactions over cell phones (about 2 percent of Zambia's GNP). In South Africa, telecoms are buying and selling $100,000 blocks of air time on cell phone networks.

Businesses are using the mobile-money system in Zambia and Democratic Republic of Congo. Bralima, the bottling and distribution subsidiary for Heineken and Coca-Cola in Zambia, hired Celpay to put its financial transactions on a cell phone system. "You can't do anything without infrastructure", says Celpay CEO Lazarus Muchenje.

"If the only thing you have is a cell phone, that's where everything is going to gravitate".

That's something Africans can look forward to.

Newsweek, July 16th, 2007

Corrigé page 196

I. Compréhension

Rédigez en français le résumé du texte en 100 mots.

II. Expression

1. Do you feel ready to pay for your purchases with your mobile phone in the near future?

2. List the pros and cons of this means of payment. Explain why you would opt for it or not, and if you don't, say what alternative you would prefer. (150 words)

Exam Paper

The British real estate crisis

London, Aug. 22 – Susan Whittaker was desperate. Four years ago, she purchased her first apartment in the town of Rochester, less than two hours east of London. But then interest rates started to rise, and the income from the small shop she ran with her partner no longer covered their adjustable-rate mortgage. In British society, "we encourage people to take on debt," said Frances Walker, a debt adviser.

Facing foreclosure, and determined to avoid moving in with her mother, Ms. Whittaker found a way out in an increasingly popular arrangement here known as a "sale and rent back." A private company bought her home, allowing her to avoid foreclosure; then the company rented the house back to Ms. Whittaker and her partner and they did not even have to move. The catch is that the company paid the couple less than the value of their apartment. Such deals are uncommon in the United States, and mortgage brokers say they discourage them because of the possibility of unscrupulous and dishonest lenders exploiting distressed homeowners. But desperate times call for desperate measures.

While Americans fear an epidemic of foreclosures, Britain is already suffering one. An estimated 125,100 households are behind in their mortgage payments. And personal bankruptcies are at an all-time record, caused largely by a crushing increase in mortgage debt. The situation has grown so dire — as has the threat of desperate homeowners being exploited – that the newly installed government of Prime Minister Gordon Brown is trying to change the fundamentals of the mortgage system. Whether they can is an open question [...]

Lawmakers are now trying to figure out how to encourage more homeowners to take fixed-rate loans, but that will not help those already facing foreclosure, or prevent the threat of predatory lending.

The liberalization of the British mortgage market in the 1980s under Margaret Thatcher's government removed some credit controls, admitting new lenders who offered mortgages with ever more competitive short-term fixed rates. Longer-term fixed-rate mortgages became even more unpopular in the 1990s when interest rates peaked at 15 percent. [...]

For Susan Whittaker the experience of having to sell her home and rent it back has made any type of loan out of the question. "We won't get a mortgage again," said Ms. Whittaker, speaking on the phone from her Rochester home. "The whole episode has put us off."

I. Compréhension **À rédiger en français**

Faites en français la synthèse de l'article ci-dessus en 100 mots.

II. Expression **À rédiger en anglais.**

1. What are the reasons for the present situation of homeowners in Great Britain? (50 words)

2. According to the article, is the situation exactly the same in the USA? (20 words)

3. Would you like to be a homeowner? State your reasons why or why not? Say what precautions you would take. (100 words)

CORRIGÉS TEST YOURSELF

Unit 1 p. 18

I. Expression

This article, dated July 12, 2007, published in *The Times*, deals with a new development in career networking via the internet, exploring the advantages of such innovation.

With the increasing popularity of on-line social and business networking sites, job networking was the next logical link. One successful website is i-resign.com, which posts resignations rather than traditional job openings. This way, an employee who has already decided to leave his or her job gives the potential job seeker inside information about a job that has not yet been listed.

Thus, the job hunter can carefully prepare his or her upcoming contact with the company based on such early information. This gives the job seeker a head start, and helps promote successful career matches by better defining the profile and enlarging the candidate pool. This career boost given from the inside by employees within a firm has given rise to the term "mole".

Moles, or employees, help market jobs from within firms. Websites such as TheCareerMole.com have the clear-cut advantage of not only providing information to jobseekers, but of providing tools for managers as well. In other words, moles help bosses find employees to fill vacancies, and the bosses reward moles financially. So it's a winning game for all parties involved. (**210 words**)

II. Compréhension

Laura, qui travaille pour un cabinet d'expertise comptable faisant partie des « Big Four », s'est inscrite comme « taupe » chez TheCareerMole.com. Ce site Internet cherche à mettre sur le marché des recommandations d'emploi personnelles en mettant en relation des chercheurs d'emploi et des taupes au sein de l'entreprise pour laquelle le chercheur d'emploi aimerait travailler. Le chercheur d'emploi reçoit des informations privilégiées de l'intérieur de telle ou telle société et la taupe reçoit une prime pour une embauche réussie dans le cadre du programme de bonification pour les recommandations.

Unit 2 p. 28

I. Expression

The article, entitled *Jobs for the disabled* was published in the issue of the *The New York Times* dated Saturday, March 11th, 2006. It explains how new technology has created many jobs for disabled people in the United States.

The columnist quotes the example of Pamela Post who works as a home-agent because she suffers from agoraphobia and is afraid to leave her house.

Today, there also exists software that helps the blind or disabled to operate computers, so that that many of them can work at home.

For companies, it is an advantage too, because even if home-agents are well paid, they cost at least 30 percent less than full-time employees in outsourced companies in India.

So, the journalist concludes by saying that computer technology is bringing jobs back to the US, which is quite an unusual remark. Since the Industrial Revolution many Luddites have maintained that machines steal their jobs from them making them redundant. (**158 words**)

II. Traduction

De tels arrangements fournissent des emplois à des milliers de gens qui souffrent de handicaps. Les ordinateurs à grande vitesse et les connexions à haut débit sont devenus si peu chers et si sûrs que le lieu de travail n'est plus une difficulté pour les emplois de service aux clients. Parallèlement, il existe une large gamme de technologies pour aider les personnes handicapées à faire fonctionner un ordinateur, tels qu'un logiciel qui permet à une personne aveugle de se servir du clavier au lieu de la souris pour se déplacer dans un programme ou des synthétiseurs vocaux qui transforment le texte en parole. Il existe aussi des solutions alternatives à la souris pour les gens qui n'ont qu'un usage limité des bras.

Unit 3 p. 38

I. Compréhension

The overall trend is a rise in wages in China.

Mr Zhang's example is significant because it shows that he made more money not only thanks to more work, but mainly because of an increase in the pay rate awarded by the factory.

This trend has consequences not only on the job market in China as it is more difficult to recruit at low salaries, but also on the prices in the USA. As a matter of fact a boomerang effect is expected in the American population's everyday life regarding prices.

Locally the issue is serious too as young people are reluctant to take underpaid jobs. Neither are they ready to work in appalling conditions such as those described in a factory in northern China.

Young people are more and more demanding which results in both complaints from executives and an overall shortage of labour in China. (**143 words**)

II. Traduction

Avec 45 heures de travail par semaine, M. Zhang perçoit l'équivalent de 263 dollars par mois, alors qu'il y a peu de temps, en février dernier, il ne percevait que 197 dollars. Une partie de ce salaire plus élevé provient d'une efficacité accrue au travail. « Lorsque j'ai commencé au tout début, je n'étais pas aussi rapide », dit il.

Mais une bonne partie correspond à une augmentation du salaire de M. Zhang, à savoir 1,45 cents pour chaque selle de bicyclette au lieu de 1,32 cents.

Cela représente une petite différence qui implique un changement majeur.

Les salaires chinois augmentent. Il n'existe aucun chiffre fiable de salaire moyen. Les dernières données économiques du gouvernement ne sont notamment pas vérifiables.

En revanche, les propriétaires d'usine et les experts qui suivent de près l'état du marché du travail à l'échelon national disent que les hommes d'affaires ont beaucoup de mal à trouver des travailleurs compétents et qu'ils sont amenés à payer davantage les travailleurs qu'ils recrutent.

De plus, la hausse des salaires en Chine est susceptible de faire augmenter les prix aux USA, dans les centres commerciaux, les épiceries et même à la pompe.

Unit 4 p. 48

I. Compréhension

Published on February 26, 2007, this article from *Newsweek*, entitled "A strike too many", raises the issue of big companies' stability.

An unexpected decrease in sales and a 10-month backlog in orders have led management at Hyundai, the world's sixth-largest car maker, to push for night shifts at their Cheonju plant in South Korea. They have been met with strong opposition from the powerful labour unions, who insist that night shifts are hazardous to workers' health. Despite the fact that Hyundai workers are paid almost as much as their counterparts in Detroit, the trade union, since its establishment in 1987, has constantly been at loggerheads with management.

Recently, Hyundai's productivity decreased significantly. This can be largely attributed to bad choices in profit allocation, where cost-effective technology comes second to employee wages. This has resulted in an ever-increasing productivity gap between Hyundai and its major Japanese and American competitors. For GM and Ford, for instance, productivity and profits have increased after cost cutting and large layoffs, and despite their own labour unions, they have managed to convince their workers that less benefits are preferable to being unemployed. At Hyundai, however, the obstinate unions have been counter-attacked by an unprecedented move - in response to the union's excessive demands, consumers have begun boycotting Hyundai cars.

I wouldn't have imagined such large companies selling millions of cars all over the world being on the brink so easily. This article underlines the necessity of mutual understanding between workers and managers to keep a company working.

II. Expression

1. Hyundai is losing money today because of its uneconomical use of profits, making it competitively inefficient when matched against other car giants such as Toyota and Ford. These companies are more productive because they have chosen to invest in labour-saving technology, rather than in wages for employees as Hyundai has done. This productivity gap, and the negative effect labour unions have had on consumer opinion, have both led to a sharp decrease of Hyundai's popularity, hence profits. (**78 words**)

2. To me, it seems that the phrase "their work might go overseas" reflects a change in perception. Previously, Western companies sought to move their businesses into Asia to profit from lower labour costs and higher productivity than what they would get at home. Now it seems that a car company such as Hyundai may profit from moving their production lines to developing African countries to have these same benefits, as the labour costs in its own country have increased while productivity has decreased. (**84 words**)

Unit 5 p. 58

I. Compréhension

This article published in *The Times* on July 21st, 2007 tackles the issue of financial support in developing countries thanks to not-for-profit organisations like Hand in Hand, hence the title.

Hand in Hand has one main purpose: to help potential entrepreneurs to get out of poverty by becoming successful business owners. The organization has already helped to found thousands of businesses, and plans to found hundreds of thousands more. It will also provide an extra million jobs within the next five years in the Indian state Tamil Nadu. It is partially backed by private money lenders such as the retired benefactor Percy Barnevik, and works with communities to help impoverished individuals manage and build up their businesses.

The concept is simple: to train people, mainly illiterate women, to be self-sufficient in running their own businesses, and to give them almost interest-free loans to get them started, which may be paid back from the profits gained. It also introduces eco-friendly initiatives, a business model based on local cooperation as well as a lending mechanism called microfinancing to further promote the growth and sustainability of the business.

To my mind, this kind of financial charity must be a boon to poor countries where banking services are reluctant to loan money to prospective entrepreneurs unable to pay it back. The system contributes to improving India's standard of living by providing jobs and creating self-supportive structures. (**179 words**)

II. Traduction

Bien qu'ayant fait un don d'environ 7 millions de livres à Hand in Hand, Mr Barnevik tient à ce que cet organisme reste autonome. « Il faut que tout ce que nous faisons soit durable, nous ne sommes là que pour faciliter et former. Tant qu'il y a des gens illettrés à chaque coin de rue il faut poursuivre cette formation. Mais c'est comme à l'école, une fois diplômé c'est à vous seul d'assumer. »

III. Expression

1. Mr. Barnevik has already donated about 7 million pounds to the not-for-profit organization, Hand in Hand so that impoverished people from the developing world, specifically in India, may start up their own businesses and get themselves out of poverty. His money goes towards promoting education, training, and loans to help the entrepreneurs build their dreams. He has helped create tens of thousands of businesses and jobs, and is slowly changing the world by his and the organization's radical approach to solving the world's poverty crisis. (**86 words**)

2. Hand in Hand is trying to eliminate poverty in the Indian state of Tamil Nadu by educating and empowering people, especially women, to take charge of their own lives and become successful, through lending schemes that will not put the people further into debt. It also promotes health, the eradication of child labour, and environmentally-friendly approaches. (**57 words**)

3. "Microfinancing" can support people in need, as donated money from an organization may be more easily accessed by impoverished communities to invest in a certain project themselves. They may have access to finance through a lending scheme that aids their progress rather than hampers it. A not-for-profit organization, for example, may give out loans that have a very low interest margin compared to other lenders, thereby allowing new business owners to first build up their business and then repay the money. There is a limit to how effective microfinancing can be, as some business owners may not be as prolific as others, hence not be able to pay the loans back, or, when collective responsibility does not work smoothly within communities. (**125 words**)

Unit 6 p. 68

I. Compréhension

The article, entitled *T-shirts might solve Middle East peace* was published in the issue of the *Cambridge Chronicle* dated July 25th, 2007.

It describes the initiative led by Zander Sebenius who launched a line of T-shirts manufactured in a factory in Palestine that is owned by a Christian and has a Muslim union. His idea was to both make money and do good in the world at the same time. He hopes it will help solve the Israeli-Palestinian conflict by giving hope to desperate citizens. He claims that creating jobs will be a deterrent to violence.

With a Muslim friend, Sebenius has already sold 500 wholesale custom-printed T-shirts to schools and organizations. At the same time they promote the environmental benefits of organic cotton, the fair-labour benefits of a unionized shop and the diplomatic benefits of economic development in Palestine.

Obviouly, Sebenius is an idealist who believes that no issue is too big to be tackled and that something as simple as buying a T-shirt can make a difference. (**171 words**)

II. Traduction

Sebenius a déclaré qu'il a rejoint le mouvement des entrepreneurs engagés parce qu'il croit qu'il est possible de faire le bien dans ce monde et de gagner de l'argent en même temps, une chose que la plupart des gens séparent. Il dit qu'il espère qu'en montrant que cela peut rapporter que de soutenir la paix, le travail équitable et les mouvements écologistes, il les aidera à se développer. « Autrefois, je pensais que certains problèmes étaient trop importants pour que l'on s'y attaque, quoi que l'on fasse » a déclaré Sebenius. « Ceci m'a montré que quelque chose d'aussi simple que d'acheter un T-shirt peut avoir un effet. »

Unit 7 p. 78

I. Compréhension

Bloom est un exemple parmi d'autres d'entrepreneurs qui profitent de la tendance actuelle de vendre des produits ou des services destinés aux enfants en séduisant leurs parents. On pourrait citer également des créateurs de vêtements, des auteurs de livres et même des consultants en décoration pour chambres d'enfants.

Certaines de ces entreprises jouent sur l'inquiétude des parents, d'autres prennent pour cible les incertitudes d'ordre politique, physique ou social de ces mêmes parents.

Par exemple, l'obésité des enfants, le diabète ainsi que d'autres problèmes liés à la nourriture, ont poussé Shazi Visram à sortir la gamme « Happy Baby » (« Bébé Heureux »).

Visram a identifié un marché de parents désirant donner une alimentation bio à leurs enfants mais qui n'ont pas le temps de cuisiner. Sa société a lancé une gamme d'aliments bio et non cuisinés pour bébé le jour de la fête des mères en 2006.

Un paquet contenant douze cubes surgelés est disponible au prix de $4.99 (3 euros) dans des épiceries bio telles que Whole Foods ainsi que dans des supermarchés plus conventionnels tels que Publix. (**182 mots**)

II. Expression

1. In most of these families both parents work, therefore their safety concerns can be well satisfied. They have less time but more money thanks to their combined income, which make them the perfect target for selling these kinds of products. Moreover, the few kids they have are often considered kings or queens, so they must have the best. These people are also influenced by advertising, which reinforces their sense of guilt.

Work pressure makes them easier victims, and some of them may also enjoy showing off a bit in front of their families, friends and neighbours.

2. The first negative aspect is that those children will automatically think that everything and anything can be bought, at any age, without limits. Thus there will be a blurring of the age barrier where children dress and behave like adults. This artificial sophistication of their lives could turn them into blasé adults, if not obnoxious and superficial beings having lost touch with reality and moral values while boasting about their stylish clothes.

3. It is a way of disengaging themselves from their children's education and guidance. These products and services will serve as a substitute for a genuine relationship between parents and children. They will not teach them any values. They will spend less time together and communication will suffer.

Parents could end up being considered as a mere source of revenue to their kids. What's more, it will be very hard to reverse this trend and make them relinquish their comfortable standard of living.

Unit 8 p. 88

I. Compréhension

La publicité d'aujourd'hui, à défaut de cibler les qualités d'un produit s'attache par souci d'efficacité, aux envies, désirs et émotions des consommateurs. Les publicitaires s'appuient sur l'attirance sexuelle et le plaisir et font de la femme un objet de prédilection.

Paradoxalement on observe que, si la publicité s'attache à montrer des normes, des valeurs, des idées, elles-mêmes révélatrices de cultures et époques, elle nous limite aussi à des stéréotypes sexistes.

La femme et l'homme sont idéalisés et deviennent des modèles inaccessibles. Les conséquences sont graves pour les consommateurs et consommatrices qui développent des problèmes psychologiques, obsessionnels, de nutrition et d'intégration dans la société. (**106 mots**)

II. Expression

Trisha Grover puts forward the idea that models are idealized, and can make women lose their balance, psychologically speaking, by realizing that they can never resemble their icons.

The strategy is to deliberately encourage this feeling among women who inevitably consume more, thus rapidly becoming fashion victims. Buying clothes and making use of cosmetics has become a need that they try hard to satisfy at any price. This is exactly what admen are after.

I believe admen do lure women into buying compulsively, thus contributing to making them develop all sorts of complexes.

I appreciate what was done in Spain when skinny models were refused catwalks because they represented a danger, not only to themselves, but also to young girls desperately trying to look like them, thus running the risk of becoming anorexic.

I wish admen would not exert that much pressure, but I also wish women would become more sensible. (**152 words**)

Unit 9 p. 98

I. Compréhension

As the title clearly indicates *Dianabilia Takes Over*, the article published in the issue of *The New York Times* dated August 27th, 2007, deals with the merchandizing of Lady Diana, Princess of Wales, nicknamed "Princess of Sales".

Indeed, he recalls that Lady Diana's death on Aug. 31st, 1997 created a powerful market of memorabilia and that the coming tenth anniversary has boosted the sales of commemorative products by both large and small companies.

A specialist explains Diana's potent global marketing phenomenon by the fact she was brilliant in reaching out and connecting to her audience, that she was a beautiful princess who did not go through the aging process and that her sons, William and Harry, keep her alive in people's minds, which perpetuates her brand, and allows the legend to continue.

The column therefore raises the issue of whether a price should be put on every aspect of a celebrity's life after his or her death. (**160 words**)

II. Traduction

Une autre raison pour laquelle il se peut que Diana continue à intriguer les gens est la manière dont la vie de ses fils se déroule. « Quand on regarde ces garçons, on ne peut s'empêcher de penser à elle », ajoute-t-il. William et Harry sont peut-être même des versions vivantes des « extensions de ligne », comme on appelle les produits dérivés dans les cercles de la mercatique. « Ils la maintiennent vivante dans l'esprit des gens, ce qui perpétue sa marque. »

Unit 10 p. 108

I. Compréhension

NewsWeek a publié le 30 octobre 2006 un article intitulé « The *Great Wal-Mart of China* » dans lequel se côtoient la culture d'entreprise américaine et la tradition commerciale chinoise.

La grande distribution recueille le suffrage des Chinois qui apprécient la variété, la qualité, la quantité et les prix pratiqués par le numéro un américain. La forte population représente un marché énorme au niveau du secteur de la consommation mais le transfert des stratégies américaines ne peut pas être un copié-collé. C'est Wal-Mart qui doit s'adapter et tenir compte de l'environnement local. En concurrence avec Carrefour pour le rachat de Trust-Mart, Wal-Mart a remporté les enchères se hissant ainsi à la première place des chaînes étrangères en Chine.

Au niveau de la qualité et de la quantité des consommateurs, la Chine offre le même profil que les États-Unis. Toutefois, le secteur de l'activité commerciale reste l'apanage des autochtones, c'est la raison pour laquelle Wal-Mart investit un minimum en Chine et renforce son monopole en terre américaine.

Cette approche du marché chinois n'est pas insignifiante ; en effet elle démontre les capacités d'adaptabilité d'une puissante structure et son respect de l'identité économique nationale. Mais elle souligne aussi les besoins de ces complexes géants à innover géographiquement et politiquement pour éviter la saturation, l'isolement et la rupture.

Cet article montre à quel point les grandes chaînes de supermarchés se battent pour rester au premier rang mais aussi à quel point elles sont fragilisées par les identités nationales. S'imposer dans un pays ne correspond pas à une épreuve de force, un mélange de diplomatie, de connaissance et d'acceptation de l'autre est incontournable. La Chine sonne-t-elle le glas de l'américanisation?

II. Expression

1. According to the table, US retail giant Wal-Mart has a 3.1% market share in China, ranking it eighth. Once it has taken over the Taiwanese Trust-Mart, it is expected that sales, market share and ranking of the two companies will combine, indicating that Wal-Mart will increase to 8.9% market share. This will catapult Wal-Mart to first position in the Chinese retail market, just 0.1% more than the current leader, the French Carrefour. Merging the two companies will be like bettering the Great retail Wall of China, a laudable feat for a foreign company in an economy dominated by domestic retailers. (**101 words**)

2. Carrefour's hesitation to invest more in the Far East cost the French chain its leadership. Its ranking of challenger may not suit its ambitions. However, Carrefour is close behind, with tight competition between these giants always a certainty. They both share new markets and have the same retail style, targeting the same middle-class, and adapting to the indigenous cultures. These giants – among others – won't disappear rapidly since they meet consumers' demands wherever they set up. People are used to one-stop shopping, with bigger supermarkets, meaning lower prices, and wider choice. These giants rely on the currently prosperous consumer society to maintain their position. (**105 words**)

Unit 11 p.118

Bill Bryson is a best-selling American-born author of books on travel, the English language and scientific subjects. He visited Britain in 1971 and decided to stay. He lived in Yorkshire for most of his adult life, before moving to Norfolk in 2003.

I. Compréhension

This text is a passage from Bill Bryson's inaugural speech as president of the Campaign to Protect Rural England published in the issue of *The Guardian* dated July 9th, 2007. It is a plea for the defence of the traditional British countryside.

First, Bryson recalls that Britain offers a sumptuous diversity of history, but that it should not be thought inexhaustible, because losing it would be a serious loss.

Therefore, Bryson advocates the limitation of the development of the English countryside, which is under pressure. He also wishes people would stop littering and fly-tipping. He hopes the 8,000 miles of high-voltage power line wires will be buried and pylons taken away because they are alien and ugly.

Bryson also believes there ought to be specific targets for woodland creation in England because the UK has less forest cover than almost any country in Europe. Eventually, pushes for the restoration and renewal of hedgerows that are fading away. (**160 words**)

II. Traduction

Vous n'avez guère besoin que je vous dise à quel point vous avez la chance d'avoir ce que vous avez dans ce pays. Être entouré par une si somptueuse diversité d'histoire et de beauté est un délice et un privilège, certes, mais c'est aussi un grand danger. Lorsque l'on possède une telle abondance de grandes choses, il est aisé de penser qu'elles sont inépuisables et de se persuader qu'elles peuvent être grignotées progressivement sans perte irréparable. Je déteste que des gens pensent de la sorte.

Unit 12 p.128

I. Compréhension

Globalization caused the acquisition of Hymall by Tesco, and Trust Mart by Wall Mart, that is to say by giants in developed countries. However, western supermarkets find it hard to implement their strategies in countries other than their own. The examples of Wall Mart, Tesco, and other giants show that they could neither fit in other European nations, nor China for cultural reasons.

Culture clash is an obstacle they find hard to overcome.

The Taiwanese, to the contrary, can easily tap the Chinese market thanks to their command of the Chinese language and their quick adaptation to Chinese culture.

The Taiwanese also strive to understand the Chinese better, and to train their own staff to overcome hurdles. They value their human resources, and teach the personnel to see more than salary as an incentive to work. That is why RT Mart remains the only successful Taiwanese chain in the market. (**150 words**)

II. Traduction

La vente au détail joue un rôle important dans l'économie d'un pays. Les pays développés mettent en place des méthodes industrialisées de pointe pour gérer les supermarchés.

Quand bien même ils sont prospères dans leurs propres pays, ils rencontrent bien souvent des difficultés ailleurs.

Wall-Mart est puissant aux USA mais a perdu la bataille en Allemagne. Tesco est implanté partout en Grande Bretagne mais n'est que très peu présent dans les autres pays européens. Les géants que sont Carrefour et Auchan n'envisagent même pas de tenter de prendre la part de marché que Wall-Mart possède aux USA.
Beaucoup de détaillants occidentaux pensent que pénétrer le marché chinois revient à s'introduire dans plusieurs pays différents, tant le dialecte, la cuisine, et les comportements d'achat diffèrent d'un endroit à l'autre. L'avantage qu'ont les détaillants Taiwanais est de maîtriser la langue.
La culture d'entreprise globale de RT Mart a influencé presque tous les membres du personnel – faire du profit est manifestement important mais lancer une marque à identité chinoise dans l'industrie est l'objectif majeur.

Unit 13 p. 138

I. Compréhension

Ce texte, tiré et adapté du *New York Times* et publié en juin 2007, analyse une nouvelle tendance dans la consommation d'articles de haute technologie.

À travers l'exemple d'une jeune cadre new-yorkaise, il est démontré que la tendance actuelle est de posséder plusieurs objets remplissant la même fonction au départ mais qui ensuite seront utilisés à tour de rôle selon le moment, l'activité pratiquée ou li lieu.

Cette tendance, initiée il y a quatre ans avec le succès des ordinateurs portables, s'est ensuite exportée vers d'autres appareils. C'est ainsi que cette jeune femme possède deux lecteurs de musique, deux appareils photo et deux lecteurs de DVD.

La démultiplication de ces objets fait bien sûr le bonheur de l'industrie.

On est loin de vouloir vendre un seul et même objet standard à toute la famille.

Cette déclinaison de l'offre correspond à l'ambition de préserver une dynamique de croissance sur des marché saturés.

II. Expression

1. Several factors can explain this new trend of repeat buyers: on the companies' side, the high technology market is now saturated and thus in need of renewal, new and dynamic growth, and of new perspectives. As disruptive innovations are rare, the only possible innovations are found in minor aspects like accessory functions. Moreover, the production cost of these items has dropped continuously and many of them are now quite affordable to a wider range of customers. Progress has also been made on the technical side (miniaturization).
On the consumer side, they like to own a product adapted to their needs and personalities: products become a way of showing who we are. It is what the notion of "extended self" is about.
For young people it is also a way to show their autonomy if they have their own equipment (telephone, tv, computer, camera). As many of them tend to stay longer at their parents' home, these items are perhaps substitutes to real independence.
2. The main drawback could be a greater dependency on objects: people now feel incapable of living without these items around them, whereas a few years ago, we didn't even know about them. Therefore, a loss of freedom follows: we feel compelled to take photos, to send messages, to check our mail every day or several times a day... in order to keep in touch with an ever changing world. We can have the impression of being taken into a swirl of hyper and continuous activity. We can even get messages on the train, or after working hours, at home, or on holiday. More time spent on these objects means less time spent reading or sharing time with people, or simply sleeping.
Also, these products change and are upgraded very quickly, and as a result people feel the need to change them very often thus spending money on them. Some of us end up over equipped.
3. Il faudra ici choisir "votre camp"! et répondre en fonction de votre attitude personnelle.
Voici quelques idées.

Yes, I do.
I will always be keen on getting the latest cell phone, or digital camera, even if it is expensive, or even if I must sacrifice other things.
Like Alison Shepard, I own .... and here is how I use all these objects. (give examples)
If I didn't have all these items with me, I would feel lost or naked!
I need to keep in touch all the time.

No, I do not
Quite the reverse (on the contrary), I try to reduce the number of these objects in my every day life: I'd rather have one object performing many different functions like a cell phone that is also an mp3 player and a camera.
I am not gadget-minded.
I hate all these devices and I adamantly refuse to own one, I would be afraid of losing my freedom, or my independence.

Unit 14 p. 148

I. Compréhension

Even if India may voice worries about China's construction of a metal road in the Himalayas, China claims to be committed to environmental protection. Tourism is becoming increasingly important to the Chinese, in view of the upcoming Olympic games. Since the increase of tourism is linked to a healthy environment, Shao Qiwei, Chairman of the National Tourism Association, has declared the environment to be the top priority. Limiting the number of tourists would be a solution that, according to Shao, requires little effort. Due to the high altitude of Mount Everest, the number of tourists able to sustain the physical strength required to endure the hike would be naturally low. Finally, although environmentalists disapprove of the road, Shao vigourously affirms that not only does China have tough environmental policies, but it enforces them as well. **(135 words)**

Questions

1. Tourists are attracted to countries with a positive image – economic, political, and social – as well as landscapes and infrastructure. Due to its amazing growth, China has developed at a rapid pace, however, building infrastructure destroys flora and fauna, displaces rural populations, and pollutes rivers.
2. China is known not only for its spectacular growth, but also for its massive environmental destruction and neglect. China must be attentive to world issues such as climate change in order to improve its negative image around the world. The environment is a priority for tourism. The Kyoto Protocol, rejected by the U.S. and China, makes tourists all the more aware of this necessity in order to ensure sustainable tourism – the way of the future.

Unit 15 p. 158

I. Compréhension

Cet article, publié fin avril 2006, dans le *Daily Mail* fait le point sur le problème de la contrefaçon dans le monde.

Les entreprises victimes de cette escroquerie ne sont pas restées les bras ballants et consacrent beaucoup d'argent à essayer d'enrayer le phénomène.

Appuyées par la police, la justice et des campagnes d'information, elles ont réussi à réduire ce commerce illégal dans toute l'Asie.

Cependant, c'est sans compter sur la capacité de réaction des réseaux de faussaires : ceux-ci ont habilement fait passer leurs marchandises des étals de marchés à Internet qui est extrêmement difficile de contrôler.

Le journaliste fait aussi très justement remarquer que les fabricants sont en partie à l'origine du problème ; en délocalisant leur production vers l'Asie, ils favorisent la fabrication de faux de très bonne qualité.

La seule façon de lutter efficacement sera d'éliminer la demande pour ces produits.

On voit bien qu'il est très difficile de contrecarrer ces réseaux qui, comme le phénix, renaissent facilement de leurs cendres.

II. Questions

1. For both economic and ethical reasons, companies are motivated to fight against the proliferation of counterfeit goods.
Firstly, the unauthorised duplication of goods is an infringement of intellectual property rights. Companies products are in direct competition with fakes so they suffer a loss in their sales. Often, fakes even dominate the market, thus creating a barrier to the entry of genuine products.
Moreover, this unfair competition can lead to job losses and redundancies in legitimate companies.
Counterfeiting also reduces innovation and the will to invest in research.
The value of the brand can suffer, and also the firm's reputation; consumers lose confidence in the company.
In some cases, the buyers of fakes also face health and safety risks, damaging the original firm's reputation and image even more.
Finally, some genuine companies might worry about the bad use made of the money generated by this illegal trade.

2. It is a well-known fact that counterfeiting is a thriving illicit activity attracting criminal networks. It is one of the most dynamic sectors of organized crime. The regulations are weak and good prospects of profit make it worth it.
They invest in the traditional sectors such as real estate, finance and industry, thus perverting normal economic functioning. These operations enable them to launder their illicit money.
If public structures are weak, they can also be bribed with the profits coming from counterfeiting. This makes the counterfeiters' lives easier by having decisions made in their favour.
But even worse, they can also be involved in violence: in gang warfare, arms trafficking and the financing of terrorist activities throughout the world.
For more details, read the article on the Internet entitled "*The true cost of faking it*", Daily Mail, July 30th, 2007.

3. The range of products being counterfeited is expanding, and we can rightly suppose that the number of unwitting buyers is low.
There are user-friendly purchasing networks on the Internet that certainly sell fakes, especially auction websites like eBay, and the people buying on those sites do not really want to know if they are buying fakes or not.
I think that the great majority of consumers are responsible for this boom. Many don't even think that it can do any harm. Therefore, shoppers should be prepared to accept the wider moral implications of what they are doing. When they buy those fakes, they are just thinking about themselves and what they want, they are not thinking about the cost in terms of loss to others, or violence and criminality.
The only way to win some of them back is for the firms to persuade them that the genuine products have got unique qualities that make them worth their price.

Unit 16 p. 168

I. Compréhension

La fuite des cerveaux touche désormais de nombreux pays de l'Est, membres de la communauté européenne qui voient leurs meilleurs employés partir vers l'Europe de l'ouest où les salaires et conditions de travail sont meilleurs.
Romag, entreprise Polonaise souffre d'un manque de travailleurs qualifiés depuis que la Pologne est entrée dans l'Union Européenne. Le maire d'une ville d'Allemagne de l'Est propose d'envoyer de la main d'oeuvre qualifiée allemande n'exigeant pas de hauts salaires, vers la Pologne, le marché du travail pour le personnel qualifié arrivant à saturation en Allemagne. Une formation des travailleurs est aussi à l'étude pour faciliter la mobilité des employés. Le nouveau visage du marché du travail en Europe fait qu'aujourd' hui il semblerait que le travail se déplace vers les demandeurs d'emploi. (**128 mots**)

II. Expression

The last sentence of the article shows that the European labour market is changing. When jobseekers used to look for jobs and leave their countries for better salaries and working conditions, it's now employers who target potential jobseekers, train them and offer them facilities to work abroad. Mobility is a key issue but it now concerns employees and employers. The brain drain has obviously had repercussions as it has deprived countries of the best of their workforce.
The opening of borders meant more opportunities for workers in emerging countries but it has also meant the impoverishment of their economic development.
The European labour market will probably be faced with problems that will range from shortage to saturation of skilled workers. It will therefore have to find a right balance.
In terms of mobility, what is also to be expected in the future is probably a different type of migration, encouraging the integration of workers' families as well as students, retired, and unemployed people. (**163 words**)

Unit 17 p. 178

I. Compréhension

Sous le titre « *Lost in translation* », paraissait, dans le *Newsweek* du 29 mai 2006, un article faisant allusion aux problèmes rencontrés par les Philippins dans les centres d'appels à cause de leurs lacunes en anglais.

Les Philippines abritent un grand nombre de centres d'appels d'entreprises délocalisées et offrent ainsi la sécurité de l'emploi à bon nombre de ses habitants. Malheureusement, le recrutement devient difficile à cause des capacités linguistiques insuffisantes des postulants. Bien qu'ayant bénéficié de l'influence américaine pendant un demi-siècle, la langue parlée est devenue un mélange d'anglais et de dialecte, incompréhensible dans les échanges téléphoniques. Ce sont pourtant les meilleures écoles qui alimentent ce secteur.

Toutes les forces sont mises en branle pour palier ce manque. Le gouvernement d'abord qui a rendu l'anglais obligatoire à l'école. Des organismes participent à cette promotion pour faciliter l'apprentissage et rompre avec les habitudes de parler le Taglish. Le président du pays a lui-même pris la parole pour annoncer une forte subvention financière pour motiver ses concitoyens. Tout cela, bien sûr, afin que les Philippines gardent le monopole de ce secteur qui pourrait bien se délocaliser à son tour si les intermédiaires s'avérraient incompétents.

Le marché des centres d'appels, s'il convient à certains pays du fait d'un investissement minime, n'en reste pas moins fragile. Une économie qui repose sur ce seul secteur d'activité risque rapidement de s'effondrer à cause d'insuffisances humaines mais aussi de concurrence étrangère. La pratique de l'anglais fait partie des pré-requis nécessaires et des atouts déterminants qui attirent les entreprises étrangères. (**251 mots**)

II. Expression

1. The BPO industry worries about having non-English-speaking employees because its business depends on its call operators being able to communicate adequately with English-speaking countries, such as the US, for example. The problem is for the employees to understand the vernacular, as well as being able to speak proper English. (**50 words**)

2. For a call-centre job catering to English-speaking countries, I do support the idea that English should be a necessary prerequisite for acquiring a job in countries such as the Philippines. Employers depend on their employees to sell their products, and communication at a higher level is needed to convince potential customers to buy their wares. Poor English skills may breed mistrust, especially when a customer is never face to face with the salesperson. Good English skills are also important to avoid misunderstandings during sales transactions. When a country such as the Philippines depends on call centres for the majority of its income, English should become a priority to increase its profits when out-sourcing. (**114 words**)

Unit 18 p. 188

I. Compréhension

L'usage du téléphone portable est devenu prépondérant en Afrique. C'est un moyen de transférer des fonds. Au Kenya où le programme M-Pesa a été lancé pour Vodafone, les usagers du portable peuvent effectuer des transactions financières sans être détenteurs d'un compte bancaire, n'engageant ainsi que de minimes commissions. On peut désormais payer ses factures d'électricité et eau par téléphone. On peut également traiter toutes sortes d'affaires grâce au mobile.
Ces programmes prétendent s'étendre à toute l'Afrique ainsi que d'autres pays du monde.
Cette infrastructure promet à l'Afrique un développement économique considérable. (**91 mots**)

II. Expression

Mobile phones have become a new means of making payments. They're easy, fast, convenient, and save you worrying about cheque books or additional credit cards. Mobile phones can replace computers, mp3 players, TV, and now banks.
The advantages are obvious as stated before. One tiny object can perform all sorts of functions and save you a lot of trouble.
The danger is that if you happen to lose it or have it stolen, you run the risk of having it hacked. Besides, are we always cautious enough with new technology? Do we know how secure our payments are on mobile phones?
The other risk is in using it carelessly or too often, to pay for purchases. You could very easily find yourself in the red without your knowing it.
I'd rather check my expenses with my bank and rely on my bank statements, or use credit cards with chips that have personal pins. (**157 words**)

Précis grammatical

DOMAINE NOMINAL

Noms

Noms dénombrables

Un nom dénombrable désigne un élément que l'on peut compter. Il peut donc être précédé d'un nombre (*one, two*...), de l'article indéfini *a/an*, d'un quantifieur et se mettre au pluriel.
***a** car, **two** telegrams, **ten** fans, **a few** journalists, **some** messages*

Pluriel

Le **-s** ou **-es** du pluriel est prononcé :
– /iz/ après les sons /s/, /z/, /ʃ/ et /ð/
*voi**ces**, si**zes**, bo**xes**, loa**thes***
– /s/ après les consonnes sourdes : /p/, /t/, /k/, /f/ et /θ/
*tem**ps**, paren**ts**, wal**ks**, roo**fs**, mon**ths**,*
– /z/ après les consonnes sonores et les voyelles :
*worke**rs**, jo**bs**, ne**ws**, lifeti**mes**, nee**ds**, ski**lls**, degr**ees**.*

Modifications orthographiques

– consonne + Y + S → ies
*a cit**y** → cit**ies***
– O + S → oes
*a tomato → tomat**oes***
mais *pianos/photos*
– SS/SH/CH/X + S → es
*a box → box**es***
– F/FE+S → ves
*a hal**f** → hal**ves**, a kni**fe** → kni**ves***

Pluriels irréguliers

*m**a**n → m**e**n, wom**a**n → wom**e**n,*
*child /ai/ → child**ren** /i/, m**ouse** → m**ice**,*
*f**oo**t → f**ee**t, t**oo**th → t**ee**th.*

Noms indénombrables

Un nom indénombrable désigne un élément qu'on ne peut pas compter. Il ne peut pas être précédé d'un nombre (*one, two*...), ni de l'article indéfini *a/an*, ni se mettre au pluriel.

Dénombreurs

Pour se référer à un élément de l'ensemble, on utilise un dénombreur ou *some* pour une quantité indéfinie :
***a piece of** news/of luggage/of furniture/of advice/of information*, une nouvelle, un bagage, un meuble, un conseil, une information
***a pint of** beer* une pinte de bière, ***a cup of** tea* une tasse de thé, ***a bottle of** milk* une bouteille de lait, ***a glass of** wine* un verre de vin, ***some** time* un certain temps
Certains mots changent de sens selon qu'ils sont dénombrables ou indénombrables.
***a** paper* : un journal, **Ø** *paper* : du papier,
***a** room* : une pièce **Ø** *room* : de la place.

Indénombrables singuliers

– les noms de matière : *coal* le charbon, *iron* le fer, *oil* le pétrole, *asbestos* l'amiante ;
– les couleurs : *purple* le pourpre, *black* le noir ;
– les noms de maladies : *AIDS* le sida, *the flu* la grippe ;
– les noms en *-ics* : *economics* l'économie, *physics* la physique, *electronics* l'électronique, *politics* la politique ;
– les noms en *-ing* décrivant une activité : *driving* la conduite, *travelling* voyager, *advertising* la publicité, *computerizing* l'informatique ;
– les noms représentant un ensemble : *advice* les conseils, *business* les affaires, *evidence* les preuves, *hair* les cheveux, *homework* les devoirs, *information* les informations, *leisure* les loisirs, *news* les nouvelles, *progress* les progrès, *transport* les transports, *trouble* les ennuis, *wear* les vêtements ;
– notions abstraites : *comfort* le récomfort, *freedom* la liberté, *happiness* le bonheur, *justice* la justice, *knowledge* le savoir, *money* l'argent, *pollution* la pollution, *poverty* la pauvreté, *unemployment* le chômage, *work* le travail.

Indénombrables pluriels

– vêtements en deux parties : *jeans* un jean, *pyjamas* un pyjama, *shorts* un short, *trousers* un pantalon ;
– instruments en deux parties : *binoculars* une paire de jumelles, *glasses* une paire de lunettes, *scissors* une paire de ciseaux ;
– les collectifs : *people* les gens, *clothes* les vêtements, *customs* la douane, *police* les policiers, *stairs* les escaliers.

Noms invariables

– *a sheep* un mouton, *sheep* des moutons ;
– *a fish* un poisson, *fish* des poissons ;
– *a fruit* un fruit, *fruit* des fruits.

Noms composés

Dans un nom composé l'élément essentiel est le second. Le premier élément sert à le qualifier et dans la plupart des cas porte l'accent.

Second nom

– un nom : *a race **horse*** un cheval de course, *a horse **race*** une course de chevaux ;
– un verbe : *a bottle-**opene**r* un ouvre-bouteille, *a taxi-**drive**r* un chauffeur de taxi ;
– un adverbe : *the have-**nots*** les démunis ;
– une particule : *a break**down*** une panne, *grown-**ups*** des adultes.

Premier nom

– un nom : *the **job** market* le marché du travail, ***job** security* la sécurité de l'emploi, ***advancement** opportunities* des perspectives de promotion, *the **work** force* la main d'œuvre, *a **college** degree* un diplôme universitaire, *a **hightech** career* une carrière dans la technologie de pointe, *a **software** engineer* un programmeur ;
– une particule : ***on**-lookers* des spectateurs ;
– un adjectif : *a **black**smith* un forgeron ;
– un nom verbal : *a **swimming**-pool* une piscine.
Le premier nom se comporte comme un adjectif et est donc toujours au singulier même s'il est précédé d'un chiffre.
– *a 24-**hour** event* un événement qui dure 24 heures ;
– *a yearlong **20,000-mile**, around the world cycling epic* une aventure à bicylette qui va durer un an et parcourir 36.000 kilomètres autour du monde.
Quelques noms pourtant portent toujours un S :
– *a **goods** train* un train de marchandises ;
– *a **customs** officer* un douanier ;
– *the **accounts** department* le service de la comptabilité ;
– *the **claims** department* le service des réclamations ;
– ***sports**wear* les vêtements de sports ;
– *a **savings** account* un compte épargne ;
– *the **arms** race* la course à l'armement.

Noms dérivés

Les noms dérivés se forment à l'aide d'un suffixe ou un préfixe.

Préfixes

***anti**militarism, **auto**biography, **dis**like, **il**literacy, **im**maturity, **in**credibility, **ir**regularity, **mis**fortune, **un**stability.*

Suffixes

arriv**al**, bak**er**, employ**ee**, free**dom**, friend**ship**, host**ess**, kind**ness**, mouth**ful**, neighbour**hood**, stupid**ity**.

Nom verbal

-ing permet de former un nom à partir d'un verbe.
- *to swim* nager → *swimm**ing*** la natation ;
- *to train* se former → *train**ing*** la formation ;
- *to type* taper à la machine → *typ**ing*** la dactylographie ;
- *to write* écrire → *writ**ing*** l'écriture.

Ces noms peuvent être :
- sujets : *Work**ing** on a computer is my favourite job.* Travailler sur ordinateur est mon travail favori ;
- complements : *I don't mind your smok**ing***. Cela ne me dérange pas si vous fumez.

Articles

Article indéfini *A/AN*

L'article indéfini *a/an* n'a pas de forme au pluriel et désigne un élément dans un ensemble.

On choisit *a* ou *an* en fonction de la prononciation de la première lettre du mot qui suit.
- ***A*** s'emploie pour un son-consonne :

***a n**ewspaper*, ***a u**niversity* /juː/, ***a h**ouse*, ***a o**ne-parent family* /wʌn/.
- ***An*** s'emploie devant un mot commençant par un son voyelle :

***an i**dea*, ***an M**P (empi :)*, ***an (h)o**ur*.

L'article a/an s'emploie
- devant un attribut :

*Her father is **a** butcher.* Son père est boucher.
- devant une apposition :

*Hitchcock, **a** famous film director, was born in Britain.* Hitchcock, célèbre réalisateur, est né en Grande-Bretagne.
- pour une répartition :

*twice **a** week* deux fois par semaine, *£20 **a** head* 35 euros par personne.
- avec une exclamation :

*He is **such a** nice man!* C'est un homme si gentil !

*He is **so** nice **a** man!* C'est un homme si gentil !

***What a** wonderful idea!* Quelle idée merveilleuse !

***How** wonderful **an** idea it is!* Comme cette idée est merveilleuse !

Article zéro Ø

Un nom employé seul, c'est-à-dire précédé de l'article zéro **Ø**, évoque une idée, une notion, une catégorie non repérée.

*I prefer **Ø** tea to **Ø** coffee.* J'aime mieux **le** thé que **le** café.

L'article **Ø** se trouve devant :
- les noms dénombrables au pluriel :

Ø *European countries* **les** pays européens ;

Ø *British people* **les** Britanniques.
- les noms de matière :

Ø *water* **l'**eau, **Ø** *butter* **le/du** beurre, **Ø** *bread* **le/du** pain.
- les noms désignant une notion abstraite :

Ø *love* **l'**amour, **Ø** *hatred* **la** haine, **Ø** *freedom* **la** liberté, **Ø** *friendship* **l'**amitié, **Ø** *humankind* **l'**humanité.
- les noms propres même précédés d'un titre :

Ø *Britain* **la** Grande-Bretagne, **Ø** *President Bush* **le** Président Bush **Ø** *Queen Elizabeth* **la** reine Elisabeth.
- les expressions :

go to **Ø** *school/* **Ø** *church/* **Ø** *hospital* aller à **l'**école/**l'**église/**l'**hôpital ;

have **Ø** *breakfast* prendre **le** petit déjeuner ;

Ø *last week* **la** semaine dernière, **Ø** *next year* **l'**année prochaine.

Article défini *THE*

L'article défini ***the*** se prononce :
- /ðə/ devant un mot commençant par un son consonne :

***the s**olution*, ***the U**SA* /ju/.
- /ði/ devant un mot commençant par un son-voyelle :

***the a**nswer*.

The reprend un élément déja isolé, déjà repéré. Il permet d'indiquer qu'une chose est :
- unique :

***the** sky*, ***the** sun*, *the moon*, ***the** media*, ***the** press*, ***the** TV*, ***the** radio*, ***the** millennium*, ***the** Arctic Circle*.
- repérée par la situation :

*Look at **the** sky!* Regarde le/ce ciel !
- repérée par le contexte :

*She saw a dog. **The** dog was her neighbours'.* Elle vit un chien. Le chien était celui de ses voisins.
- de parler de tout un groupe :

***the** Italians* les Italiens, ***the** French* les Français, ***the** British* les Britanniques, ***the** Finns* les Finlandais.

Pronoms

Pronoms personnels

Les pronoms personnels permettent de reprendre un groupe nominal.

Pronoms personnels sujets	Pronoms personnels compléments
I	*me*
he/she/it	*him/her/it*
we	*us*
you	*you*
they	*them*

Pronoms sujets

It reprend un nom qui n'est ni masculin ni féminin.

*Janet lives in a little **house**. **It**'s very comfortable.* Jeanne vit dans une petite maison. Elle est très confortable.

*Listen to the **baby**. **It**'s crying.* Ecoute le bébé. Il/elle pleure.

It est aussi employé pour annoncer une proposition qui est en fait le sujet réel de la phrase.

***It's** Mary Pierce.* C'est Mary Pierce.

Pronoms compléments

Ils n'ont qu'une forme en anglais et se placent toujours après le verbe qu'il soit simple ou prépositionnel.

*I like **them**.* Je **les** aime bien

*She looks like **him**.* Elle **lui** ressemble.

Les pronoms ***me*** et ***him*** ne peuvent être que compléments.

*My brother and **I** are twins.* Mon frère et **moi** sommes jumeaux.

***He** and his wife were late.* **Lui** et sa femme étaient en retard.

Adjectifs et pronoms possessifs

Adjectifs possessifs	Pronoms possessifs
my	*mine*
his/her/its	*his/hers/its*
our	*ours*
your	*yours*
their	*theirs*

À la différence du français, l'adjectif possessif reprend le genre et le nombre du possesseur.
- féminin singulier → ***her***

Mary *twisted* ***her*** *ankle.* Marie s'est tordu la cheville.
– masculin singulier → ***his***
John *shouldn't pitch* ***his*** *tent under that tree.* Jean ne devrait pas monter sa tente sous cet arbre.
– pluriel → ***their***
They *were unable to find* ***their*** *way back.* Ils furent incapables de retrouver leur chemin pour rentrer.

Pronoms réfléchis
Pour faire référence à soi-même on utilise un pronom réfléchi.

Singulier	Pluriel
myself	*ourselves*
yourself	*yourselves*
himself, herself, itself	*themselves*

Ils ont parfois une valeur d'insistance.
I did it ***myself****.* C'est moi qui l'ai fait.
Certains verbes ne sont pas réfléchis en anglais : *dress* s'habiller, *feel* se sentir, *meet* se rencontrer, *shave* se raser, *wash* se laver.

Pronoms réciproques
Pour renvoyer à l'autre ou aux autres on utilise *each other* ou *one another.*
Comparez :
They were looking at ***themselves*** *in the mirror.* Ils se regardaient dans la glace.
They were looking at ***each other/one another*** *lovingly.* Ils se regardaient amoureusement.

Pronom *ONE(S)*
One(s) permet de reprendre un nom déjà apparu dans le discours.
'Give me plates' 'White ***ones*** *or blue* ***ones****?'* « Donne-moi des assiettes ! » « Des bleues ou des blanches ? »

Mise en relation de deux noms

En français pour mettre deux noms en relation, on utilise la préposition « de ». En anglais, on utilise
– la préposition ***of*** si le nom qui la suit désigne une chose.
The leg ***of*** *a chair.* Un pied de chaise.
– une préposition différente :
an article ***by*** un article de, *taken* ***from*** tiré de, *a decrease* ***in*** une diminution de, *a cheque* ***for*** un chèque de
– Le génitif si le premier nom est :
• une personne :
his parents' car la voiture de ses parents,
*my brother****'s*** *bike* le vélo de mon frère,
*the children****'s*** *toys* les jouets des enfants ;
• un groupe de personnes :
*the world****'s*** *population* la population du monde, *the government****'s*** *warning* la mise en garde du gouvernement ;
• une unité de temps :
*an hour****'s*** *drive* une heure de voiture,
*today****'s*** *paper* le journal d'aujourd'hui,
a *day****'s*** *work* une journée de travail ;
• un lieu public :
*the baker****'s*** (sous-entendu *shop*) chez le boulanger,
*St Patrick****'s*** (sous-entendu *Cathedral*) la Cathédrale St Patrick,
at the Joneses' (sous entendu *home*) chez les Jones.

Si le nom au génitif est un singulier ou un pluriel irrégulier, on le fait suivre de ***'s.*** S'il se termine par *-s*, il est suivi de l'apostrophe seule.
Le second nom ne prend jamais d'article.
The woman's **Ø** *child.* L'enfant de la dame.

Adjectifs

Généralités

Les adjectifs sont toujours invariables.
These are ***difficult*** *problems.* Ce sont des problèmes difficiles.
Les adjectifs épithètes se placent devant les noms qu'ils qualifient.
I can't stand chatting about ***famous*** *people.* Je ne peux supporter de bavarder au sujet de gens célèbres.
Les adjectifs commençant par ***a-*** ne peuvent être qu'attributs.
The child is ***asleep****.* L'enfant est endormi.

Ordre des adjectifs

En anglais, l'adjectif qui indique un jugement se place en premier, vient ensuite celui qui décrit une caractéristique fondamentale :
an intelligent young lady une jeune femme intelligente.

Adjectifs composés

Les adjectifs composés se forment de plusieurs manières :
– adjectif + adjectif :
light-blue bleu clair,
– nom + adjectif :
sky-blue bleu ciel,
– adjectif + nom-*ed* :
long-legged qui a de longues jambes,
– nom + participe passé :
heart-broken qui a le coeur brisé, *home-made* fait à la maison,
– nom + nom-ed :
snow-capped couvert de neige,
– adjectif + verbe-*ing* :
easy-going décontracté, *far-reaching* qui porte loin, *hard-working* qui travaile dur, *fast-moving* qui avance rapidement ;
– nom + verbe-*ing* :
French-speaking qui parle français, *law-abiding* qui respecte la loi,
– adjectif + participe passé :
open-minded à l'esprit ouvert,
– adverbe + participe passé :
well-known célèbre,
– numéral + nom :
twenty-nine-year old âgé de vingt neuf ans, *15-month old* âgé de quinze mois, a *two-year forecast* une prévision sur deux ans.

Adjectifs dérivés

Comme les noms, les adjectifs peuvent être dérivés par un suffixe ou un préfixe.
– Préfixes donnant une idée de contraire :
il*legal* illégal, ***im****patient*, impatient, ***in****expensive* peu cher, ***inca****pable* incapable, ***ir****regular* irrégulier, ***un****real* irréel, ***un****wanted* indésirable, ***un****shakable* inébranlable, ***un****disputed* incontesté, ***un****likely* peu vraisemblable, ***un****challenged* sans concurrent.
– Préfixes donnant une idée d'erreur :
dis*loyal* déloyal, ***dis****satisfied* mécontent, ***mis****interpreted* mal interprêté, ***mis****leading* trompeur.
– Nom + ***less/ful*** :
*use****ful*** utile, *use****less*** inutile, *beauti****ful*** beau, *care****ful*** prudent, *care****less*** imprudent, *harm****ful*** qui fait mal, *harm****less*** inoffensif, *point****less*** inutile, *home****less*** sans abri.

Adjectifs nominalisés

L'article défini ***the*** devant un adjectif a une valeur de généralisation. Il renvoie à la classe complète des membres du groupe.
L'adjectif ne prend pas de ***s*** mais s'accorde avec un verbe pluriel.
the *poor* les pauvres, ***the*** *unemployed* les chômeurs, ***the*** *young* les jeunes, ***the*** *English* les Anglais.

Adjectifs de nationalité

Adjectif et nom semblables

– *Asian, an Asian, the Asians*
African, American, Australian, Austrian, Belgian, Brazilian, Egyptian, European, Indian, German, Italian, Jamaican, Mexican, Nigerian, Norwegian, Russian, Singaporean
– *Saudi, a Saudi, the Saudis*
Iraqi, Israeli, Pakistani, Bangladeshi

Adjectif et noms semblables et invariables

– *Chinese, a Chinese, the Chinese*
Japanese, Lebanese, Portuguese, Senegalese, Vietnamese
– *Swiss, a Swiss, the Swiss*

Adjectif et nom différents

– *Spanish, a Spaniard*
Arabic an Arab, British a Briton, Danish a Dane, Finnish a Finn, Jewish a Jew, New Zealand a New Zealander, Polish a Pole, Scottish a Scot, Spanish a Spaniard, Swedish a Swede, Turkish a Turk

Adjectif et nom dérivé

– *English, an Englishman, English people, the English*
a Dutchman, a Frenchman, an Irishman, a Welshman

Adjectifs à deux formes

Certains adjectifs ont deux formes qui ont un sens légèrement différent qu'il convient de mémoriser.
– ***Economic*** : qui concerne l'économie.
*The governement's new **economic** policy favours full employment.* La nouvelle politique économique du gouvernement encourage au plein emploi.
Economical : économe de son temps ou de son argent.
*You should be **economical** of your time.* Vous devriez être plus économe de votre temps
– ***Historic*** : qui marque l'histoire.
a historic event un évènement historique
Historical : qui parle de l'histoire.
Robin Hood *is a **historical** novel.* *Robin de Bois* est un roman historique.
– ***Electric*** : qui marche à l'électricité.
*an **electric** guitar* une guitare éléctrique
Electrical : qui s'occupe d'électricité.
*an **electrical** engineer* un ingénieur en éléctricité
– ***Comic*** : qui fait rire.
*a **comic** film* un film comique, *a **comic** strip* une bande dessinée, *a **comic** opera* un opéra comique
Comical : ridicule, étrange.
*She alwayswears **comical** old hats.* Elle porte toujours de vieux chapeaux ridicules.

La comparaison

Pour comparer deux éléments on utilise le comparatif, tandis que le superlatif indique qu'un élément est supérieur ou inférieur à tous les autres.

Comparatif d'égalité

– ***The same … as, as … as*** exprime une équivalence.
*They have **the same** difficulties **as** I do.* Ils ont les mêmes difficultés que moi.
La forme négative nie cette équivalence.
*The budget used by Smart is **not as** considerable **as** the one used by BMW.* Le budget utilisé pour la Smart n'est pas aussi élévé que celui de BMW.
– ***As many… as, as much … as***
*What we need is **as much** information **as** possible on their intentions.* Ce dont nous avons besoin c'est d'autant d'informations que possible concernant leurs intentions.

Le groupe ***as many/much*** peut être précédé de multiplicateurs.
*There are **twice as many** mobile users in the South **as** in the Norh of England.* Il y a deux fois plus d'utilisateurs de portables dans le Sud que dans le Nord de l'Angleterre.
La forme négative nie cette équivalence.
*I do not have **as many** employees under my responsibility **as** you do.* Je n'ai pas autant d'employés sous ma responsabilité que vous.

Comparatif et superlatif de supériorité

– adjectifs de deux syllabes ou plus :
Comparatif : ***more*** + adjectif + ***than***
*Today's companies are **more competitive than** they used to be.* Les entreprises d'aujourd'hui sont plus performantes qu'autrefois.
Superlatif : ***the most*** + adjectif
*It's **the most expensive** advertising campaign I have ever seen.* C'est la camapgne publicitaire la plus chère que j'ai jamais vue.
– adjectifs d'une syllabe ou de deux syllabes terminés en *-y, -er, -ly* :
Comparatif : adjectif-***er*** + ***than***
*They go **faster** and **higher**.* Ils vont plus vite et plus haut.
*It is **easier**.* C'est plus facile.
Superlatif : ***the*** + adjectif-***est***
*It is one of **the tightest** budgets.* C'est l'un des budgets les plus réduits.
*She is the **happiest** person I know.* C'est la personne la plus heureuse que je connaisse.

Il y a doublement de la consonne finale si l'adjectif se termine par consonne/voyelle/consonne. Comparez.
big → *bi**gg**er than, strong* → *stron**g**er than*
vcc cvc

Formes irrégulières

adjectif	comparatif	superlatif
much/many beaucoup	*more than* plus que	*the most* le plus
little peu	*less than* moins que	*the least* le moins
good bon(ne)	*better than* meilleur que	*the best* le mieux
bad mauvais(e)	*worse than* pire que	*the worst* le pire
old vieux(elle)	*elder than* plus âgé que	*the eldest* l'aîné
far lointain(e)	*farther than* plus loin que *further than* davantage que	*the farthest* le plus loin *the furthest* le plus loin

Comparatif et superlatif d'infériorité

*Today's companies are **less** competitive **than** before.* Aujourd'hui les entreprises sont moins concurrentielles qu'auparavant.
*I bought **the least** expensive present I could find.* J'ai acheté le cadeau le moins cher que j'ai pu trouver.

De plus en plus/De moins en moins

*Women are **more and more** determined to work and have children.* Les femmes sont de plus en plus déterminées à travailler et à avoir des enfants.
*Their chances to succeed are **fewer and fewer**.* Leurs chances de réussir sont de moins en moins grandes.
*They seem **less and less** interested.* Ils semblent de moins en moins intéressés.

THE + comparatif, *THE* + comparatif

The richer *he is,* ***the richer*** *he wants to be.* Plus il est riche, plus il veut être riche.
The more *experienced you are,* ***the better***. Plus vous êtes expérimenté, mieux cela vaut.
The more *you'll type,* ***the*** *fast****er***. Plus vous taperez à la machine, plus vite vous taperez.
The less *overworked I am,* ***the better***. Moins je suis débordée de travail, mieux c'est.

ALL THE MORE (SO)... AS / SINCE

– **D'autant plus/moins que + adjectif**
The competition is ***all the*** *harsh****er/more*** *important* ***as*** *Marks & Spencer's image is ageing.* La concurrence est d'autant plus dure/importante que Marks & Spencer a une image vieillissante.
His victory was ***all the less*** *predictable* ***since*** *he was sick.* Sa victoire était d'autant moins prévisible qu'il était malade.
– **D'autant plus que sans adjectif**
We have to hurry up, ***all the more so as*** *the plane takes off in 20 minutes.* Il faut se dépêcher, d'autant plus que l'avion décolle dans 20 minutes.

AS et *LIKE*

– ***Like*** est une préposition qui se trouve devant un nom pour établir une comparaison.
Like *father* ***like*** *son.* Tel père tel fils.
She looks ***like*** *her mother.* Elle ressemble à sa mère.
What was the weather ***like****?* Comment était le temps ?
He is dressed ***like*** *a tramp.* Il est habillé comme un clochard.
– Lorsque ***as*** est préposition, il signifie « en tant que ».
I speak to you ***as*** *a friend.* Je te parle en tant qu'ami.
He was dressed ***as*** *a tramp.* Il était déguisé en clochard.
– ***As*** peut aussi être une conjonction.
Do ***as*** *you like.* Fais comme tu veux.

Quantifieurs

Les quantifieurs permettent de désigner une plus ou moins grande quantité.

Adjectifs cardinaux

0 zero	19 nineteen
1 one	20 twenty
2 two	21 twenty-one
3 three	22 twenty-two
4 four	23 twenty-three
5 five	24 twenty-four
6 six	25 twenty-five
7 seven	26 twenty-six
8 eight	27 twenty-seven
9 nine	28 twenty-eight
10 ten	29 twenty-nine
11 eleven	30 thirty
12 twelve	40 forty
13 thirteen	50 fifty
14 fourteen	60 sixty
15 fifteen	70 seventy
16 sixteen	80 eighty
17 seventeen	90 ninety
18 eighteen	100 one hundred

– ***Dozen, hundred, thousand, million*** et ***billion*** sont invariables quand ils sont précédés d'un nombre.
Mais s'ils désignent une quantité indéfinie, ils portent la marque **-s** du pluriel et sont suivis de ***of***.
*dozen****s****/hundred****s****/million****s*** ***of*** des douzaines/des centaines/des millions de.

200 two hundred
2,000 two thousand
20,000 twenty thousand
200,000 two hundred thousand
2,000,000 two million
20,000,000 twenty million
200,000,000 two hundred million
2,000,000,000 two billion
20,000,000,000 twenty billion

Lire les chiffres

– Là où le français utilise un point, l'anglais utilise une virgule et vice versa.
3.14 *three point fourteen,*
18.6% *eighteen point six percent,*
3,464 miners *three thousand four hundred and sixty-four miners*
– Les dizaines et les unités sont précédées de ***and***.
752 *seven hundred* ***and*** *fifty-two*
– dates :
1980 *nineteen eighty,*
2009 *two thousand and nine,*
in the '80s/eighties dans les années quatre-vingt,
– mesures :
– 10° *minus ten degrees,*
– prix :
£6 *six pounds,* $20 *twenty dollars*
– téléphone :
233 00 42 *two double three double o four two*

Adjectifs ordinaux

Ils permettent de repérer la place dans une série.
*1****st*** *fir****st****, 2****nd*** *seco****nd****, 3****rd*** *thi****rd****,*
*4****th*** *four****th****, 5****th*** *fif****th****, 11****th*** *eleven****th****, 12****th*** *twelf****th****, 13****th*** *thirteen****th****,*
*20****th*** *twentie****th****, 21****st*** *twenty-fir****st****,*
*31****st*** *thirty-fir****st****, 100****th*** *one hundred****th.***
On utilise les adjectifs ordinaux pour les dates.
*July 22****nd*** *= on July the* ***twenty-second***

Petite quantité

– ***Little / a little / less / the least*** s'emploient devant un nom indénombrable.
I'm afraid we have very ***little*** *time to find it.* J'ai peur que nous ayons peu de temps pour le trouver.
Jack tried to give her ***a little*** *advice.* Jack a essayé de lui donner quelques conseils.
I have ***less*** *time than before.* J'ai moins de temps qu'autrefois.
We have ***the least*** *money.* C'et nous qui avons le moins d'argent.
– ***Few / a few / fewer / the fewest*** s'emploient devant un nom dénombrable.
We have ***few*** *people ready so far.* Nous avons peu de gens prêts jusqu'à présent.
Only ***a few*** *Germans work for this company.* Seuls quelques Allemands travaillent pour cette société.
He has ***fewer*** *friends than we do.* Il a moins d'amis que nous.
I made ***the fewest*** *mistakes.* J'ai fait le moins de fautes.

Ensemble de deux

– ***Both*** exprime un ensemble de deux.
They ***both*** *wanted to set up their own business.* Ils voulaient tous les deux créer leur propre entreprise.
He was not able to run ***both*** *of them.* Il n'était pas capable de diriger les deux.
– ***Either*** désigne l'un ou l'autre élément d'un ensemble de deux.
You can park on ***either*** *side of the street.* Tu peux te garer d'un côté ou de l'autre de la rue.

– ***Either … or*** désigne le choix entre deux alternatives.
Either *you stay* ***or*** *you go.* Ou bien tu restes, ou bien tu pars.
– ***Neither*** désigne un ensemble de deux éléments de manière négative.
I know ***neither*** *of them.* Je ne les connais, ni l'un ni l'autre.
– ***Neither … nor*** désigne le rejet de deux alternatives.
I like ***neither*** *fish* ***nor*** *seafood.* Je n'aime ni le poisson ni les fruits de mer.

Quantité non précisée

Some s'emploie pour se référer à une quantité non précisée d'éléments dont on suppose qu'ils existent.
Some *people claim it is not true.* Certaines personnes disent que ce n'est pas vrai.
Do you want ***some*** *tea?* Tu prendras bien du thé ?
Any s'emploie pour parcourir tout l'éventail des éléments dont on ne sait pas s'ils existent. On trouve donc *any*
– après une negation :
He doesn't have ***any*** *time.* Il n'a pas le temps.
– dans les questions où l'on attend une réponse négative :
Is there ***any*** *problem?* Il n'y a pas de problème, n'est-ce pas ?
Les composés de ***some*** et ***any*** suivent les mêmes règles d'emploi dans les phrases affirmatives.

Somebody/someone quelqu'un	*something* quelque chose	*somewhere* quelque part
anybody/anyone n'importe qui	*anything* n'importe quoi	*anywhere* n'importe où
nobody/no one personne	*nothing* rien	*nowhere* nulle part

La plupart

Most précède un nom non déterminé.
Most Ø *people have a car.* La plupart des gens ont une voiture.
Most of précède un nom déterminé par un article défini ou un possessif.
It rains ***most of the*** *time.* Il pleut la plupart du temps.
Most of my *friends have a mountain bike.* La plupart de mes amis ont un VTT.

Assez

Enough indique une quantité ou un degré suffisant.
– Adjectif + ***enough*** :
Is the water warm ***enough****?* L'eau est-elle assez chaude ?
– ***Enough*** + nom :
Have you got ***enough*** *time?* As-tu assez de temps ?
– ***Rather*** signifie « plutôt ».
He behaved ***rather*** *stupidly.* Il s'est comporté assez bêtement.
– ***Quite*** signife « assez » avec un adjectif graduable.
It's ***quite*** *a long way.* C'est assez loin.
It's ***quite*** *cold.* Il fait assez froid.

Beaucoup

Much s'emploie devant un nom indénombrable aux formes interrogative et négative pour désigner une grande quantité.
Do you need ***much time?*** As-tu besoin de beaucoup de temps ?
She was determined ***not*** *to do* ***much business****.* Elle était déterminée à ne pas faire beaucoup d'affaires.
Many s'emploie devant un nom dénombrable.
Many *family* ***businesses*** *are hard to manage.* Beaucoup d'entreprises familiales sont difficiles à gérer.
A lot of / lots of / plenty of peuvent s'employer dans tous les cas.
There were ***a lot of / lots of / plenty of*** *people.* Il y avait beaucoup de gens.

Totalité

All exprime la totalité.
He's read ***all*** *the books.* Il a lu tous les livres.
The whole insiste sur l'intégralité.
He's read ***the whole*** *book.* Il a lu le livre entier.
Every et ses composés se réfèrent à chacun des éléments d'un ensemble. C'est pourquoi ils s'accordent avec un nom et un verbe au singulier.
Everybody *knows I cycle* ***every*** *day.* Tout le monde sait que je fais du vélo chaque jour.
Each accorde plus d'importance à chaque élément considéré.
Each *of you* ***has*** *to do so.* Chacun de vous doit le faire.

Démonstratifs

THIS / THESE

This / these est utilisé pour désigner ce qui est proche
– dans l'espace :
this *book here* ce livre-ci, *in* ***this*** *country* dans ce pays (où je suis)
– dans le temps :
these *days* de nos jours, *this week* cette semaine
– affectivement :
this *heart of mine* ce coeur qui est le mien.

THAT / THOSE

That / those est utilisé pour désigner ce qui est loin
– dans l'espace :
in ***that*** *country* dans ce pays là,
– dans le temps :
at ***that*** *time/in* ***those*** *days* dans ce temps là,
– affectivement :
that *friend of yours* cet ami à toi,
oh, ***that*** *girl* oh, cette fille là !

Prépositions

Prépositions de lieu

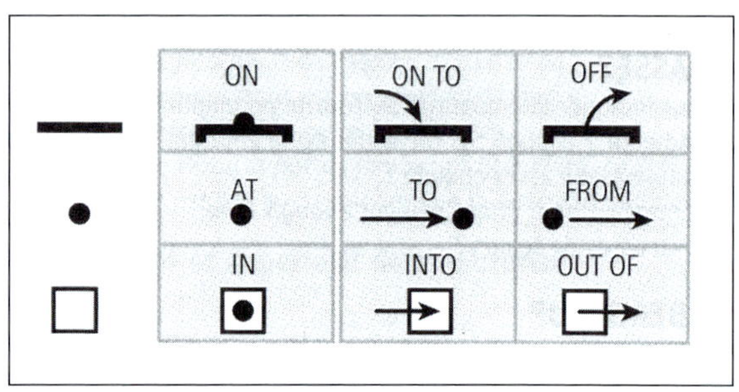

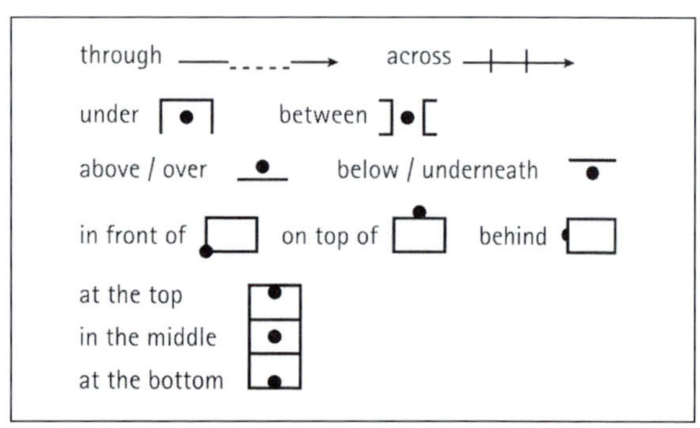

along le long de
at the bottom en bas
at the top en haut
beside à côté
beyond au delà de
in the background à l'arrière plan
in the foreground au premier plan
near/next to près de
on the left /right à gauche/ droite
on the side of sur le flanc de

He went ***from*** *Liverpool* ***to*** *London* ***by*** *train and waited* ***at*** *the station.* Il est allé de Liverpool à Londres en train et a attendu à la gare.

Prépositions de temps

after *2.30* après 14h30
at *8 p.m.* à 20 heures
before *noon* avant midi
between *November 1992* **and** *March 1998* entre novembre 1992 et mars 1998
by *2009* avant 2009
during *the war/summer/holidays* pendant la guerre/l'été/les vacances
in 1998 en 1998, **in winter** en hiver
on *Saturday evenings* le samedi soir
since *mid-August* depuis la mi-août
throughout *the night* durant toute la nuit
till/until *the time comes* jusqu'à ce que le moment vienne
within *six months* dans les 6 mois

Verbes et adjectifs prépositionnels

Certains verbes et adjectifs sont suivis d'une préposition différente du français qu'il convient de mémoriser.

about
certain about : sûr de
complain about : se plaindre de
crazy about : fou de
curious about : curieux de
glad about : satisfait de
happy about : heureux de
sad about : triste de
sorry about : déso1é de
uneasy about : mal à l'aise de
worried about : inquiet de

at
aim at : viser
amazed at : surpris par
amused at : amusé par
angry at : fâché avec
astonished at : étonné de
bad at : mauvais en
good at : bon en
hint at : faire allusion à
hopeless at : incompétent en
laugh at : se moquer de
look at : regarder
surprised at : surpris de, étonné de
wonder at : s'étonner de

by
decrease/drop/fall by : diminuer/chuter/ tomber de
frightened by : effrayé de
increase/rise by augmenter/s'élever de
profit by : profiter de
written by : écrit par

for
account for : justifier, expliquer
apologize for : s'excuser de
apply for : des présenter à un poste
blame for : accuser de
congratulate for : féliciter de
hope for : espérer
look for : chercher
long for : désirer fortement
necessary for : nécessaire à
pay for : payer
prepared for : prêt à
ready for : prêt à
responsible for : responsable de
sorry for : désolé pour
thank for : remercier de
wait for : attendre
yearn for : désirer fortement

from
absent from : absent de
benefit from : bénéficier de
borrow from : emprunter à
buy from : acheter chez
deprive from : priver de
die from : mourir de
differ from : différer de
different from : différent de
far from : loin de
flee from : s'enfuir de
hide from : cacher de
independent from : indépendant de
part from : se séparer de
prevent from : empêcher de
protect from : protéger de
rob from : voler à
separated from : séparé de
suffer from : souffrir de

in
consist in : consister à
interested in : intéressé par
succeed in : réussir à

into
burst into : éclater en
divide into : diviser par
integrate into : s'intégrer à
translate into : traduire en
turn into : transformer en

of
approve of : approuver
hear of : entendre parler de
remind of : rappeler
short of : en manque de
think of : penser à

on
comment on : commenter
depend on : dépendre de
keen on : féru de
insist on : insister pour
operate on : opérer

to
listen to : écouter
look forward to : attendre avec impatience

with
agree with : être d'accord avec
amused with : amusé de
angry with : fâché envers
charge with : accuser de
compare with : comparer à
content with : content de
cope with : faire face à
correspond with : correspondre à
deal with : traiter de
delighted with : enchanté de
interfere with : se mêler de
pleased with : content de
reproach with : reprocher de
satisfied with : satisfait de

Verbes à particules

Les particules changent le sens du verbe :
– *give* donner / *give* ***up*** abandonner,
– *break* casser / *break* ***down*** tomber en panne.
Si le complément est un pronom, il se place avant la particule.
Comparez :
– Préposition : *Look* ***at*** *it.* Regarde-le.
– Particule : *Look it* ***up*** *in a dictionary.* Cherche-le dans un dictionnaire.

Adverbes

Les adverbes se placent généralement devant le mot ou groupe de mots qu'ils modifient.
Is it ***really*** *what you think?* Est-ce vraiment ce que tu penses ?
Les adverbes de manière et de temps imprécis se placent devant le verbe.
Paul ***always*** *reads* Newsweek. Paul lit toujours *Newsweek.*
Have you ***ever*** *worked as a volunteer?* As-tu déjà travaillé comme bénévole ?

Adverbes de manière

Ils se forment en ajoutant le suffixe **-ly** à l'adjectif :
definitely certainement,
drastically radicalement,
decidedly décidement,
dramatically fortement,
lavishly sans compter,
mainly principalement,
shamefully honteusement,
sharply brusquement,
slightly légèrement,
steadily régulièrement,
undoubtedly sans aucun doute,
unfortunately malheureusement,
unmistakably immanquablement

Double forme

Certains adjectifs peuvent fonctionner comme adverbes et ont une forme en **-ly** qui a un sens différent. Comparez :
He works ***hard.*** Il travaille d'arrache-pied.
He ***hardly*** *works.* Il travaille à peine.

They arrived ***late***. Ils arrivèrent en retard. *Have you met him* ***lately****?* L'as-tu vu dernièrement?
Do you feel all ***right****?* Te sens-tu bien?
He answered quite ***rightly*** *that...* Il répondit à juste titre que...

Adverbes d'intensité

little peu, *a little* un peu,
almost / nearly presque,
rather / fairly / quite relativement,
very très, *so* tellement, *too* trop.

Même

– Adverbe :
Even *you can do it.* Même toi tu peux le faire.
– Adjectif :
It's always ***the same*** *thing.* C'est toujours la même chose.
– Adjectif d'insistance :
These are his ***very*** *words.* Ce sont ses paroles mêmes.
– Pronom réfléchi :
I did it ***myself****.* Je l'ai fait moi-même.
– De même :
in the same way, similarly, likewise.
– Tout de même, quand même :
all the same, even so, for all that.

Encore

– Toujours :
He is ***still*** *here.* Il est toujours ici.
– Davantage :
We want ***more*** *responsibilities.* Nous voulons plus de responsabilités.
– À nouveau :
Could you say it ***again****?* Pourrais-tu le redire?
– Encore :
He is **always** complaining! *Il est encore en train de se plaindre!*
– Pas encore :
I have ***not*** *understood* ***yet***. Je n'ai pas encore compris.

DOMAINE VERBAL

Auxiliaires

BE

Formation

Présent		Prétérit	
I ***am***	*we* ***are***	*I* ***was***	*we* ***were***
you ***are***	*you* ***are***	*you* ***were***	*you* ***were***
he, she, it ***is***	*they* ***are***	*he, she, it* ***was***	*they* ***were***

Valeur lexicale

Be sert à indiquer une propriété du sujet.
My name ***is*** *Elison McKinly. I* ***am*** *22 (years old).* Mon nom est Elison McKinly. J'ai 22 ans.

There + be

There + ***be*** conjugué indique l'existence et s'accorde en nombre avec le nom qui suit.
There is *a lot of noise.* Il y a beaucoup de bruit.
There are *different points of view.* Il y a divers points de vue.
There were *many people.* Il y avait beaucoup de gens.
There will be *sun.* Il y aura du soleil.
There must be *solutions.* Il doit y avoir des solutions.
There will have been *a problem.* Il y aura eu un problème.

HAVE

Formation

Présent		Prétérit	
I ***have***	*we* ***have***	*I* ***had***	*we* ***had***
you ***have***	*you* ***have***	*you* ***had***	*you* ***had***
he, she, it ***has***	*they* ***have***	*he, she, it* ***had***	*they* ***had***

Have sert à indiquer une possession.
He ***has*** *two children.* Il a deux enfants.
He ***doesn't have*** *any brother.* Il n'a pas de frère.

Have correspond à «prendre» dans les expressions suivantes :
to ***have*** *breakfast / lunch / dinner / a drink* prendre le petit déjeuner / le déjeuner/ le dîner / un verre
to ***have*** *a bath / a shower* prendre un bain / une douche

Opérateur

– ***Have*** + participe passé : *present perfect.*
He ***has*** *rais****ed*** *their children alone.* Il a élévé leurs enfants seul.
– ***Have*** *something* ***done*** : faire faire quelque chose.
He ***had*** *a house* ***built***. Il s'est fait construire une maison.
– ***Have to*** : obligation.
*'****Do*** *I* ***have to*** *do it? 'No, you don't* ***have to***.*'* « Faut-il que je le fasse? » « Non, ce n'est pas nécessaire. »

Formes simples

L'anglais n'a que deux temps grammaticaux *(tenses)* : le présent simple *(Ø/-s)* et le prétérit simple *(-ed)*. Pour se référer à d'autres temps on emploie des auxiliaires.

Présent simple

Formation

Affirmative	Interrogative	Négative
I like	*Do you like?*	*I don't like.*
He likes	*Does he like?*	*He doesn't/ does not like.*

Le -*s* se prononce :
– [iz] après /s/, /z/, /ʃ/ :
*kis****s****es, advi****s****es, wat****ch****es,*
– [s] après /f/, /k/, /p/, /t/, /ð/ :
*lau****gh****s, ma****k****es, kee****p****s, expec****t****s, fro****th****s,*
– [z] dans tous les autres cas :
*ca****ll****s, carr****i****es, gi****v****es, sa****y****s.*

On emploie le présent simple pour décrire une action de manière neutre, objective, sans ajouter son opinion. On le trouve donc pour indiquer :
– une action habituelle avec des adverbes de fréquence tels que *always* (toujours,) *currently* (actuellement), *usually* (habituellement), *often* (souvent), *sometimes* (parfois), *seldom* (rarement), *never* (jamais).
We ***often go*** *on holidays in July.* Nous partons souvent en vacances en juillet.
– une action vraie en toutes situations, permanente :
Every Englishman ***wears*** *a mackintosh.* Tous les Anglais portent un imperméable.
– une référence à l'avenir :
The plane ***leaves*** *at 6 PM.* L'avion part à 18 heures.

– une hypothèse réalisable dans une subordonnée conditionnelle :
*If the bridge is open we **take** it.* Si le pont est ouvert nous le prenons.

Prétérit simple

Formation

	Verbes réguliers	Verbes irréguliers
affirmative	*He worked.*	*She went.*
interrogative	*Did he work?*	*Did she go?*
négative	*He didn't/ did not work.*	*She didn't/ did not go.*

***-ed* se prononce :**
– [t] après /f/, /k/, /s/, /ʃ/, /p/, /ð/ :
*lau**gh**ed, wor**k**ed, noti**c**ed, wa**sh**ed, co**p**ed, fro**th**ed,*
– [id] après /d/ ou /t/ :
*soun**d**ed, deci**d**ed, gradua**t**ed, las**t**ed,*
– [d] dans les autres cas :
*fi**ll**ed, vie**w**ed, accu**s**ed, recei**v**ed, challen**g**ed, ear**n**ed.*

Pour le prétérit des verbes irréguliers se reporter à la liste page 211.

Le prétérit simple indique qu'une action a eu lieu à un moment précis du passé, coupé du présent. C'est l'aspect ponctuel de l'action qui est important.
*I **read** your job ad in yesterday's* Daily Mail. J'ai lu votre petite annonce dans le *Daily Mail* d'hier.
*I **passed** my A' levels in 2008.* J'ai été reçu au bac en 2008.
*The concept **was** pioneered more than ten years ago.* Le concept a été lancé il y a plus de dix ans.

Prétérit modal

Le prétérit modal s'emploie pour évoquer des faits non-réels, imaginaires ou hypothétiques, après certaines conjonctions *(if, as if, as though, even though, if only)*, certains verbes *(wish, imagine, suppose)* et expressions *(I'd rather, it's high time)*.
*I **wish** I **had** access to the Internet.* J'aimerais avoir accès à Internet.
Le *past perfect* renvoie à un souhait ou un regret sur le passé.
*I **wish** I **hadn't bought** this dress.* Je regrette d'avoir acheté cette robe.

Used to do

Used to /ju:st tu:/ s'emploie pour parler de faits passés qui ne se produisent plus et se traduit par « avant/autrefois » + imparfait. Il est souvent opposé à ***no longer*** « ne ... plus ». Les formes négative et interrogative se forment avec ***did***.
*Where **did** he **use to** live?* Où habitait-il avant ?
*He **used to** be poor but he **no longer** is.* Autrefois il était pauvre, mais ce n'est plus le cas.

Il ne faut pas le confondre avec ***be used to*** + *V-ing* /ju:zd/ qui indique une habitude actuelle.
*You need to **be used to** driv**ing** on the left in Britain.* Il faut être habitué à conduire à gauche en Grande-Bretagne.

Formes composées

À l'aide des auxiliaires ***have*** et ***be***, celui qui parle peut indiquer la manière dont il considère l'événement : soit comme inachevé (*be*+ *V-ing*), soit dans le lien présent/passé (*have* + *V-en*).

Be + *V-ing*

Les formes continues (ou progressives) se forment avec l'auxiliaire ***be*** suivi du verbe en ***-ing***.

Présent en *be* + *V-ing*

Le présent en ***be*** + ***V-ing*** indique que celui qui parle envisage l'événement comme inachevé au moment où il parle.
*Be careful! You'**re** walk**ing** on my toes.* Attention. Tu me marches sur les pieds!
*Look! He'**s** wear**ing** a mackintosh.* Regarde! Il porte un imperméable.

Le présent en ***be*** + ***V-ing*** indique aussi qu'une action est présentée du point de vue de celui qui parle pour exprimer :
– une intention, un projet :
***I'm** not cook**ing** tonight.* Ce soir, je ne fais pas la cuisine.
– une irritation, un reproche :
***You're** always sleep**ing**!* Tu dors tout le temps!

Prétérit en *be* + *V-ing*

Le prétérit en ***be*** + ***V-ing*** s'emploie lorsqu'un événement est perçu dans son déroulement dans le passé.
*He **was** liv**ing** happily at the time the war broke out.* Il vivait heureux lorsque la guerre éclata.

Have + *V-en*

Le *present perfect* se forme avec ***have/has*** suivi du verbe au participe passé.
En utilisant le *present perfect* celui qui parle fait un bilan. C'est le résultat de l'action dans le présent qui importe.
*The group's goal **has** be**en** revised.* L'objectif du groupe a été revu.
Le ***present perfect*** : s'emploie donc avec :
– ***already, just, recently, ever, never, not ... yet.***
*We **have alreday seen** that film.* Nous avons déjà vu ce film.
– ***for*** + durée, ***since*** + point de départ :
*I **have** liv**ed** in Glasgow **for** ten years now.* Je vis à Glasgow depuis dix ans maintenant.
*They **have been** based here **ever since** they started.* Ils sont installés ici depuis qu'ils ont commencé.
– ***how long*** et ***since when*** :
***How long have** you liv**ed** here?* Depuis combien de temps habites-tu ici ?
***Since when** has he manag**ed** this company?* Depuis quand gère-t-il cette entreprise ?

Has / have been + *V-ing*

Les deux **formes *be*** + ***V-ing*** et ***have*** + ***V-en*** peuvent être combinées.
*They **have been** try**ing** to develop that approach for more than ten years.* Ils essayent de mettre au point cette approche depuis plus de dix ans.

Had + *V-en*

Le ***past perfect*** se forme avec ***had*** suivi du verbe au participe passé.
En utilisant le *past perfect* celui qui parle établit un lien entre deux moments révolus.
*He **had passed** his exam the first time he **had taken** it.* Il avait réussi son examen la première fois qu'il l'avait passé.

Parler de l'avenir

Le temps grammatical *(tense)* du futur n'existe pas en anglais. Pour se référer à l'avenir, on utilise différentes formes verbales.

Will + base verbale

Will s'emploie. si la réalisation de l'action parait évidente à celui qui parle.
*I am certain I **will** be sick.* Je suis sûr que je serai malade.

Be + going to + base verbale

***Going to* + base verbale** indique que la prédiction s'appuie sur des indices présents.
*Look, it's **going to** rain.* Regarde, il va pleuvoir.

Be + V-ing

Avec ***be + V-ing*** la personne qui parle exprime une intention, indique ce qui est prévu.
*Tomorrow, Michael **is** leav**ing** New York.* Michael quitte New York demain.

Présent simple

Le **présent simple** avec une expression de temps se référant à l'avenir donne une information brute.
*The plane **leaves** at six.* L'avion part à six heures.

Subordonnées de temps

Dans les subordonnées introduites par ***when, as soon as, as long as, while, before, after*** on trouve le présent ou le prétérit et jamais *will* ni *would*.
*What will he do when he **finishes** school?* Que fera-t-il quand il aura fini l'école?
*He said he would call as soon as he **arrived**.* Il a dit qu'il téléphonerait dès qu'il arriverait.

Modaux

Les **auxiliaires de modalité** sont suivis de la base verbale.
*They **must do** it at once.* Ils doivent le faire tout de suite.

Les **auxiliaires de modalité** ont deux valeurs pour celui qui parle et seul le contexte permet de faire le choix :
- soit il porte un jugement ou exerce une pression sur autrui.
- soit il exprime une opinion sur les chances de réalisation de ce qui est énoncé.

Jugement ou pression

***Can* exprime une capacité ou une permission.**
***I can** use a word processor.* Je sais me servir d'un traitement de texte.
*Yes, you **can** do so.* Oui, tu peux faire ainsi.

Cannot / can't indique une incapacité ou une absence de permission :
*She **cannot** resist any interesting offer.* Elle ne sait pas résister à une offre intéressante.
*You **can't** park your bike here.* Tu ne peux pas garer ton vélo ici.

***May* indique une permission.**
***May** I borrow your car?* Puis-je emprunter votre voiture?

***May not* indique une interdiction de manière polie.**
*You **may** not park here.*Vous ne pouvez pas vous garer ici.

***Must* indique que l'obligation est imposée par celui qui parle.**
*You **must** be here by six.* Tu dois être ici avant six heures.

Have to et ***have got to*** indiquent que l'obligation est imposée de l'extérieur par un état de fait, un réglement ou une nécessité.
*Students **have to** be silent in the library.* À la bibliothèque les élèves doivent être silencieux.

Must not / Mustn't indique une interdiction.
*Students **must not** park their bikes here.* Les élèves ne doivent pas garer leurs vélos ici.

Needn't / don't have to expriment une absence d'obligation.
*These students **needn't/don't have to** show a pass.* Ces élèves n'ont pas besoin de montrer un laisser-passer.

Will exprime une demande d'aide à la forme interrogative une acceptation à la forme affirmative :
Will you help me, please? Veux-tu m'aider s'il te plaît?
*He **will** do it.* Il accepte de le faire.

Will not / won't exprime un refus.
He won't do it. Il refuse de le faire.

***Would*, forme passée de will , exprime :**
- une requête polie à la forme interrogative :

***Would** you answer me as soon as possible?* Auriez-vous l'obligeance de me répondre aussi rapidement que possible?
- une bonne volonté :

*I wish you **would** stop shouting.* J'aimerais que tu veuilles bien cesser de crier.
- une preference :

***We'd rather** go to Spain than stay in France.* Nous préférerions aller en Espagne plutôt que de rester en France.
***I'd sooner** you came tomorrow.* Je préférerais que vous veniez demain.
- la répétition d'une action dans le passé :

*He **would** smoke a cigar after lunch.* Il fumait un cigare après le déjeuner.

Would not / Wouldn't exprime un refus dans le passé.
*I tried to speak to him, but he **wouldn't** listen.* J'ai essayé de lui parler, mais il n'a pas voulu écouter.

Shall exprime une pression de l'énonciateur sur le sujet grammatical, une demande de l'accord des autres ou une mise à la disposition de quelqu'un d'autre :
*You **shall** do as I tell you!* Tu feras ce que je te dis de faire.
***Shall** we go to the pub? Let's go to the pub, **shall** we?* Et si on allait au café?
***Shall** I help you?* Puis-je vous aider?

Should exprime un conseil ou une obligation atténuée :
*A think tank **should** be set up.* On devrait créer un comité de réflexion.
*They insist that you **should** go back.* Ils insistent pour que tu rentres.

Should not / Shouldn't exprime un conseil.
*You **shouldn't** cross here.* Tu ne devrais pas traverser ici.

Expression de la probabilité

Pour porter un jugement sur les chances de réalisation de ce qui est énoncé en anglais on utilise un modal plutôt qu'un adverbe.
*He **may** be sick* est plus courant que *Perhaps he is sick*.

Must indique une quasi-certitude et équivaut à *certainly*. Le locuteur pense ne pas se tromper.
*The quality **must** be excellent.* La qualité doit être excellente.

Will indique que la réalisation est probable.
*That'**ll** be Peter.* C'est sans doute Pierre.

May exprime une éventualité. Il y a autant de chance que l'événement se produise, qu'il ne se produise pas (50/50).
*There **may** be trouble ahead.* Il se peut que cela crée des problèmes.
*He **may have** arrived.* Il se peut qu'il soit arrivé.

Could exprime que la réalisation de l'action est imaginable.
*It **could** be dangerous.* Il se pourrait que cela soit dangereux.

Might indique l'incertitude : l'ignorance est plus grande qu'avec ***may***.
*You **might** like this job better.* Il se pourrait que tu préfères ce travail.

Should correspond à une probabilité ou une hypothèse peu vraisemblable :
*The doctor **should** be here by now.* Le médecin devrait être ici maintenant.
*If there **should** be a problem, let me know.* Si par hasard il y a un problème préviens moi.

Can't / cannot indique une impossibilité; en toute logique, la chose n'est pas possible.
*It **can't / cannot** be true.* Il est impossible que cela soit vrai.

Formes complexes

Les modaux ne peuvent pas être combinés entre eux, mais ils peuvent être suivis d'un auxiliaire.

L'emploi d'un modal suivi de ***be*** + ***V-ing*** indique que l'action est vue dans une situation précise, en cours de déroulement.
They ***must be*** *demonstrat****ing***. Ils sont sûrement en train de manifester

L'emploi d'un modal suivi de ***have*** + ***V-en*** exprime une opinion sur un fait passé.
He ***must have*** *travel****led*** *abroad*. Il a dû voyager à l'étranger.
He ***shouldn't have*** *taken his pledge*. Il n'aurait pas dû prêter serment.
Be sure to / ***be bound to*** / ***be (un)likely to*** permettent d'exprimer une plus ou moins grande certitude dans le présent ou le passé.
He is bound to have *forgot****ten***. Il y a de fortes chances qu'il ait oublié.
You are likely to *have a successful interview*. Vous allez vraisemblablement réussir votre entretien.

Passif

Be + participe passé

Le passif se forme avec le verbe *be* conjugué suivi du participe passé.

Présent	*It* ***is*** *estimat****ed***
Présent en *be* + *V-ing*	*It* ***is being*** *estimat****ed***
Prétérit	*It* ***was*** *estimat****ed***
Prétérit en *be*+*V-ing*	*It* ***was being*** *estimat****ed***
Present perfect	*It* ***has been*** *estimat****ed***
Past perfect	*It* ***had been*** *estimat****ed***
Infinitif	*It will* ***be*** *estimat****ed***
Infinitif passé	*It might* ***have been*** *estimat****ed***

Avec la voix passive l'énonciateur met l'accent sur l'objet de l'action et correspond à la tournure impersonnelle « on » en français.

Les verbes qui se construisent avec deux compléments ont deux formes passives selon ce que l'énonciateur veut mettre en relief :
– la personne (complément d'attribution)
He ***was*** *giv****en*** *a promotion*. Il a reçu une promotion.
– la chose (complément d'objet)
A £15 voucher ***was*** *giv****en*** *to her*. Un bon de 30 euros lui a été remis.

Il ne faut pas confondre ***be said*** et ***be told***.
This manager ***is said*** *to be unable to make decisions collectively*. On dit que ce directeur ne sait pas prendre de décisions collectivement.
He ***was told*** *to leave at once*. On lui a dit de partir sur le champ.

On peut combiner passif et modaux, ainsi que passif et aspect.
It ***cannot be*** *deni****ed***. On ne peut le nier.
It ***must*** *not* ***be*** *forgot****ten***. On ne doit pas l'oublier.
It ***should be*** *remember****ed***. On devrait s'en souvenir.
This issue ***is being*** *debat****ed***. On est en train de discuter de cette question.
It ***may have been*** *do****ne***. Cela a peut-être été fait.

Impératif

L'impératif est utilisé pour donner des ordres, des consignes, faire des suggestions ou interdire.
– 2e personne
Take *a map and compass*. Prends / prenez une carte et une boussole

– 1re personne
Let me *go!* Laisse-moi partir !
Let's *go!* Allons-y !
– Forme négative
Do not / don't *litter*. Ne jetez pas vos papiers gras.

Constructions verbe + verbe

En français, lorsqu'un verbe suit un autre verbe il est à l'infintif. En anglais, il y a trois possibilités.

Verbe + base verbale

La base verbale se trouve après :
– les auxiliaires de modalité (voir ci-dessus)
– ***let*** et ***make***
Too much pressure ***makes*** *her* ***cry***. Trop de pression la fait pleurer.
I ***won't let*** *you* ***say*** *such things!* Je ne te laisserai pas dire des choses pareilles !
– ***had better***, et ***would rather***
You ***had better listen***. Tu ferais mieux d'écouter.
I ***would rather go***. Je préférerais partir.

Verbe + V-*ing*

La forme en ***V-ing*** renvoie à quelque chose de connu et s'emploie donc pour donner une appréciation avec des verbes tels que *like, love, enjoy, be keen on, be fond of, appreciate, be crazy about, prefer, dislike, hate, can't stand/bear, can't put up with, I don't mind...*
*I don't mind work****ing*** *a lot*. Cela ne me dérange pas de beaucoup travailler.
*I don't like be****ing*** *disturbed by the telephone*. Mais je n'aime pas être dérangé par le téléphone.

Lorsque ***to*** fait partie de la construction d'un verbe prépositionnel, il est suivi de ***V-ING***.
The manager is ***used to*** *hir****ing*** *tax lawyers*. Le directeur a l'habitude de recruter des avocats de la fiscalité.
He ***took to*** *drink****ing*** *when he lost his wife*. Il s'est mis à boire quand il a perdu sa femme.

Verbe *to* infinitif

To permet d'envisager la réalisation de l'action dans l'avenir. On le trouve donc après les verbes indiquant une pression sur autrui tels que *allow, ask, expect, force, order, hope, persuade, tell, want, would like...*
Do you ***want*** *them* ***to*** *come with us?* Veux-tu qu'ils viennent avec nous ?
La négation se place devant ***to***.
I hope ***not to be*** *late*. J'espère ne pas être en retard.

Deux constructions

Certains verbes admettent deux constructions.
– ***V-ING*** si le verbe renvoie à de l'accompli :
I've ***stopped*** *work****ing***. J'ai cessé de travailler.
I ***remember*** *post****ing*** *your letter last week*. Je me souviens d'avoir posté ta lettre la semaine dernière.
– ***to*** s'il renvoie à un but ou à l'avenir :
We ***stopped to*** *have lunch*. Nous nous sommes arrêtés pour déjeuner.
Please, ***remember to*** *post the letter*. S'il te plaît, souviens-toi de poster la lettre.
Pour les verbes de perception
– ***V-ING*** renvoie à une action en cours de déroulement :
I ***hear*** *a child cry****ing***. J'entends un enfant en train de pleurer.
– la base verbale indique que l'action est vue comme complète :
I ***heard*** *a woman scream*. J'ai entendu le cri d'une femme.

ÉNONCÉS

Énoncés simples

Forme affirmative

Sujet + Verbe

I like *English very much.* J'aime beaucoup l'anglais

Forme interrogative

Questions fermées

Auxiliaire + Sujet + Verbe?
Do you understand? Comprends-tu?
Could I speak to Mr Barns? Pourrais-je parler à M. Barns?

Questions ouvertes

Mot interrogatif + Auxiliaire + Sujet + Verbe?
What's her nationality? De quelle nationalité est-elle?
How much does this cell phone cost? Combien ce téléphone portable coûte-t-il?

Mots interrogatifs

How *are you?* Comment allez-vous?
How far *is the station from here?* À quelle distance est la gare?
How deep *is the lake?* Quelle est la profondeur de ce lac?
How long *have they been talking now?* Depuis combien de temps parlent-ils maintenant?
How many *passengers will it carry?* Combien de passagers peut-il transporter?
How much *time should be dedicated to training?* Combien de temps faut-il consacrer à une formation?
How often *can they meet?* Tous les combiens peuvent-ils se rencontrer?
How old *are you?* Quel âge avez-vous?
What *do you think about your working conditions?* Que pensez-vous de vos conditions de travail?
What *do you want to put it on the agenda* ***for****?* Pour quelle raison voulez-vous le mettre à l'ordre du jour?
When *did supermarkets begin paying customers one penny for reusing a shopping bag?* Quand les supermarchés ont-ils décidé de donner 1 centime aux clients réutilisant un sac à provisions?
Where *do you think we should meet?* Où pensez-vous que nous devrions nous rencontrer?
Which *do you prefer?* Lequel préférez-vous?
Who *would you rather negotiate with?* Avec qui préfèreriez-vous discuter?
Whose *salaries will be first discussed?* Les salaires de qui seront-ils discutés en premier?
Why *are you cross?* Pourquoi êtes-vous fâché?

Forme négative

Sujet + Auxiliaire + Négation + Verbe
I ***don't*** *want to.* Je ne veux pas le faire.
I ***can't*** *believe you.* Je ne peux te croire.

Forme interro-négative

Auxiliaire + Négation + Sujet + Verbe + ?
Hasn't *a company developed a new type of maize?* Une société n'a-t-elle pas récemment mis au point un nouveau type de maïs?

Tags (reprises d'auxiliaires)

Pour demander confirmation de ce qui vient d'être dit on utilise un *question tag*.
– Énoncé négatif → *tag* positif
It is ***not*** *a strong disagreement,* ***is it****?* Ce n'est pas un profond désaccord, n'est-ce pas?
*A virus ca****n't*** *develop,* ***can it****?* Un virus ne peut pas se développer, n'est-ce pas?
– Énoncé positif → *tag* négatif
She bought a cell phone, ***didn't she****?* Elle a acheté un portable, n'est-ce pas?
You've read it, ***haven't you****?* Tu l'as lu, n'est-ce pas?

Confirmation ou renforcement

Sujet + *do/does/did* + Verbe
I do like *English very much.* J'aime vraiment beaucoup l'anglais

Les subordonnées nominales en V-*ing*

On trouve un gérondif après :
– un verbe d'appréciation ou d'aversion.
I don't ***like*** *be****ing*** *disturbed by the telephone.*
Je n'aime pas être dérangée par le téléphone.
– une préposition :
Work instead ***of*** *los****ing*** *your time!* Travaille au lieu de perdre ton temps!
After *clos****ing*** *the door, he burst out laughing.* Après avoir fermé la porte, il éclata de rire.
He left ***without*** *say****ing*** *goodbye.* Il sortit sans dire au revoir.

For + ***-ing*** exprime la cause.
Thank you ***for*** *listen****ing*** *to me.* Merci de m'avoir écouté.

On + ***-ing*** exprime la simultanéité.
She jumped for joy ***on*** *hear****ing*** *the news.* Elle sauta de joie en entendant la nouvelle.

By + ***-ing*** exprime le moyen.
I learn typing ***by*** *train****ing*** *hard.* J'apprends à taper en m'entrainant beaucoup.

Exclamatives

What (a) et ***such (a)*** portent sur un nom.
What a *lovely* ***day****!* Quelle belle journée.
It's ***such a*** *funny* ***ad****!* C'est une pub si amusante!
They are ***such*** *big* ***firms****!* Ce sont de si grandes sociétés!

How et ***so*** portent sur un adjectif. L'ordre des mots reste celui d'une phrase affirmative : sujet + verbe.
How lovely *she is!* Comme elle est charmante!
She's is ***so lovely****!* Elle est si charmante!

Énoncés complexes

Infinitives

L'infinitif se forme avec la particule ***to*** suivie de la base verbale.
I want ***him to leave****.* Je veux qu'il parte.
À la forme négative, la négation se place avant la particule *to* afin de ne pas séparer les deux éléments de l'infinitif.
I want ***them not to be*** *late.* Je veux qu'ils ne soient pas en retard.
Si ce sujet de l'infinitive est un pronom, on utilise les pronoms : *me, him, her, it, us, you, them.*
They don't want ***us*** *to help them.* Ils ne veulent pas que nous les aidions.
On trouve une proposition infinitive après les verbes qui indiquent une volonté, un désir, un ordre ou une interdiction : *want, would like, expect, plan, desire, refuse, ask, tell, order, force, hope, etc.*
I would like to *have a tutor to help me.* J'aimerais avoir un tuteur pour m'aider.

Relatives

Une subordonnée relative est une proposition qui apporte des renseignements sur un groupe nominal (l'antécédent) de la proposition principale.

Le choix du pronom relatif dépend à la fois de sa fonction dans la subordonnée relative (sujet ou complément) et de la nature de l'antécédent (animé ou non-animé).

	Animé	Non-animé
Sujet	***who***	***which / that***
Objet	***(whom/that)***	***(which / that)***
Complément prépositionnel	***at whom***	***at which***
Complément de nom	***whose***	***of which / whose***

Who : animé, sujet
The manager ***who*** *was recently appointed is expected to help the company recover.* On s'attend à ce que le directeur qui vient d'être nommé redresse l'entreprise.

Which/that **: non-animé, sujet**
They wanted to close the sites ***that*** *the firm found useless.* Ils voulaient fermer les sites que l'entreprise jugeait inutiles.

That **ou Ø : complément**
He is the friend ***(that)*** *I like best.* C'est l'ami que j'aime le mieux.
It is a book ***(that)*** *I don't fancy so much.* C'est un livre que je n'apprécie pas baeucoup.

Après un superlatif
Le relatif est toujours *that* ou Ø
She is the most gorgeous girl ***(that)*** *I have ever seen.* C'est la plus belle fille que j'ai jamais vue.

Where / when / why
Where s'emploie si l'antécédent est un lieu.
The place ***where*** *he works is quite pleasant.* L'endroit où il travaille est tout à fait agréable.
When s'emploie si l'antécédent est une époque, un moment ou un jour.
I remember the day ***when*** *I got my first job interview.* Je me souviens du jour où j'ai eu mon premier entretien d'embauche.
Why s'emploie si l'antécédent est une cause.
He could not understand the reason ***why*** *his scheme had failed.* Il ne parvenait pas à comprendre pourquoi son projet avait échoué.

Traduction de « dont »
Si « dont » indique une possession, on emploie ***whose***.
That department manager ***whose*** *results are so good has never been to college.* Ce chef de service dont les résultats sont si bons n'est jamais allé à l'université.
Si « dont » peut être remplacé par « au sujet duquel, à propos de laquelle... » on emploie ***whom*** ou ***which***. À l'oral, il est plus courant de supprimer le relatif et de placer la préposition en fin de phrase.
She is the girl of ***whom*** *I dream. She is the girl* **Ø** *I dream* ***of***. C'est la femme dont je rêve.
It is a topic about ***which*** *I know nothing. It is a topic* **Ø** *I know nothing* ***about*** C'est un sujet dont je ne sais rien.

Ce que / ce qui
What correspond à *the thing(s) that* et annonce ce qui suit.
I did not understand ***what*** *he meant.* Je n'ai pas compris ce qu'il voulait dire.
Which s'emploie si la proposition relative est un commentaire de l'énoncé précedent.
He arrived late for his interview, ***which*** *is very much like him.* Il est arrivé en retard à son entretien, ce qui est tout à fait son genre.
Comparez : *I do* ***what*** *I want,* ***which*** *is my right.* Je fais ce que je veux, ce qui est mon droit.

Conditionnelles

Dans les subordonnées conditionnelles introduites par ***if*** (si), ***provided*** (pourvu que), ***even if / even though*** (même si), ***whether*** (si oui ou non) ou ***unless*** (à moins que) la concordance des temps se fait comme en français.

Le présent **indique que la condition est réalisable et que l'évènement peut se produire.**
If you ***meet*** *him, tell him I will calll at six.* Si tu le rencontres dis-lui que j'appellerai à six heures.
In business, whether you ***want*** *it or not, you often need to risk it all not to end up a loser.* En affaires, qu'on le veuille ou non, il faut souvent tout risquer pour ne pas perdre.
We will visit Finland, unless something important ***prevents*** *us from going.* Nous allons visiter la Finlande à moins que quelque chose d'important ne nous empêche d'y aller.

If **+ prétérit modal**
Le prétérit ne renvoie pas ici à des événements passés. Il indique que des faits sont soumis à une condition irréelle : c'est le prétérit modal.
If I ***had*** *time, I would help them find a solution.* Si j'avais du temps, je les aiderais à trouver une solution.
If I ***were*** *you, I would call that help line.* Si j'étais toi, j'appelerais ce numéro.
If I ***could*** *do it, I would volunteer for a charity.* Si je pouvais, je serais bénévole dans une organistaion caritative.

Le *past perfect* indique que la condition ne s'est pas réalisée dans le passé.
He would have been able to do it if he ***had tried*** *harder.* Il aurait pu le faire s'il avait essayé davantage.

Discours direct et indirect

Le discours direct permet de citer les paroles de quelqu'un.
'Go away,' he ***said***. « Va-t-en ! » dit-il.
– Les verbes pour rapporter les dires :
• ***ask*** ou ***wonder*** pour une question :
'What's on the agenda?' → *She* ***asked*** *what was on the agenda.* Elle a demandé ce qu'il y avait à l'ordre du jour.
'Can we find a better room?' → *He wondered whether they could find a better room.* Il se demanda s'ils pourraient touver une meilleure salle.
• ***tell*** pour un ordre :
'Don't wait for the tip.' → *Our boss* ***told*** *us not to wait for the tip.* Notre patron nous a dit de ne pas attendre le pourboire.
• ***advise*** pour un conseil :
'You should be careful.' → *He* ***advised*** *them to be careful.* Il leur a conseillé d'être prudents.
• ***regret*** pour un regret :
'It's too bad *we cannot get them directly on the database.'* → *The manager* ***regretted not*** *being able to get them directly.* Le directeur regretta de ne pas pouvoir les avoir directement.

Le discours indirect conduit à changer :
– les pronoms personnels, adjectifs et pronoms possessifs :
*"****I*** *am not sure but* ***I*** *think* ***we****'ll have to talk about salaries."* → *The secretary said* ***she*** *was not sure but that* ***she*** *thought* ***they*** *would have to talk about salaries.* La secrétaire a dit qu'elle n'était pas certaine mais qu'elle pensait qu'il faudrait qu'ils parlent salaires.
– les marqueurs de temps :
'Why weren't you there ***yesterday****?'* → *He ashed why I hadn't been there* ***the day before***. Il a demandé pourquoi j'avais été absent la veille.
'Jim called ***last night****.'* → *She said that Jim had called* ***the night before***. Elle a dit que Jim avait appellé la veille au soir.
'I will see you ***tomorrow****.'* → *He said that he would see me* ***the next day***. Il a dit qu'il me verrait le lendemain.

'I will go to London **next week**.' → She said she would go to London **the following week**. Elle a dit qu'elle irait à Londres la semaine suivante.

– **les temps :**

• *présent* → *prétérit*

'What ***do*** *you expect from me?'* → *The lawyer asked what Jim* ***expected*** *from him.* L'avocat a demandé ce que Jim attendait de lui.

• *prétérit* → *past perfect*

'I ***had*** *no life.'* → *She admitted she* ***had had*** *no life.* Elle admit qu'elle n'avait pas eu de vie.

• *present perfect* → *past perfect*

'I ***have stopped*** *working with women.'* → *He claimed he* ***had stopped*** *working with women.* Il prétendit qu'il avait cessé de travailler avec les femmes.

• *will* → *would*

*'****Will*** *I give the firm the image I want'?* → *She wondered if she* ***would*** *give the firm the image she wanted.* Elle se demandait si elle donnerait à la société l'image qu'elle voulait.

'The company will never associate with the AT&T brand' → *The executive said that the company* ***would*** *never associate with the AT&T brand.* Le cadre a aussi déclaré que la société ne s'associerait jamais à la marque AT&T.

• *can* → *could*

*'****Can*** *I get a compensation for my unfair layoff?'* → *He asked whether he* ***could*** *get a compensation for his unfair layoff.* Il demanda s'il pourrait obtenir un dédommagement pour son licenciement injuste.

LES MOTS DE LIAISON/LINK WORDS

Addition

above all : par dessus tout
also : aussi
besides : d'ailleurs
furthermore : en outre
in addition : de surcroît
moreover : de plus
on top of that : par dessus le marché
or else : sinon
too : aussi
what's more : qui plus est

Cause

because : parce que
because of : à cause de
due to : dû à
for : car
given that : étant donné que
owing to : en raison de
since : puisque

Comparison

in comparison : en comparaison
in the same way : de la même manière
likewise : également
similarly : de même

Concession

after all : après tout
all the same : tout de même
anyway : de toute façon
despite : malgré
even so : quand même
in any case : en tous cas
in spite of : en dépit de

Consequence

as a result/consequence : par conséquent
consequently : en conséquence
for this reason : pour cette raison
so : ainsi
then : donc
therefore : par conséquent
thus : ainsi

Contrast

but : mais
conversely : en revanche
either... or : soit... soit
however : cependant
instead of : au lieu de
neither... nor : ni... ni
nevertheless : néanmoins
nonetheless : malgré tout
notwithstanding : néanmoins
on the contrary : au contraire
on the one hand : d'une part
on the other hand : d'autre part
still : cependant
though : pourtant
unlike : contrairement à
whereas : alors que
while : tandis que
yet : pourtant

Degree

above all : par-dessus tout
in many respects : à bien des égards
in other respects : à d'autres égards
in so far as : dans la mesure où
in some way : d'une certaine manière
in this connection : dans cet ordre d'idées
in this respect : à cet égard
one way or another : d'une manière ou d'une autre
somehow : d'une façon ou d'une autre
to a certain extent : dans une certaine mesure
to a large extent : en grande partie

Example

e.g. (exempli gratia) : par exemple
for example/instance : par exemple
i.e. (id est) : c'est-à-dire
namely : à savoir
such as : tel que
that is : c'est-à -dire
that is to say : c'est-à -dire

Opinion

as far as I am concerned : en ce qui me concerne
as for me : quant à moi
in my opinion : à mon avis
to my mind : selon moi

Reinforcement

actually : en réalité
as a matter of fact : en fait
indeed : en effet
in fact : en fait
last but not least : enfin, et c'est un point important
not only... but also : non seulement... mais encore
really : vraiment

Summary

all in all : tout bien pesé
to begin with : pour commencer
to conclude : pour conclure
eventually : finalement
finally : pour terminer
first : premièrement
first of all : tout d'abord
in a nutshell : en deux mots
in conclusion : en conclusion
in other words : en d'autres mots
in short : en bref
in a word : en un mot
in the end : en fin de compte
in the first place : tout d'abord
lastly : enfin
to make a long story short : bref
next : ensuite
roughly : en gros
secondly : deuxièmement
to sum up : pour résumer
then : puis

ABRÉVIATIONS/ABBREVATIONS

A.F.L.-C.I.O. *American Federation of Labor and Congress of Industrial Organization*
A.G.L. *Annual General Meeting* Assemblée générale annuelle
A levels *Advanced Levels* Baccalauréat dans une matière
am *Ante Meridiem* avant-midi
APR *Annual Percentage Rate* taux de pourcentage annuel
a.s.a.p. *as soon as possible* aussitôt que possible
A.S.E.A.N *Association of South-East Asian Nations* Association des Nations d'Asie du Sud-Est
B & B *Bed and Breakfast* Chambre et petit déjeuner
BC *Before Christ* avant Jésus-Christ
bl *barrel* (mesure de capacité) un baril (160 litres)
B.L. *Bill of Lading* connaissement
bn *billion* **m** milliard
B.Sc. *Bachelor of Science* Licence ès-sciences
C.A.F. *Cost and Freight* coût et fret
C.D. *Compact Disk* C.D.
C.E.O. *Chief Executive Officer* P.D.G.
C.E.T. *Central European Time* Heure de l'Europe Centrale
C.I.A. *Central Intelligence Agency* Surveillance du Territoire
C.I.F. *Cost Insurance Freight* CAF coût assurance frêt
C/O *Care Of* aux soins de
Co. *Company* Compagnie
C.O.D. *Cash on Delivery* envoi contre remboursement
C.P.A. *Certified Public Accountant* Expert Comptable
C.P.U. *Central Processing Unit* Unité centrale de traitement
C.V. *Curriculum Vitae* C.V. Curriculum Vitae
C.W.O. *cash with order* paiement à la commande
D.I.Y. *Do It Yourself* Bricolage
Dr *Doctor* Docteur
D.S.S. *Department of Social Security* Ministère de la Sécurité Sociale
D.T.I. *Department of Trade and Industry* Ministère du Commerce et de l'Industrie
E.C.B. *European Central Bank* **B.C.E.** Banque Centrale Européenne
E.E.A. *European Economic Area* **E.E.E.** Espace Économique Européen
E.E.C. European Economic Community C.E.E. Communauté Économique Européenne
E.F.T.A. *European Free Trade Association* Association Européenne de Libre Échange
e.g (exempli gratia) *for example* par exemple
E.M.S. *European Monetary System* Système Monétaire Européen
E.M.U. *Economic and Monetary Union* Union Économique et Monétaire
Enc: / *Encl* / *Encs* / *Enclosures* P.J. / Pièces jointes
E.U. *European Union* Union Européenne
F.B.I. *Federal Bureau of Investigation*
F.D.A. *Food and Drug Administration* Office du Contrôle Pharmaceutique et Alimentaire
F.O.B. *Free on Board* franco à bord
F.T.A. *Free Trade Area* Zone de libre Echange
G.A.T.T. *General Agreement on Tariffs and Trade* **GATT** Accord Général sur les Tarifs et le Commerce
G.B. *Great Britain* Grande-Bretagne
G.C.S.E. *General Certificate of Secondary Education* Baccalauréat
G.D.P. *Gross Domestic Product* **P.I.B.** Produit Intérieur Brut
G.E.P. *Genetically Engineered Products* Produits Manipulés Génétiquement
G.M. *General Manager* Directeur Général
G.M.O. *Genetically Modified Organisms* **O.G.M.** Organismes Génétiquement Modifiés
G.M.T. *Greenwich Mean Time* heure G.M.T.
G.N.P. *Gross National Product* **P.N.B.** Produit National Brut
G.P. *General Practitioner* médecin généraliste
H.C.R. *High Commissioner for Refugees* Haut Commissariat aux Réfugiés
H.R. *Human Resources* Ressources Humaines
http *hypertext transfer protocole*
i.e (id est) *that is to say* C'est-à-dire
I.M.F. *International Monetary Fund* **F.M.I.** Fonds Monétaire International
I.L.O. *International Labor Organization* **O.M.T.** Organisation Mondiale du Travail
IOU I owe you reconnaissance de dette
I.S.O. *International Standard Organisation* Organisation des Normes Internationales
I.T. *Information Technology* Technologies de l'information
Inc. *Incorporated*
£ *pound (100 pence)* livre
lb *pound (450 grams)* livre
L.C.D. *Liquid Crystal Display* Affichage à Cristaux Liquides
LDC's *Less Developed Countries* Pays Moins Avancés
Ltd *Public Limited Company* **S.A.** Société anonyme
M.B.A. *Master of Business Administration* Maîtrise de gestion
M.D. *Doctor of Medecine* Docteur en médecine
M.D. *Managing Director* P.D.G.
MoT *Ministry of Transport* Ministère des Transports
M.P. *Member of Parliament* un parlementaire
mph *miles per hour* miles par heure
Mr. *Mister* **M.** Monsieur
Mrs. *Missis* **Mme** Madame
Ms. *Miz* Madame ou mademoiselle
N.A.F.T.A. *North America Free Trade Agreement* **A.L.E.N.A.** Accord de Libre-Échange Nord-Américain
NASA *National Aeronautics and Space Administration* Agence nationale de l'aéronautique et de l'espace
N.A.T.O. *North-Atlantic Treaty Organization* **OTAN** Organisation du Traité de l'Atlantique Nord
NGO *non-governmental organization* **ONG** organisation non-gouvernementale
N.H.S. *National Health Service* Sécurité Sociale
N.I.C.'s *Newly Industrialized Countries* **N.P.I.** Nouveaux Pays Industrialiés
No.1 *Number 1* Numéro 1
N.V.Q. *National Vocational Qualification* Qualification professionnelle
NYSE *New York Stock Exchange* Bourse de New York
O.E.C.D. *Organization for Economic Cooperation and Development* **O.C.D.E.** Organisation de Coopération et de Développement Économiques
O'levels *Ordinary Levels* Examen de fin de 1er cycle
O.P.E.C. *Organization of Petroleum Exporting Countries*
O.P.E.P. Organisations des Pays Exportateurs de Pétrole
Oz *ounce (32 g.)* une once
P.A. *Personal Assistant* Assistante de Direction
P.A.Y.E. *paye as you earn* impôts retenus à la source
pm words *per minute words* mots à la minute
P.C. *Personal Computer* ordinateur domestique
P.L.C. *Private Limited Company* **SARL** Société à Responsabilité Limitée
pm *post meridiem* après-midi
P.M. *Prime Minister* Premier Ministre
P.O. *Box Post Office Box* Boîte Postale

P. & P. *Postage & Packing*, frais d'expédition
P.R. *Press Realease* Communiqué de Presse
P.R. *Public Relations* Relations Publiques
P.T.O. *Please Turn Over* **T.S.V.P.** Tournez s'il vous plaît
pw *per week* par semaine
R.A.M. *Random-Access Memory* R.A.M.
rBHG *recombinant Bovine Growth Hormone* Hormone de Croissance pour Bovins
R.O.M. *Read-Only Memory* R.O.M.
R.R.P. *Recommended Retail Price* Prix de détail conseillé
R.S.A. *Royal Society of Arts*
R.S.I. *Repetitive Strain Injury* microtraumatismes répétés
R.S.P.C.A. *Royal Society for the Prevention of Cruelty to Animals* **S.P.A.** Société protectrice des animaux
$ *dollar* dollar
sq.m. *square meter* mètre carré
S.E.C. *Security and Exchange Commission* Commission américaine des échanges en bourse
S.I.B. *Securities and Investment Board* Commission britannique des échanges en bourse
S.M.E. *Small and Medium-sized entreprises* **PME** Petites et Moyennes entreprises
S.M.I. *Small and medium-sized industries* **PMI** Petites et Moyennes industries
U.H.T. *Ultra High Temperature* Ultra Haute Température
U.K. *United Kingdom* Royaume-Uni
U.N.O. *United Nations Organization* **O.N.U.** Nations Unies
U.R.L. *Uniform Resource Locator* adresse Internet
U.S.A. *United States of America* États-Unis d'Amérique
V.A.T. *Value Added Tax* **TVA** Taxe à la Valeur Ajoutée
V.C.R. *Video Cassette Recorder* magnétoscope
V.I.P. *Very Important Person*
W.H.O. *World Health Organization* **O.M.S**. Organisation Mondiale de la Santé
WP *Word Processor* traitement de texte
W.T.O. *World Trade Organization* **O.M.C.** Organisation Mondiale du Commerce
W.W. *World War* Guerre Mondiale
W.W.W. *World Wide Web*
Y2K *Year Two Thousand* l'an 2000

VERBES IRRÉGULIERS/IRREGULAR VERBS

Prononciation semblable des voyelles dans les trois formes

to bet	bet	bet	*parier*
to burst	burst	burst	*éclater*
to cost	cost	cost	*coûter*
to cut	cut	cut	*couper*
to hit	hit	hit	*frapper*
to hurt	hurt	hurt	*blesser*
to let	let	let	*laisser*
to put	put	put	*mettre*
to quit	quit	quit	*abandonner*
to set	set	set	*placer*
to shut	shut	shut	*fermer*
to split	split	split	*fendre*
to spread	spread	spread	*étendre*
to bend	bent	bent	*courber*
to build	built	built	*construire*
to burn	burnt	burnt	*brûler*
to learn	learnt	learnt	*apprendre*
to lend	lent	lent	*prêter*
to send	sent	sent	*envoyer*
to smell	smelt	smelt	*sentir*
to spell	spelt	spelt	*épeler*
to spend	spent	spent	*dépenser*
to spoil	spoilt	spoilt	*gâcher*
to have	had	had	*avoir*
to make	made	made	*faire*
to lay	laid	laid	*poser*
to pay	paid	paid	*payer*
to mow	mowed	mown	*tondre*
to saw	sawed	sawn	*scier*
to sew	sewed	sewn	*coudre*
to show	showed	shown	*montrer*
to sow	sowed	sown	*semer*
to beat	beat	beaten	*battre*

Prononciation semblable des voyelles dans deux formes

	/e/	/e/	
to deal	dealt	dealt	*distribuer*
to dream	dreamt	dreamt	*rêver*
to lean	leant	leant	*pencher*
to mean	meant	meant	*signifier*
to read	read	read	*lire*
to lead	led	led	*mener*
to leave	left	left	*partir*
to bleed	bled	bled	*saigner*
to feed	fed	fed	*nourrir*
to speed	sped	sped	*se hâter*
to creep	crept	crept	*ramper*
to feel	felt	felt	*ressentir*
to keep	kept	kept	*garder*
to kneel	knelt	knelt	*s'agenouiller*
to meet	met	met	*rencontrer*
to sleep	slept	slept	*dormir*
to sweep	swept	swept	*balayer*
to weep	wept	wept	*pleurer*
	/ɔː/	/ɔː/	
to bring	brought	brought	*apporter*
to buy	bought	bought	*acheter*
to fight	fought	fought	*combattre*
to seek	sought	sought	*chercher*
to think	thought	thought	*penser*
to catch	caught	caught	*attraper*
to teach	taught	taught	*enseigner*
to bear	bore	borne	*porter, supporter*
to swear	swore	sworn	*jurer*
to tear	tore	torn	*déchirer*
to wear	wore	worn	*porter un vêtement*

to forget	forgot	forgotten	*oublier*
to get	got	got	*obtenir*
to lose	lost	lost	*perdre*
to sell	sold	sold	*vendre*
to shine	shone	shone	*briller*
to shoot	shot	shot	*tirer, abattre*
to tell	told	told	*raconter*
	/ʌ/	/ʌ/	
to hang	hung	hung	*pendre*
to stick	stuck	stuck	*coller*
to strike	struck	struck	*frapper*
to swing	swung	swung	*balancer*
to win	won	won	*gagner*
	/əu/	/əu/	
to awake	awoke	awoken	*se réveiller*
to break	broke	broken	*casser*
to choose	chose	chosen	*choisir*
to freeze	froze	frozen	*geler*
to speak	spoke	spoken	*parler*
to steal	stole	stolen	*voler*
to wake	woke	woken	*éveiller*
	/i/	/i/	
to bite	bit	bitten	*mordre*
to hide	hid	hidden	*cacher*
to light	lit	lit	*allumer, éclairer*
to slide	slid	slid	*glisser*
	/e/	/e/	
to say	said	said	*dire*
	/əu/	/əu/	
to blow	blew	blown	*souffler*
to grow	grew	grown	*croître; grandir*
to know	knew	known	*savoir*
to throw	threw	thrown	*jeter*
	/ʌ/	/ʌ/	
to become	became	become	*devenir*
to come	came	come	*venir*
to run	ran	run	*courir*
to be	was	been	*être*
to draw	drew	drawn	*dessiner*
to eat	ate	eaten	*manger*
to fall	fell	fallen	*tomber*
to find	found	found	*trouver*
to forbid	forbade	forbidden	*interdire*
to forgive	forgave	forgiven	*pardonner*
to give	gave	given	*donner*
to hear	heard	heard	*entendre*
to hold	held	held	*tenir*
to lie	lay	lain	*être allongé*
to mistake	mistook	mistaken	*prendre (pour) par erreur*
to see	saw	seen	*voir*
to sit	sat	sat	*être assis*
to spit	spat	spat	*cracher*
to shake	shook	shaken	*secouer*
to stand	stood	stood	*se tenir debout*
to take	took	taken	*prendre*
to understand	understood	understood	*comprendre*
to wind	wound	wound	*enrouler*

Prononciation différente des trois voyelles

to begin	began	begun	*commencer*
to drink	drank	drunk	*boire*
to ring	rang	rung	*sonner*
to sing	sang	sung	*chanter*
to sink	sank	sunk	*couler*
to spring	sprang	sprung	*s'élancer*
to stink	stank	stunk	*puer*
to swim	swam	swum	*nager*
to drive	drove	driven	*conduire*
to ride	rode	ridden	*chevaucher*
to rise	rose	risen	*se lever*
to write	wrote	written	*écrire*
to do	did	done	*faire*
to go	went	gone	*aller*
to fly	flew	flown	*voler*
to take	took	taken	*prendre*

The English-speaking world

Historic data

17th century: British colonists establish permanent **settlements** in North America, then India, Africa, the West Indies, Australia and New Zealand.

1783: The British lose the **13 colonies** of **America**.

1907-1910: Canada, Australia, New Zealand and South Africa become **independent dominions**.

1931: As the 30 British colonies gradually become independent, they join the **Commonwealth**, a system of mutual consultation and voluntary co-operation in international economic, social and political affairs, including rural development, food production, youth programmes, science, technology, law and health.

1991: Heads of Governments issue a Declaration in Harare, Zimbabwe, that sets the Commonwealth on a new course promoting democracy and good governance, human rights and the rule of law, gender equality, and sustainable economic and social development.

The 53 member states of the Commonwealth

Africa: Botswana, Cameroon, Gambia, Ghana, Kenya, Lesotho, Malawi, Mauritius, Mozambique, Namibia, Nigeria, the Seychelles, Sierra Leone, South Africa, Swaziland, Tanzania, Uganda, Zambia.

America: Antigua and Barbuda, the Bahamas, Barbados, Belize, Canada, Dominica, Grenada, Guyana, Jamaica, Saint Kitts and Nevis, Saint Lucia, Saint Vincent and the Grenadines, Trinidad and Tobago.

Asia: Bangladesh, Brunei, India, Malaysia, Maldives, Pakistan, Singapore, Sri Lanka.

Europe: Cyprus, Gibraltar, Malta, the United Kingdom.

Pacific: Australia, Fiji, Kiribati, Nauru, New Zealand, Papua New Guinea, Samoa, Solomon Islands, Tonga, Tuvalu, Vanuatu.

Immigration policy in Britain

1962: The Commonwealth Immigrants Act marked a break with the policy of free entry into Britain for Commonwealth citizens, reflecting a general concern about the increase in unemployment. It was disapproved of by some as making possible a "colour bar".

1981: The British Nationality Act limited access to British nationality.

January 1st 2004: All new applicants for British citizenship must attend a **citizenship ceremony** to take an **Oath of Allegiance** and a **Pledge** to the United Kingdom. They must also meet English language requirements.

November 1st 2005: All new applicants for naturalisation as a British citizen must prove they have passed the **Life in the United Kingdom Test.**

Ethnic breakdown in the U. K.: 60.5 million

Ethnic minorities: 4.8 million (7.9%)
Indians, Pakistanis, Bangladeshis: 1.9 million (3.1%)
West Indians and Africans: 1.2 million (2%)
Others: 1.7 million (2.8%)

Today

– Nearly two billion citizens live in the 53 Commonwealth countries.
– 400 million people speak English as their first language in 12 countries.
– 1.5 billion other people speak English as their second language in more than 90 other countries.
– 70% of the world's scientists write in English.
– 75% of the world's mail is written in English.
– 85% of the information stored in computers throughout the world is in English.

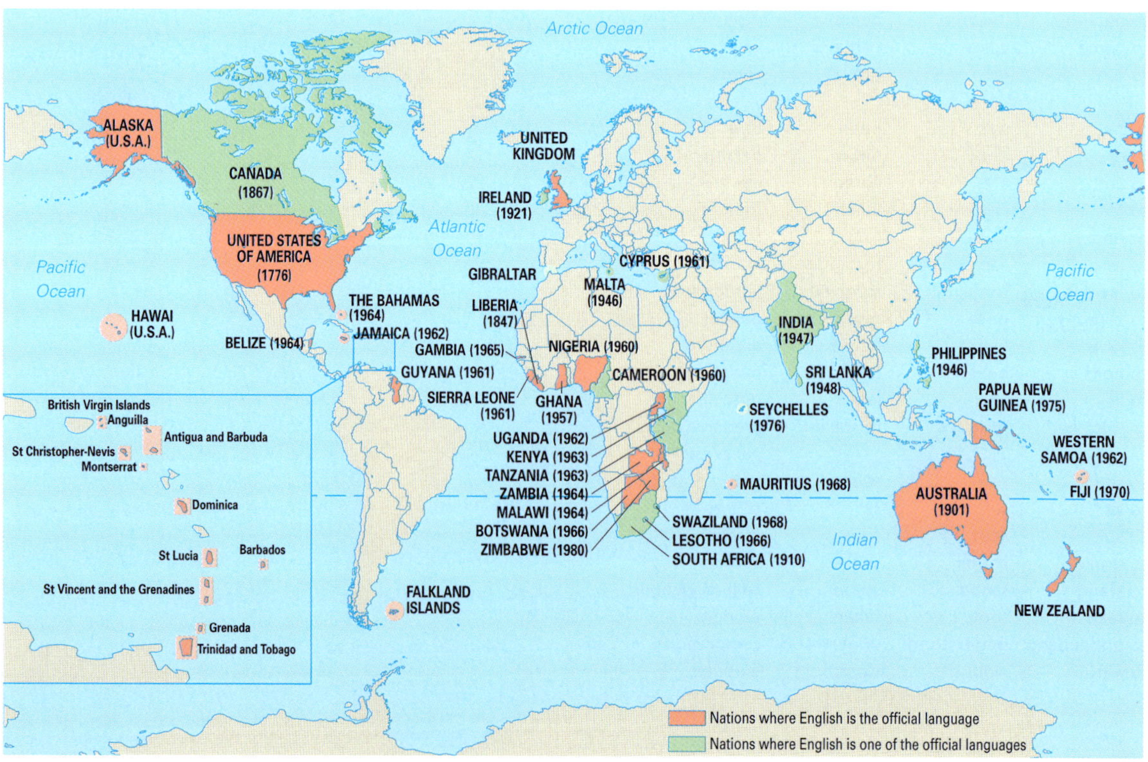

The United Kingdom

A multiple country

The British Isles is the geographical name for all the islands off the northwest coast of the continent of Europe. They include the Irish Republic (capital: Dublin), a country that is independent from the U.K.

The United Kingdom (capital: London) is a political union which includes Britain, Northern Ireland, and many small islands.

Great Britain (G.B.), the main island, contains three nations: England (capital: London), Scotland (capital: Edinburgh) and Wales (capital: Cardiff).

A constitutional monarchy

Queen Elizabeth II has been the head of the United Kingdom since February 1952. The Queen is head of the Church of England and commander-in-chief of all the armed forces. She is also head of the judiciary, and her signature has to be on all new laws and many state papers. But she has very little direct power over her government, which is run by the **Prime Minister** and the **cabinet** of Secretaries of State (Home and Foreign Offices) and Ministers (Ministries of Defence, Education and Health). The Prime Minister is the leader of the political party that wins the General Election.

A parliamentary democracy

The British Parliament has two chambers. **The House of Commons** is an assembly of 650 MPs (Members of Parliament), who are each elected by voters in one constituency. It decides on national policies.

Members of the House of Lords are judges, bishops, and heads of aristocratic families, who are hereditary peers. Other Lords are personalities appointed by the Queen according to merit (actors, industrialists, singers, sportsmen...). Their status has recently been changed.

The political parties

The Conservative Party, or **Tories,** is attached to Britain's traditional values concerning the monarchy, the Establishment and education. Tories want to limit the role of the State to encourage private initiative, and have serious reservations about European integration. Famous Conservative Prime Ministers: Winston Churchill (1951-54), Harold Macmillan (1957-63), Margaret Thatcher (1979-90) and John Major (1990-94).

The Labour Party, whose most famous Prime Ministers were Clement Atlee (1945-51) and Harold Wilson (1964-70), believes the reduction of Welfare State services will make the poor poorer and the rich richer, thus dividing Britain into two nations. However in recent years, Tony Blair (1994-2007) has made political decisions departing from the traditional line of the party. Gordon Brown has been Prime Minister since June 2007.

The Welfare State

In 1945, a comprehensive state scheme was established aimed at guaranteeing protection to every citizen. Money from taxes was used to provide free education, free medical care, and social security for those unemployed or too ill to work. The system is still working today even though the NHS (National Health Service) has frequently been the target of criticism over the years for its waiting lists and its super-bugs.

THE U.K. IN FIGURES

Parliamentary democracy and Constitutional monarchy
Monarch: Queen Elizabeth II,
Prime Minister: Gordon Brown
Capital: London (7.5 million)
Area: 244,820 km^2
Population: 60,587,300
National language: English (de facto)
Major religions: Protestantism, Roman Catholicism, Judaism, Orthodox Christianity
GNP: $2.5451 trillion
Average income per capita: $38,624

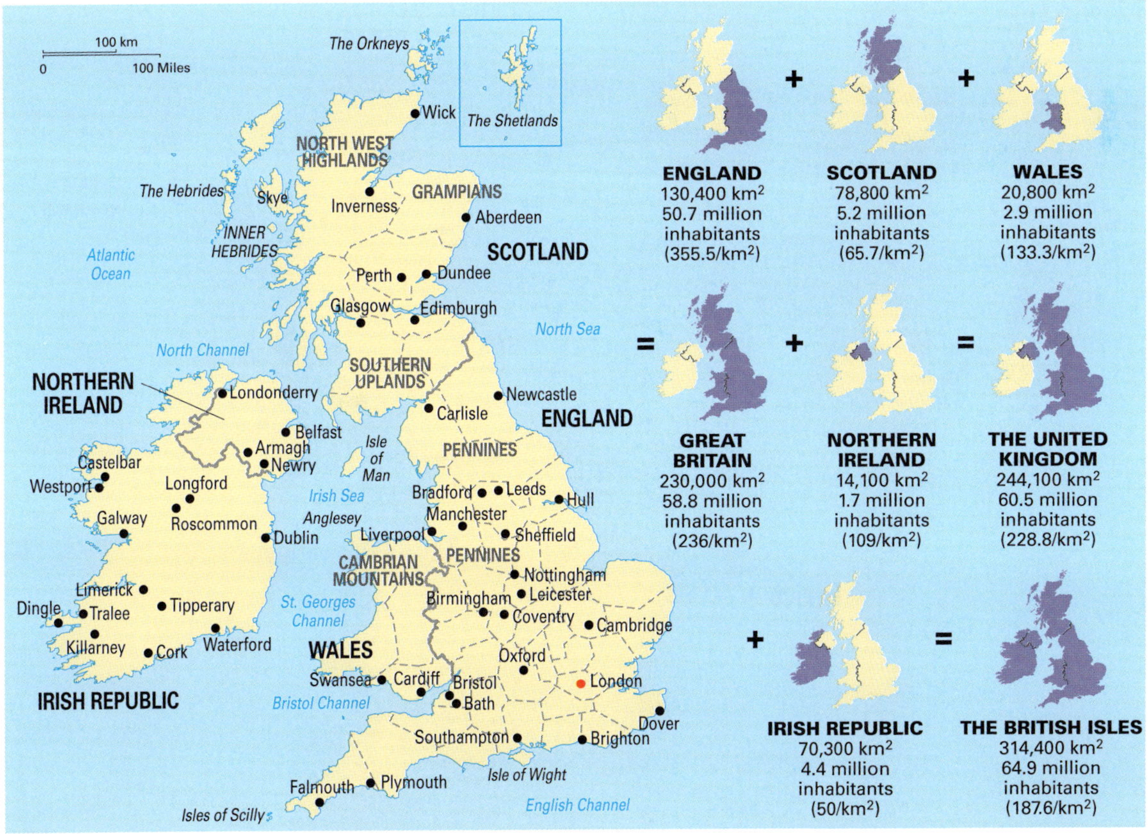

The United States

A democracy

In 1789, the Constitution established the political system aiming at securing stability. The first ten amendments of 1791, called the Bill of Rights, guarantee the basic rights of individual Americans (including the right to keep and bear arms - 2nd Amendment). The Constitution has been amended 26 times since, to ban slavery (1865) or give women the right to vote (1920).

The constitution is based on three principles.

1. The Constitution sets up a federal system of 50 states with a strong central government. Each state has its own government with a governor, a congress and a supreme court. It can set state taxes and pass state laws, especially as concerns the drinking of alcohol in public places, marriage, gambling or the speed limit.

2. The three branches of the federal government have separate powers.

• **The Executive** is headed by a **President** elected for four years, who appoints the Secretaries of State. He is the commander-in-chief of the armed forces, proposes laws and appoints federal judges and senior government officials. He is also responsible for relations with foreign countries.

• **The Legislature** is headed by **Congress**, made up of the **Senate** (two senators for each state) and the **House of Representatives** (435 representatives elected for two years). It makes federal laws, sets federal taxes and in the event of serious hostilities, declares war on other countries.

• The **Supreme Court** is the highest body of **the Judiciary** - nine judges appointed for life by the President and confirmed by the Senate by a majority vote.

3. Each power is carefully checked and balanced by the powers of the other two. The actions and appointments of the Executive must be approved by Congress. The President can veto a Congressional Bill. The main function of the Supreme Court is to make sure that the actions of Congress and the President do not go against the Constitution.

Political parties

There are two leading political parties in the United States.

• **The Republican Party or G.O.P. (Grand Old Party),** symbolized by an elephant, is conservative. Most Presidents have been Republicans, from Lincoln (1861) to the Great Depression (1933). Recent Republican presidents were Richard Nixon, Gerald Ford, Ronald Reagan and George W. Bush.

• **The Democratic Party**, symbolized by a donkey, tends to be liberal and defend the rights of minorities. Democrats have almost continuously held the majority in Congress since 1931. J.F. Kennedy, Lyndon Johnson, Jimmy Carter and Bill Clinton are recent Democratic Presidents.

THE U.S. IN FIGURES

Political subdivisions: a federation of 50 states
Capital: Washington D.C. (600,000)
Area: 9 628 382 km^2
Population: 303 million
Largest city: New York (8.3 million)
National language: English (de facto)
Major religions: Protestantism, Roman Catholicism, Judaism, Orthodox Christianity, Islam
GNP: $10 trillion
Average income per capita: $46,326

Canada

A wide country

Canada is so wide that it has six time zones. About 80% of Canadians are classified as urban. 90% of the country is uninhabited. Canada is one of the world's most sparsely populated nations.

A dual cultural heritage

The British and the French settled Canada in the 18th century. French Canadians are concentrated in the province of Quebec. The threat of separatism has been an issue since the 1980s, yet it has been defeated in several referendums. Indians and Eskimos (Inuits) account for a small percentage of the total population but are a major element in the north. The ethnic composition of Canada continues to change with the arrival of many immigrants from Europe, Asia, the West Indies and Africa.

An affluent high-tech industrial society

The Canadian economy has been transformed from agricultural production into a high-tech industrial economy with leading manufacturing and service sectors. Canada has an abundance of mineral, forest and water power resources. Canada is one of the world's largest exporters of wood products. Hydroelectric power is a leading source of energy. The leading industries are transport equipment, food and beverages, paper and allied industries, primary metals, chemicals, electrical and electronic products, and fish-related products. The United States is Canada's main economic partner, representing 75% of all exports and 65% of imports.

CANADA IN FIGURES

Political subdivisions: a federation of 10 provinces and 2 territories
Prime Minister: Stephen Harper
Capital: Ottawa (820,000)
Area: 9,984,670 km^2 (the second largest country in the world)
Population: 33,157,200
French Canadians: 27% of the population
Density: 3.2 persons per km^2
Largest cities: Toronto (5,5 million), Montreal (3,6 million), Vancouver, Ottawa Edmonton, Calgary, Winnipeg, Quebec and Hamilton,
Official languages: English, French
Major religions: Roman Catholicism (46%), Protestantism (United Church of Canada, Anglicans, Presbyterians, Lutherans, and Baptists), Animism
GDP: $1 trillion
Average income per capita: $32,614

Repères culturels

Ireland

Ireland's history

It has been marked by British political involvement since the 12th century. After the intensive English colonization of Ireland in the 17th century, the growing agitation for Home Rule gave way to the Anglo-Irish Treaty of 1921, by which 26 counties gained dominion status as the Irish Free State (Eire), the other six counties remaining part of the United Kingdom (Ulster). In 1948, the 26 counties declared their independence as the Irish Republic. With the rise of the Ulster Defence Association, a militant Protestant group, and of the Catholic Irish Republican Army, the British army was sent to Northern Ireland in 1969. Several thousand civilians were killed on both sides in Ireland and Britain. Following a Provisional IRA cease fire and multi-party talks, the Belfast Agreement was concluded and ratified by referendum in 1998. Violence decreased greatly after the signing of the accord and on July 28, 2005, the Provisional IRA announced the end of its armed campaign and agreed to a full decommissioning of the Provisional IRA's weapons. The power-sharing assembly was restored from May 8, 2007.

IRELAND IN FIGURES

The Republic of Ireland (Eire)

President: Mary McAleese / **Taoiseach**: Bertie Ahern, TD
Area: 70,273 km^2
Population: 4.4 million
Capital: Dublin (1 million)
Official languages: English, Irish
Religion: Roman Catholicism (92%)
GDP: $203 billion
Average wealth per head: $190,000

Northern Ireland (Ulster)

Monarch: Queen Elizabeth II, **Prime Minister**: Gordon Brown, **First Minister**: Ian Paisley
Area: 24,481 km^2
Population: 1.7 million
Capital: Belfast (580,000)
Official language: English, Irish and Ulster Scots
Religions: Roman Catholicism (60%), Protestantism (35%)
GNP: $33.2
Income per capita: $19,603

The Celtic tiger

Despite their decline in relative importance, stock raising, fishing and dairy products remain significant. Manufacturing of metals, chemicals, electronics and pharmaceuticals accounts for more than one-fifth of total employment and about a third of GNP. Attracted by favourable tax conditions, more than a thousand foreign companies have established bases in Ireland, and they account for about 55% of manufacturing output and more than 75% of manufacturing exports.
A prodigious economic boom began in the mid-1990s fuelled by a surge in investment in high-end industries and services, lower taxation levels, and low interest rates. The Republic of Ireland was ranked the second wealthiest per capita country in the world behind Japan in July 2006. Ireland was also ranked by The Economist as the best place to live in the world for health, freedom, unemployment, family life, climate, political stability and security, gender equality and family and community life. Since the 1960s, traditional Irish music has undergone a revitalization and enjoyed great popularity with U2, Clannad, Enya, Sinead O'Connor, Paul Brady, Van Morrison, Christy Moore, the Cranberries, and the Saw Doctors.

Australia

A vast country

Australia is the world's smallest continent, but the sixth largest country in the world. 64% of all Australians live in the cities while the vast interior ('the Outback') remains little developed and sparsely populated. Air transportation is important with four domestic airlines and many ranches (stations) with their own aircraft and airstrips.

A country of immigration

Aborigines have occupied Australia for at least 75,000 years. In 1788, the British founded a penal colony where Sydney is now. The discovery of gold in the 1850s boosted the migration of settlers. Since 1945, almost 5 million people from more than 130 countries have settled in Australia. Today 40% of Australians are immigrants or first-generation children of migrants and some 30% of settler arrivals are from Asia.

One of the world's most economically developed countries

Australia possesses enormous mineral resources. It is one of the world's leading producers and exporters of agricultural products which account for about 25% of total exports and 75% of the G.D.P. Manufacturing accounts for the rest with food processing, metallurgy, chemical, petroleum and coal products, the manufacture of transportation equipment and electronic and information technology industries.

Medicare insures residents for medical care, hospital costs, eye care, and pharmaceuticals. The famous Flying Doctor Service provides health care to inhabitants in isolated rural areas.

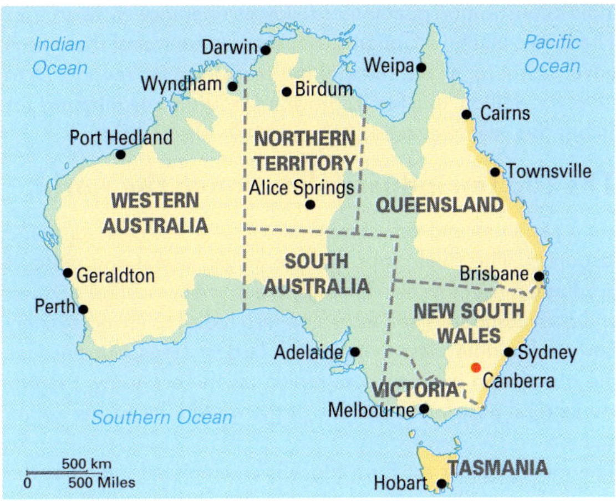

AUSTRALIA IN FIGURES

Political subdivisions: a federation of 6 states, 3 territories, and 6 dependent areas
Prime Minister: Kevin Rudd
Capital: Canberra (350,000)
Area: 7,741,220 km^2
Population: 21.2 million
Aborigines: 1.5%
Population density: 2.4 persons per km^2
Religions: Anglicanism (52%), Roman Catholicism (25%), Animism
Largest cities: Sydney (4 million), Melbourne, Brisbane, Adelaide, Perth and Hobart
GNP: $890 billion
Average income per capita: $42,553

New Zealand

An isolated island nation

New Zealand consists of two major islands and numerous tiny islands. Its nearest neighbour, Australia, is some 2,250 km to the northwest.

A mixed population

The Maoris, of Polynesian origin, reached the islands in 900. Although the Dutch were the first Europeans to arrive in 1642, the area remained relatively unknown until the arrival of Captain James Cook in 1769. Today, Maoris are far outnumbered by people of European descent, yet the Maori population is increasing at a faster rate than that of non-Maoris.

An economy dependent on trade

25% New Zealanders live in the city. Although only 1% of New Zealand's people are farmers, agricultural production has generated most of the nation's wealth. New Zealand is the world's third-largest producer and second-largest exporter of wool, and produces approximately 50% of the world's lamb and mutton exports. Sheep in New Zealand outnumber people by more than 15 to 1. There are also more than 8 million cattle, and the country is the world's largest and most efficient exporter of dairy products. New Zealand is also a major exporter of fresh fruit, beef, and fish.

A social welfare state

New Zealand was the first country to give the right to vote to women in 1893. Citizens are eligible for the unemployment benefit, and to retire at the age 60 with a pension equalling as much as 80% of the average pay. Medical care and secular education for all are free. All students who qualify for university studies receive a government scholarship.

NEW ZEALAND IN FIGURES

Political subdivisions: Parliamentary democracy without a written constitution
Head of State: HM Queen Elizabeth II, **Governor-General**: Anand Satyanand, **Prime Minister**: Helen Clark
Area: 269,000 km^2
Population: 4.240 million
Maoris: 14%
Official languages: English and Maori
Largest city: Auckland (1,300,000)
Capital: Wellington (400,000)
Religions: Anglicanism (24%), Presbyterianism (18%), Roman Catholicism (15%)
GDP: $103.900 billion
Average income per capita: $29.698

India

The world's second most populous nation

The population of India doubled from the late 1940s to the late 1980s and continues to increase by nearly 15 million a year although the government encourages family planning. India has one of the world's most diverse populations, representing a wide variety of physical types and cultural traditions.
Although 200 languages are spoken, the Constitution recognizes Hindi, which is spoken by 30% of the population, as the official language. English, although only spoken by about 3% of the population, remains important in government, education and science.

Independence

India gained its independence from the British on Aug. 15, 1947. When the two Muslim regions in the north-western and north-eastern corners of the subcontinent became the separate states of Pakistan and Bangladesh some 17 million Hindus and Muslims were uprooted to join their new homelands. There were at least one million casualties in the ensuing sectarian violence, despite efforts to restore calm by Mahatma Gandhi, the revered father of modern India. He was assassinated on January. 20, 1948, by a militant Hindu who believed he was too kind to Muslims. Today, India's constitution guarantees religious tolerance to all groups. The Indian National Congress remained in control of the central government for all but three of the years from independence to 1996. In addition, one family provided India's prime ministers for all but five years between 1947 and 1989 - the Nehrus.

INDIA IN FIGURES

Political subdivisions: a federal republic, parliamentary democracy
President: Pratibha Patil **Prime Minister**: Manmohan Singh
Capital: New Delhi (14 million)
Area: 3,287,590 km^2 - 3,000 km wide
Population: 1.12 billion
Largest cities: Calcutta (13 million), Bombay, Madras
Religions: Hinduism (83%), Islam (11%), Sikhism (2%), Jainism (1%) and Buddhism (1%)
GDP: $9,6.268 billion
Average income per capita: $863

The top ten industrial nation in the world

India has a rich and varied mineral-resource base and vast land resources. The chief crops are rice, millet, wheat and pulse. It produces most of its own chemicals, automobiles, steel, textiles, and even computers and television sets. India has an increasingly powerful middle-class living in the largest cities, but because the population is growing as rapidly as the economy, the primarily rural population has one of the world's lowest per-capita income.
The most popular art form today is cinema, and India has the world's largest filmmaking industry, with Bombay (Bollywood) and Madras as centres.

English-Speaking Africa

Historic data

The Rift Valley in the centre of Kenya has been established "the cradle of mankind" after the discovery of hominoid skulls estimated to be 31/2 million years old. From the 8th century on, powerful empires emerged from across the continent: Ghana, Mali, Songhai, Ashanti, Dahomey... After 1550, the demand for slaves in America led Europeans to set up trading posts along the coasts of Senegal and the Gulf of Guinea, and about 10 million Africans were forcibly removed from Africa. The colonization of Africa by the Europeans began in the second half of the 19th century with considerable imperialist rivalry between the French, Germans, Dutch, Portuguese and British. Gambia, Sierra Leone, Liberia, Ghana, Nigeria and Cameroon in West Africa, and Uganda, Kenya, Malawi, Tanzania, Zambia and Zimbabwe came under British administration. Liberia, peopled by the descendants of freed American slaves, was the first country to gain its independence in 1847. In the 1960s, the awakening of nationalism led other countries to independence.

The bad news and the good news

Overall, the economic situation in Africa is bleak, with the world's poorest countries (Sierra Leone being at the absolute bottom) and lowest human development (based on life expectancy and adult literacy). Yet, there are some success stories. Ghana is still the show-case of Africa while Nigeria continues to expand.

South Africa

It is the most economically advanced of African countries producing 70% of all electricity on the continent. It is rich in minerals, coal, foodstuffs, cattle and sheep. Leading industries include food processing, metalworking, and the manufacture of clothing, textiles, iron, steel, and machinery. Yet, there are significant economic, social, and political differences between the Whites and the other racial groups. Life expectancy is 59 years for Blacks and 72 years for Whites, and black infant mortality is more than six times the rate for Whites due to the system of Apartheid implemented in 1948 by the white minority of Dutch descendants (the Afrikaners) and English settlers. In April 1994, South Africa's first free and full elections were held and Nelson Mandela, the leader of the anti-apartheid African National Congress (ANC) and winner of the Nobel Peace Prize in 1993, became the first Black president. The new government announced an ambitious program to improve life for the black majority by building 1 million homes generating 2.5 million jobs and redistributing 30% of the agricultural land. It also decreed that children under 6 years of age and pregnant women must be given free treatment, and children between 7 and 17 compulsory schooling.

A vast cultural heritage

English-speaking African countries can boast a great number of artists and intellectuals. Writers include Ayi Kwei Armah of Ghana, Camara Laye of Guinea, Meja Mwangiwhose and Ngugi wa Thiong'o of Kenya, Chinua Achebe, Ben Okri, Amos Tutuola and Wole Soyinka (who was the first African writer to be awarded the Nobel prize for literature in 1986) of Nigeria, Andre Brink, J. M. Coetzee, Nadine Gordimer, Albert Luthuli, Ezekiel Mphalele and Alan Paton of South Africa.

The West Indies

A chain of 1,000 islands 2,500 miles long

The West Indies extend from Florida to South America in the Caribbean Sea. They are divided into three groups: the Bahamas Islands, Greater Antilles (Cuba, Hispaniola, Jamaica and Puerto Rico) and Lesser Antilles (Windward and Leeward Islands, Barbados, and Trinidad and Tobago). The climate is tropical, with temperatures averaging 27 degrees and rainfall 1,000 mm.

Racial mixture

Originally peopled by Indians, the islands were colonized by Europeans who brought African slaves to work on the plantations. The present population consists of descendants of African slaves, European settlers and Asian workers.

A fragile economy

The West Indies produce a wide variety of tropical fruits, spices, sugar, coffee, and cacao. Industries include sugar, rum, tobacco, and fruit processing, textile manufacturing and mineral refining. Tourism is a major source of income. Due to joblessness and lack of economic opportunities many West Indians migrated to Britain in the 1950s and 1960s. They hold a carnival in West London at the end of August, known as the Notting Hill Carnival.

THE WEST INDIES IN FIGURES

Bahamas

Political subdivisions: Parliamentary democracy and Constitutional monarchy

Monarch: Queen Elizabeth II, **Governor-General**: Arthur Dion Hanna, **Prime Minister**: Hubert Ingraham

Population: 330,600

Capital: Nassau (210,000)

Official language: English

Average income per capita: $17,843

Jamaica

Political subdivisions: Parliamentary democracy and Constitutional monarchy

Monarch: Queen Elizabeth II, **Governor-General**: Kenneth Hall, **Prime Minister**: Bruce Golding

Population: 2,651,000

Capital: Kingston (651,000)

Major religions: Church of God, Baptism, Anglicanism, Roman Catholicism, Rastafarianism (5%)

GDP: $9,730 billion

Average income per capita: $3,658

Repères culturels

The press

It is estimated that worldwide some 8,000 dailies, and 52,000 weeklies exist with a combined circulation of 500 million. Countries with the highest readership are Britain, Norway, Denmark, Sweden, Japan and the United States.

The press in Great Britain

There are about 130 dailies with a total circulation of 20 million. Most of them have a special Sunday paper.
The quality press: *The Times, the Guardian, the Independent,* and *the Telegraph*
The popular press: to refer to newspapers that are smaller in size (28cmÐ38cm) the word 'tabloids' is used. They present brief news items in sprightly style, appeal to interest in crime, sex and disaster and also include a profusion of large headlines and pictures, while advertisements may account for 60% of the total space. Because tabloids place so much stress on gossip, the unusual and the shocking, they are called "scandal sheets" or the "sensational press".
Magazines are issued weekly, fortnightly, monthly or quarterly. The Economist analyses current events throughout the world.

The press in the United States

The first Amendment to the US Constitution guarantees the freedom of speech and of the press.
Of the 1,556 dailies, with a combined circulation of 60 million in 1994, the 'Big Three' enjoy strong national and global reputations: *the New York Times, the Washington Post,* and *the Los Angeles Times.* They stress foreign and national news, science, politics, economics and culture. There are also *the International Herald Tribune, USA Today,* and *the Wall Street Journal.*

Time (1923, circulation 4 million), *Newsweek* (1933, circulation 3 million) and *US News* and *World Report* are weekly news magazines.
Most other magazines target a special group: *The National Geographic* 'for the increase and dissemination of geographic knowledge' defends wildlife. *The New Yorker* is a New York City weekly magazine that has a major influence on the quality of writing and humour. *Ebony, Jet* and *Essence* are addressed to African-Americans. Others target the military, university students, prison populations, sports fans...

Average circulation in Britain in 2007

The popular press (Tabloids)

Sun (1964)	3,126,900
Daily Mail (1896)	2,353,800
Daily Mirror (1903)	1,930,000
Star (1978)	770,000
Daily Express (1900)	761,630

The quality press

Daily Telegraph (1855)	882,400
Times (1785)	692,580
Guardian (1821)	355,750
Independent (1986)	240,110
Financial Times (1888)	140,000

Free Trade Areas (FTAS)

ASEAN Association of South-East Asian Nations (Brunei, China, Hong Kong, Indonesia, Malaysia, Papua New Guinea, Philippines, Singapore, Taiwan, Thailand)

APEC Asia-Pacific Economic Cooperation (Australia, Canada, Chile, Japan, Mexico, New Zealand, South-Korea and the United States + ASEAN): founded in 1989, all eighteen countries signed a nonbinding "declaration of common resolve" to create a Pacific free-trade zone by the year 2020.

NAFTA North America Free Trade Agreement (Canada, USA and Mexico)

Jan. 1, 1994. Advertising, trucking, bank and insurance company ownership are free of restrictions. All barriers to trade in farm products and some 10,000 other products are to be eliminated over 15 years.

MERCOSUR Southern Common Market (Brazil, Argentina, Uruguay and Paraguay)

On Jan. 1, 1995 the world's fourth largest trade association, eliminated tariffs on more than 90% of the goods traded among the four member nations and established common tariffs on imports from outside the Mercosur trade zone. Combined gross national product: $500 billion. Combined population: 190 million.

EFTA European Free Trade Association

EEA European Economic Area

EU European Union

The making of a united Europe was made necessary by the fast-growing populations of European countries and the inappropriate regulations that divided their economies and legislations.

Eurozone states		
State	**Adopted on**	**Population**
Austria	1 January 1999	8,316,487
Belgium	1 January 1999	10,584,534
Cyprus	1 January 2008	766,400
Finland	1 January 1999	5,289,128
France	1 January 1999	63,392,140
Germany	1 January 1999	82,314,906
Greece	1 January 1999	11,125,179
Ireland	1 January 1999	4,239,848
Italy	1 January 1999	59,131,287
Luxembourg	1 January 1999	476,200
Malta	1 January 2008	404,962
Netherlands	1 January 1999	16,372,715
Portugal	1 January 1999	10,599,095
Slovenia	1 January 2007	2,013,597
Spain	1 January 1999	45,116,894
Eurozone		**320,143,372**

The European Union is currently composed of twenty-seven countries known as member states: Austria, Belgium, Bulgaria, Cyprus, the Czech Republic, Denmark, Estonia, Finland, France, Germany, Greece, Hungary, Ireland, Italy, Latvia, Lithuania, Luxembourg, Malta, The Netherlands, Poland, Portugal, Romania, Slovakia, Slovenia, Spain, Sweden, the United Kingdom.
The term **Schengen Agreement** is used for two agreements concluded between European states in 1985 and 1990. The main purpose of the Schengen rules is the abolition of physical borders among European countries.
The E.U. is regulated by a number of institutions, primarily the Council of the European Union, the European Commission, and the European Parliament.

The official launch of the Euro on January 1, 1999 gave birth to the Eurozone which currently includes 15 member states with over 320 million people.
Coins and banknotes were introduced on January 1, 2002.

Growth of the European population	
Year	**Population**
1300	73,000,000
1750	140,000,000
1850	266,000,000
1900	420,000,000
1995	728,000,000
2005	732,380,859
2007	732,938,773

The euro has been designed to help build a single market by, for example: easing travel of citizens and goods, eliminating exchange rate problems, providing price transparency, creating a single financial market, price stability, low interest rates, having a currency used internationally to protect against shocks due to the large amount of internal trade within the Eurozone. It is also intended as a political symbol of integration and stimulus for further integration. In recent years speculation has grown so much that if the Eurozone continues to enlarge, and the U.S. dollar continues to fall, the Euro could well become the main reserve currency in the world.

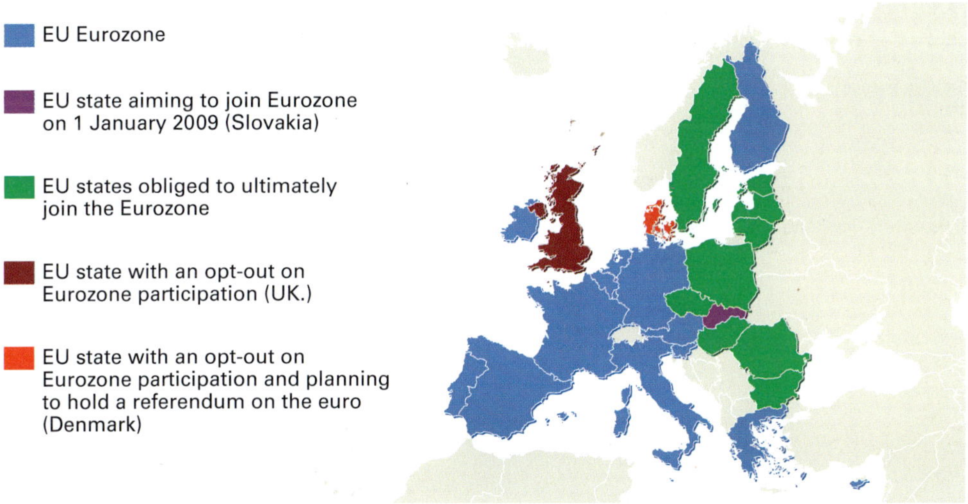

Repères culturels

Table des illustrations

Maquette
François Lecardonnel

Mise en page
Ici & ailleurs

Iconographie
Éliane Usaï

Illustrations
Didier Crombez, Anne Gallet, Julien Noirel

Infographies
Illustratek

Éditions Foucher – Vanves – juillet 2010 – 04 – RG-DL/DC

Imprimé par Loire Offset Titoulet – Saint Etienne